Friends

BEHIND THE SCENES

BACKSTAGE PASS TO THE SERIES
A COMPREHENSIVE HISTORY

Dennis Bjorklund

PRAETORIAN PUBLISHING

Library of Congress Cataloging-in-Publication Data
Bjorklund, Dennis
Friends Behind the Scenes: Backstage Pass to the Series, A Comprehensive History / Dennis Bjorklund.
p. cm
"A Maizeland Books book"

1. Friends (Television program)–Miscellaneous. I. Title.

First published in the United States of America in 2004

Table of Contents

Author

Dennis Bjorklund is an accomplished and well-respected television programming authority who published many small-screen books covering some of the best sitcoms in network television history. In addition to writing books, the author provided literary contributions to numerous entertainment magazines as well as authoritative interviews for A&E network, E! Entertainment, The Biography Channel, Bio channel, and FYI.

Bjorklund is considered one of the foremost authorities on network television sitcoms, and the only one to write multiple in-depth and thoroughly comprehensive books in this genre. He has written numerous books on some of the best sitcoms. Here is a listing of his most famous works:

Seinfeld

Seinfeld Reference: The Complete Encyclopedia

Seinfeld Behind the Scenes: Backstage Pass to the Series, A Comprehensive History

Seinfeld Secrets: 1500 Fun Facts About the Show

Seinfeld Secrets: 180 Episodes, Thousands of Facts

Seinfeld Exposed: 1500 Fun Facts About the Show

Seinfeld Trivia: Everything About Nothing

Seinfeld Trivia: Everything About Nothing, Challenging

Seinfeld Trivia: Everything About Nothing, Multiple Choice

Seinfeld Ultimate Episode Guide

Friends

Friends Behind the Scenes: Backstage Pass to the Series, A Comprehensive History

Friends Secrets: 236 Episodes, Thousands of Facts

Friends Exposed: 1500 Fun Facts About the Show

Friends Challenging Trivia: Channel Your Inner Unagi

Friends Ultimate Episode Guide

Cheers

Cheers Reference: A Comprehensive History

Cheers Behind the Scenes: Backstage Pass to the Series, A Comprehensive History

Cheers Secrets: 275 Episodes, Thousands of Facts

Cheers Exposed: 2500 Fun Facts About the Show

Cheers Trivia: It's a Little Known Fact...

Cheers Ultimate Episode Guide

The Big Bang Theory

The Big Bang Theory Trivia, Casual Fan

The Big Bang Theory Trivia, Challenging

Modern Family

Modern Family Trivia: Early Years, Challenging

The author continues to reside in Southern California so he can remain close to the heart of network television programming.

Series Backstory

Creators

Friends creators David Crane (b. 8.13.57) and Marta Kauffman (b. 9.21.56) were raised in the Philadelphia (PA) area but did not meet until they attended Brandeis University in Waltham, Massachusetts. They were both cast in the Tennessee Williams play *Camino Real;* Kauffman was a prostitute and Crane a street waif. The thespians quickly became thick as thieves. They shared a mutual love of network television and an insatiable desire to perform onstage. As youths, both had entertainment aspirations, but not the same: one wanted to be an actor, the other a writer.

Born an only child to a Jewish family in the city of brotherly love, David, the son of Joan Crane (née Meyers) and veteran Philadelphia television personality Gene Crane, had only one youthful aspiration—to be an actor. While watching his favorite television shows, like *The Dick Van Dyke Show, The Mary Tyler Moore Show, The Bob Newhart Show* and *Happy Days*, he daydreamed about living the life of a Hollywood star. He wanted to follow his father's path in show business but sought greater heights beyond the confines of the keystone state. While attending Harriton High School in Rosemont, Pennsylvania, David Crane performed in all the school productions. After graduating in 1975, he moved away, but not too far, to enroll at Brandeis University. He instantly gravitated toward the school's drama department but after a few years of limited success as an actor, he realized that his childhood dream would never become a reality. He was still enchanted with theater, but his new role would feature himself tucked away behind the velvet curtain.

The youngest of two daughters, Marta Kauffman was born to Dorothy R. "Dot" (Cohen) and Herman M. Kauffman. Her sister, Andrea, was born six years earlier and became an entertainment manager in Brigantine, New Jersey, her most noteworthy client being Frank Sinatra Jr. Marta was an aspiring thespian but her initial interest was writing, that is, until an AP English teacher told her that she was the least perceptive student he ever had and that she would never make it as a scribe. Devastated, she abandoned writing and spent her senior year as an actor and student director working on school productions such as *Our Town*. In 1974, Kauffman enrolled at Brandeis University to pursue acting but during her junior year she realized that she enjoyed writing much more than acting, though continued to do both. Interestingly, she was inspired as a playwright after watching endless hours of *The Dick Van Dyke Show*; Kauffman believed that if Sally Rogers (portrayed by Rose Marie) could be a television writer, even in a fictional universe, so could she. Her epiphany became a reality after meeting her future writing partner David Crane.

After *Camino Real*, Kauffman was asked to direct a school production of *Godspell* so she offered an acting role to Crane but he turned it down. He had just come to the realization that he was not meant to be in the limelight so he offered to codirect the play. She agreed and thereafter the pair became an inseparable team. As incipient thespians, they realized there were no roles for undergraduates so they set out to change this inexplicable theatrical roadblock. "We wrote something undergraduates could do," Kauffman noted. "It was fun being on the other side." Although they didn't lose the desire to perform onstage, they did become equally spellbound by playwriting.

After graduating with a Bachelor of Arts degree in theater in 1978, Kauffman followed the same path traversed by nearly all serious aspiring actors and relocated to New York, choosing to hone her skills at the Neighborhood Playhouse School of the Theatre, which is a full-time conservatory offering postsecondary training in Dramatic Arts Acting. In 1980 she graduated their two-year program and teamed up with Crane who had previously moved to New York after graduating from Brandeis University in 1979.

By now, their mutual goal was to become playwrights. They were told it takes seven years to get a play on Broadway or off Broadway so they buckled down and got busy. They contributed musical and sketch material to the off-Broadway revue *Upstairs at O'Neal's* (1982) starring Bebe Neuwirth (*Cheers*), and then quickly teamed with composer Michael Skloff—who roomed with Crane while dating Kauffman—to work on a series of shows for TheaterWorksUSA, which commissioned musical theater for inner-city children. One such project was *Rapunzel*—a musical fairy tale that debuted on December 3, 1984, at Village Performers Theatre, which offered matinee shows ($5 for kids and $7.50 for adults). The trio also worked on more serious theatrical ventures such as Off Broadway's *A... My Name Is Alice* (1983) and a stage adaptation of the 1981 comedy movie *Arthur*, which floundered for five years before stalling, and then miraculously its corpse was resuscitated a few years later. *Arthur, The Musical* made its stage debut on August 12, 1991, at Goodspeed Opera House in East Haddam, Connecticut. (In their shared office at Warner Bros. Studios, above their desks, which faced each other, Kauffman and Crane displayed playbills from their theatrical shows.)

The success of *A... My Name Is Alice,* which *New York Times* theater critic Frank Rich called "delightful," caught the attention of International Creative Management (ICM) talent agent Nancy Josephson, who agreed to represent them. The pair then penned the musical *Personals*, starring Jason Alexander (*Seinfeld*), which opened off Broadway on November 24, 1985, at the Minetta Lane Theater. It was a musical revue with comedic scenes and songs about people writing and responding to newspaper personal advertisements. Rich characterized it a "misconceived show" but *New York Post* critic Clive Barnes celebrated it as the "brightest revue of the year." *Personals* was nominated for four Outer Critics Circle Awards (winning one) and four Drama Desk Awards including Best Score and Best Musical (winning none).

The theater scene was barely paying the bills so to make extra money, David Crane's father arranged a gig at WCAU-TV for the fledgling playwrights to pen questions about math and history for a local Philadelphia game show called *The Knowledge Bowl.* In 1984, the pair also contributed comedy sketches and cabaret songs to the New York–based CBS series *Comedy Zone* but their efforts were uncredited. The one-hour "almost live" series only lasted four episodes.

As the years continued to pass, the co-collaborators were experiencing fleeting success —both professionally and financially—so Josephson urged them to move to Los Angeles to write for television. Crane and Kauffman resisted the idea because they saw themselves as musical theater people, not television writers. Nevertheless, in 1987, they submitted a spec script (unsolicited) for the CBS sitcom *Everything's Relative* (ep It Had to Be You and You) starring Jason Alexander. The scribes chose this particular sitcom because they had just finished working with Alexander in the musical revue *Personals* so they felt they could craft dialogue for his comedic sensibilities. According to Crane, "literally not one word was the same when it aired."

Discouraged by the network's unceremonious dismissal of their work, the duo focused on *Arthur, The Musical,* their pet project since 1982. When the seventh year approached, the playwrights were at a crossroad: Kauffman just had a baby, neither playwright had any money, and their professional success appeared illusory. Josephson convinced them to come up with 10 ideas for new television shows so she could peddle them to production companies to see if there was any industry interest. The duo finally acceded to the idea; they needed a change.

Crane and Kauffman completed the assignment and Josephson discovered there was some interest in her client's writing, so the playwrights periodically traveled to Los Angeles to pitch their ideas in person. Theater was riveting and personally fulfilling but Kauffman and Crane were in their early 30s and not making any money, so they said, "The hell with it, we're going," but vowed never to work on other people's shows. They had to have control. They wanted their voice heard, not someone else's. The tandem understood different writing styles but they still wanted it done their way. They felt uncomfortable receiving writing credit when it was not their words or style, which was exactly what had occurred to their script for *Everything's Relative.*

Lacking any knowledge about the television industry or its production schedule, Crane and Kauffman (and her husband Michael Skloff) relocated to Los Angeles in the spring of 1989. Their timing, however, was ill-conceived. They missed the all-important pilot season; the period of time when most aspiring writers earn their keep. During the 1980s, networks paid writers to come up with ideas for shows. The naive playwrights actually believed that writers were paid for scripts the networks never intended to air. So that's what they did. As David Crane recounted, "We just started coming up with ideas for TV shows and trying to sell them."

Kevin Bright, Marta Kauffman and David Crane in September 1994 and May 2021

Their agent instructed them to write an original script so the tandem worked on a pilot called *Dream On*. Josephson then arranged a meeting with producer Norman Lear (*All in the Family*). He liked the work and signed them to a developmental deal, but their debut was rather inauspicious. The inaugural script was a disaster. Lear hated it—the script was deemed "shallow and superficial" (a descriptive catchphrase the writers later embraced over the years to motivate them)—so they worked on developing another sitcom for Lear while furtively pitching their *Dream On* script to HBO. The pair kept delaying Lear's project as they awaited a final decision which came in the form of a cable series. The scribes had only written one or two specs before *Dream On,* so their meteoric success was relatively abrupt. Unfortunately, they were still under contract with Lear to complete one more project.

In a perfunctory effort to fulfill their obligation, Crane and Kauffman opted to pen a script that was guaranteed to be rejected—a politically themed sitcom, which, at the time, was considered taboo for television. The concept involved a US senator having an affair with his executive assistant, his lesbian wife being physically abusive to their maid, a bulimic daughter, and suicidal son-in-law. "All the characters were reprehensible," Crane admits but "we were having a good time writing." In the opening scene the son-in-law tries to kill himself by hanging, using the curtain cord, but his futile effort only opens the drapes, and later in the episode the wife slaps the maid and the senator is in bed with his mistress. "Ironically, this pilot was shallow and superficial; there were no feelings or emotions," said Crane. The tandem pitched the idea to Lear and he started laughing. The scribes thought, "No, no, this isn't happening!"

CBS purchased the pilot, *The Powers That Be*, but wanted the script doubled in length. Crane and Kauffman were proud of the original version they penned but displeased with their expanded effort. The series costarred Holland Taylor, Tom Forsythe, Peter MacNicol, David Hyde Pierce, Valerie Mahaffey and Joseph Gordon-Levitt, and aired from March 7, 1992 to January 16, 1993, producing 21 episodes. CBS didn't trust newbies to oversee a network show so Lear and other executives took the reins, which was fine with the creators because they had *Dream On*, a show they loved. The HBO series was also the venue where they met and quickly gelled with executive producer Kevin Bright, their future business partner.

In July 1993, Les Moonves was hired as president and chief executive officer of Warner Bros. Television (when WB and Lorimar Television merged). He immediately hired David Janollari from FOX, whose first order of business was to hire Kauffman, Crane and Bright. Disney was offering more money for the triumvirate so Moonves stressed that WB had more shows on television than Disney, "so do you want 10 cents more or 100 million?" The trio liked the pitch so they formed Bright/Kauffman/Crane Productions (BKC Productions) and signed a developmental deal with Warner Bros. The threesome made a good team. Crane and Kauffman were talented writers and Bright had vast entertainment industry experience and impeccable production expertise.

BKC Productions promptly sold two scripts, *Couples* and *Family Album*. From a writer's perspective, one effortlessly flowed and the other was like pulling teeth: *Couples*, a witty, single-camera, three-couple sitcom was written in a week, while *Family Album*, a multi-camera, extended-family farce was painstakingly difficult to put to paper.

Couples involved the interconnected lives of three New York couples sharing the same apartment building, starring Helen Slater, Jonathan Silverman and Megan Mullally. The network was not thrilled with the telepilot so it delayed airing until July 2, 1994, during the television off-season, aptly dubbed Garbage Dump Theatre by industry executives, the landing spot and often final resting place for all unsold pilots. As expected, *Couples* was never picked up.

Naturally, the most arduous project of the two, *Family Album*, was picked up by CBS. What should have been easy to write—it was modeled after the writers' personal lives while growing up in Philadelphia with characters based on their parents—turned out to be very difficult. The series was canceled after six episodes. It aired from September 24, 1993 to November 12, 1993.

Within two months after *Family Album* was canceled, the trio experienced déjà vu. In January 1994 the duo sold two more scripts, "Reality Check" and "Insomnia Cafe" (aka *Friends*). The former required the jaws of life to extract dialogue while the latter flowed like melted butter. Fortunately, for Crane and Kauffman, the network chose the right pilot.

"Reality Check" was a single-camera high school–musical show—a PG version of *Dream On* meets *Glee* featuring Giovanni Ribisi and Hilary Swank. The story followed a high school student (played by David Lipper) who frequently lapsed into elaborate fantasies while his classmates expressed their feelings by bursting into song. The FOX pilot went through "a gazillion" rewrites, as Kauffman noted, and even after the final version was approved, FOX executives were concerned it was not risqué enough. The network wanted the show to be raunchier like *Dream On*, yet tame enough for network television. Despite all the network meddling and tweaking of the show to fit their conceptualization, FOX passed on the pilot. Warner Bros. hoped the show would be a hit on the fledgling WB network (which started broadcasting on January 11, 1995) but costar Hilary Swank dropped out once the project switched networks so the show ended there.

"Insomnia Cafe" (aka *Friends*), as everyone knows, became the flagship series of BKC Productions. After the series debuted and became an immediate success, NBC executives wanted the creative team to develop additional projects for the network. The trio created *Veronica's Closet* (1997-2000) starring Kirstie Alley, and worked as executive producers on *Jesse* (1998-2000) starring Christina Applegate. With *Friends* in the mix, the triumvirate unwittingly bit off more than they could chew. David Crane honestly admitted: "I spend my time running back and forth between the three shows. … It's crazy, and I miss being on all of them full-time, but that's just the reality of taking on more." Crane and Kauffman later acknowledged their lack of involvement precipitated the early demise of the other sitcoms.

After a dry spell, the writing partners experienced creative differences and eventually split. David Crane and his husband Jeffrey Klarik partnered to create the Showtime comedy series *Episodes* (2011-17) starring Matt LeBlanc, while Marta Kauffman and Howard J. Morris cocreated Netflix's comedy series *Grace and Frankie* (2015-21) starring Jane Fonda and Lily Tomlin.

Kevin Bright

Although frequently forgotten because he worked behind the scenes, executive producer Kevin Bright was equally instrumental in the success of *Friends*. Born November 15, 1954, to a Jewish-American family in New York City, Bright attended East Side Hebrew Institute on the Lower East Side of Manhattan. He was raised in a showbiz family. His father, Jackie, a vaudeville comic who later worked as a talent manager for Catskills acts, often dragged his son to the Concord Resort Hotel to watch incomparable talent such as Sammy Davis Jr.

Being raised on live comedy, Bright gravitated toward variety shows for entertainment. He was not a big fan of scripted television shows like *The Dick Van Dyke Show* or *The Mary Tyler Moore Show*; he was captivated by Flip Wilson, Redd Foxx, Andy Williams, Sonny and Cher, and the Osmonds. His first foray into variety programming was *The Ed Sullivan Show* (1948-71).

Kevin Bright's childhood upbringing provided ample firsthand knowledge of the life of an entertainment hustler, so he decided at an early age that he wanted no part of it. When he entered college at State University of New York College Plattsburgh (SUNY Plattsburgh) in 1972, his calling was philosophy, a far cry from vaudeville. Then, an elective film course in his sophomore year altered his career path. Suddenly, the entertainment industry shined a vastly different light than his father's life had illuminated. Prior to his junior year, Bright transferred to Emerson College, which had a highly regarded film and television program, and he immersed himself in the coursework, graduating magna cum laude in 1976.

The era of vaudeville was dying but its media-driven offspring, the variety show, was taking center stage in the television industry. Bright fused his childhood experience with his collegiate studies to create a passionate career path. After graduation, his father pulled some strings to get him a job working in New York at Joseph Cates Company as an intern, which led to him being hired as a personal assistant. Bright slowly learned the business and within three years was an associate producer for one-shot variety shows and specials, including four Johnny Cash segments, and countless country music specials for superstars such as Glen Campbell and Tennessee Ernie Ford. Bright also produced a couple David Copperfield specials. If there was a television variety show produced in New York, he had a hand in it. But he also saw the writing on the wall. As the 1980s arrived, variety shows were fading in popularity and television production in New York City was drying up. David Letterman moved his talk show to Los Angeles and sitcoms were being produced exclusively on the West Coast. Bright realized he had to either go down with the ship or set sail for new shores.

In 1982, Bright quit his job and moved to Los Angeles. Producer Walter Miller had a deal with the Osmond family, who were starting the Osmond Family Network, so he lured Bright to work on their pilot. After six weeks without pay, Bright discovered the Osmonds were financially strapped and that he needed to find a new job that actually paid. His wife had just moved from New York so he was desperate for work. He made a few calls and talent manager Tisha Fein gave him a lead on a new syndicated sitcom called *Madame's Place*. He contacted the show's producer, Don Van Atta, and even though the position had been filled, Bright finagled an interview and then bluffed his way into being hired for the job by insisting he was the man for the job.

The first-run syndicated series *Madame's Place* (1982-83) required shooting 75 episodes in 15 weeks. At one point, they started filming at 9am and finished at 3am, every weekday, shooting two episodes per day. When series star Wayland Flowers finally cracked from the pressure, he demanded they do no more than one episode per day. It was a chaotic work environment but it taught Bright everything he needed to know about television production.

Bright spent the rest of the decade producing cable comedy specials for George Burns, Martin Mull, and Harry Shearer, and had a hand in several other network television and cable specials. He won a CableACE Award as producer of the mockumentary *The History of White People in America* (1985) starring Martin Mull, and served as executive producer for the critically acclaimed syndicated talk show *The Ron Reagan Show* (1991).

In early 1990, Bright hit another bump in the road, going six months without a job, but this time his predicament was more urgent—his wife was pregnant with twins and he had no money in the bank. Once again, he was desperate for a job. Any job would do. When two projects became available, he agreed to do both, practically sight unseen. There was a new comedy sketch series on FOX called *In Living Color* that needed a supervising producer, and an unspecified show for HBO where he would be an executive producer. Despite accepting both offers, Bright actually preferred working for FOX, since commercial network television was preferable to cable at the time. After the pilot for *In Living Color* was picked up, Bright was not asked to return. He was initially hired for the series to be a numbers guy but he could not resist interjecting his thoughts on ways to creatively improve the show. Despite only being involved in the pilot installment, Bright won an Emmy Award for Outstanding Comedy Series for his one-episode role as supervising producer on the hit show.

Despite losing the FOX gig, Bright still had a fallback series. Legendary director John Landis (*Animal House, Coming to America*) was venturing into television so he had to hire someone with production expertise to navigate the packaging and producing for television. Universal Television President Sid Sheinberg told the filmmaker to create a program using the studio's massive movie and television archive. Landis had an idea for a game show and another involving *Mystery Science Theater 3000* meets *Animal House* where frat members make snide remarks about the vintage shows. It was only after he met with the *Dream On* creators that everything synced.

While Crane and Kauffman were living in New York, they had a meeting with Universal executives and Landis. They were shown black-and-white television and movie clips and asked, "What would you do with them?" and the pair responded, "I dunno." On the flight home, however, they came up with the idea for a sitcom that later became *Dream On*. David Crane noted, "That became our first show, which became everything else. When we went into that meeting, we thought, 'This is stupid,' and then it ended up leading to everything." The writing tandem suggested using the old movie and TV clips in their *Dream On* series as a way of expressing the inner thoughts of their protagonist. Landis fell in love with the idea and agreed to executive produce the cable show. In 1992, the series won a CableACE Award for Best Comedy Series.

After three years working together on *Dream On*, Bright, Kauffman, and Crane were in the office when Kauffman expressed wonderment at their seemingly perfect professional arrangement. "This is so great," she exclaimed, "Wouldn't it be great if we could just keep doing this?" Bright quickly replied, "Well, we could. We just need to become partners." So they did. In 1993, the triumvirate formed Bright/Kauffman/Crane Productions, primarily because they felt underappreciated by Universal. Since Kauffman and Crane were nearing the end of their contractual commitment to *Dream On*, they decided to shop around for a developmental deal. Universal was the only studio disinterested in working with them. The trio promptly cemented a deal with Warner Bros. to produce original television programs. When they told Universal of the developmental deal, the executives precipitously expressed interest in signing the triumvirate and were even willing to match the offer. However, it was too late. Bright still had one year left on his contract so he finished it out while the writing duo ruminated sitcom ideas.

Crane and Kauffman immediately generated four pitches, two of which received pilot orders: *Family Album* and *Couples*. The next year two more pilot episodes were ordered, one of which became the pinnacle of their business association. Bright directed 54 episodes of *Friends*, including the series finale. In later years he would produce the sitcoms *Veronica's Closet*, *Jesse*, and then *Joey* (Crane and Kauffman wanted nothing to do with the *Friends* spinoff series).

In 2006, Bright hit a personal and professional low point in his life. After spending a dozen years working 60 to 80 hours per week on *Friends* and *Joey*, the time commitment finally took its toll at home—he was an absentee father for much of his sons' lives and an emotionally distant husband which resulted in a separation from his wife Claudia. As a nonwriting producer, Bright was an industry pariah so he moved to Boston, leaving behind his wife and kids and his career. He taught television production classes at his alma mater, Emerson College, and a decade later returned to the industry to executive produce and direct small-scale projects tailored to his liking, such as documentaries on Doc Severinsen and Martin Mull, and an episode of Matt LeBlanc's sitcom, *Man with a Plan*. Bright and his wife eventually reconciled; she moved east to reconnect with her childhood roots, and the couple currently divides time between Boston and their vacation retreat in Sarasota, New York.

NBC's Mindset

In the mid-1980s, Brandon Tartikoff was president of NBC and his studious protégé was Warren Littlefield. During an advertising meeting, the research department presented a study comparing two shows, one based on viewership and the other on advertising revenue. The results were cataclysmic. One showed that CBS's top-10 hit *Murder, She Wrote* had a large audience base but generated very little ad revenue. In contrast, NBC's critical darling *St. Elsewhere* had depressed viewership (hovering around 50th) but earned substantially more income for the network. Although seemingly incongruous, the reason was surprisingly logical. NBC was able to charge more for advertising because its series attracted viewers that were 18 to 49 years old, the target group for advertisers.

Littlefield took the revelation to heart. He realized that times were changing in network television, and noticed FOX was blazing a new trail to capitalize on this shift to economic programming. After becoming president of NBC in the summer of 1990, Littlefield made it his mission to develop programs specifically designed to attract young viewers. He quickly realized that tenderfoot FOX had proven his theory correct when it began loading its time-slots with popular and successful youth-oriented shows (*Married... with Children*, *In Living Color*, *The Simpsons*, etc.). Of course, Littlefield had the advantage because upstart FOX still lacked credibility and respectability in the industry.

At the start of the 1993-94 television season, NBC was in a predicament. Under the tutelage of Tartikoff, the network dominated the competition through much of the 1980s with smash hits like *Cheers*, *The Cosby Show*, and *L.A. Law*, and solid performers like *Hill Street Blues*, *Hunter* and *The Golden Girls*. As Tartikoff's successor, Littlefield had his hand in developing prosperous comedies, such as *Seinfeld* and *Frasier,* but NBC still slipped into third place in the ratings behind ABC and CBS.

As NBC entered pilot season in the winter of 1993, Littlefield went about his ordinary daily routine of studying the overnight ratings from the major markets but his mind started to aimlessly wander. "I found myself thinking about the people in those cities, particularly the twentysomethings just beginning to make their way," he divulged. "I imagined young adults starting out in New York, LA, Dallas, Philly, San Francisco, St. Louis, or Portland all faced the same difficulties. It was very expensive to live in those places as well as a tough emotional journey. It would be a lot easier if you did it with a friend."

The epiphany became an obsession for the network executive. "Addressing that general idea became a development target for us. We wanted to reach that young, urban audience, those kids starting out on their own, but none of the contenders had ever lived up to our hopes," he surmised. "Then Marta Kauffman and David Crane showed up with their pitch for a show called 'Six of One.'" (In reality, their pitch was for a show called "Insomnia Cafe." It was later called "Six of One" when the pilot was filmed.)

Pilot Concept

Marta Kauffman and David Crane met as students at Brandeis University and after graduation moved to New York City to write musicals. Although they lacked money and job opportunities, the pair nurtured newfound friendships which became their extended family. Their inner circle of best friends included Michael Skloff (Kauffman's future husband), Billy Dreskin (college friend and musical collaborator), and a lesbian couple (Deborah Franzblau and Rona Oberman).

After moving to Los Angeles, Kauffman and Crane's first successful sitcom pilot was the cable series *Dream On* (1990-96), which revolved around the family, romance and career of Martin Tupper, a divorced New York City book editor. The show was notable for its frequent use of clips from old movies and TV shows to express Tupper's inner life and feelings, which lent to much of its quirky appeal, reminding viewers about the impact of television on their consciousness. It was also one of the first American sitcoms to use uncensored profanity and nudity. To this day, the static shown on the TV screen near the end of the *Dream On* title sequence is part of the opening credits for every show made by HBO.

The cable success of *Dream On* opened the door to television networks. After teaming with Kevin Bright and signing a developmental deal with Warner Bros., the duo created the sitcom *Family Album*, which was quickly canceled after airing six episodes. With the failure of *Family Album* weighing heavy on their minds, Kauffman and Crane started reminiscing about their struggles and aspirations after college. It was a time dominated by friends—hanging out together, going out together, doing everything together; the stage of life where friends become paramount and function as an extended, sort of surrogate, family. "We had a group of friends and we were all very tight. We look back on those years really fondly," Crane recalled. "We wanted to write about that time in your life when you left home, you left college, you don't know what you're doing but it's okay because you have this group of people around you who are terrific and make it alright."

The initial concept had six friends heavily involved in each other's lives, spending time together in their apartments, and coping with the daily travails that most twentysomethings encounter. It was a time for firsts: first career, first apartment, first shot at independence (personal and financial), first serious romance, etc. But the scribes were adamant that the series had to be an ensemble. Their biggest complaint about *Dream On* was having every storyline revolve around one character. In an ensemble sitcom, all the characters were to be given equal screen time and equal importance. (At the time, the pilot concept had four main costars and two secondary characters.)

An ensemble comedy was a novel idea to television. No sitcom in the history of network television was a true ensemble. Many shows came close but there was always one dominant star featured in the series. The most famous sitcoms that have been labeled as ensembles include *The Mary Tyler Moore Show*, *Taxi* and *Cheers*, but each of these shows focused on the main star: Mary Tyler Moore, Judd Hirsch and Ted Danson, respectively. Crane and Kauffman were determined to change history.

The inspiration for *Friends* came at a low point in their careers. The two sitcoms they created the prior year had failed so their reputation of having the Midas touch after the success of *Dream On* was tarnished. "We were looking at a time when the future was more of a question mark," Marta Kauffman recalled. "Maybe because that's what we were feeling at the moment, but looking at that question mark and going: that's interesting. Everybody knows that feeling."

In early December 1993, Marta Kauffman exited her Hancock Park abode on a typical drive to work. While cruising along Beverly Boulevard she passed an offbeat coffee shop called Insomnia Cafe, across the street from an Orthodox synagogue. She thought it may be a unique, fun setting for a sitcom, "sort of an over-caffeinated feel for the show." Kauffman ventured inside for a peek and was captivated by the esoteric venue filled with Christmas lights, tattered couches, mismatched club chairs, and mammoth bookshelves bulging with tomes. A hangout congregated with hipsters, artists and philosophers from the Fairfax–La Brea area. The setting seemed right for a sitcom, and also jived with other recent successful comedies—*Seinfeld* had a diner, *Cheers* had a bar—yet it was entirely different. "Oh, that would be a cool place to put these people," she concluded.

To her credit, the coffeehouse setting was a novel business concept at the time. In 1992, Starbucks launched a public stock offering and was largely still seen as a regional chain in the Pacific Northwest. The first international Starbucks location didn't open until 1996, two years after *Friends* premiered. In fact, the two seemingly unrelated businesses shared a symbiotic relationship—as Starbucks introduced a new social environment, *Friends* helped popularize the location as a cool hangout and communal setting.

Kauffman and Crane sketched a rough outline which quickly turned into a seven-page treatment titled "Insomnia Cafe." Their premise: "It's about sex, love, relationships, careers, a time in your life when everything is possible. And it's about friendship because when you are single and in the city, your friends are your family." The original treatment also offered a description of the characters:

> Monica—Smart. Cynical. Defended. Very attractive. Had to work for everything she has. An assistant chef for a chic uptown restaurant. And a romantic disaster area.

> Rachel—Spoiled. Adorable. Courageous. Terrified. Monica's best friend from high school. Has worked for none of what she has. On her own for the first time. And equipped to do nothing.

> Phoebe—Sweet. Flaky. New Age waif. Monica's former roommate. Sells barrettes on the street and plays guitar in the subway. A good soul.

> Ross—Intelligent. Emotional. Romantic. Monica's brother. Suddenly divorced. Facing singlehood with phenomenal reluctance. A paleontologist. Not that it matters.

> Joey—Handsome. Macho. Smug. Lives across the hall from Monica and Rachel. Wants to be an actor. Actually, wants to be Al Pacino. Loves women, sports, women, New York, women and most of all Joey.

> Chandler—Droll. Dry. A wry observer of everyone's life. And his own. Works in front of a computer doing something tedious in a claustrophobic cubicle in a nondescript office building. Survives by way of his sense of humor. And snacks.

All are in their 20s. All trying to figure it out. (This is the actual document the creators used when pitching the sitcom concept to the networks.)

Concept Not Original

Although not entirely unique to television, the sitcom premise was relatively new to the Big Three networks (ABC, CBS and NBC). Kevin Bright opined, "I had never seen on TV a show about people in their 20s in primetime living away from a family situation and friends are your extended family. That was basically the theme—friends is family." Nevertheless, there were several similar notions circulating throughout the smaller, newer networks. In fact, FOX led the charge for youthful programming.

There were several rival shows in development around the same period: (1) in August 1993, one year prior to *Friends*, FOX debuted the sitcom *Living Single* which featured six black twentysomething professionals living in a Brooklyn brownstone; (2) on September 4, 1994, FOX debuted the sitcom *Wild Oats*, a group of twentysomething friends in Chicago; (3) on January 23, 1995, UPN aired *Pig Sty*, five slobby roommates in Manhattan; and (4) in late December 1993 Matthew Perry pitched the sitcom "Maxwell's House," a group of active and attractive twentysomethings taking their first steps in the real world. He sold the pilot to Universal Television but his pitch was turned down by NBC because it, coincidentally, was already developing a similar project—"Insomnia Cafe" (aka *Friends*).

Since *Living Single* premiered in 1993, it is most often referenced as the precursor to *Friends*, while others go so far as to say the entire premise was pirated by *Friends* and then whitewashed for corporate sponsorship. Both comedies feature attractive, young adult male and female characters who love to hang out together. Both are set in New York. Both are dominated by themes involving sex and the search for true love. And both featured sexual tension within the groups of characters that boiled over at times, though more frequently on *Living Single*. The most obvious difference is the composition of the ensembles. *Living*

Single has an all-black cast. *Friends* has an all-white cast. *Living Single*'s Erika Alexander snidely remarked, "*Friends* is a really good sample of *Living Single*," (a term regularly used in rap music to describe a recycled recording). "But the minute they start referring to us as 'Black *Friends*,' that's when I'll go off," actress Kim Fields Freeman joked. "It's better to call them 'The White *Living Single*.'"

David Janollari, executive vice president of creative affairs for Warner Bros. Television, denied there was a great deal of similarity between the two situation comedies. "Both shows have different tones and different attitudes, and are about different things," he explained. *Living Single* was originally developed as a vehicle for Queen Latifah and Kim Coles, "and what happened in the casting was that it emerged as an ensemble of six people," Janollari clarified. "*Friends* began life as a show that would center on two men and two women, with one other man and woman as supporting characters." There are certain stylistic differences between the two shows as well. *Living Single* was developed as a hipper, edgier show for the younger FOX audience while *Friends* was aimed toward the young, more leisurely *Seinfeld* audience. Moreover, *Friends* has three different storylines running together in every episode and is filmed like a movie with more sets and faster pacing, Janollari added.

Nowadays, there are numerous TV shows about young people hanging out in the big city, but in 1994, the idea of a show about aimless twentysomethings was new and scary to the Big Three networks. It had always been the unwritten policy of networks to steer clear of change, to never venture into uncharted waters, and to stick with the same programming formula that worked in the past. NBC President Warren Littlefield thought it was time for a change; a new way of network thinking.

Pitching the Pilot

Television pilot season runs from early fall to late spring. A pilot is a standalone episode of a television series that is used to sell the show to a network. At the time of its creation, the pilot is meant to be the testing ground to gauge whether a series will be successful. Executives from each of the major networks (ABC, CBS, NBC and FOX) listen to hundreds of writers pitch pilot ideas. Within each network, a few dozen are chosen to advance to the script writing stage, of which only 8 to 10 projects are deemed worthy of production. This group is further culled to merely four or five new sitcoms that will make it on air. By the time the fall schedules are finalized, sometime in mid-May, roughly 99 out of 100 of the initially proposed pilots will be rejected.

During development season, a network's objective is strictly a cost-benefit analysis—find the best prospective hit show for the least amount of money. A pilot pitch is free; it costs a network nothing to hear the idea. The pilot cost begins to skyrocket as the process advances toward production. A network pays anywhere from $50,000 to $100,000 for a script, and up to $1.2 million for a pilot. (The writers and producers get their cut but most of the money goes to the cast, crew and studio.)

During the 1993-94 television season, there were only four major broadcast networks producing original programming, and independent production companies like Warner Bros. created shows to sell to the networks. The cable success of *Dream On* earned Kauffman and Crane sufficient Hollywood clout to freely pitch their ideas. In December 1993 the former playwrights pitched their concepts to the networks, but only one was near and dear to their hearts. The following excerpt is the original treatment used to pitch "Insomnia Cafe" to the major networks:

> "This show is about six people in their 20s who hang out at this coffeehouse. An after-hours insomnia cafe. It's about sex, love, relationships, careers ... a time in your life when everything is possible, which is really exciting and really scary. It's about searching for love and commitment and security ... and a fear of love and commitment and security. And it's about friendship, because when you're young and single and in the city, your friends are your family."

At its inception, the pilot concept for "Insomnia Cafe" was somewhat different from the final version that later became known as *Friends*. The sitcom was much more dramatic and not as lighthearted and playful, fusing elements from the creators' dramedy series *Family Album*. However, as the creators negotiated with network and studio executives and began to compromise on production matters, the series slowly evolved from dramedy to comedy.

In the hierarchy of pilot pitching, CBS was given precedence because it took a chance on the duo's first network project, *Family Album*. After the series flopped, Kauffman and Crane felt a sense of loyalty and obligation to CBS. As a form of appreciation, the tandem slotted FOX in second position because it purchased a pilot (*Couples*) though it was never picked up. Warner Bros., the producer of "Insomnia Cafe," was hoping for NBC because the network had a programming vision that meshed well with the pilot concept for "Insomnia Cafe."

In December 1993, Kauffman and Crane had three pilot pitches: (1) "Insomnia Cafe," six people in their 20s making their way in Manhattan; (2) "Reality Check," an adolescent boy and his fantasy life; and (3) an unnamed proposal that was basically a 1990s updated version of *Grease*. In reality, only the first two were given serious consideration. Although "Insomnia Cafe" was best suited for FOX, which had hip programming aimed at youthful viewers, CBS was given the right of first refusal. But, in all honesty, CBS was not the right network for their proposed project, and if they had picked up the pilot, it would have likely faltered. After fretting the thought of having another failed pilot on their résumé, their fears were allayed when CBS passed on both proposals.

After the CBS rejection, Kauffman and Crane joyously sauntered to FOX and pitched both pilot concepts. The network was given the choice of which show to sign, and the suits surprised everyone by ordering a script for both shows. Nonetheless, Warner Bros. was still interested in cutting a deal elsewhere. Although FOX was a good fit, it was still an upstart network lacking the panache and swagger of the Big Three. ABC was approached but the bigwigs expressed no interest—they had a look on their faces like deer caught in headlights. That didn't matter to Warner Bros. executives because NBC was a better fit.

NBC Entertainment President Warren Littlefield was seeking a comedy involving young people living together and sharing expenses. He wanted the group to exchange memorable periods of their lives; he wanted a group of friends who had become "new, surrogate family members." Unfortunately, he was having difficulty bringing the concept to life because the scripts in development were terrible. Then Kauffman and Crane delivered their tagline: "It's about that time in your life when your friends are your family."

The ensuing pitch detailed the characters, the setting, and some of the adventures the creators fathomed transpiring. Littlefield was impressed with how well the characters were developed. "Their pitch was wonderful, and funny, and relatable," he stated. It was perfect. Exactly what he was looking for. He, too, was interested in ordering a script.

Warner Bros. executives were salivating at the thought of a bidding war on "Insomnia Cafe." Studio President Les Moonves brazenly called FOX and demanded a script order with penalty, which is basically a pilot commitment. In other words, FOX would have to bypass the script ordering stage—where the network reviews a single script from the writers before deciding whether to proceed—and commit to filming a pilot without first getting to see the script. At the time, filming a subpar pilot that did not make it to air would be the equivalent of a $250,000 penalty. FOX refused and passed on the sitcom, primarily because it already had a similar project in the works with *Wild Oats*, starring Paul Rudd. (*Wild Oats* only aired four episodes before it was canceled.) Nevertheless, FOX remained interested in the other project pitched by Crane and Kauffman, a high school drama called "Reality Check," which ultimately never made it to air.

Undeterred, Moonves immediately called NBC President Warren Littlefield to gauge his interest. Moonves never mentioned that FOX had already expressed interest in the show, or even that it had been pitched to other networks at all, yet audaciously demanded a pilot commitment. It was the same offer he proposed to FOX but NBC accepted the offer, which is called a put pilot. In Littlefield's opinion it was a very reasonable request. If the pilot was terrible, it was the cost of doing business; if the pilot was at least adequate, it had a chance at becoming a series. Besides, he had been searching for the right series to attract youthful viewers and wholeheartedly believed "Insomnia Cafe" would fill the void, so he did not want to miss a broadcasting opportunity for a paltry $250,000 penalty. Also, he did not want to risk the show going to another network. (He didn't know at the time that at all the other networks had passed on the project.)

It was déjà vu for the scribes. In 1993 they had two pilots purchased, one was easy to write and the other was excruciatingly painful, and both appeared to be heading for the airwaves. One year later, they were in the same position. The creators were thinking, "No, no, no. We've been through that!" They were rooting for only one survivor, "Insomnia Cafe," because "Reality Check" was extremely difficult to write. Nevertheless, they had to prepare as if the FOX pilot was going to be picked up so they rented dozens of teenage movies, such as *Risky Business* and *Say Anything*, started watching the TV drama *Beverly Hills, 90210*, and studied the entire genre to ascertain any commonalities to its mass appeal. "The actors are all very good looking," was Marta Kauffman's astute synopsis. All their efforts were in vain. FOX passed on the pilot for "Reality Check."

First Draft

In the weeks following NBC's decision to order a pilot, the creators reviewed unsolicited scripts written for other series, primarily *Seinfeld* episodes. They looked to the hit sitcom to help them find their voice. Besides *Seinfeld*, the tandem also drew creative inspiration from other well-known "ensembles" such as *The Mary Tyler Moore Show*, *Taxi* and *Cheers*—three successful shows rooted in dialogue and the art of conversation. Their goal was to create a sitcom that would parallel a stage play with fast-paced production.

The *Seinfeld* episode structure also inspired Kauffman and Crane to devise multiple storylines with equal weight. Prior to *Seinfeld*, all sitcoms had a major plot with one or two minor subplots. The groundbreaking sitcom set a new standard in the industry, and the tandem was committed to incorporating this novel concept into their pilot. "When we wrote the pilot we cut back and forth between three stories so it doesn't feel like your traditional sitcom—one big A story and maybe a B story," David Crane interjected. "The feeling was with six actors they needed to tell a bunch of stories."

After all their preparation, the scribes were finally ready to write the pilot script but didn't know where to begin. They only had a rudimentary framework for the show concept and their treatment (story idea) had undeveloped characters. "When you write pilots, you keep coming up with ideas and characters, and characters and ideas, so you never fully develop characters," Crane explained. "You basically say, 'we have six characters, okay let's pitch it.' You do not write a pilot expecting to spend the next 10 years of your life writing about them." The creators knew they had to further define the characters before crafting a script.

Inspirations

The pair drew inspiration from within, utilizing personality traits from themselves, as well as people they knew, such as friends and relatives, not to mention acquaintances and other actors, to create an amalgamation of characteristics that would form loosely based profiles for their protagonists. But first they drew from within.

David Crane is partially represented in Chandler and Ross. "There's a bit of Chandler in me, in terms of his insecurities and defending himself with his humor," he acknowledged. Crane then went on to say that his neurotic tendencies are incorporated into both Chandler and Ross. Marta Kauffman inspired Phoebe's spiritualism, as well as Monica's obsessive compulsive disorder, while her mother was the foundation for Judy Geller but "an extreme version of her." (Just like Monica, Kauffman felt she could do nothing right to please her mother.) Ross' ex-wife Carol and her lover (Susan) were based on friends of the creators, Deborah Franzblau and Rona Oberman, who are the godmothers to Kauffman's daughter Hannah.

The showrunners wanted a sitcom about life as twentysomethings but since they were now in their late 30s, the pair felt a bit out of touch. "We were part of a group of six in New York in our 20s but people today in their 20s are different than what we were," she stated. "When we wrote this we were like anthropologists; we had to ask 20-year-olds what it's like to be in your 20s now. Still the same, but we were pre-AIDs." To get a better idea of how her sitcom characters would behave, Kauffman interviewed several of her children's twenty-something babysitters.

According to Kauffman, the "pilot wrote itself" and was finished in three days. They had a solid first draft but it still needed to be polished. Freelance writers often volunteer their time to improve a script for pilot creators. It establishes goodwill, and may parlay into paid work if the series is picked up. Kauffman and Crane chose three trusted advisors: Jeffrey Klarik (Crane's life partner), and their protégés, the writing team of Jeff Greenstein and Jeff Strauss. Greenstein and Strauss had penned episodes for *The Charmings*, *Mr. Belvedere* and *Charles in Charge*, before joining the *Dream On* staff, and had previously volunteered their time to polish the creators' other pilots, *Couples* and *Family Album*.

Remarkably, the original pitch for "Insomnia Cafe" closely mirrored the actual series that aired except the central love story involved Joey and Monica, not Ross and Rachel. The creators believed these were the two most sexually charged characters so it made sense to have them hook up—a hot young actor and an unlucky-in-love vixen, it seemed obvious and inevitable. The creators were aware of the sexual tension between Ross and Rachel, but were disinclined to develop it further.

Naming the Characters

Rachel's surname was originally Robbins. Of course, it was later changed to Green but there were spelling inconsistencies throughout the series. In most episodes it was Green (without an "e" at the end), but in a couple shows it was Greene.

There have been many false reports that the *Friends* characters were named after *All My Children* characters: Monica (Monique Cortland), Rachel Green (Janet Green), Phoebe (Phoebe Tyler Wallingford), Ross (Ross Chandler), Joey (Joey Martin) and Chandler (the Chandler family). This is merely a coincidence. The creators drew from their personal lives and then randomly picked names until one sounded right.

Chandler was named after a college friend of Marta Kauffman. Monica was selected to honor Kauffman's niece. Phoebe was named after a friend of David Crane's parents because it was a really bizarre moniker. Joey was chosen because he was an actor and the creators wanted something short and simple. The other two character names were randomly chosen.

NBC Critique

When Marta Kauffman and David Crane delivered the pilot script for "Insomnia Cafe," network executives were impressed. NBC President Warren Littlefield felt the creators were venturing into uncharted water. "This is great young adult television, they nailed it," he boasted after seeing the first draft. He thought "Insomnia Cafe" was the type of program to "represent Generation X and explore a new kind of tribal bonding." Despite the adulation, Littlefield felt the script needed a few adjustments to fit the corporate sitcom model.

Limited Settings

The network's first concern was the limited number of scene settings. Littlefield believed the characters were spending too much time in the neighborhood coffeehouse. The initial script had nearly every scene set in the cafe. The network president wanted to feature the characters' apartments. The creators agreed and split the scenes between both locales.

The initial script draft had Chandler living alone. Littlefield suggested having Joey as a roommate and then placing their apartment directly across the hall from Monica's. The executive believed proximity would facilitate additional scenes as the characters flowed from one apartment to the other with the adjoining hallway becoming another meeting spot. Crane concurred so the script was changed accordingly. He honestly stated, "Once we got into making the show, I don't think we'd realized how important having them across the hall would be. We just hadn't done that much four-camera television."

Demographics

One major point of contention was audience demographics. Littlefield wanted an age-diversified cast so the program would appeal to both younger and older viewers. The key advertising demographic is 18- to 49-year-old viewers, and the pilot, in his opinion, only captured the under-30 generation. Network protocol catered to age diversification to entice national advertisers.

It wasn't just network executives who questioned such a youthful cast. Actor-comedian Paul Reiser (*Mad About You*) wondered how the show could function with only a group of twentysomethings. After Lisa Kudrow was cast for the part, she told him about the pilot and he said, "Where's the adult?" It was standard network practice in sitcoms to cover all demographics. Reiser then quizzically quipped, "I don't get it. It's six people sitting on a couch. That's a show?"

Network executives suggested adding an older character into the series—a permanent cast member or frequent recurring character—to entice older viewers to watch the show. The older character would appear periodically in the coffee shop ostensibly as a patriarch figure offering sagacious life and relationship advice to the youthful protagonists. He was someone who would magically appear at the most opportune times to sprinkle magical wisdom as needed. Although Littlefield praised the show as representing Generation X, he quickly reversed course and criticized it as being "too Gen X, too narrow."

The creators did not share this characterization of their show. David Crane defended the pilot as not being one generational, stating that it embraced common themes that made it relatable, accessible, and interesting to all generations. "It's really a show about a rite of passage that's really universal," said Kevin Bright. "What do you want to do for the rest of your life, and where are your romantic interests?" The creators vehemently resisted such an imperious alteration to their script, but in the end, they had no leverage to flat-out reject NBC's proposals. Consequently, they made every effort to incorporate an older character into the script but it never really worked.

NBC President Warren Littlefield (left), and WB President Les Moonves (right)

Pat the Cop

Based on NBC's recommendation to add an older character, Greenstein and Strauss suggested adding the character affectionately known as Pat the Cop, a police officer who would regularly pop by Central Perk for coffee and conversation. The staff writers named the character after a police officer who used to hang out in the Somerville, Massachusetts, movie theater where they used to work during their college days at Tufts University. The creators unilaterally rejected the idea. Instead, they proposed an older coffeehouse owner known as Coffee Joe.

"[NBC] wanted to have an older demographic represented somehow," David Crane said. "We felt that it was fine for an episode, but you wouldn't want to see the character more than once or twice. For us, it just kept coming back to these six friends." Marta Kauffman pointed out that a wisdom-dispensing mentor would actually have stunted the personal growth of the core characters. "Our feeling was that the show existed on these identifiable characters and conflicts. It's about being in your 20s and starting your life. The show is not about the advice they get from an older coffee shop owner."

The creators knew NBC wielded the power to influence and mold the series. Unlike their cable series *Dream On*, the showrunners did not have complete autonomy to formulate and develop their concept. Although they could offer alternative suggestions or tweak an idea, if NBC insisted, the creators had to acquiesce. They had to pick their battles. Pat the Cop was one of the proposals that NBC would not concede.

Kauffman and Crane knew it was a poor idea and one that may ultimately destroy the show but they had no power or control. They set out to rewrite the script by incorporating the character into a scene or two. Coffee Joe began as a coffeehouse owner but then the showrunners realized he was present in too many scenes so they needed a more transient character, which took them back to the original idea of Pat the Cop, an NYPD officer who frequented the cafe. They even cast the role despite loathing the script. Crane found the storyline to be terrible, and Kauffman joked, "You know the kids' book, *Pat the Bunny*? We had Pat the Cop."

In desperation, the showrunners begged NBC executives to yield, and in exchange, they suggested introducing the characters' parents in supporting roles and featuring older guest stars. In their minds, the compromise would satiate the network's desire to attract a more mature audience. NBC consented, so Pat the Cop was axed, but a new script had to be written featuring Rachel's parents visiting the coffee shop in search of their runaway-bride daughter. Hence, the revised script had a more traditional story where Rachel's parents arrive just before the act break (commercial break) but the story was eventually scrapped because "It was awful," Crane acknowledged with a laugh. "After one draft, we said, 'We can't do it.'"

Cafe Setting

Another major sticking point was the setting for the series. New York City wasn't the issue, it was the coffeehouse. Until *Seinfeld* became a megahit, the Big Apple was not a desired setting for sitcoms. Former NBC President Brandon Tartikoff, remarked, "Who will want to see Jews wandering around New York acting neurotic?" As a Jewish man from New York, he was not convinced *Seinfeld* would work, and characterized it as "Too New York, too Jewish." *Seinfeld*'s biggest network supporter, Rick Ludwin, retorted, "I'm not from New York, I'm not Jewish, and I thought it was funny." The show's success allayed all concerns.

Central Perk set from its typical filming angle (left), and a view from the restrooms (right)

NBC thought a coffee shop was too hip and trendy as a hangout for close friends. They wanted the gang to socialize in a diner, much like *Seinfeld*. Kevin Bright put the network's concern in context: "You gotta remember what time it was. Starbucks hadn't really taken hold yet." Coffee shops were new and unknown. Networks like to stick to any formula that worked in the past. Since *Seinfeld* was successful with a diner setting, NBC preferred a diner over a coffeehouse. On the other hand, the creators wanted something different so they held their ground. They did not want to use a diner like *Seinfeld* because then they would *be* like *Seinfeld* and they did not want to be like *Seinfeld*. NBC backed down but executives still had other concerns.

Script Format

NBC executives were not thrilled with the script format. First, the act break (commercial break) was unorthodox; there was no big event to signal the break. Instead, a commercial is forced where it would not normally occur—after Phoebe claims she doesn't want to help the guys assemble furniture. The script designates the Act I break nearly three-quarters into the episode, as Ross and Rachel stare out the window. David Crane commented, "In a pilot, that seems crazy. You couldn't do it today, and I'm surprised we did that then." Although NBC didn't like the stylistic format, executives decided to drop the issue. Instead, they focused on the plots and subplots.

Limit Plots

The traditional network approach to situation comedies is having a main plot with one or two secondary plots behind it. The showrunners opted for three storylines having equal footing. Naturally, NBC requested that the script be changed to feature one dominant plot with one or two minor ones. NBC's discord was a common contention by all broadcasters at the time. Executives paid lip service to the idea of breaking the rules, but in nearly every instance they eased back into their comfort zone—a system of well-established rules—since they feared the potential chaos lurking behind the new and unknown.

The network also had an ulterior motive for encouraging one main plot with two minor subplots. Executives were angling for the pilot to have one dominant star. The showrunners refused. According to Kauffman, "We didn't want it to be like every other sitcom." In this instance, NBC did not stick to their guns, especially since *Seinfeld* established a precedent where coplots can exist in a successful sitcom and the featured star can commensurately share storylines with costars.

Ensemble

The final network objection was to the sitcom format of having an ensemble cast. No successful sitcom ever had a truly ensemble cast, and the shows typically characterized as such—*The Mary Tyler Moore Show*, *Taxi*, *Cheers* and *Seinfeld*—were in fact anchored with one predominant star. The broadcast networks preferred at least one lead actor for every series because it allowed for easier advertising and promotion as well as instant viewer recognition. NBC didn't push the issue until it came time for casting actors for the roles.

Kauffman and Crane always envisioned an ensemble show. After working on *Dream On* where every episode centered on actor Brian Benben, the creators wanted something new and different. If the lead actor was ill, indisposed, or contentious, the entire production had to be shut down. Moreover, writing every plotline around one character became taxing and stifling. An ensemble opened up storylines for each character.

Casts for *Everything's Relative* (1987) (left) and *Dream On* (1990) (right)

Of course, when the pilot was pitched, the ensemble only had four main protagonists and two supporting characters. "When we first pitched the show, we always said it was an ensemble show, we kind of thought Phoebe and Chandler as a little more secondary. They would provide humor when we need it," Marta Kauffman stated. Of course, that all changed once Lisa Kudrow and Matthew Perry were added to the cast. "They gave us much, much more than that. They became so central to the ensemble," she added.

Single Camera

David Crane and Marta Kauffman's involvement in *Dream On* influenced their decision to champion the single-camera filming concept, which is common in feature films. Although it is widespread in television today with scores of successful shows, such as *Modern Family* and *The Office*, back in 1994, this was objectionable to network executives. Single-camera filming usually involved a closed set with no studio audience and the use of a laugh track. Despite its industrywide disfavor, the creators decided to pitch the idea of a single-camera series. Their primary experience was single-camera so it felt more familiar and comfortable. "Marta and David and I had really just been starting out doing multiple-camera sitcoms, it was only our second one," Kevin Bright confided. But the network executives insisted on sticking to their level of familiarity and comfort, which was a three-camera setup. "They all said no, thank God," Kauffman ecstatically proclaimed.

In retrospect, the showrunners were glad the novel filming concept was rejected. They came to embrace live studio filming. It offered instantaneous feedback which allowed the writers to revamp jokes and bits that flopped in front of the studio audience. And the actors welcomed the cheering and spectator enthusiasm because it actually helped improve their performance on each take. The creators noted the difference a crowd made on the cast's performances. When the cast filmed preshoots or on location, often their energy level waned and they gave subpar performances.

Final Thoughts

Despite conceding and compromising on numerous points of contention, Kauffman insisted the show was always about six friends, and that she and Crane were "prepared to live or die by that." This is a bold definitive statement much easier uttered in hindsight. In reality, the creators did not live or die by their initial concept; instead, they were fortunate the resulting network conflicts and resolutions kept their pilot framework mostly intact.

Final Details

After meandering through the quagmire of network politics, David Crane and Marta Kauffman were given the green light to produce the pilot. The endless hours of negotiation and compromise, writing and rewriting, had finally paid off. NBC's agreement to buy the pilot did not guarantee success but it was a step in the right direction.

Once a network orders a pilot, many show creators have the daunting task of finding a production company to pay the tab for producing the installment. For example, when NBC approached Jerry Seinfeld to star in a television series, he did not have a contract with a production company to produce a project. After the network ordered a pilot for *The Seinfeld Chronicles*, he and Larry David had to locate a production company to produce the show. Seinfeld's manager called his friend Carl Reiner who encouraged his son Rob to finance the project through Castle Rock Entertainment. Seinfeld and David were extremely lucky. They had connections. Freelance writers without a studio developmental deal are hard-pressed to find backers to finance their pilot project.

At the time, the cost of producing a sitcom pilot cost around $500,000 (today it hovers in the $2 million range). Generally, the network will not pay the entire cost of production, so the production company is looking at taking on the project knowing it is going to lose money. Not a very attractive business proposition for many studios.

Production Company

Writing a script is one thing but having it produced is an entirely different animal. The project goes from theoretical to practical. No longer is it pulling concepts out of thin air to create a work of art. It requires putting the ideas into practice, which entails a myriad of nuts-and-bolts details. Final production involves meticulous work because the entire series' future hinges on the quality of one show. Thus, significantly more time and money is spent on assembling a pilot episode than one for a regularly scheduled series.

Fortunately, for Kauffman and Crane, they went into the network executive meeting with a developmental deal with Warner Bros. in hand. Despite the scribes having two prior disappointing series in 1993 (*Family Album* and *Couples*), Warner Bros. was excited about this project, especially since it was able to manipulate NBC into paying a penalty if it was not produced. The next important task was picking the director for their pilot.

Pilot Director

Kauffman and Crane were assigned the daunting task of finding a director for the pilot. They contemplated hiring Betty Thomas who previously directed 18 episodes of *Dream On* and the *Couples* pilot, but she was not known singularly as a comedy director. Knowing their poor track record for hiring directors, the duo deferred to someone with considerably more expertise and experience, WB President Les Moonves—and he wanted the best in the business, James Burrows. Moonves wanted a skilled visionary with immense knowledge of the craft and substantial industry experience, and Burrows was perfect because he could handle the assignment without oversight or direction. The renowned director could take the creators under his wing and guide them through the network maze of pilot production.

Although most television viewers do not know his name, in the entertainment industry James Burrows is a legend. He expanded traditional three-camera-sitcom filming to four cameras, and specialized in adult-themed material. He is well respected and was always in high demand. His résumé includes *The Mary Tyler Moore Show*, *Taxi,* and *Cheers* (which he also cocreated), three of the best ensemble sitcoms in television history. If he chose to direct a pilot, there was a strong probability it would be a hit. Burrows had an eye for talent and a vision for artistic excellence.

James Burrows with wife Debbie (left), Ted Danson (top right), and *Friends* cast (bottom right)

James Edward Burrows was born December 30, 1940, in Los Angeles, California, the son of Ruth (née Levinson) and Abe Burrows, a Pulitzer Prize–winning writer and legendary Broadway director. James has one sister, Laurie Burrows Grad. When he was still a young child, his family moved to the Big Apple where he attended New York City's High School of Music & Art. Raised in the then unfashionable Upper West Side of Manhattan, James was introverted and rarely spoke, but he enjoyed singing, especially for the Metropolitan Opera Children's Chorus and downtown in *Carmen* and *Boris Godunov* for $3 a show. After high school, he earned a Bachelor of Arts degree from Oberlin College (Ohio) and a Master of Fine Arts from Yale School of Drama.

Although college did not pique any interest, Burrows attended Yale to avoid the draft. After taking an inspirational directing class, and applying some skills learned from summer musical theater and Off Broadway, he was hired as a stage manager for *Holly Go Lightly* (an adaptation of *Breakfast at Tiffany's*) which was directed by his father and costarred Mary Tyler Moore. Under the tutelage of his masterful father, Burrows gradually incorporated all the technical skills and artistic creativity necessary to build the foundation for a prolific directorial career. The musical bombed on Broadway, but Burrows impressed the star and her then husband Grant Tinker, who would subsequently recruit the younger Burrows to apprentice at their production company, MTM Enterprises, Inc. Despite lacking knowledge about television directing, Burrows was hired for his skill at relating to, and motivating, actors. (MTM became a comedy factory for writers in the 1970s and 1980s, spawning such television sitcom hits as *The Mary Tyler Moore Show*, *The Bob Newhart Show*, *Rhoda* and *Lou Grant*.)

While working for *The Mary Tyler Moore Show*, Burrows learned the craft from skillful director Jay Sandrich, and together they captured most of the directorial awards in the 1970s. In 1978, four MTM veteran writers left to create their own television show, *Taxi*, and recruited Burrows as their director. After four years, two of the *Taxi* cocreators (Glen and Les Charles) teamed up with Burrows to create a new comedy show, *Cheers*.

Burrows' track record of success and experience made him a prime candidate to direct a multitude of television pilots with the expectation that his talents and skills would elevate the show to unprecedented success. He launched many successful sitcoms such as *Dear John*, *Night Court*, *Wings*, *Frasier* and *Friends*.

Each spring, during pilot season, he would wade through a mound of scripts sent by his agent. In March 1994, the one pilot that seized his attention was "Friends Like Us" (aka *Friends*). It was well written, witty, and seamlessly introduced all six protagonists. He liked the dramatic elements which often characterized *Cheers*, and fancied staging both poignant and humorous moments. For example, in the apartment doorway scene where Monica is saying goodbye to Paul the wine guy, Joey and Chandler keep moving the dining table to eavesdrop. The table movement idea was all Burrows. Also, at the end of the episode where Ross splits an Oreo with Rachel, the cookie prop was suggested by Burrows.

Having Burrows agree to direct the pilot was like anointing the series as the season's best of the lot. Just his presence gave the show an advantage over the competition. If he thought it was a great show, there was a good chance it would make it on the fall schedule. But signing him comes at a great cost. His knowledge, skill, experience, and reputation translates into a hefty price tag, and in this instance it was $100,000. By the time he was approached by WB President Les Moonves, Burrows had previously signed on to do three other pilots. He agreed to do a fourth but only because he liked the script. "I read it, and I said, 'I can't let anyone else do this,'" he recalled. But he could not commit to any future episodes beyond the pilot. "I literally had no time," he acknowledged. When the series was picked up with a guarantee to air 6 episodes, Burrows directed the next 3, but thereafter only oversaw 11 more in the first four seasons.

Kevin Bright reflected on the significance of hiring Burrows. "The choice of Jim Burrows directing was a no-brainer because Jim was very well known as executive producer and director of *Cheers,* which had been for all of us one of our favorite shows on television, and also *Taxi,*" Bright stated. "Having the opportunity to have the experience of somebody like Jimmy who had done so many of them was an amazing thing." He succinctly added, "We were very lucky."

Show Title

Throughout the entire pilot process, from inception to pick up, the show title became an endless debate for the creators. Literally, hundreds of ideas were proposed, though only a dozen or so were seriously considered.

When the show concept was pitched in December 1993, the seven-page treatment was titled "Insomnia Cafe." It was based on a cafe by the same name, the very establishment that first inspired Marta Kauffman to write a sitcom with a coffeehouse setting. When FOX and NBC expressed interest in the pilot, the creators opted to change the title to avoid any potential trademark infringement with the real business upon which it was based so they came up with "Central Perk Cafe" (the creators' wordplay on Central Park, the famous New York landmark).

After NBC bought the pilot, it suggested changing the focus away from the coffeehouse. Thus, to comport with this location shift, the showrunners began searching for a series title that would encompass the local neighborhood, not a specific business. Their initial outline was for a show called "Bleecker Street," after the Manhattan street where Kauffman resided during the 1980s, specifically 77 Bleecker St. in New York. Although it was a working title, it still didn't feel right to the creators.

The next naming idea went along with the dramedy theme of the proposed pilot and was called "Once Upon a Time in the West Village." However, after the show switched to a more comedic vibe, the title did not seem to fit. After NBC agreed to buy the pilot, the first draft of the script was aptly titled "NBC Pilot Which Still Needs a Title."

During one of the meetings, NBC President Warren Littlefield recommended Joey and Chandler be roommates that live across the hall from Rachel and Monica. Based on this conceptual change, he proposed changing the title to "Across the Hall." David Crane was not enamored with the title so he sarcastically remarked, "Or just have it *be* across the hall." Nevertheless, since the creators did not have a better title in mind, they went with Littlefield's suggestion.

Since the titling ideas were not flowing, in early February 1994 Warner Bros. Studios sponsored an internal "name-that-show" contest. The big winner was David Crane's life partner Jeffrey Klarik, who suggested "Friends Like Us." The creators finally unearthed a moniker they liked so it became the pilot title when NBC received the final script from the creators.

Once casting commenced in late February, "Friends Like Us" was the official pilot title. But the name was short-lived. On March 29, 1994, ABC debuted *These Friends of Mine,* a sitcom about adults hanging out and looking for romance. The show was given the best timeslot in television—following No. 1 smash *Home Improvement*—so naturally it became an instantaneous top-10 hit. This caused trepidation among NBC executives. They worried there may be audience confusion because both sitcoms were quite similar in title, genre (sitcoms), demographics (young adults), themes (daily travails), etc., and the network did not want "Friends Like Us" to get lost in the shuffle. Ironically, one year later, during the summer of 1995, ABC renamed *These Friends of Mine* because it was being overshadowed by *Friends.* The new rebranded series was called *Ellen,* after the lead character who had the same name as the actress who played her, Ellen DeGeneres.

To mollify NBC's fears, the creators reluctantly changed the pilot title to "Six of One," which was the actual name of the series when filming commenced in early May. It was only after the final edit was delivered to NBC that network executives expressed displeasure with the title and requested another name change. One day before NBC was set to announce its fall lineup on Friday, May 13, 1994, the producers reflected upon the one title they actually liked, "Friends Like Us," but opted to shorten it to "Friends." After notifying the network, NBC executives called the title "generic," "too Gen X," "way too narrow" and "such a snore" but were under the gun to make their official public announcement so they reluctantly acceded.

Upon further reflection, network executives embraced the title after realizing it had a vibe similar to other singularly titled smash hits, namely *Seinfeld*, *Cheers*, *Frasier* and *Taxi*, which they considered a harbinger. Executive producer Kevin Bright did not care one way or the other: "If you put us on Thursday nights, you can call us Kevorkian for all I care." This is a rather obscure reference that many younger fans of the show may not understand. Jack Kevorkian (1928–2011) was an American pathologist and euthanasia proponent. He publicly championed a terminal patient's right to die by physician-assisted suicide ("Dying is not a crime"). He admitted to assisting at least 130 terminal patients and was eventually convicted of murder in 1999, earning him the media moniker "Dr. Death." Astonishingly, there was massive support for his social cause, and he ultimately helped set the platform for reform.

Casting

The creators finished writing the pilot script in early March 1994, though the laborious casting process commenced a month earlier with a preliminary list of actors, and then at the end of February an eight-line character breakdown was sent to acting agencies in Los Angeles, New York and Chicago. Agents promptly sifted through their clients and submitted photos and résumés of actors they thought, or at least hoped, might fit the descriptions. During television pilot season, actors would fly from Chicago or New York and live in Los Angeles for three months to audition for pilots, hoping to be selected for one of the few that would get picked up and made into a series.

Kauffman and Crane only had eight weeks to complete the task. The three cocreators expressed a desire to be open about race and ethnicity, except for the characters Ross and Monica which were designated as Caucasian siblings. The remaining four castmates were race neutral. Casting director Ellie Kanner compiled an enormous list of prospective actors which included numerous African-American and Asian-American performers.

The project created a buzz in the industry. Once it became apparent that the series was a favored project, NBC President Warren Littlefield was inundated with calls. "There was a clarion call for young acting talent throughout the industry going 'How do I get an audition for this?'" he recalled. Auditions for the lead roles took place in New York and Los Angeles.

Casting director Ellie Kanner received more than 1,000 glossy black-and-white headshots for each role. She meticulously culled the prospective crop of applicants to 75 actors for each part and scheduled callbacks for the performers to read a scene from the pilot. The most promising candidates received another callback to audition for Marta Kauffman and Kevin Bright. Cocreator David Crane purposely abstained from the early screening process because he wanted to hire every actor who came in and felt guilty rejecting them.

All six lead roles were cast at the same time which made the casting process immensely cumbersome, time consuming and arduous. It was not a simple matter of finding an actor to play Joey, then moving on to the next costar; each part was cast simultaneously which made it exceptionally difficult to ascertain whether the actors hired would have chemistry together in an ensemble.

At the end of March, the number of prospective actors had been reduced to three or four for each part, so the next step was to read for, most notably, Les Moonves, president of Warner Bros. Television, along with Kanner, the executive producers, and other WB execs. The session took place in studio casting director Barbara Miller's office. They all received a list of the actors and their agency representatives, as well as prospective actors unable to appear for various reasons, such as prior television commitments or pregnancies (of which there were a few). The actors were called into the room one by one and seated in a director's chair, which was surrounded by studio and network executives, the creators, and casting personnel with their chairs arranged in a semi-circle facing the actor.

The session lasted about 75 minutes. According to Moonves, it was "not a bad session, but not a great session." Some of the actors were considered "too theatrical or too sitcomy" while others failed to replicate an earlier dazzling performance. The overall consensus was that only a few of the actors were ready for the next phase: auditioning for NBC executives.

Prior to the final network audition, it was standard practice for the studio (in this case Warner Bros.) to negotiate a salary with each actor. The typical industry contract required a pilot commitment plus five years on the series. While salaries may vary, at the time, it was common practice for an actor to receive $25,000 or more just for the pilot, depending on their experience, industry clout, and agency representation. An excellent example of salary disparity in an ensemble series occurred in *Modern Family* when it debuted in 2009. Actor Ed O'Neil earned $200,000 for the pilot, after Craig T. Nelson (*Coach*) rejected the offer as too low; meanwhile, his costars earned between $30,000 and $90,000.

Final casting decisions are made by the network. If there is disagreement between the network and the creators as to the best actor for the part, the production company almost unilaterally sides with the former. Its objective is to have the pilot picked up as a series so it often acquiesces to the network's demands by bullying the show's creators into acceding. Since very few creators have bargaining power with network executives, they must relent or risk capsizing production of their project.

In the realm of casting, there are no guarantees. Even the brightest minds often fail at assembling the perfect cast despite their best efforts to create a viable series. All the diligent screening, painstaking interviews, scrutinizing auditions and repeated callbacks is worth nothing once the cast is assembled onstage. Their chemistry as a team, as a cohesive unit, will make or break the project, validating or vitiating the entire casting process. Assembling the perfect cast is a fluid concept. Actors initially chosen for roles are rapidly replaced for various reasons (e.g., they accept other roles, become ill, unavailable or pregnant, or the network wants someone else. This instability occurs at every phase of the casting process, up to the time of filming, and occasionally afterwards.

The audition process is terribly frustrating for everyone—talent agents, actors, casting agencies, creators, studio executives and network executives. But, it is a necessary evil. It's an endless cattle call of actors with limited range or inconsistent performances. Casting for "Friends Like Us" was no different. After more than two months of casting, which involved hundreds of actors (and nearly 1,000 auditions), the creators were not making any progress at signing the six leads. They began doubting their writing. "There was even a point during the casting process where we weren't even sure the script was funny anymore because so many people had come in and done it and were unable to make it come to life," said Kevin Bright. According to David Crane, there were only six actors who "nailed" their parts. Not surprising, it was the final chosen cast.

The order of casting decisions was Schwimmer, Kudrow, LeBlanc, Cox, Aniston, and Perry. The order in which the actors were signed was Cox, Kudrow, LeBlanc, Perry, Aniston, and Schwimmer. Although Schwimmer was first to be cast, his agent held out the longest to negotiate a higher salary than his costars. Technically, Aniston was the last cast member to become part of the ensemble since her contract with CBS didn't officially terminate until mid-September; incredibly, at that point in time, four *Friends* episodes had already been filmed.

Ross Geller

Ross' character profile was simple: "Intelligent. Emotional. Romantic. Monica's brother. Suddenly divorced. Facing singlehood with phenomenal reluctance." David Crane reflected upon his specific influence on the character: "I've always connected with ... Ross because he's always trying to do the right thing. There's kind of a woebegone quality about him I can relate to."

Having worked with David Schwimmer in the past as a guest performer on *Dream On* and during casting for *Couples* a year prior, the creators had him in mind when writing the character Ross, so he was the first actor cast. "There was something so unique about him," Marta Kauffman proclaimed. "When we wrote Ross, he was in our heads. ... His hangdog expression stuck with us, so when we started doing Ross, that was on our mind."

The role of Ross was specifically written for Schwimmer even though he had never been approached to appear in the pilot. He was their one and only choice for the role. "The first person we approached was David Schwimmer because we had an experience with him in another pilot that we did, *Couples*, he went to the network on that [final audition] but didn't get the part," Kevin Bright recalled. When Schwimmer was finally approached and offered the "Friends Like Us" (aka *Friends*) role without an audition, he turned it down.

When it became apparent that Schwimmer was steadfast in his denial, the creators had no other choice but to open casting for the part. NBC was thrilled because they wanted a big-name star to anchor the new pilot. It was common practice at the time for networks to hire an established, successful actor with a loyal fan base because it effectively guaranteed a built-in audience for the series.

Jonathan Silverman

With David Schwimmer out of the picture, NBC pushed hard for Jonathan Silverman, a perennial favorite among networks because he was an attractive, successful, established star. According to Kevin Bright, NBC perceived Silverman as a handsome Jew, and one who could pass as a leading man, whereas Schwimmer was not. Silverman stayed at the top of the casting list to play Ross until Schwimmer reconsidered his earlier decision.

This wasn't the first time NBC chose Silverman over Schwimmer. One year prior, NBC insisted on signing Silverman instead of Schwimmer for the male lead in *Couples*. Although Kauffman and Crane lobbied for Schwimmer, the network had final veto authority which it used on him.

Eric McCormack

During the open casting, Eric McCormack (*Will & Grace*) was brought in to read for the part. He made it through three auditions and read for the studio but did not make it any further. McCormack was hopeful and expressed his thoughts to director James Burrows. "Years later I told Burrows the story, and he said, 'Honey, you were wasting your time. They wrote the part for Schwimmer,'" the actor honestly admitted.

Noah Wyle

During TV pilot season, series creators experience intense competition to sign the best actors. Since actors audition for multiple pilots and usually accept the first offer, Kauffman and Crane were often left in the dust. They had difficulty finding the right performer and by the time they did, the actor had already signed with another series. Case in point, Noah Wyle. The creators chose Wyle to test (final audition) for the network, but in the meantime, he also auditioned for the drama series *ER*, and was offered a costarring role, which he did accept. This left Kauffman and Crane forced to sign Wyle in second position, meaning the actor could star in "Friends Like Us," but only if *ER* was not picked up. Since there was no guarantee he would be available, the creators had to find a replacement. *ER* became a hit with Wyle as an important costar, and yet he still took the time to have a guest appearance on *Friends* in the first season, along with George Clooney, as doctors on a double date with Rachel and Monica.

Mitchell Whitfield

With Noah Wyle in second position, relatively unknown actor Mitchell Whitfield became a top prospect. He is better known to *Friends* fans as orthodontist Barry Farber, Rachel's ex-fiancé. Immediately after reading the script for "Friends Like Us," he called his agent and said, "We have to make this happen." The audition process went well and he was a finalist pitted against Noah Wyle. Of course, Wyle won the role, but after he became unavailable, Whitfield received a call from a staffer who indicated that he was going to get the lead. At the last minute, however, the producers stated, "We're bringing in one more guy to read." That guy turned out to be David Schwimmer.

David Schwimmer

In early 1993, after being bypassed for Kauffman and Crane's sitcom *Couples*, David Schwimmer was immediately cast for NBC's new pilot *Monty*. It starred Henry Winkler as a conservative radio talk show host with a brash personality who clashes with his listeners and then goes home to his family, where more conflicts arise. The network opted to pass on the project but FOX picked it up and commissioned 12 more episodes. Despite taping 13 installments, the network only aired 6 before summarily canceling the series. The sitcom aired from January 11, 1994 to February 15, 1994.

The news of *Monty*'s cancellation was a relief for Schwimmer. His time on the show was exasperating. The creative team never listened to his ideas and he was basically told to shut up and say his lines. The series left him with the impression that television was a medium where ideas were ignored and everyone reports to work to engage in mediocre performances that were personally unsatisfying and professionally unfulfilling. With the noose removed, Schwimmer vowed never to return to television. He wanted a collaborative, creative environment, which, up until that point in his career, he only experienced in the theater. Thus, in late 1993 he moved back to Chicago to work on projects for Lookingglass Theatre, which he cofounded with classmates after graduating from Northwestern University in 1988. The nonprofit stage company had just completed moving to a new location at Steppenwolf's, and Schwimmer finally felt at home. He immediately joined the new theatrical production of Mikhail Bulgakov's *The Master and Margarita*, a fantastical world of Soviet totalitarianism tempered with magical realism, and explicitly instructed his agent Leslie Siebert to reject all television projects.

Siebert honored his request for several months before the pilot script for "Friends Like Us" (aka *Friends*) crossed her desk. She urged him to read it but he firmly refused. Siebert called a few more times, persistently prodding her client to read the script. Then she found a new angle. She eased him into the conversation by stating the pilot was written by David Crane and Marta Kauffman, who admired his craft. She knew he had a pleasant experience with them on *Dream On* and during casting for *Couples*. After Schwimmer gave a favorable response, "Oh, yes. I remember loving the writing," Siebert uttered the magic words: "It's an ensemble show. There's no star. There are six people, all similar age." Her client succumbed and said, "Okay, I'll read it, but I'm not going to do it."

Schwimmer was enticed by the idea of an ensemble show. It had the potential to be a television series that functioned like a theatrical troupe. Despite loving the script, he was still disenfranchised by the television industry. He stood firm. The creators were next in line to persuade Schwimmer to change his mind. "We were sending him flowers and lunch and deli, whatever we could do to get him to agree to do the show," Kauffman stated. They were adamant in their quest to obtain the crown jewel for their series. According to David Crane, they had "to beg" and "beseech" Schwimmer to join their ensemble. "We assured him that whatever his past experience was, this was going to be different. We promise," Crane said. Schwimmer still said no.

Then he received two game-changing telephone calls. The first from Robby Benson, a friend of Kauffman and Crane, and the other was from James Burrows. Schwimmer had positive experiences with both directors while working on the set of *Monty*, so he was happy to indulge the pair. After a pleasant conversation, Benson urged Schwimmer to take some action, "Look, I really think you should consider doing this. At least go and meet Marta and David and talk about it." Although impressed with Benson's work, Schwimmer remained unaffected.

The next phone call tipped the scales. It was from one of Schwimmer's idols, legendary director James Burrows. Although Burrows espoused the same thoughts as Benson, he sweetened the pot by confessing that he agreed to personally direct the pilot episode, and then doubled-down by revealing the role of Ross was specifically written for the thespian. Schwimmer was flattered and thought to himself, "Well, it's quite disrespectful [to continue refusing] with all this talent asking to meet and just consider it. I'd be an idiot not to go." He called the creators, who told him it would be fun and that since it was merely a pilot, it would probably never go anywhere.

Although there was no formal audition, David Schwimmer was required to read for the part. It was an informal gathering with the producers and casting director Ellie Kanner; there were no studio or network executives involved. He read the part with Kanner and she immediately knew he was perfect for the role of Ross. Everyone in the room knew it.

Phoebe Buffay

According to the original pitch, Phoebe was "sweet, flaky, a waif, a hippie" and a free spirit who played bad folk songs on her guitar and dated a lot. The character was originally supposed to be goth. When the casting call went out for a "New Age waif," many actresses arrived for the audition sporting "bell bottoms and clunky shoes and nose rings."

The audition required the actresses to recite a monologue from the pilot script where Phoebe discusses her sad life:

> "I remember when I first came to this city. I was fourteen. My mom had just killed herself and my step-dad was back in prison, and I got here, and I didn't know anybody. And I ended up living with this albino guy who was, like, cleaning windshields outside port authority, and then he killed himself, and then I found aromatherapy. So believe me, I know exactly how you feel."

Jane Lynch

Numerous sources falsely reported that Jane Lynch auditioned for the role of Phoebe. She said it was a "Hollywood myth" that she almost joined *Friends*. "I would have loved that audition," Lynch exclaimed. "At that time in my life I wasn't getting that level of audition, that's for sure!" She is best known as Sue Sylvester in *Glee* (2009-15), which earned her an Emmy Award and Golden Globe Award. Lynch eventually appeared in the last season of *Friends* as Ellen, a real estate agent selling the house next door to the one the Bings were under contract to purchase.

Megan Mullally

A wonderful, talented actor, Megan Mullally advanced quite far in the audition process but her age was a hindrance (she was 35). The future award-winning sitcom star made it through several callbacks but never became a finalist. She is best known as Karen Walker in *Will & Grace* and Chief Lydia Dunfree in *Childrens Hospital*. FYI: Mullally tested for the role of Elaine on *Seinfeld*, which was awarded to Julia Louis-Dreyfus.

Kathy Griffin

The creators were familiar with Kathy Griffin and her acting skills because she was a guest actor in an episode of *Dream On*. She could play the part of a flaky woman but lacked experience and was too old (33). Griffin received one callback but never advanced further. She is best known as Vicki Groener in *Suddenly Susan*.

Lar Park Lincoln

The casting director was initial interested in Lar Park Lincoln because of her successful recurring role in *Knots Landing* as Linda Fairgate from 1987 to 1991. She also appeared in several horror films, such as *House II: The Second Story*, *Friday the 13th Part VII: The New Blood* and *Freddy's Nightmares*. Lincoln was a bit too old (33) so she did not make it far in the audition process.

Janeane Garofalo

Although initially considered to play the part of Monica, Janeane Garofalo was asked to audition for the role of Phoebe. This was very early in the casting process when Phoebe was a goth girl. "Long ago before *Friends* was *Friends*, when it was in its infancy, it was a show called 'Friends Like Us,' and I was being considered for a role, like a goth girl, which I think morphed into Phoebe," Garofalo recalled. Instead of pursuing the sitcom role, she opted to join *Saturday Night Live* for its infamous 1994-95 season. This was a fallow period in *SNL*'s history, during which the sketch show wasn't particularly friendly to women. Garofalo later referred to her season at *SNL* as "the most miserable experience of my life." Coincidentally, she was given the assignment after Jennifer Aniston turned down an offer to join *SNL*.

Ellen DeGeneres

Contrary to numerous reports, Ellen DeGeneres did not audition for the role of Phoebe. Her name was at the top of a list of potential candidates when casting commenced but she had already been hired to star in her own sitcom *These Friends of Mine* (aka *Ellen*) which debuted on March 29, 1994. Most sources misreported her involvement in "Friends Like Us" (aka *Friends*) because the titles were similar.

Lisa Kudrow

In 1985, long before costarring in *Friends*, Lisa Kudrow was a Vassar College graduate with a degree in biology (with an emphasis in neurobiology), and in 1994 co-authored a scientific research paper on "Handedness and Headache" with three others, including her father, Dr. Lee Kudrow, who founded the California Medical Clinic for Headache, which is now headed by her brother, Dr. David Kudrow. It was her intention to continue her father's work as a headache researcher.

"I started off doing research, because my goal was still to go to graduate school and I wanted to be published," Kudrow stated. "But after a few months I realized if I wanted to try acting, now was the time to do it. My father agreed. So I just stopped the research after that one project and became a receptionist for him." She worked on her father's staff for eight years while breaking into acting.

Her first big break was being cast as a regular cast member on *Frasier* where she would play radio producer Roz Doyle. However, once the show began production, cocreator Peter Casey noticed that Kudrow was not able to play a formidable foil to Frasier; she was rather milquetoast. The writers tried to tone down the dialogue and then Kelsey Grammer began giving a weaker performance so he wouldn't overwhelm her. Kudrow saw the writing on the wall: "I knew it wasn't working. I could feel it all slipping away, and I was panicking, which only made things worse." Casey consulted with director James Burrows and they agreed to fire Kudrow after three days of rehearsals. The role was recast and the part was awarded to Peri Gilpin, another finalist for the role.

A few months later, Kudrow received an unusual call: there was an offer for a role on *Mad About You* but her agent discouraged her from accepting it, because she had to be on set in one hour without first reading the script. Her agent deemed the request "insulting and demeaning." Nonetheless, Kudrow was desperately low on cash so she jumped at the opportunity.

Kudrow did so well in her inaugural performance that *Mad About You* cocreator Danny Jacobson immediately offered her a recurring role, with at least five more appearances over the course of the season. She also impressed staff writer Jeffrey Klarik, who gushed to his life partner, David Crane, about Kudrow's talent playing Ursula, a ditzy waitress. "You have to see Lisa Kudrow. She absolutely is Phoebe," he earnestly proclaimed. Shortly thereafter,

Crane called Kudrow and invited her to audition for a new sitcom he was cocreating. She thought an audition would leverage Jacobson into offering her a permanent part on *Mad About You*. The ploy didn't work. He actually encouraged her to pursue the costarring role.

After reading the script, Kudrow was more drawn to the Rachel character. "It's funny because when I first read the script, and I was going to be auditioning for Phoebe, I saw Rachel and I just went, 'Oh, that's like a Long Island JAP—that could be hilarious. I can identify with that more,'" she recalled. But the producers were against the idea and told her, "No, no. Phoebe."

Due to Klarik's recommendation, Kudrow was able to bypass a preliminary audition with the casting director and perform directly for Kevin Bright and Marta Kauffman. She was given the same monologue other actors were required to deliver. Bright already knew of her from *Mad About You* and thought she had a lot of potential. He was not disappointed. "When Kudrow came in to audition she hit Phoebe out of the park, better than we could have imagined it," he surmised. "It was one of those few moments where Marta and I were able to say, 'This is the person.'" Bright went on to say, "She was great at delivering the unexpected. The way you envisioned the line to be said in your head was different but her delivery was better or a more original twist I had not envisioned." Marta Kauffman was in awe and added, "Phoebe ran the risk of being cartoonish, and Lisa brought so much humanity to her."

Kudrow tapped into personal experience to perform the scene comically. For inspiration, she harkened back to her days at Vassar College:

> "That reminds me of my friend from college who had to leave school because her parents thought it was making her irreligious, and they didn't want to pay for it anymore. And she had to work in a nursing home. And she never got down about it, ever. It was always like, 'It's so funny where I work, there's this one woman who's so funny because she can't think straight anymore, and it's very funny.' She found things to love about working in the nursing home. What an attitude! I always admired that, and it stuck with me. And I thought, 'Okay, that's what this person needs to have—that attitude. Doesn't feel sorry for herself at all.'"

At the callback, she performed in front on the executive producers, casting directors Lori Openden and Ellie Kanner, and director James Burrows. Kudrow was particularly worried about performing for Burrows because he was instrumental in having her fired from *Frasier*. Much to her relief, though, he was a nonfactor. All he said was "No notes … Okay, thank you, Lisa." According to Openden, the actress "owned the role from the start."

On the next callback, which was held in a studio theater, Kudrow read for the executive producers, studio casting director, and Warner Bros. executives. The venue was supposed to connote a theatrical play to make actors feel at ease. Instead, most of the actresses were freaking out and several walked out before their audition. Kudrow was confounded. She thought to herself, "How was this audition different than performing in a play or in front of a studio audience?" She credits her good coping skills as the reason for her advancement to the next round. According to Kudrow, several actresses were perfect for the part but they panicked. WB President Les Moonves felt that many of the actors were "too theatrical" for a television comedy.

When Kudrow finally received a callback a month later to test for the role, she wanted to play the part differently. Her agent was alarmed so she arranged a preliminary audition with Kanner and Kauffman. The new interpretation was good but it lacked the indefinable ditziness that Kudrow displayed in her prior performances. Kudrow was advised to stick with her original portrayal.

The final audition involved the executive producers, and executives from WB and NBC. It was down to Kudrow and one other actress. "Every time I auditioned it was a different actor going for the role of Phoebe," she remarked. "I had no idea what was going on." She passed the test and became the second actor to be cast, approximately one month after Schwimmer came aboard.

Numerous sources claim Lisa Kudrow was the only *Friends* actor to audition twice, but in truth most of the cast auditioned numerous times before getting their respective parts. Kudrow had at least three auditions. Matt LeBlanc claims he was subjected to the casting process six times. Only David Schwimmer was cast without an audition. Courteney Cox had the chance to accept the role of Rachel after one tryout but turned it down. She, too, had numerous callbacks before being cast as Monica.

Although excited about earning a costarring role as Phoebe, Kudrow was more worried whether a failed pilot would impact her recurring role on *Mad About You*. "Pilots work and don't work," she told the NBC executives, "but we have to protect *Mad About You*, please." Kudrow was relieved that both sitcoms shared the same network because she thought NBC would protect her interest on *Mad About You*. Nevertheless, in the first couple months of the series she kept pulling the *Friends* producers aside during rehearsal breaks to ask, "Are the ratings good enough?" Kudrow needed to know her level of job security and whether she should prepare for another round of pilot auditions. Even though the show proved to be successful, the *Friends* producers encouraged her to continue the dual role on *Mad About You* and vowed to work around her filming schedule.

Joey Tribbiani

The Joey character was written as a lothario, city slicker, and arrogant, self-centered jerk. He performs in children's theater, which he finds unfulfilling, and works a variety of gigs to make the rent, like a bouncer, bike messenger, and "the guy in the department store saying 'Aramis? Aramis? Aramis?'"

In the casting call for actors, Joey was described as a "handsome, smug macho guy in his 20s." According to casting director Ellie Kanner, there was a slew of actors displaying ample chest hair. The casting call apparently triggered an unexpected image in the minds of all the candidates. It was nothing the showrunners had in mind for the character, but that didn't really matter since none of the actors conveyed the proper pacing and delivery the creators imagined for Joey.

All the actors read the same pilot script dialogue from the "grab a spoon" scene where Joey refutes Ross' belief that there is only one woman for every man:

> "What are you talking about? One woman? That's like saying there's only one flavor of ice cream for you. Let me tell you something, Ross. There's lots of flavors out there. There's Rocky Road, and Cookie Dough, and Bing Cherry Vanilla. You could get 'em with jimmies, or nuts, or whipped cream! This is the best thing that ever happened to you! You got married, you were, like, what, eight? Welcome back to the world! Grab a spoon!"

Hank Azaria

Skill and experience highlighted Hank Azaria's résumé. He was a regular performer in *Herman's Head* and prolific voice artist in *The Simpsons*. Azaria thought he was perfect for the role of Joey and had his heart set on playing the part. After reading the script, he "knew it was great" and was "desperate to be in it." In fact, after receiving the first rejection, he begged for a second chance. "I went and auditioned for Joey and got rejected. But—and this was the first and only time I've done this—I asked to go back in. I said, 'I know you said no to me once, but I just want to try it again, because I like that show that much.' And I went back in ... And I got another very quick no. As quick as the first time." He concluded, "They liked my audition, they just thought Matt LeBlanc was better."

Despite the setbacks, Azaria's opinion of himself playing the role didn't change. He still thought he was suited for the part and truly believes he could have been funnier than Matt LeBlanc in the first season. "At first, in my opinion, in the first few episodes of *Friends* he hadn't really found it. And all that first season I was like, 'I could've been funnier than him!'" But Azaria conceded that "LeBlanc really found himself in that role."

It was bad enough losing the costarring role to LeBlanc, but then Azaria had to further endure the frustration associated with his longtime friend, Matthew Perry, being cast for the show. "I had to tell him, 'Bud, I'm burning with jealousy. I'm consumed with hatred for you right now.'" However, he did qualify his response, "Once you express it and are honest about it, it kind of goes away. You can just be happy with your friend. I needed to say, 'You have to know that a part of me's dying.'" Azaria ended up having a five-episode arc on the show as Phoebe's scientist boyfriend David.

Vince Vaughn

At the time of the audition, Vince Vaughn was youthful (23) and inexperienced. He had only seven episodic appearances and two bit parts in movies. Although he showed decent potential, Vaughn didn't have the proper skill set for the role. Casting director Ellie Kanner admitted that Vaughn was "handsome and tall" (6'5) and a "good actor" but he didn't quite fit the role the way Matt LeBlanc did.

Louis Mandylor

The final audition was narrowed down to two actors: Louis Mandylor and Matt LeBlanc. Mandylor had more experience; he costarred in the FOX sitcom *Down the Shore* (from 1992 to 1993), playing the part of Aldo, a noted lothario, and had a recurring role in ABC's hit comedy *Grace Under Fire* (from 1993 to 1994) as Carl, a coworker of Grace Kelly (played by Brett Butler). FYI: In *Grace Under Fire*, Cole Sprouse (Ben in *Friends*) and his twin brother Dylan played the youngest child, Patrick Kelly, from 1993 to 1998.

Prior to the final audition, LeBlanc's agent received a character breakdown—Joey was an Italian-American struggling actor in New York City—so her client dressed accordingly, yet somehow, Mandylor came dressed in a denim jacket, jeans, cowboy boots and stetson. LeBlanc looked at him and thought, "One of us is way off the mark. God, I hope it's you." The showrunners were leaning towards Mandylor because LeBlanc was raw talent and less experienced. Warner Bros. casting director Barbara Miller tipped the scales when she gave her opinion to Kauffman, "[LeBlanc] is the actor who will get better every episode. He can do it." The producers trusted her judgment and cast him.

Matt LeBlanc

Casting assistant Stacy Alexander brought Ellie Kanner a videotape of an actor gaining accolades on FOX's *Married... with Children*, *Top of the Heap* and *Vinnie & Bobby*. Granted, the sitcom material was notably different, but Kanner felt there was something about Matt LeBlanc that could possibly work for the role of Joey. "He could be perfect," she thought.

Long before *Friends*, LeBlanc was a struggling actor. He was so poor that he once saved money by doing his own dental work. After a headshot photographer suggested getting an uneven tooth filed down, LeBlanc visited a dentist and learned it would cost $80 without insurance. He went to a drug store and bought a three-pack of emery boards, and did the work himself. When he went back for the headshot, the photographer said, "They did a nice job."

In his early days as a struggling actor, LeBlanc was down on his luck, and admits to sleeping in some of the worst hotels imaginable. He was almost homeless at certain points of his life as well. In early 1994, LeBlanc's mother came for a visit. At the time, LeBlanc was destitute, living in squalor and living on snacks and food he mooched from his friends. She begged him to move home and give up acting. He promised himself that if the "Friends Like Us" audition didn't go through and he ran out of money, he would quit acting and return home. When the final test was held, LeBlanc had $11 to his name. After he got paid for the audition, the first thing he did was go to the nearest restaurant and buy a hot meal. He did not even know whether he won the part. In his words, "It was far from certain I would get the role."

After initially receiving the "Friends Like Us" (aka *Friends*) pilot script from his agent, LeBlanc thought it "sucked and was not believable." But he was still going to the audition because he needed the paycheck. The night before the audition, an actor-friend persuaded him to go out drinking with friends, assuring him that group carousing would help him get into character for an ensemble comedy. After an evening of heavy partying, LeBlanc passed out at his friend's place and during the night he needed a bathroom break. "I got up too fast and I kind of blacked out, as you do, and fell face-first into the toilet," he explained. "I hit my nose on the bottom of the toilet seat and a huge chunk of meat came off my nose. I'm looking in the mirror and it's bleeding." He continued, "I went to the audition with this huge scab on my face, and Marta said, 'What happened to your face?' I said, 'Aw, it's a long story.' She thought it was funny and laughed, and that kind of set the tone for the room."

At the initial audition, LeBlanc put a "different spin" on the character. Since the Joey character was not fully developed in the script, he decided to play it like "this Italian, kind of dim character" from *Vinnie & Bobby*, more simpleminded than the creators had intended, but he gave the character heart. Initially, the creators didn't like his portrayal, and rejected him. They had a different vision of Joey and LeBlanc's rendition was not a good match. But, NBC loved him, and forced the producers to reconsider their casting decision. "We didn't want him," Kauffman admitted, while David Crane said, "He was shoved down our throats!" The network saw the actor as something special, and the creators eventually realized that Joey's obtuseness could be the source of many comedic moments. They learned to accept and ultimately embrace the casting decision. As Kevin Bright noted, "Matt LeBlanc in real life is a guy's guy, and that's what we needed Joey to be."

LeBlanc's final audition was with Courteney Cox to test their chemistry because they were supposed to be a romantic couple. Although they had acting chemistry, it was never romantic in nature. Interestingly, Cox was secretly hoping LeBlanc would be cast because, in her opinion, he was "so dang cute." As part of the final casting decision, LeBlanc also read with Jennifer Aniston.

Monica Geller

In the creators' original sketch of the Monica character, she was "darker and edgier and snarkier." While writing the script dialogue they had Janeane Garofalo's voice in their head. Basically, the character was cynical, wisecracking and tough. Monica was a blue-collar girl (in upbringing and attitude) with lofty aspirations of opening a fine-dining establishment so she worked at Le Cirque, an upscale restaurant, to gain experience. The writers liked the contrast of blue-collar girl in a white-collar world. As David Crane explained, "it would be fun to see this tough, downtown woman in this uptown, French bull's arena."

Monica was not maternal, caring, or nurturing. In fact, she did not want the runaway bride (Rachel) to live with her because she was bitter over not being invited to the wedding. Moreover, she was highly sexualized. If men were womanizers, then Monica was a manizer. One-night stands were not uncommon. The casting agency was told to find someone having "the attitude of Sandra Bernhard or Rosie O'Donnell and the looks of Duff" (Karen Duffy, an MTV veejay and model). With those parameters in mind, the showrunners set out to find an actor who could exhibit these qualities.

Janeane Garofalo

At the top of the audition list was comedian-actor Janeane Garofalo (*SNL*, *Reality Bites*). After all, she was the archetype for the Monica character. Surprisingly, after her audition, the creators felt she was better suited to play Phoebe, so she was invited to read for the goth girl, which was Phoebe's character profile at the time. The showrunners had too many fabulous actors to play Monica and too few to play Phoebe, so Garofalo was repurposed to fill a casting void.

Jennifer Aniston

When casting director Ellie Kanner assembled a lengthy list of potential candidates for the role of Monica, Jennifer Aniston made the final cut because she was young and had experience playing edgier roles. At the time, she was under contract to costar in *Muddling Through*, a new CBS sitcom. The pilot was shot but unaired, which meant if it were picked up, she would be required to honor the contract. Kanner decided to take a chance and have Aniston read in second position.

Early in the casting process, Jennifer Aniston was the top choice to play Monica and it appeared inevitable that she would be offered the part. But, shortly before making the final casting decision, Kanner received the telephone call she was hoping would never come— *Muddling Through* had been picked up; CBS ordered six episodes. This practically ensured that Aniston would not be available to play Monica so a casting call went out to find a new actress to play the part.

Leah Remini

Loaded with talent, experience and beauty, Leah Remini cruised through several rounds of auditions, including going in front of the head of the network. She recalled the day where she and an actress friend were leaving the Burbank studio: "We walked out of the building and into the completely empty parking lot. We chatted on the way to our cars, wishing each other the best, and then we saw Courteney Cox walking toward us, then past us and right into the building. Motherf*cker! We both knew it right away: she had the part of Monica." Remini continued, "I was devastated that I didn't get it. We all knew it would be a huge hit. We just knew it."

The casting director kept Remini in mind for a guest starring role, and at the end of the first season she was cast as Lydia, a woman in labor being consoled and comforted by Joey. Remini subsequently landed a costarring role as Carrie Heffernan in the CBS sitcom *The King of Queens* (1998-2007).

Jessica Hecht

Another potential candidate was Jessica Hecht. She was new to the industry and had never appeared in a television program. Her inexperience showed in the casting process but her performance wasn't without merit. The casting director kept Hecht in mind and later offered her a recurring role as Susan Bunch, the girlfriend and future wife of Carol, Ross' ex-wife.

Maggie Wheeler

After an unsuccessful bid to costar in *These Friends of Mine* (aka *Ellen*), Maggie Wheeler was offered a recurring role in Ellen DeGeneres' series. Eager to find a permanent position as a cast regular, Wheeler auditioned to portray Monica in "Friends Like Us" (aka *Friends*). Although she did not get too far in the process, Wheeler impressed the producers enough to be cast as Chandler's vexing girlfriend, Janice, in "The One with the East German Laundry Detergent" (1.05). It was supposed to be a one-time-only role but she turned it into one of the most memorable recurring characters in television history.

Jami Gertz

The future *Still Standing* star was initially considered for the role of Monica. NBC was extremely interested in having her join the cast because she had name recognition and star power, having starred in *Square Pegs* and *Sibs*. She fit the character profile of being cynical and tough but the competition for Monica was fierce. It was a casting director's nightmare —too many suitable actors for Monica with no definitive options for Rachel. Thus, to ease the burden, network executives decided to cast Gertz as Rachel.

Nancy McKeon

Sitcom veteran Nancy McKeon (*The Facts of Life*) was originally considered when the producers were looking for someone with a darker and snarkier tone. She impressed the creators with her audition so it came down to her and Courteney Cox. "She gave a terrific performance," exclaimed casting director Lori Openden. At the time, the producers wanted Monica to have an attitude and be the mean one of the group. McKeon played it well. NBC President Warren Littlefield thought it was a toss-up so he deferred the final decision to Bright, Kauffman and Crane.

The executive producers meandered around the Warner Bros. studio lot debating their decision. The trio liked the idea of Cox being relatively unknown. "Because we were doing an ensemble there was something very appealing about not using someone as known as Nancy McKeon," Kauffman confided. They opted for Cox because she brought something fresh to the role which they thought may prove beneficial in the long run. As David Crane explained, "Courtney brought a whole bunch of other colors to it."

Courteney Cox

Contrary to most media reports and published books, Courteney Cox never auditioned for the role of Rachel. In reality, the creators approached her to audition for the part but she insisted on trying out for the role of Monica. "We originally went to Courteney to play Rachel and she said, 'I really want to do this show but I want to play Monica,'" Kauffman said. "And it was so not what was in our heads." Cox confirmed this fact. "People think that I was auditioning for Rachel. I wasn't. But they were considering me for that," she declared. "When I read the script, I thought, 'I should be up for Monica.' So I kind of lobbied for that. They let me do it."

It was actually the day prior to the Rachel audition that Cox asked if she could try out for Monica. The creators were initially hesitant. Cox appeared too wholesome and sweet so she did not seem to fit the part. Casting director Ellie Kanner also had Cox in mind to play Rachel because she was "adorable" and had a "cheery, upbeat energy," which was not how they envisioned Monica. The creators were looking for someone slightly less glamorous who could potentially play a harried, occasionally bitter woman. Besides, they liked Jennifer Aniston for the part of Monica.

Director James Burrows also wanted Cox for the role of Rachel. "It's like lightning in a bottle," he said. "You don't know what will work until you try it. When Courteney read for the show I thought she would be great as Rachel. But she wanted to play Monica, and she was right." Cox felt a deep, personal connection to the "strong" character. Although the producers remained hesitant, Warner Bros. casting director Barbara Miller came to Cox's defense and told them, "She can do it. She can do it."

Unfortunately, Cox's first audition was not stellar. Kanner concluded that the audition was "good," and Cox was a "definite maybe" for the role, but not a lock for the spot. After Cox's performance, the producers were convinced they wanted her as Rachel. Besides, they already endured hundreds of auditions for Monica, and had several strong candidates, so they did not need one more.

In an effort to persuade Cox to accept the role of Rachel, the producers upped the ante by tempting the actress with a test option deal, which guaranteed her the role of Rachel without an audition. Cox was flattered but remained adamant about pursuing the role of Monica. In fact, she gave an ultimatum: if she was not chosen as Monica, she was would quit the show. In other words, by rejecting a test option deal, she was willing to sacrifice losing both roles rather than accepting a guaranteed deal. She told her manager (Bernie Brillstein) to demand an audition. Cox insisted, "I will read for Monica and that's it."

Kanner and the producers agreed to one final audition, figuring all along they would offer her the part of Rachel immediately after the audition, hoping all the while that the ensuing excitement would overshadow her desire to play Monica. Instead, Cox came in and knocked it out of the park. "Holy crap!" Kanner thought to herself. "She's great as Monica! Why didn't we see that before?"

Rachel Green

According to the creators, Rachel was an incredibly hard role to cast. The character was potentially unlikable because she was "spoiled and whiny, and upset and crying, and no one likes to see that." But, they also wanted her to be portrayed as "charming and warm and modestly clueless." Finding an actor to pull it off was highly improbable. In the wrong hands, Rachel would be perceived as a spoiled, petulant, fiancé-fleeing mess. They needed the right actress to project Rachel's more attractive personality traits.

All the actresses performed the same monologue where Rachel first enters Central Perk after leaving her fiancé at the altar:

> "Oh God ... well, it started about a half hour before the wedding. I was in the room where we were keeping all the presents, and I was looking at this gravy boat. This really gorgeous Lamauge gravy boat. When all of a sudden—[to the waitress that brought her coffee] Sweet'N Low?—I realized that I was more turned on by this gravy boat than by Barry! And then I got really freaked out, and that's when it hit me: how much Barry looks like Mr. Potato Head. Y'know, I mean, I always knew he looked familiar, but ... Anyway, I just had to get out of there, and I started wondering 'Why am I doing this, and who am I doing this for?' [to Monica] So anyway I just didn't know where to go, and I know that you and I have kinda drifted apart, but you're the only person I knew who lived here in the city."

Courteney Cox

At the time of her audition, Courteney Cox was a hot commodity. She costarred in the series *Misfits of Science* (1985-86) and played Alex Keaton's girlfriend (Lauren) in the hit sitcom *Family Ties* from 1987 to 1989. The producers remembered her from a *Dream On* episode in 1992. But, ironically, it was a failed sitcom that proved she had the comedic chops to star in a sitcom. Few people remember the 1993 series *The Trouble with Larry* starring Bronson Pinchot (*Perfect Strangers*), which taped six episodes but was canceled after three. The one bright spot was Courteney Cox. She credited the sitcom's epic failure for launching her comedy career. "No one had ever seen me like that," she said. "I was mean and I was the funny one, and from that I was recommended for *Friends*."

Cox's acting portfolio provided everything the producers needed to conclude she was perfect for the Rachel character. But to her, it just didn't feel right. After Cox nailed the audition for Monica, the showrunners offered her the part, especially since Jennifer Aniston appeared contractually unavailable due to her commitment to the CBS series *Muddling Through*. Nevertheless, the creators still wanted to find a part for Aniston so they asked her to audition for Rachel. During casting, she proved perfect for the role, but they had to sign her in second position due to her commitment to *Muddling Through*. Thus, the producers needed to cast a replacement.

Téa Leoni

Casting director Ellie Kanner spent the next month looking at headshots and overseeing auditions, but no one was more captivating than Aniston. The role was offered to Téa Leoni, a superlative actress and comedian, but she seemed too sophisticated to play Rachel. NBC encouraged casting her because they wanted a big-name star to anchor the show. Although interested in the part, she declined the offer because she preferred a starring role, which was offered to her the following year with *The Naked Truth*, a situation comedy that lasted 2.5 television seasons and aired 48 episodes.

Jami Gertz

After Téa Leoni declined the part, NBC executives made a bold, impetuous move—they offered the role of Rachel to Jami Gertz (without consulting the creators). Gertz previously auditioned for Monica but the competition was overwhelming, especially after Courteney Cox nailed the part. NBC was hellbent on finding an actor to anchor the show so Gertz was the next best option. Although a great actor, the executive producers did not believe Gertz was right for the part but they had no say in the decision. They had worked with her in two installments of *Dream On* so they knew she was not a good fit for the role. It was a tense 24 hours as they awaited her final decision.

Fortunately for the cocreators, the actress overplayed her hand. While negotiating the deal, Gertz, a Sabbath-observant Jew, asked the showrunners to commit to a Wednesday-to-Tuesday schedule, where filming would take place on Tuesday nights, instead of Friday nights, like most shows. The showrunners respected her beliefs but could not commit to such an arrangement. Kevin Bright would later refer to her as "the Sandy Koufax of show business" (the legendary Jewish pitcher who refused to pitch Game 1 of the 1965 World Series because it fell on Yom Kippur).

Kauffman and Crane did their best to manipulate the situation by preying upon Gertz' vanity. They knew she was an egomaniac interested in a starring role, so they stressed their vision of an ensemble show where nobody would take center stage. The showrunners did their best to dissuade Gertz, and the following day she declined the offer. She would later appear in the movie *Twister* (1996) and costar in the sitcoms *Still Standing* (2002-06) and *The Neighbors* (2012-14).

Jane Krakowski

Although unknown at the time, Jane Krakowski auditioned for the producers but never received a callback. "I wish I had gotten that one. ... I didn't go very far," she frankly stated. Krakowski didn't have to wait long before her talents were appreciated. She found future success in *Ally McBeal* (1997-2002) as Elaine Vassal, *30 Rock* (2006-13) as Jenna Maroney, and *Unbreakable Kimmy Schmidt* (2015-19) as Jacqueline White. Coincidentally, while she was living in New York in 1982, Krakowski beat out Jennifer Aniston for the role of a 13-year-old runaway on the soap opera *Search for Tomorrow*. It was Aniston's very first acting audition; she surreptitiously read for the part without her father's knowledge and thought she was a shoo-in since he starred in the serial.

Tiffani-Amber Thiessen

One surprising candidate for the role of Rachel was Tiffani-Amber Thiessen. She had a strong pedigree, having graduated from a successful stint in the *Saved by the Bell* franchise (TV series, spinoff, and movie) as Kelly Kapowski. The producers liked her but thought she was too young to mesh with the older castmates. "I was a little too young to [be paired with] the rest of them," she confessed. Thiessen was only 20 years old at the time, while Jennifer Aniston, the youngest female costar, was 25 when she joined the cast. Although rejected for "Friends Like Us," Thiessen was promptly signed as Valerie Malone in *Beverly Hills, 90210* (1994-2000).

Denise Richards

Another unknown and callow candidate was Denise Richards who was a little too young for the role. She was 23 at the time and her inexperience showed. She didn't make it past a callback but did earn a guest starring role in the series seven years later playing Cassie, the Gellers' alluring cousin. She is generally recognized as Carmen Ibanez in *Starship Troopers* (1997), Kelly Van Ryan in *Wild Things* (1998) and Bond girl Christmas Jones in *The World is Not Enough* (1999).

Elizabeth Berkley

Although beautiful and experienced, having costarred in the *Saved by the Bell* franchise as Jessie Spano, Elizabeth Berkley was too youthful to play the role of Rachel. She was only 19 years old at the time of her audition. The following year she starred in *Showgirls* (1995), Paul Verhoeven's controversial film featuring abundant sex and nudity.

Anita Barone

On paper, Anita Barone had everything the producers wanted in a lead but onstage she simply did not fit their image for the character. Although she lost the lead role, Barone was offered a recurring role as Ross' ex, Carol.

Jane Sibbett

Very few *Friends* fans are aware that Jane Sibbett was offered the role of Rachel. At the time, she was over three months pregnant, though not showing. She urged her agent to be honest with the show's producers because it was only a matter of time before the "secret" would be inconceivable. The pilot was scheduled to be shot a month later so the creators withdrew the offer. To this day Sibbett has no regrets about how things turned out. "There's no way anybody could have come close to what Jennifer Aniston did with Rachel. She was so perfect," Sibbett confided.

Interestingly, both Sibbett and Barone also auditioned to portray Carol. They were the two finalists for the part. However, after Sibbett revealed her pregnancy, the showrunners said, "Thanks, but no thanks." They decided to go with Barone instead. Ironically, after the second episode was filmed, Barone was replaced by Sibbett, who played the recurring role throughout the series' run.

Melissa Rivers

In an effort to join the ranks of acting, Melissa Rivers was age-appropriate (26) but had no formal training or experience. She was quickly dismissed. Rivers is best known as Joan Rivers' daughter. Together they hosted fashion interviews on the red carpet for the E! cable network and in 2003 accepted a more lucrative deal with the TV Guide Channel which was valued at between $6 million and $8 million.

Nicollette Sheridan

Beautiful and experienced, having played Paige Matheson on *Knots Landing* (1986-93), Nicollette Sheridan was on the fringe of age-appropriateness (31) at the time of casting. She had the physicality the showrunners wanted but not the sweet girl-next-door look nor the convincing delivery to elevate the character to audience likability. Sheridan would later costar as Edie Britt in *Desperate Housewives* from 2004 to 2009.

Parker Posey

Inexperience was the key to Parker Posey not earning the role of Rachel. She also lacked the voice and delivery needed to make the character sweet, adorable and lovable. Posey has since performed in dozens of indie films but never achieved stardom.

Lisa Whelchel

The Facts of Life alum, who is a devout Christian, explained that her faith kept her from really going after the role. "There were many opportunities I maybe could have pursued, but I didn't feel comfortable," Lisa Whelchel said. "I remember reading the pilot episode and I said to my husband, 'This is the funniest script I have ever read and this is going to be a huge hit. But I can tell it's just going to be all about sex.'" While she candidly admitted, "I don't regret not taking that opportunity," her kids felt differently. "I remember my daughter once said, 'Are you telling me Brad Pitt could have been my father?'"

Jennifer Aniston

The journey to casting Jennifer Aniston for the role of Rachel followed a very long and winding road. First, there is one major false rumor that needs to be addressed regarding her weight. Neither the *Friends* producers nor her agent told her that she had to lose 30 pounds to secure the role of Rachel. Numerous internet sources and even published books by respected authors have spread this false rumor. In reality, Aniston was given this advice, but it was in 1988, while living in New York City as a struggling actor. She had a callback but it required her to wear a leotard and tights. She knew she was doomed. Her agent sat her down and gave it to her straight—she was not getting roles because she was fat. She took the advice to heart and the following year she became the Nutrisystem Success Story Spokesmodel. Aniston appeared on *The Howard Stern Show* where she praised the product for helping her lose 15 pounds in six weeks. Aniston eventually lost 30 pounds and began getting more gigs before moving to Los Angeles later that year.

Although acting jobs were lining up, Aniston nearly quit the profession because every program in which she costarred had crashed and burned. She was cast in five pilots, four made it to the airwaves—*Molloy, Ferris Bueller, The Edge* (with Wayne Knight) and *Muddling Through*—but none lasted more than a year. She was genuinely frustrated. In late 1993, Aniston approached NBC President Warren Littlefield at a gas station on Sunset Boulevard in Hollywood, and discouragingly asked, "Is it ever going to happen?" Littlefield remembered her from *Ferris Bueller* and offered reassurances that she was talented and her big break would come. Less than a year later, it did.

Cutthroat competition reigned supreme as networks battled for the services of Jennifer Aniston. In early 1994, she was under contract with CBS for the series *Muddling Through*. The network was not particularly fond of the show but ordered six episodes because it knew NBC wanted Aniston for a pilot. The strategic move prompted NBC to pass on her for the role of Monica but NBC President Warren Littlefield was still committed to signing the relatively unknown actress. He felt she was the next big star in the making so he urged the producers to cast her as Rachel. The producers were hesitant. Rachel was a very difficult role and so far no one was able to capture the essence of the character. It seemed like a big waste of time but they acquiesced. Aniston was very pleased. "I auditioned for Rachel. They wanted me to come in for Monica. But I liked Rachel," she stated.

Her first audition floored the showrunners. She was perfect for the part. Aniston had the potential to be the focal point of the series. Three hours after the final audition, she was given the part but it was in second position. "It happened so fast," says Aniston. "I went in, read the script, laughed out loud, got home and an hour later had the part." The producers concurred. "She *was* the part," Kevin Bright declared. "She was funny. She was pretty. It all came through in one big stroke."

There was still one problem. If CBS delayed broadcasting *Muddling Through* until the fall, Aniston would be unavailable for NBC's "Friends Like Us" series. Something had to be done. First, the creators tried diplomacy. David Crane approached Barton Dean, the creator of *Muddling Through*, and asked him to release Aniston from her contract so she could join the cast of "Friends Like Us." Not surprisingly, Dean declined. Crane later admitted that had the table been turned, he would never agree to the terms he proposed to Dean. It would be absurd to spend all the time and effort finding the perfect actor for a role and then allow another series to feature the performer.

Second, the creators used business logic. It was obvious that CBS didn't favor *Muddling Through* since it only ordered six episodes and withheld the series from its spring lineup as a midseason replacement. However, it was now late April and the filming for "Friends Like Us" was only two weeks away so a decision had to be made on Aniston. The showrunners decided to watch unaired episodes of *Muddling Through* and they concluded it was weak but not a guaranteed failure. Be that as it may, they still wanted to take a major chance by casting Aniston because she was wonderful and worth it. Kevin Bright added: "The idea of going with someone who didn't bring to it what she brought to it, we thought 'Let's roll the dice.'" However, Warner Bros. had a contrary opinion. Since they were ultimately paying the tab, studio executives wanted to sign a different actress. They wanted stability and security in casting, and Aniston's situation was pure chaos.

Third, the executive producers sought counsel. With no definitive plan, the triumvirate contacted NBC President Warren Littlefield for advice. He was determined to cast Aniston for the series so WB executives suggested that he cover the cost of reshooting the pilot if she was forced to honor her CBS contract. Littlefield agreed. To him, it was well worth the gamble. He saw "Friends Like Us" as having considerable potential, but only if it had the best possible cast, which in this case needed Aniston to survive.

NBC prepared for battle, heavily arming itself in anticipation of a long, protracted war with CBS. Littlefield was on the warpath. He watched *Muddling Through* and thought it was a "horrible show" and then contemplated to himself, "They won't pick up this horrible show just to f*ck us, will they?" He ordered WB to shoot the pilot episode with Aniston. She was also included in the upfronts—fall and midseason series previews with cast promotional segments presented by networks for advertisers—but was purposely excluded from the fall schedule announcement on May 13, 1994. When CBS President Peter Tortorici caught wind of NBC's plan to use Aniston, he was incensed. He immediately ordered three additional episodes of *Muddling Through* to see if Littlefield would back down. But the NBC chief held his ground.

A few weeks later CBS announced it would be broadcasting *Muddling Through* during its summer schedule, though a date was not specified. It was a common practice at the time for networks to air unsold pilots and disfavored shows in the summertime (aka Garbage Dump Theatre) which was where *Muddling Through* landed; it was the network equivalent of banishment to the island of misfit toys. Tortorici knew the series was unsalvageable but network programming strategies utilize military-grade tactics to destabilize the competition. His thoughts were simple; his intents were devilish. As he pondered his options, Tortorici fathomed a July airing date because it would extend the series into September, which was only a couple weeks before the start of the fall season on network television. In his mind, this would derail NBC's plan to cast Aniston. Tortorici now had the upper hand. But NBC was not out of moves.

Jennifer Aniston was beside herself. She wanted to join *Friends* (by then the title had changed from "Friends Like Us") but knew her contractual obligation to *Muddling Through* took precedence. She was determined to find a way out of the contract, which included a heart-wrenching appeal to Warner Bros. President Les Moonves. He made a telephone call, but Tortorici refused to relent, so Moonves tried to outflank the CBS president.

Moonves approached his good friend Jon Feltheimer, executive vice president of Sony Pictures Entertainment, the company producing *Muddling Through*, and they struck a deal. Feltheimer would allow Aniston to shoot the first six episodes of *Friends*, but CBS would retain first position. In other words, if *Muddling Through* was picked up for the fall or as a midseason replacement, then CBS would retain the rights to Aniston, and consequently, *Friends* would have to reshoot all her scenes with another actress. Feltheimer knew CBS was lukewarm about the series because it withheld the show from its midseason lineup, shelved the project for six months, and then unceremonious scheduled it in its summer lineup. With respect to the agreement with Moonves, Feltheimer later admitted to regretting the programming decision. As he stated to Moonves, "I could have gotten 1% of the profits of that show, which would have meant a lot of money, and you would have given it to me." Moonves replied, "You're probably right."

Moonves then contacted NBC President Warren Littlefield to finance the sitcom project. Littlefield was all in to bankroll the endeavor. NBC was prepared to shoot six episodes with Aniston, and then halt production if CBS remained noncommittal on *Muddling Through*. The stakes were high. A pilot commitment was $250,000 but reshooting six episodes would cost millions of dollars, decimating a network's developmental budget.

Littlefield knew CBS was playing a cat-and-mouse game with him. Tortorici was doing exactly what Littlefield would do in the same predicament. CBS continued to procrastinate before announcing that it was airing the first episode of *Muddling Through* on Saturday, July 9. This was the break NBC was waiting for. A summer airing meant it was perceived as a weak show so only solid summertime ratings would warrant picking up the series for the fall or as a January midseason replacement. Littlefield contacted Preston Beckman, NBC's scheduling guru, and ordered him to "Kill it."

Beckman's plan was ingenious. NBC had four unaired telefilm adaptations of Danielle Steel romance novels which were guaranteed to attract a large female audience. And since *Muddling Through* also catered to the same demographic, the telefilms were sure to siphon some of the viewers. He scheduled two movies to coincide with the first two sitcom airings, and then two more over the next four weeks. The plan worked perfectly. *Muddling Through* had abysmal ratings (No. 72) and after six episodes the series was switched to Wednesday night in an effort to save the sitcom. But it was too late. The damage was done and the series withered in the process.

During the networks' summertime programming hijinks, the *Friends* creators continued casting a suitable replacement for Aniston. But the options were limited. All the talented actors were already committed to other projects. Only a few would slip through the cracks if their pilot was not picked up by the networks.

In late August, *Friends* started production on the second episode (the pilot was filmed in May). NBC promised to air six episodes of the series, which coincided with its commitment to pay for the filming of six installments with Aniston. Nonetheless, the employment status of the embattled actress remained in limbo and she continued to hear rumors from actress friends claiming they just read for the role of Rachel. In fact, a couple weeks before *Friends* debuted, NBC withheld her from some of the publicity photo shoots. No one was sure she would be a cast member.

As production rolled into the fourth episode, there was still no decision on the fate of Aniston so she decided to take matters into her own hands. "I went to the producer of the show I was on, and said, 'Please release me from this show. I love this show that I'm doing right now,'" she recalled. *Muddling Through* creator Barton Dean said, "I saw that show. I'm going to tell you something—that show is not going to make you a star. This show is going to make you a star." The *Friends* premiere was only a couple weeks away and still there was no decision as to her fate.

Tensions were high as the uncertainty persisted. Everything hinged on CBS President Peter Tortorici. In early September he had to make a decision to cancel *Muddling Through* or order more episodes simply to spite NBC. He pondered the options and waited until two weeks before the *Friends* premiere to announce his decision. Tortorici took the moral high road. "It went against the grain for me to deprive an actress of a chance for real success just so I could play the game by investing $3 million in something I didn't believe in, all just to hope for, but not guarantee, damage to a competitor," he honestly confessed. Ironically, the following year, in June 1995, Les Moonves replaced Peter Tortorici as president of CBS.

At long last, Aniston could officially join the cast. Director James Burrows celebrated by taking the entire *Friends* cast to Las Vegas.

Chandler Bing

Cocreator David Crane partially modeled Chandler after himself, most notably his dry, acerbic wit. "I've always connected with Chandler in terms of his sense of humor," he noted. Crane, who is openly gay, originally considered writing the Chandler character as gay but after casting Matthew Perry, the direction of the character changed to a straight man often mistaken for gay. (Marta Kauffman's college friend Chandler jokingly accused her of ruining his life by naming a *Friends* character after him.) The showrunners decided to stick to gay references, innuendos, mannerisms and stereotypes. After Perry was cast, the creators had no intention of having Chandler come out of the closet.

Chandler was written to be the witty commentator on everybody's lives as well as his own. An office drone who knows his job is "killing his brain cells and his sperm, but it's a place to make long distance calls from." He was unlucky in love yet somehow seemed to attract beautiful, eccentric women. Chandler believes himself to be funny and uses humor as a defense mechanism. Thus, casting required an actor who could sell both the humor and personal insecurities. The character breakdown described Chandler as a droll, dry guy.

Kauffman and Crane knew what they wanted when casting the role of Chandler but didn't know where to find it. The character needed to have a certain timbre to the way he delivered his lines. "I always assumed Chandler was going to be the easiest role to cast," Crane declared. "He's a wise guy. He's sarcastic and has a joke." But sometimes the easiest task in theory is the most difficult in practice.

When the showrunners and casting directors compiled a list of potential candidates, Matthew Perry was near the top but they knew he was committed to another sitcom pilot. Jennifer Aniston and Noah Wyle were already cast in second position so Warner Bros. execs refused to allow Kauffman and Crane to cast another actor whose employment status was to remain in limbo. With Perry off the table, the producers had to cast someone else. All the actors came dressed for the part and read the same scene from the pilot script:

> *Chandler:* Alright, so I'm back in high school, I'm standing in the middle of the cafeteria, and I realize I am totally naked.
> *All:* Oh, yeah. Had that dream.
> *Chandler:* Then I look down, and I realize there's a phone ... there.
> *Joey:* Instead of ...?
> *Chandler:* That's right.
> *Joey:* Never had that dream.
> *Phoebe:* No.
> *Chandler:* All of a sudden, the phone starts to ring. Now I don't know what to do, everybody starts looking at me.
> *Monica:* And they weren't looking at you before?!
> *Chandler:* Finally, I figure I'd better answer it, and it turns out it's my mother, which is very-very weird, because she never calls me!

Casting director Ellie Kanner portrayed all the other roles in the scene. A couple actors improvised lines, for instance, one added "on *that* line," which earned laughs but did not win the favor of the writers. Kauffman and Crane loathed actors who improvised lines. Ad-libs, even during auditions, were frowned upon. "We get kind of defensive," Crane admitted.

Mitchell Whitfield

Early in the casting process, Mitchell Whitfield read for both Ross and Chandler. "I went back multiple times, and then they realized Ross was the role for me," he proclaimed. The producers thought he was better suited as a dull, ne'er do well lump, than a wisecracking commentator on life. Although Whitfield was never cast in a costarring role on *Friends*, he did earn a part as Rachel's cheating fiancé Barry.

Jon Favreau

Although a relatively unknown actor at the time, Jon Favreau was offered the part of Chandler. He didn't actually wow the producers with his auditions, but he was the best of the lot. With Matthew Perry committed to another project, the producers were left with a string of good-but-not-great actors for the role. Favreau rejected the offer but subsequently appeared in the third season as Pete Becker, Monica's wealthy boyfriend with a penchant for UFC fighting.

Jon Cryer

Over a decade before *Two and a Half Men* hit the airwaves, Jon Cryer was in London performing theater when he received a call from the "Friends Like Us" creators asking him to audition for their pilot. They faxed the script and Cryer agreed to audition. He went in and read with a British casting director. They took the tape and sent it to Ellie Kanner. A few days later he was told the producers never saw the videotape because it was held up in customs. Cryer never received a second chance.

Craig Bierko

NBC had signed Craig Bierko to a deal and was intent on finding a role for him in one of their upcoming pilots. Since Crane and Kauffman were having such a difficult time finding the perfect Chandler, the network urged them to cast Bierko for the role. The producers brought Bierko back for another audition and, according to Kauffman, he was the person who came closest so they offered him the part.

Kevin Bright was distraught at the casting decision. He knew Bierko was a good actor but not right for the part. The actor lacked the instinctive comic pop that was imperative for the role. He could deliver the sarcasm but did not come off as a sensitive, likable character. Bright was at wits' end awaiting the actor's decision. Kauffman and Crane agreed because they had experience with Bierko in four episodes of *The Powers That Be*. They, too, thought he was a good actor but not quite right for the part of Chandler.

Fortunately, the creators had help in their corner. There were a few network executives who did not concur with casting Bierko for the role. Karey Burke, NBC's executive VP of primetime programming, was instrumental in persuading Bierko to reject the role. "We kind of talked Craig Bierko out of being in *Friends*. Ultimately, he made his own decision, sort of." Burke focused on the actor's vanity by manipulating him into believing "Friends Like Us" was not the right project. She convinced Bierko that he was leading man material so an ensemble project like "Friends Like Us" would impede his career. Network executives then tempted him with the lead role in another sitcom pilot titled, coincidentally, "Best Friends." Bierko took the bait, and like most developmental projects, the pilot was never produced. NBC remained committed to finding a role for Bierko so he was immediately added to the cast of *Madman of the People*, NBC's treasured new sitcom series for the 1994-95 television season.

NBC President Warren Littlefield also resisted casting Bierko in "Friends Like Us," and was pleased the actor passed on the project. "Thank God!" he joyously exclaimed. "There was something Snidely Whiplash about Craig Bierko. He seemed to have a lot of anger underneath, more of a guy you love to hate. The attractive leading man who you love and can do comedy is very rare."

Years later, Bierko wrote a letter to Bright expressing his regret for turning down the part of Chandler, something he characterized as "the role of a lifetime." The actor eventually found success portraying Chet on Lifetime channel's drama series *UnReal* (2015-18).

Although Bierko passed on "Friends Like Us," all the credit for his successful auditions belongs to someone else. In 1990 he costarred in Valerie Bertinelli's sitcom *Sydney*, where he met and befriended series costar Matthew Perry. In preparation for the "Friends Like Us" audition, Bierko asked Perry to run lines with him. Perry believed the role was perfect for himself but he was committed to another project so he coached Bierko into the mindset of the Chandler character. In fact, Perry advised several actors on how to perfect their line delivery ("just imitate what I'm doing") to the point where a few of them advanced far into the casting process. When Perry was finally able to audition for the "Friends Like Us" pilot, the creators admitted that Bierko was "merely a reflection of Matthew Perry."

Matthew Perry

Although relatively unknown, Matthew Perry was surprisingly in demand to costar in pilot projects because he had experience and was respected for his work. In late 1993, he was contacted by his business manager and told he was broke. "I desperately, *desperately*, needed the money," he unabashedly admitted. Perry begged his agent to find him any work that was available, and what popped up was a pilot called *LAX 2194*, a dark horse project highly unlikely to get picked up. Perry was dolorous (and dollarless) so he accepted an offer to costar in the sci-fi sitcom. It was an easy 20 grand in his pocket.

LAX 2194, which also costarred Ryan Stiles (*The Drew Carey Show*, *Whose Line Is It Anyway?*) and Kelly Hu (*Nash Bridges*), involved Los Angeles baggage handlers working at LAX airport in the year 2194. According to Perry, the characters wore futuristic shirts and sorted the luggage of aliens, who were played by little people (dwarfs).

When "Friends Like Us" commenced casting in February 1994, the creators were very interested in Perry because they worked with him in one episode of *Dream On*. Perry was equally interested in the project. He knew about the sitcom project because his friends were auditioning for the role and he was running lines with them. Perry believed the role was perfect for himself because he identified with the character. "The part of Chandler leaped off the page, shook my hand, and said, 'This is you, man!'" Perry immediately requested an audition but was denied due to his involvement in *LAX 2194*. Warner Bros. President Les Moonves would not allow another actor to be signed in second position.

Casting the role of Chandler was excruciatingly difficult. "We saw guy after guy after guy. Many talented. It just wasn't popping. It just didn't feel fresh and it wasn't even that funny," Crane frustratingly recalled. As the swarm of actors came and went, Perry's name kept showing up on the list and the creators kept reminding themselves, "No, we don't want him in second position, he's got another pilot."

Two months later it was mid-April and the producers were still looking to cast the role of Chandler. Crane began doubting himself. Maybe the problem wasn't the actors, maybe it was the script. The creators inquired about Perry and discovered the nature of the project, and said to themselves, "That's a risk we're gonna have to take." They watched the pilot for *LAX 2194*, and it became clear to them that it would not be picked up for a series so they approached Moonves to reconsider his viewpoint regarding Perry.

The deadline for filming the pilot was less than two weeks away. Although Warner Bros. initially refused to allow Perry to audition because they did not want another lead actor in second position, Moonves was cognizant of the casting imperativeness so he backtracked on his original stance. He knew Perry was an excellent actor because he remembered him from an unaired pilot that was even worse than *LAX 2194*. In the atrocious sitcom, Paul Sand starred as a talking dog in love with his female owner who had a jerk boyfriend played by Matthew Perry.

WB executive David Janollari was instructed to view the pilot and provide his honest opinion whether the series was likely to be picked up by FOX. After his private screening, he concluded the pilot would fail so he spoke with casting director Ellie Kanner and said, "Look, I know he's not available, but I think he's great as Chandler, and he should go as second position." She arranged an audition. The timing couldn't have been better. Matthew Perry was going out of his mind. He was about to lose the role of a lifetime because of some ridiculous sci-fi pilot. Finally, somebody at FOX told the producers, "We've seen this. It's the worst show we've ever seen in our lives, so he's available. You can hire him."

Perry arrived at the audition empty-handed. He did not need a script because he had memorized it over the past two months from repeatedly running lines with his friends. The moment he auditioned, the creators knew they found the perfect actor. "The first time we heard him read we just looked at each other and went 'Oh my God. So the writing doesn't suck. We just hadn't found the guy yet," David Crane fondly recalled. "Marta and I were thinking 'Chandler is just poorly written.' Then Matthew came in and you went, 'Oh, well, there you go. Done. Done. That's the guy.'"

During the callback, Perry read his lines with Aniston, Cox and LeBlanc, with another actor filling in for Schwimmer (he was in Chicago appearing in a play). Once again, Perry impressed the producers with his refreshing delivery of Chandler's lines, and they knew that no other performer would come as close to what they imagined their character would sound like. "You hear Matthew talking and no one ever sounded like that on television before. He's got such a distinctive rhythm," Crane remarked.

Even the casting director was impressed. While escorting Perry into an adjoining room, she told him to wait while she conferred with the producers. The group huddled to discuss their notes, and unanimously agreed that Perry was their best and only real choice for the part. In a rarity, Kanner was able to personally deliver the news that he was hired. Perry was flabbergasted, "What?! Really? What?" Kanner reiterated the decision, "Yeah, you got the job." The audition was on Friday, April 22, and Perry appeared for work the following week.

Perry was signed in second position but it was merely a legal technicality. Although he was still committed to the sitcom pilot *LAX 2194*, WB President Les Moonves was given assurances by FOX executives that the project would not be picked up. Thus, Perry was free to join the cast and begin production on the pilot episode for "Friends Like Us."

Shooting the Pilot

By the time the pilot began production, the series title was changed to "Six of One." The first table read (read-through) occurred on Thursday, April 28, 1994. It was the inaugural gathering of each crucial element of the series pilot: cocreators Marta Kauffman and David Crane, executive producer Kevin Bright, director James Burrows, and the six costars.

First Table Read

When the workday started, the cast had a casual meet and greet and then everyone congregated around a massive conference room table. A few of the actors had previously met during the audition process, but Lisa Kudrow didn't know any of them. She knew of David Schwimmer from the TV series *Monty* and that he was a really good actor, and she definitely knew of Courteney Cox because she was the famous one, but Kudrow could not remember Jennifer Aniston's last name. She knew it wasn't Anderson, so she kept referring to her simply as "Jennifer Not Anderson." Aniston and Matthew Perry had been friends since 1990, shortly after she moved to Los Angeles; they had previously partied together with her "hill people" friends in Laurel Canyon.

Many of the lead actors came dressed for their parts. Kudrow wore a bunch of seashell necklaces with a white linen hippie shirt, and her hair was pulled up in two small clips with little blonde tendrils. Courteney Cox was wearing a pink baby tee with white trim, and Matt LeBlanc had leather jeans and a plain white t-shirt to expose his biceps.

Typically, the first pilot table read is awkward and tentative because the actors are not familiar with each other, the material is new and untested, and the show has no history or direction. But this read-through was different. There was an inexplicable level of comfort, confidence and competence. The attendees were not only laughing, they were cracking up.

David Schwimmer commented on the first read-through, "Oh. You could feel it. The energy." Matthew Perry stated, "We all just read through the script and it was amazing. It was sort of the time I realized the kind of magic that was existing in my life." Matt LeBlanc opined, "I remember the first table read and thinking, 'Wow, these guys are great. I better pay attention.'" Jennifer Aniston remarked, "There was just something about their unique sound." Finally, Lisa Kudrow expressed amazement at each actor's take on their character. After reading the script, she thought Chandler was gay and was shocked that Perry was able to play the character straight. "It was like a magic trick." She was also impressed with the timing and comedic voice of both Perry and Schwimmer.

It was lightning in a bottle. The characters' voices resonated with everyone in the room. The actors' distinctive deliveries seemed to coalesce with their respective characters. David Crane observed, "They all have such amazingly distinctive voices. It's the pilot and they're already completely fully formed." Jennifer Aniston agreed, "They filled it the way I imagined it sounding." David Schwimmer then chimed in, "Not one of us could have been traded out. It was like the six of us were like the perfect pieces of this puzzle." Despite functioning as a cohesive unit, the presence of Courteney Cox somewhat intimidated the other actors. She was the only big-name TV star of the cast, which earned her a certain level of professional deference from her colleagues.

Rehearsals

The first rehearsal is really a conversation. The actors talk about the script and listen to each other's thoughts about the story. Ideas are exchanged. Good and bad. The actors take the suggestions they like and fit it into the story, but they also discuss the rejected ideas and as a collective, they try to brainstorm alternative options to improve their performance. Basically, it is a collaboration founded on discourse.

David Schwimmer perceived the first rehearsal as "something special." Marta Kauffman added, "The first time I saw the six of them together, I got chills up and down my spine." She had a feeling it would be a hit. "You never know if something's going to be successful or not, but there was magic with the six of them. It just felt like the stars were aligned and we were given these six incredible actors and it looked like they had been together forever."

Despite all the magic that appeared onstage throughout the second day of production, it was Cox's selflessness that changed the course of history for the sitcom. As the de facto leader of the ensemble, she became a driving force in uniting the cast. During a rehearsal break, the cast had congregated outside the soundstage to chat. As they conversed about their craft, Cox said, "Listen, I just did a *Seinfeld* episode and they all help each other. They say 'Try this,' and 'This would be funny.'" Since "Six of One" was supposedly an ensemble show, she firmly advocated for mutual collaboration. "This is an ensemble show. I think we should really all try to help each other out," she asserted. "I know I'm the one who's been on TV, but this is all of us." Cox recommended that her colleagues adopt a new approach to rehearsals: "You guys, feel free to tell me. If I could do anything funnier, I want to do it." She stressed that, as an ensemble, "We all need to make this thing great."

Her five costars were nonplussed. "There's a code with actors. Actors don't give each other notes under any circumstances," Lisa Kudrow said. "So she was giving us permission to give her notes, and we all agreed that that would be great." Schwimmer was in accord with this sentiment, though in his mind, he was most taken by "the spirit of collaboration" among the cast. From there, a true ensemble was born.

First Run-Through

A run-through is an uninterrupted rehearsal where the actors quickly read the script out loud and perform all the scenes in chronological order to practice or prepare for a show, without makeup or costumes. Typically, the first run-through is performed for the writers, producers and director. This allows the creative team to assess the acting, writing, jokes and scene structure to determine what works and what needs work.

The first run-through is an opportunity to see the actors working as a team. There is no assurance any group of actors, even the best in the business, will mesh onscreen. But it was different for this group. They seemed like seasoned veterans in a long-running series. Director James Burrows felt there was something special in the making. Marta Kauffman agreed. "I remember the atmosphere being electric," she said. "I knew we had something special."

Not everyone was exhilarated. Lisa Kudrow was justifiably terrified. Burrows expressed concern that Phoebe's quirkiness did not mesh with the other characters and she might interfere with the group dynamic. Kudrow was experiencing déjà vu, reliving the *Frasier* catastrophe where Burrows had her fired during the first week of production on the pilot episode. And now it was happening again. "At one point he thought it would be funny if I deliver my monologue under the table," Kudrow recalled. "They're all sitting around the table. Instead of being with them, I'm under the table, because I'm 'quirky.'" At that point in time she thought, "This is the run-through where Marta and David are going to say, 'This character doesn't work. We have to reconceive it. She's just not part of the group.'" Luckily, when the creators balked at the idea, Burrows accepted blame and said, "No, that was me. We were just trying it."

The cast's ability to gel as a cohesive unit was partly due to Burrows creating an actor-friendly environment where everyone had input during production week. Actors could freely suggest ideas on how to improve their performance or the script. "Don't just say the words, act the words," was a motto he lived by. He wanted to be inspired by their performance and encouraged adding movement, action or physical comedy to the scenes. For instance, after Ross courageously asks Rachel for an unspecified future date, Burrows recommended that Schwimmer punctuate Ross' personal achievement by emphatically popping an Oreo into his mouth. It was little additions to the scenes that made the sitcom's moments special or memorable.

But not all suggestions were accepted or incorporated into the script. During one run-through, Matthew Perry improvised a gesture while delivering a line which received laughs so he repeated it during a later rehearsal. Burrows approached the fledgling comedian and tactfully said, "I just want to tell you, you shouldn't do that after the line." He was worried about stereotyping the acting. "Because if this show is a success, which I think it will be, that will be all you're known for." Perry accepted the critique and excised the gesture from his performance.

In the world of television, some gestures are good (like Fonzie's thumbs-up) and some are bad, just like certain vocal tics are positive (Janice's laugh) while others are negative. Burrows had intuition at discerning behaviors that made a character classic versus turning them into a caricature. The youthful sextet was wise enough to internalize his suggestions rather than going rogue.

As the days passed, the cast became more comfortable working together. Each actor gradually found their character's voice and learned how to play off the other actors while performing. According to Kevin Bright, "they could have simply turned the cameras on for the first run-through and come away with an impressive show." The week of rehearsals had one other significant revelation: the inexplicable chemistry between David Schwimmer and Jennifer Aniston. It was unparalleled. The creators quickly realized that Ross and Rachel had to take center stage as the primary romantic couple in the series.

Script Changes

The initial "Bleecker Street" draft in December 1993 had several script variances that did not make it into the final "Six of One" pilot in May 1994: (1) the episode starts with Monica describing how she never wants to go on another date, but reconsiders her original statement after Phoebe offers to lend her a stunning black dress; (2) Ross' crush on Rachel was the main plot with Monica's one-night stand and Rachel's adjustment to singlehood as subplots; (3) Ross' unrequited love was the basis for much of the pilot's comedy and its emotional core; and (4) after Chandler finishes his dream monologue, a character adds, "One word for you: therapy."

In other drafts, Phoebe didn't live with her grandmother, Monica was older than Ross, and Monica was very reluctant to reconnect with Rachel because she was jealous of her wealth and upset she wasn't invited to the wedding. In fact, Monica didn't offer Rachel a place to stay and even after they became roommates, she was persistent in trying to get her to move out. The showrunners also discussed Monica taking in a young pregnant woman. Lastly, Joey was cocky and arrogant, not lovable and dimwitted.

Although many script revisions were made prior to production, the actual number of revisions during filming was minimal. "I can't think of too many changes we made while we were shooting the pilot," David Crane recalled. As the years went on, however, the number of script revisions that occurred while filming increased exponentially.

Emotional Moments

When formulating the pilot script, the showrunners insisted upon one critical thematic element: an emotional component to the series. It was never only about laughs and giggles. There had to be some semblance of drama. As a director, Kevin Bright insisted on a specific cinematic flair to the series. For example, in the bittersweet moment where lovelorn Rachel is gazing out a window, he wanted a closeup of Aniston from the balcony, which is generally resisted because it requires constructing a fourth wall (to conceal the audience bleachers). James Burrows balked at the idea but Bright insisted. The disgruntled legendary director haphazardly shot the segment in a matter of moments but it was not to Bright's satisfaction or creative style. These types of incidents, and the general displeasure with the directorial style of Burrows, led to him not being invited back to the series after the fourth season.

Cast Unity

From his vast directorial experience, James Burrows knew the importance of having a close-knit cast on and off screen. He encouraged the youthful actors to view each other as colleagues, not rivals. He did not want the series to devolve into a bitter competition for lines or jokes. Burrows knew the key to success was unity, a collective effort. The creators concurred so they purposely wrote episodes so each actor was equally accounted for in the series.

In his effort to facilitate cast cohesion, Burrows—the true star of the series if stardom was measured by dressing room size and square footage—offered his regal quarters as a meeting place for the sextet between rehearsal breaks. During the first season, the cast had tiny dressing rooms located under the audience bleachers so there was no space to gather. Thus, at Burrows' urging, the sextuplet would gather in his dressing room to play poker, joke around, and discuss their craft. According to Kevin Bright, Burrows was "instrumental in working with the six actors and making them feel like an ensemble."

The costars' tiny dressing rooms also made them the butts of jokes from fellow actors on the Warner Bros. lot, and the recipients of pranks. Since the freshman medical drama

ER filmed in the soundstage next door, a couple of its costars liked to partake in harmless shenanigans. According to a close production source, George Clooney and Noah Wyle were known to "personally deface the signs on the doors of the *Friends* minuscule, windowless dressing rooms."

Camera Blocking

A typical sitcom has four or fewer main actors in a setting and utilizes three cameras, which is perfect for blocking shots. In contrast, "Six of One" (*Friends*) had six costars, and often the entire cast occupied the same room during a scene, which became too congested and untenable for traditional three-camera filming. Thus, a fourth camera was introduced to capture all the necessary framing angles, but this caused blocking issues. Blocking each scene involves carefully orchestrating actor movements in relation to the camera. It's like choreographing a dance or ballet. All the elements on the set (actors, extras, vehicles, crew, equipment, etc.) should move in perfect harmony with each other. With four cameras, the director had to worry about the cameramen running into one another with their equipment.

Kevin Bright directed 54 *Friends* episodes so he was well aware of the mental challenges of blocking for the series. "Having scenes with six actors, all of them having to be covered at the same time, and only having four cameras, tells us that this was gonna be a tough series to follow as far as keeping the cameras on the dialogue." For pilot director James Burrows, this was his first foray into the quagmire. "This is the only show that has ever made my ears bleed," he confessed to Bright while working on the project.

Part of the problem with blocking and filming multi-camera shows was the cumbersome nature of the equipment. Schwimmer, who directed ten episodes of *Friends* (and two of its spinoff, *Joey*) marveled at the modern cameras used in 2021, as compared to what they used on *Friends* over two decades earlier. These, he indicated, could be operated by one person, but back then, each camera required three. "It was a huge crew," he said. "[With] four cameras, the choreography was incredible."

Network Run-Through

Whenever James Burrows directs a pilot episode, he often requests a studio audience preview about four days into production. It helps him gauge where the show stands—the progress made and the work that needed to be done. Adjustments are made and then the next day they do it all over again for studio and network executives in a production phase known as a network run-through. The cast is in full costume and performs the script as if filming the episode. Executives offer notes on all aspects of the performance from makeup, clothing and set design, to dialogue, script content and innuendos, including any violations of the network's standards and practices (i.e., studio censorship issues). The results from both screenings are meant to improve the script and actor performances before the pilot is filmed, which usually occurs a day or two later.

On Monday, May 2, 1994, the cast held a network run-through. This particular event was different than a typical network run-through because it occurred as part of the studio audience preview. Although it is not a preferred way to evaluate the series, the combined evaluation was necessary because there was not enough time to do them separately. The announcement of NBC's fall schedule was less than two weeks away so time was of the essence.

The performance went well but there was one major point of contention among NBC executives. In one coplot, Monica has a first date with Paul the wine guy, who confides that he's been impotent for two years, ever since his wife left him. Monica is moved by his pitiful story so she sleeps with him to buoy his spirits. The next day, she cannot remember his name and soon discovers that his "impotency" was a pickup line to get laid. NBC's West Coast President Don Ohlmeyer insisted on a script rewrite because it portrayed Monica as a slut. In his mind, it was totally acceptable for Joey to be a womanizer but Monica had to be sanctimonious.

The creators defended the story's plot so Ohlmeyer demanded they poll the audience. He purposely prepared a biased questionnaire to skew the results: "For sleeping with a guy on a first date, do you think Monica is: (A) A Slut, (B) A Whore, (C) A Tramp, (D) None of the Above." Before the results were tabulated, he insisted on having Monica written out of the show. The creators laughed at the request and vehemently refused the demand.

In all fairness, Ohlmeyer's antiquated beliefs must be viewed in context. It was the mid-1990s and youthful sexuality was taboo on television. *Seinfeld* was cutting inroads into the draconian standard but its characters were older, in their 30s, whereas the characters in

"Six of One" (*Friends*), despite being twentysomethings, were likened to innocent children exploring their sexuality. The network's predominate concern was to ensure the characters remained likable and marketable. Ohlmeyer's credo was very moralistic: "I did not like to put on TV something I did not want my kids to watch."

The questionnaire results came back overwhelmingly "none of the above" so director James Burrows championed the cause and persuaded Ohlmeyer to stand down. Spitefully, Ohlmeyer remarked, "Well, I'm okay with it because she gets what she deserves when the guy sort of screws her over." Marta Kauffman was livid, so in a passive-aggressive manner, she sent him a basket of pantyhose, tampons, lipstick and nail polish to help him get in touch with his feminine side. In a similar vein, he sent Kauffman a Harley-Davidson leather jacket to help her get in touch with her masculine side. That's how it was resolved. But, to appease network executives, the creators rewrote the script so Monica would be emotionally invested in the relationship. Surprisingly, they preferred the new version, as it made the scene "smart and subtler."

Ohlmeyer also claimed he found the show confusing—there were too many characters to follow and too many storylines. He was entrenched in the old school train of thought. He wanted the show to focus on Monica (relegating the other characters to secondary status), since Courteney Cox was the only legitimate headliner. The network was already planning on featuring her in the fall promotions. Normally, the creators would be forced to appease NBC's requests but in this instance director James Burrows, a man with considerable clout in the industry, came to bat for the creators and told Ohlmeyer, "Well, that's not the show I signed on to do." Ohlmeyer could not risk offending or losing the esteemed director so he immediately dropped the request.

To put the network run-through in a layperson's perspective, it is safe to say the level of micromanagement had no limit. For example, NBC executives offered a note to cut the "Mr. Potato Head" line from Rachel's opening monologue. In the segment, she compares her ex-fiancé Barry to the toy character. The showrunners disregarded the request since it was so insignificant, besides, they thought the bit was funny. Another request was to replace the couch because it was too tattered. Burrows convinced them to keep the sofa with minor adjustments. Basically, executives nitpicked everything.

Although the screening audience did not rave about the pilot, Burrows believed their response was immensely positive. In his mind, he likened the reaction to the pilot episodes of *Cheers* and *Frasier*. Those were lofty comparisons to live up to, but it merely reinforced his belief that this pilot was the beginning of something special.

Pilot Testing

After spending the evening processing all the network notes and rewriting the script, the next morning the creators distributed the final draft to the cast and crew for one last run-through. The pilot was filmed the following day, Wednesday, May 4, 1994, at Warner Bros. Studios in Burbank, California, in front of a live studio audience. Attendees were given a brief summary of the series to familiarize themselves with the six main characters, and a comedian was hired to entertain the crowd before the premiere, between scene breaks, and during wardrobe and makeup changes. After the pilot was shot, it was developed overnight and then rushed to the editing room where Kevin Bright proceeded to cut roughly eight hours of filmed material (two hours from each of the four cameras) down to 22 minutes.

Bright submitted the final cut to NBC on the morning of Tuesday, May 10, merely 72 hours before the fall lineup was scheduled to be publicly announced. Not surprisingly, of all the developmental projects ordered by the network, "Six of One" was the last pilot delivered to NBC. Network executives—which included official representatives from every important department such as programming, scheduling, marketing, and public relations—screened the pilot in the early afternoon. Their primary objective was to document all the flaws in the show. After the screening, they issued their results: the pilot was out of touch with the real world, and the characters were not well defined and somewhat indistinguishable from past sitcom characters. The executives thought the characters spent too much time in the coffee shop, and the locale was too New York and too downtown for the audience to relate. "Don't worry," Bright stated, "Everybody will be going to the coffee shop after they see this show." Eric Cardinal, head of programming research, despised the show, and he was not alone.

Later that afternoon, NBC executive Don Ohlmeyer returned the pilot with a variety of executives' notes, the biggest complaint being the opening scene. Ohlmeyer insisted the opening was too slow and wanted dialogue cut from the beginning. The creators objected, "No, no, no. This has always been in. This is how the show starts. We wanted that sort of slow, talking feeling." The network executive unequivocally stated, "You don't cut some of the dialogue and pace it up, you're not on the air."

The showrunners loved the opening scene. They thought it was perfect and didn't want to change it. So they used a little sleight of hand. Kevin Bright spliced together a 90-second title sequence using pulls (clips) from the pilot episode and then overlaid it with R.E.M.'s "Shiny Happy People." Everything else remained intact. He delivered the cut and much to their surprise, Ohlmeyer loved it.

The final step was to have it screened by focus groups (aka pilot testing). During this process, the network assembles a group of ordinary people to watch the episode and offer constructive criticism (including their feelings) through a preset questionnaire. A similar process was implemented by the studio so they could have market research evidence to tout positive aspects of the show or rebut negative network data. This phase of the pilot process is most taxing on show creators. They have no control. Their fate rests in the hands of others—audience participants, studio executives and network executives. The honchos take the audience data and use the results as part of their posturing when negotiating the fate of the pilot.

In the world of television pilots, the month of May is often the time of final judgment. Networks solidify their fall lineups, so last-minute decisions must be made on which pilots to include on the schedule. The odds of survival are less than one in three. Network notes can send writers into a frenzy with requests to add storylines, eliminate characters, change scenes, etc., all of which have to be done in mere days, or even hours, before filming the pilot. Compliance is mandatory or the pilot does not get picked up.

Prior to announcing their fall schedules, networks also determine which timeslots will be available on which nights, and then executives decide the best shows for each opening.

Studios are also privy to this timeslot management so their executives begin jockeying for position to place one of their pilots in the most coveted slot. Final placement can make or break a television series. Thus, effective negotiating, by both network and studio executives, is premised on quality focus group research.

The path to pilot testing is long and arduous, spanning nearly six months from pitch to final edit. During the process, each draft is color coded to distinguish one from the others. The original "Friends Like Us" script in March was printed on white paper, and then later scripts were blue, pink, yellow, and lastly, green. During that time frame, the series title also changed from "Friends Like Us" to "Six of One."

On May 12th, about 100 people were seated in NBC's screening room to view the pilot for "Six of One." The following is the original NBC Program Test Report dated May 27, 1994:

PILOT PERFORMANCE: Weak   SHOW PREDICTOR: 41 Percentile

CONCLUSIONS:

Overall reactions to this pilot were not very favorable. Interest in the show was very narrow—best among young adults 18-34—but responses even among this group were just okay. Young women (18-34) seemed to connect slightly better with the individual characters. While there was no pronounced sex skew, men showed more interest than women in both the story and premise of the show. Monica (Courteney Cox) fared best with women and young adults 18-34, but her appeal even among these groups was well below desirable levels for a lead. She earned sympathy mostly from women who felt sorry for her after she was conned by Paul. None of the supporting cast members reached even moderate levels with the target young adult audience: Phoebe and Chandler had marginal appeal with both men and women 18-49; Rachel, Ross and Joey scored even lower, and the little they did have came primarily from women. Teens rated Joey highest of all the characters, but he was still below the moderate range. Young adults (18-34) thought the show was funny, and men generally responded better to the humor than women. But most viewers felt the show was not very entertaining, clever, or original. Many considered it sexually suggestive, but not in poor taste, a good sign given the storyline. Stated viewing intentions for a series based on this pilot were not encouraging.

SUMMARY:

The group of friends who were the focus of the show did not come across very well, and viewers found it hard to get to know them in this pilot episode. Younger adults 18-34 and teens felt most of the characters seemed like nice people, and felt they could be potentially interesting since they had room to grow. For some, they offered a "90s point of view" on young people and their relationships. Others found it refreshing that it was a show about a group of friends that was not a soap like MELROSE PLACE. But older adults 35+ were more critical, and felt this group did not really care about each other the way real friends would. They found the characters smug, superficial, and self-absorbed. These older viewers also found it hard to relate to this group of friends, and felt they were not really like people they would want to know.

Courteney Cox was familiar to many viewers. As Monica, she came across as charming, attractive, confident, and motivated—the leader of the group. Among her group of friends, she seemed to be the one who was the most stable and together. Men thought she was sexy, and women liked her sense of humor. Many were bothered that she had sex with Paul, the wine guy, on the first date, but they didn't seem too critical of this indiscretion, feeling sympathy more than disdain for her. Some adults commented that Paul's "impotence" story was very convincing and did not fault her for believing it, and she drew laughs when she exacted revenge on Paul by stomping on his watch.

Basically, the results were tolerable. The research concluded that the pilot was WEAK (but a high weak). It was not a death knell. The grade simply meant the show had potential to grow. Nevertheless, the inconclusive test results started a fury of media rumors. First the show was going to broadcast on Saturday night, then Tuesday night. It was even confused with "Best Friends," an NBC pilot that was not picked up, so the media began reporting that *Friends* didn't make the cut for the fall schedule. ("Best Friends" was the sitcom pilot starring Craig Bierko, the actor who declined the role of Chandler.)

Pilot Pickup

After submitting the final edit for "Six of One," the creators had a harrowing 72 hours that included enduring the network screening, learning of the somewhat poor focus group results, and then awaiting NBC's fall schedule announcement. Listening to the rumors of their show not being picked up merely intensified their anxiety. Finally, on the evening of Thursday, May 12, just 12 hours before NBC was due to publicly announce its fall lineup, the creators received a call. They were told to pack their bags and travel to New York City for the network's promotional celebration at Avery Fisher Hall. Although a pickup seemed inevitable, the triumvirate didn't pop the champagne corks until the official announcement at 10:30 the next morning.

Before the announcement, NBC had one final request. They didn't like the show title, "Six of One," and wanted the producers to come up with something better. The trio had 12 hours to make their decision. While pondering the possibilities, they kept coming back to the original title, "Friends Like Us." Of course, this title was unfeasible because NBC had previously rejected the moniker due to its potential confusion with ABC's upstart sitcom *These Friends of Mine*. The triumvirate began going through a list of other hit sitcoms like *Seinfeld*, *Frasier*, *Cheers* and *Taxi*, and liked the simplicity of the naming so they settled on *Friends*.

After the network announced the fall schedule, which included *Friends*, the trio boarded a Warner Bros. corporate jet en route to New York, celebrating the entire way (and well into the evening). "It's a lot like winning the lottery," Marta Kauffman exalted.

The reason *Friends* made it to the airwaves despite poor testing results was simple: (1) NBC needed to fill a blank space on its schedule, (2) it was better than most of the other produced pilots, (3) it had a promising cast of rising stars, and (4) it fit the vision of NBC President Warren Littlefield. He was very confident a show about six humorous, attractive twentysomethings would play well with youthful audiences, but there was no guarantee the viewing audience could expand beyond its core. Most importantly, though, it catered to the key demographic (18- to 49-year-olds) that advertisers primarily targeted. NBC vehemently sought to appeal to the younger demographic to generate ad revenue for the network.

Littlefield believed there was a huge untapped audience of younger viewers who wanted to see themselves reflected onscreen but that type of network programming was currently unavailable on TV, except on FOX. "There was a fear of telling stories about first jobs or first serious relationships or roommates—these shared, collective experiences that weren't being told at the time," he surmised.

NBC already knew it was retooling its Thursday night lineup around their No. 1 sitcom, *Seinfeld*, which included shifting *Mad About You* from Wednesday. The notion of adding a third New York–based sitcom was appealing, so *Friends* was tentatively penciled in for the 8:30pm slot, between *Mad About You* and *Seinfeld*. In reality, there was little expectation of *Friends* succeeding so NBC only ordered 12 episodes with a guarantee to air 6.

Still, NBC saw potential for the series, especially if it was tweaked to comport with their pilot testing results. For instance, the report suggested that the male characters were too similar, possibly due to their near-identical brown hair color, so NBC considered recasting one of the starring roles. Another idea was adding supporting characters to jump-start the show. Finally, executives urged more emphasis on the professional lives of the characters, rather than limiting interactions to their apartments and the coffee shop.

Jamie Tarses, senior vice president of primetime series for NBC, and David Janollari, head of comedy development for Warner Bros., firmly resisted the other executives' efforts to meddle with the project. They were intent on preserving the creators' original vision for the series. Only one of the three suggestions made it into the scripts: incorporating more occupational scenes for the characters. Thus, early installments focused on Chandler's job dilemma, Ross' museum involvement, Phoebe becoming a masseuse, Monica having more restaurant scenes, and Joey's onstage and backstage activities.

Overall, the television industry was not entirely enthralled with *Friends*. Karey Burke, NBC's executive VP of primetime programming, discretely confessed, "There was more buzz about FOX's version of the same concept, a show called *Wild Oats* with Paul Rudd." Even NBC felt lukewarm about *Friends*. It was most excited about *Madman of the People*, starring Dabney Coleman as a cantankerous newspaper columnist dismayed to find himself working for his daughter (Cynthia Gibb). The sitcom was given the network's best timeslot, 9:30pm on Thursdays, following *Seinfeld*. Coincidentally, the *Madmen* pilot was also directed by the *Friends* director, James Burrows.

Time would prove NBC executives wrong. *Friends* became an instant hit, earning both respectable viewership numbers and the highest ratings of any debut program that year, en route to becoming a pop culture phenomenon that still resonates with audiences to this day. Meanwhile, the network's pet project, *Madman of the People*, only lasted 16 episodes and was effectively canceled five months after its debut. In fact, the series was panned right out of the gate. The *Los Angeles Times* called it one of "the fall season's least likable new comedies" and undeserving of its comedy label.

Creative Team

The moment it was announced that *Friends* had been picked up, the entire industry was abuzz and everyone wanted a piece of the pie. At the Warner Bros. studio office, Crane and Kauffman were inundated with telephone calls from writers' agents wanting to get their clients a job on the series. Within the first half hour, Kauffman astoundingly admits, "we got calls from agents saying, 'Are you ready to talk about the writer I sent you?'"

Freelance writers also threw their hats into the ring. Many forwarded unproduced spec scripts for other sitcoms, most notably a towering stack of *Seinfeld* episodes. In the next few weeks, the *Friends* team would rifle through innumerable résumés and scripts before signing seven staff writers.

Hiring Writers

Crane and Kauffman acknowledged that the inspiration for *Friends* came from that time in their lives when they were struggling playwrights in their 20s living in Manhattan, but 15 years had passed and they were now in their late 30s. In other words, they were more than a decade older than their twentysomething characters. Despite being only 37 or 38 years old, they felt out of touch with the younger generation. After all, they were both born in the 1950s, and their sitcom characters were presumably born in the late 1960s to early 1970s. Thus, to fully understand Generation Xers (born 1965 to 1980), the scribes researched the subject, compiling dozens of books, magazines, and research articles, to comprehend all the nuances of youth culture (e.g., music, lingo, slang, clothing and favorite hangouts). It gave them the background they needed to get into the mindset of youths.

It occurred to them that the best way to access this mindset was to hire recent college graduates; to take a chance on inexperienced writers with fresh ideas. Their new dictum became: "When you're 40, you can't do it anymore." The showrunners figured they could easily oversee the projects and mold the raw scripts into polished pieces.

Creative Environment

During the first few episodes of *Friends*, director James Burrows developed a rapport with the cast and encouraged the free flow of ideas. In fact, the entire creative team, writers and showrunners alike, encouraged an environment of collaborative creativity. "I would give so much credit to David and Marta and the other writers because they really invited our ideas," David Schwimmer commented. "They created an atmosphere in which we could play and fail and pitch stuff, and because of that, it wasn't about any individual—it was about all of us trying to come up with the funniest and the best and the most emotional material we could." He further expounded, "It was thrilling to be part of, and it was hands down the best creative experience I've had professionally as an actor. That kind of collaboration with your director, with those writers, and with the other actors—it's a huge high, and it spoils you for life. It does."

Matt LeBlanc confirmed the showrunners' willingness to listen to different ideas: "There was a conversation I had early on, when the show was just starting to take shape, and I remember standing back and being as objective as I could about Joey and thinking, 'This thing could go a long time. Does my character fit if it goes a long time?' Because in the beginning I was hitting on the girls all the time." Strictly out of self-preservation, he went to the creators and said, "What if Joey hits on every girl in New York but these three? What if I'm like a big brother to these three?" The creators agreed and LeBlanc's character went in a different direction, making Joey a better fit for the group.

The collaborative creative environment was so inclusive the creators invited Matthew Perry, the youngest cast member, into the writers room. This may be standard practice for sitcoms featuring comedic geniuses like Tim Allen or Jerry Seinfeld, but it is a rarity for unseasoned actors. The showrunners and staff writers respected his opinion, insight and comedic sensibilities. In fact, many of his one-liners and comedy bits were included in the final scripts. Perry also worked with the directors and his fellow castmates to craft jokes, tweak punch lines and add physical comedy routines for the show.

It was during rehearsals and run-throughs that all the cast members were included in the process of fine-tuning the script and pitching jokes. The writers would take notes and make adjustments for their evening rewrites. Many times the staff writers were in sync with other members of the creative team. "Whenever the actors come up with ideas it's always a collaborative thing," Kevin Bright noted. "Many times when the actors had questions about whether something would work, the writers often had the same questions and concerns." And the entire production was overseen by the watchful eyes of Crane and Kauffman. They may not have written every show but they did have final say, and impeccable judgment.

Christina Pickles (Judy Geller) praised the showrunners as being "the giant stars of the writing team." She was always aware of their presence on set because it terrified her, but she remained awestruck by their masterful management of the entire process. "David and Marta would come down from the office to watch the run-throughs. ... They'd sit in a row of chairs with the writers and NBC executives. And you could see they were thinking, and they'd give comments and then go back upstairs and change it all."

Script Writing

Marta Kauffman believes her stage experience was instrumental in honing her television writing skills. "It's really good to study theater before television—it teaches you a lot about structure ... and that people don't just talk to each other, but are doing things," she stated. In the writers room, there were two rules that guided each episode's storyline: "You had to care, and it had to be funny." According to Crane, "We would throw out a whole story and replace it with something that had some emotional stakes. And if the show wasn't funny enough, we would stay up until the sun came up coming up with more jokes." With the series producing as many as 25 episodes a season, the writers never had, as Kauffman so eloquently stated, "the luxury of writer's block."

The creators had a sizable office on the Warner Bros. studio lot. Crane and Kauffman shared a large desk and sat facing each other. "Marta and I generally write with the two of us together in a room debating every line, going back and forth," he recalled. "We are at our best when it's just the two of us sitting there. How 'bout this, how 'bout that. It takes longer and sometimes there isn't the time for it." In the beginning the duo always wrote every word together. Their writing styles and conceptual fortes meshed well as a creative team—Crane was detail oriented and Kauffman was more emotionally driven.

Once a writing staff was assembled, the showrunners encouraged the callow scribes to share their Gen-X perspectives. "When we finally started doing the show, the writers were so much younger than us that we felt like anthropologists," Marta Kauffman admitted. The pair were hoping the staff writers would channel their personal life experiences to develop fresh storylines with youthful relevance.

In the writers room, the showrunners and staff writers openly exchanged their beliefs, thoughts and opinions. After an idea was pitched, everyone would offer ideas or suggestions or pose a question. This was, in part, because the duo were still relatively new to television and not indoctrinated into the old school protocol. They had a malleable hierarchy and very lax meeting structure with no preconceived creative process. In this environment, the staff writers' inexperience was a bonus, not a hindrance. More than anything, Kauffman and Crane did not want to hear from their staff writers that this was the way it had always been done on *Who's the Boss?* They preferred the company of young writers who did not know "how it was done on television."

Although staff writers were encouraged to share ideas and thoughts, the creators had final say. They were the writing overlords for the series. However, the tandem often deferred to the majority. "It's not an official democracy. We certainly don't vote. There is a consensus in the room, and generally, if somebody feels vehemently about something one way or another, that will have the day," Crane declared. "If someone hates something passionately, generally it won't go in. If there's a group of people who just love something, they can very often just power an idea through." Case in point, in "The One Hundredth" (5.03), Phoebe's obstetrician is obsessed with the TV character Fonzie. The showrunners thought the *Happy Days* homage was ridiculous, but the staff writers insisted it was great comedy. The tandem deferred to the majority, and to this day, many fans believe the playful bit is hilarious. But, the creators still do not get the humor.

Besides sharing ideas, the script writing process was equally collaborative. "People will come in with ideas. They'll all get thrown into the mix, and then we'll sort of group them together into an episode because you don't generally pitch episodes with the three stories attached. You'll have a whole bunch of story ideas floating around," Crane explained. "Then you'll go, okay, this is kind of the main story we're doing and then you see which characters don't have a story or are left out of that, and then you say okay well, we know we've got this Ross–Rachel thing, now we need something for the other four."

Assigning scripts was very diplomatic. Once a story was conceived, the creators would discuss the various staff writers—their strengths and weaknesses, which one hadn't written a script in a while, and who would be perfect to write this particular episode—in advance of designating a scribe to ink the first drafts and receive writing credit. The assigned writer usually penned two drafts and then the entire staff weighed in with ideas and suggestions. Everyone was responsible for improving each line, each joke, and each emotional beat of the show. Every word was up for debate. Every idea was scrutinized. For instance, one area of debate was "How dumb can Joey be?" so the writers scrutinized all his dimwitted jokes. It was a selfless process. (As an inside joke, a rubber stamp was given to the staff that read "I Pitched That!")

Writers endured endless hours of their script being slowly, steadily and systematically dismantled and then rebuilt. Authorial defensiveness was discouraged. The scribes quickly learned it was far better to fix the script than defend the original work. It was a team effort where everyone had to check their ego at the door. Somehow, the writers didn't seem to mind having their drafts critiqued and torn apart. Through it all, every script went through three to five drafts and then continued to be rewritten during rehearsals, run-throughs, and even while filming the episode.

Accepting the collaborative process didn't make it easy to abide. The staff was unified in their occupational assessment: being a sitcom writer was extremely difficult. Adam Chase admitted, "The way life works is: you're not always on. Today I might not be at my funniest for whatever reason." Greg Malins then chimed in, "It's not hard to be funny. It's hard to be funny in a way that will translate to the show and that you can air on television." Marta Kauffman continued the train of thought, "Everybody thinks they can do it. It's not as easy as it looks, otherwise we wouldn't be there until five, six, seven in the morning, with 14 incredibly smart people." Chase concluded, "You don't have time to worry about not being funny. You just have to be."

The most difficult aspect of the writing process was coming up with fresh stories and quality plots. The creative team was in complete agreement: writing for the characters was easy, coming up with new storylines was difficult. "It's easier and easier to write for [the characters] because you just know how they talk, that's not a question. It's just coming up with new ideas that's hard," David Crane revealed. But it does justify the multiple instances where the writers inadvertently duplicated jokes and bits in several episodes.

Before an installment went into production, Crane and Kauffman made one final pass to edit anything that didn't seem right for the series in general or characters in particular. But the writing process didn't end there. Once the final draft was approved, often times the staff writers had the arduous task of condensing the script because its runtime was too long. This can entail anything from trimming excessive dialogue to excising entire scenes. After one rehearsal, for example, the episode runtime extended over nine minutes so the writers needed to cut seven pages from the script.

One noticeable scriptwriting change occurred after the third season. *Friends* was known for its non sequitur jokes but as the soap opera of the series took over, there was no time for jokes unrelated to the storyline. "The first season has a lot of the gang sitting around watching TV and making fun of it," David Crane recounted. "As time went on, the episodes became more story intensive and there just isn't time anymore." He also mentioned that the change was partially due to the television networks cutting episode runtime so they could generate more advertising revenue. Although writers kept including non sequitur jokes in nearly every script, those tangential bits were always the first items cut because they were unrelated to the plot.

Since the show was an ensemble with no headlining star, and the costars were treated equally, the creators wanted equity within the scripts. Thus, the assignment of jokes, lines, and bits was diligently monitored to ensure fairness to all. "We try very hard to make sure everybody has enough jokes, enough lines, enough stories, enough beats," Kauffman said. The staff writers had a pie chart on the office wall to track the number of lines and jokes to ensure each character balanced out to the same amount. The creators wanted an ensemble so it was imperative that no particular actor hoarded the limelight.

Story Inspirations

The writers often relied on personal experience to craft storylines. Nearly every episode has multiple examples. For instance, famed English author Jane Austen inspired a couple plots. Writer Jeff Greenstein read all her novels because his wife wrote a senior thesis on the author. So, when it came time to script a romantic climax at the end of the first season, "The One Where Rachel Finds Out" (1.24), Greenstein was motivated to come up with the story of Ross giving Rachel a brooch for her birthday, only to leave on a trip to China just before she realizes his feelings for her, which she reciprocates, but it is too late because he returns from China with a new girlfriend.

Similarly, in "The One with the List" (2.08), the pros-and-cons list that Ross composes to compare Rachel and Julie is textbook Jane Austen from her novel *Pride and Prejudice*. There is a parallel between Ross' major blunder and Mr. Darcy's first marriage proposal. Ross emphasizes Rachel's limitations, not her positive attributes; similarly, in Mr. Darcy's overture, he spends more time focusing on Elizabeth's lower rank than asking her to marry him.

Infomercials were the basis for several comedy bits because the writers were addicted to this form of late-night television programming. They often worked into the early morning hours and would unwind by watching television, but back in the 1990s, the programming options were quite limited so infomercials ruled the airwaves, which inevitably became a source of comedic inspiration. For example, "The One with the Metaphorical Tunnel" (3.04) features an *Amazing Discoveries* infomercial segment, "The One the Morning After" (3.16) premieres Waxine, a fictional infomercial leg waxing product, and "The One with the Free Porn" (4.17) has Phoebe demonstrating a Ginsu knife. All these bits were motivated in part by late-night infomercials.

On-set activities also influenced installment plots. For instance, "The One with All the Poker" (1.18) was inspired by director James Burrows getting the cast to play poker in his dressing room. He had the largest on-set accommodations so he encouraged the cast to congregate there to bond. The girls didn't know how to play poker so the guys taught them the game. With the help of Matthew Perry, the writers recreated the dialogue and added the group's interactions into the script.

The *TV Guide* periodical being addressed "Miss Chanandler Bong" was a joke used in "The One with the Embryos" (4.12). It was influenced by a childhood incident where writer Seth Kurland's surname was misspelled on an address label.

A *Saturday Night Live* skit was the basis for Phoebe's past-life experiences in "The One with All the Thanksgivings" (5.08). In two segments, she is a military nurse who has an arm blown off during an explosion causing blood to squirt from her severed extremity. Her war injuries were inspired by *SNL*'s 1978 "Julia Child" skit where Dan Aykroyd dressed as the famed chef to parody a real-life incident where she cut her finger during a live segment. He took the event one step further by having his severed finger spray blood everywhere.

One of Matthew Perry's dental procedures became a major plotline. Following the fourth season, he had porcelain veneers attached to six top teeth. The whiteness of his false teeth was glaringly apparent. This became the foundation for Ross' teeth whitening product in "The One with Ross's Teeth" (6.08).

The storyline of Ursula being a porn star was inspired by Paul Reiser's sitcom. In the *Mad About You* series finale on May 24, 1999, a flash forward segment to the year 2021 revealed that Ursula was elected governor of New York after a successful career as a porn star. The *Friends* writers decided to incorporate that revelation into a memorable episode.

Activities within the writers room were eased into the scripts. In "The One with All the Haste" (4.19), Joey's neighbor sings "Morning's Here" using the catchy melody from Chuck Mangione's jazz-fusion hit "Feel So Good." The writers often jammed to the song on their boom box during sunset. Sometimes their dinner order would arrive at the same time so they would burst into a Mangione-inspired song: "The food is here, the food is here." Their lyrical parody inspired the "Morning's Here" song for this episode.

Another installment, "The One with All the Cheesecakes" (7.11), evolved from one of the writers receiving a package that was intended for someone else. "Somebody on staff had got sent a box of fruit that was not for him, and he ate it with the justification that by the time he tracked down the person it was supposed to go to, it would have gone bad. So he was really doing the world a favor," writer Shana Goldberg-Meehan explained. The staff writers didn't think a box of fruit was tempting enough so they opted for irresistible cheesecake.

Even the actors inspired plotlines. When Jennifer Aniston lived in Laurel Canyon, every now and then her female friends (the hill people) would go into the woods and form a circle filled with candles and personal mementos, hold hands, and talk. As she pensively recalled, "I remember the first time we did it, this one girl was silent through the whole thing, and then at the end she was just weeping. She just had this huge sort of enlightening kind of experience being with these women, and it was, like, women are awesome, especially together as a group, so kind and warm and wonderful." This ceremony was the basis for the boyfriend cleansing ritual in "The One with the Candy Hearts" (1.14).

Recycled Jokes

The failure to assign a staff member to be responsible for documenting or researching past episodes ultimately resulted in the repetition of numerous jokes and comedy bits. There are too many to recount so here are the highlights:

- Having a character wearing two belts appears in "The One with Monica and Chandler's Wedding, Part 2" (7.24) and "The One with the Fertility Test" (9.21).

- Characters purposely sitting in another character's chair is written into three episodes: "The One Where No One's Ready" (3.02), "The One with the Race Car Bed" (3.07) and "The One with Ross's Grant" (10.06).

- A character practicing dirty talk and then being embarrassingly caught by another person who discretely enters the room takes place in "The One with the Stoned Guy" (1.15) and "The One with Rachel's Dream" (9.19).

- Two characters going out to eat and then forgetting to pay for the food happens in "The One with All the Cheesecakes" (7.11) and "The One with Ross's Tan" (10.03).

- Chandler having a tear rolling down his cheek occurs in "The One Without the Ski Trip" (3.17) and "The One Where the Stripper Cries" (10.11).

- Throwing a glass of water in Joey's face can be seen in "The One After the Superbowl, Part 1" (2.12) and "The One with Joey's New Brain" (7.15).

Writing Dramedy

There was an unwritten understanding among the staff writers that it was their duty to be funny and overload each script with as many killer jokes as possible, and withhold the emotional, heart-wrenching dialogue for the creators because that was their forte. Crane and Kauffman were also masterful at dovetailing the storylines with comedy and drama to keep the audience emotionally invested in the characters and the series. The showrunners always stressed the need for balance between comedy and drama. It was their mantra that all the jokes in the world could never convince an audience to feel affection for the show's characters. There had to be an emotional element. They believed sentimentality made the characters endearing and the emotional undertow kept the audience invested in the series. For example, in "The One with All the Poker" (1.18), Ross concedes a poker hand to give Rachel a much-needed victory. This episode infuses such a level of unexpected sentiment that it catches audiences off guard, and makes them say, "Oh wow, that was cool."

Crane, Kauffman, and later Alexa Junge, were among the best at scripting emotional nuances for the show. Without Ross and Rachel, and the audience's emotional investment in the characters, viewers would never have bothered to watch the show, no matter how many one-liners were delivered. This was television based on the *Cheers* model: joke, joke, joke, joke, until suddenly the ground falls away and a moment of unexpected sentiment retroactively justifies and enriches all the effortless humor that preceded it.

Despite all the sentimentality, the program was a situation comedy so the series' writers often provided comedic relief for every emotional or dramatic segment to ease the tension. Sometimes it's a lot easier to laugh the hard moments away rather than allow the audience to become depressed and start bawling like babies. The showrunners do regret one instance where they failed to offset an emotional moment with light humor. In "The One with Barry & Mindy's Wedding" (2.24), Monica and Richard decide to break up and the scene fades to black without a humorous offset. Marta Kauffman opined that the ending was sad, and just didn't work.

Friends **writers (from left): Alexa Junge, Adam Chase, Jeff Astrof, and Jeff Greenstein**

Sexual Innuendos

At its core, *Friends* is an adult-oriented sitcom so there are tons of sexual metaphors, innuendos and symbolism scattered throughout every episode, covering the gamut from erections, vaginas and masturbation, to fellatio, cunnilingus and copulation. There are certainly enough examples to fill a book, so only some of the highlights will be mentioned, primarily ones that may have been missed by many of the more youthful, naive *Friends* fans.

Premature Ejaculation

- Sexual symbolism starts with the very first episode. After Rachel is reintroduced to Ross, they approach each other for a hug and he inadvertently opens an umbrella which kills the moment. This was meant to symbolize premature ejaculation.

- In "The One Where Ross and Rachel...You Know" (2.15), as Ross and Rachel are making out in the planetarium, she rolls over, makes a surprised sound, and then says, "Honey, that's okay." Ross explains, "What? Oh, no, you just rolled over the juice box." She then responds, "Thank God!" Due to the sexual nature of the innuendo, this segment is often excluded from the syndicated release.

- According to writer Adam Chase, there is a scene in "The One with the Jellyfish" (4.01) that is a direct nod to "the juice box moment" (mentioned above). In the episode, Ross and Rachel have a fight and after he storms out, she shouts, "Just so you know. It's *not* that common, it *doesn't* happen to every guy, and it *is* a big deal!" The original joke submitted by writer Greg Malins had Rachel saying, "Well, one time, when you prematurely ejaculated, I told you it was okay and it wasn't." As with most ideas in the writers room, after the line was pitched, it was tweaked and polished.

Erection

- In "The One with the Cop" (5.16), Chandler claims the tape measure is in his bedroom, and Monica agrees. This is a sexual connotation related to them measuring the size of his erect penis.

- Another illustration occurs in "The One with Phoebe's Cookies" (7.03). In the scene, Rachel is teaching Joey how to sail and asks him, "How do you get the mainsail up?" to which he replies, "Uh, rub it?" The mainsail is a metaphor for penis.

- In "The One After Joey and Rachel Kiss" (10.01), Ross and Charlie are making out on the bed but he stops because he wants to talk to Joey first. Ross then needs a moment before standing up so he repeats the word "grandma" and concentrates on that image. The implication is that he has a hard-on and the image of his grandmother will quickly facilitate flaccidity.

- One erection inference was censored by NBC. In "The Pilot" (1.01), Paul the wine guy was lying in bed under the covers and the bedsheet was elevated like he had just pitched a tent. Network executives bristled at the idea and nixed the sexual imagery from the episode.

Hand Job

- In "The One with Rachel's Inadvertent Kiss" (5.17), Monica and Phoebe practice handshakes, and afterwards, Monica asks if she squeezed too hard, to which Phoebe replies, "Let's just say, I'm glad I'm not Chandler." The insinuation relates to Monica giving him hand jobs.

Fellatio

- There was a clever reference to fellatio using a fictional female empowerment book. In "The One Where Eddie Won't Go" (2.19), Rachel utters the line, "How do you expect me to grow, when you won't let me blow?" Ross then sheepishly replies, "You, you know I, I don't, have a, have a problem with that." Obviously, this is a sexual innuendo about a blow job. Jennifer Aniston had the hardest time saying the line. Numerous takes had to be done because she could not stop laughing.

- In "The One with the Bullies" (2.21), Monica explains her stock trading principles: "MEG was good for me but I dumped her. You know, my motto is get out before they go down." Joey retorts, "That is so *not* my motto," implying he sticks around for a blow job ("going down" is slang for oral sex). This segment is often cut from syndication.

Cunnilingus

- Oral sex on a female was a rich comedic area for the writers. In "The One Where Rachel Finds Out" (1.24), Joey participates in a fertility study which entails him donating sperm. Since he is not allowed to partake in private donations, he discovers a new way to pleasure his girlfriend—with oral sex. Melanie is impressed with his selflessness in the bedroom, and comments, "I guess I just had you pegged as one of those guys who are always 'me, me, me.' But you ... you're a giver. You're like the most generous man I ever met. I mean ... you're practically a woman."

- In "The One with the Baby on the Bus" (2.06), Joey remarks that his Uncle Sal has a really big tongue, so Chandler quips, "Is he the one with the beautiful wife?" This is a subtle allusion to Sal being quite skilled at cunnilingus.

- Actress Jane Sibbett pitched a sexual innuendo that made it into the script. In "The One Without the Ski Trip" (3.17), Ross interrupts Carol and Susan's anniversary celebration of their first time being intimate together. As Carol and Ross speak in the doorway, she removes a pubic hair from her tongue to imply that she was performing cunnilingus on Susan.

- In "The One with Phoebe's Uterus" (4.11), Chandler tries to conceal his ignorance about female erogenous zones by claiming he was looking at the drawing upside down. Rachel then comments "Well, you know, sometimes that helps." The sexual overtone refers to the 69 position. Of course, this reference pertains to cunnilingus and fellatio.

Masturbation

- By far, the most frequent sexual allusion was masturbation. In "The One with the Prom Video" (2.14), after gifting Chandler a bracelet, Joey queries, "[Do] you have any idea what this'll do for your sex life?" Chandler, looking at the bracelet dangling from his right wrist, replies: "Well, it'll probably slow it down at first but, once I get used to the extra weight, I'll be back on track."

- In "The One with the Tiny T-shirt" (3.19), Rachel rejects Mark's sexual advances by claiming she is only on a date with him to get back at Ross. Mark then says: "If you want to get back at Ross, I am here for you. I say we get back at him right on this couch." After she declines, he adds, "I can just go home and get back at him by myself." The carnal nuance refers to him being sexually frustrated and relieving himself through self-pleasuring.

- Women were also the subject of masturbation innuendos. In "The One with the Dollhouse" (3.20), Ross panics when Phoebe's dollhouse catches fire so he rushes into the bathroom to extinguish the flames in the shower, only to discover Monica in there with her friend, Mr. Showerhead. "By the way, I was just checking the shower massager," she tells him later. The erotic allusion is that she was using the showerhead to masturbate.

- In "The One with All the Haste" (4.19), the guys agree to trade their apartment if Rachel and Monica kiss for one minute. After witnessing the girl-on-girl action (offscreen), the guys beeline for their bedrooms and close their doors, intimating their need for sexual privacy.

- Many of the sexual allusions were very subtle. In "The One with All the Resolutions" (5.11), Ross proclaims: "You know what? I am gonna be happy this year. I am gonna make myself happy." Chandler curiously inquires: "Do you want us to leave the room?"

- In "The One Where Joey Loses His Insurance" (6.04), Ross, frustrated at the criticism from his friends, dejectedly comments: "I'm just gonna do it on my own with no naked chicks." Chandler quickly turns the remark into a sexual connotation by proclaiming: "That's the way I did it until I was 19."

- Some innuendos stretched the boundaries of reality. In "The One Where Ross Got High" (6.09), Rachel is making a dessert which ends up being half trifle and half shepherd's pie. When Ross checks the recipe, he discovers the cookbook pages are stuck together. Joey accusingly yells, "Chandler!" to imply that ejaculatory fluids caused the pages to stick together. David Crane thought this was one of the dirtiest jokes on the show. This was not in the original script but something added during production. Of course, the joke is a bit of a stretch since the universal understanding is that an adult magazine would have pages stuck together, not a cookbook.

Vagina

- In "The One with the Sonogram at the End" (1.02), the female protagonists claim a kiss is equally important to sex, whereas Chandler likens a kiss to the comedian you must sit through until Pink Floyd arrives. This is a metaphor for the vagina.

Female Orgasm

- There was a classic scene in "The One with Phoebe's Uterus" (4.11) where Monica teaches Chandler the seven female erogenous zones. She seems to reach climax after repeatedly screaming "Seven!!!" Chandler's girlfriend Kathy reinforces the allusion by blithely thanking Monica for teaching Chandler the art of pleasuring a woman.

Copulation

- In "The One with the Giant Poking Device" (3.08), after Monica accidentally bangs Ben's head on the overhead archway, Rachel tries to help the situation by banging her head against a wooden beam in the apartment. Afterwards she states, "You know, if it's not a headboard, it's just not worth it." This implies a couple having wild sex where each forceful thrust by the man pushes the woman's noggin into the headboard.

- The *Friends* writers even delved into sexual positions. In "The One with Joey's Porsche" (6.05), Monica asks, "I wonder what age it is when you stop being able to put both legs over your head?" Phoebe replies, "Oh, I can still do that." Monica then comments, "How are you still single?!" The insinuation relates to a woman's flexibility during sexual intercourse.

- In "The One with the Truth About London" (7.16), as Monica and Chandler prepare to have sex, he quickly removes his clothes, to which she remarks, "Wow, you are really fast." He then replies, "It bodes well for me that speed impresses you." The overtone is that he doesn't last very long during sexual intercourse.

Sodomy

- There were a couple references to sodomy. In "The One with the Birthing Video" (8.15), in the uncut DVD version, Rachel is watching what she thinks is a birthing video but it's actually a porn movie. In her thoughts, she ponders whether the movie starts with how the couple gets pregnant, but once they start having sex, she comments, "No, nope. You can't get pregnant that way."

- In "The One Where Joey Speaks French" (10.13), Monica informs Chandler that the father of Erica's child is not the guy in prison because "it'd be pretty hard to make a baby that way." Chandler then asks, "What was it? The thing that we hardly ever do or the thing we never do?" Monica quickly clarifies, "The thing we *never* do."

Bestiality

- Nothing was off limits in the realm of sexual innuendos. In "The One Where No One's Ready" (3.02), Rachel is annoyed when Ross picks out a Little Bo Peep outfit for her to wear, but he says he didn't recognize it without the inflatable sheep. Rachel then comments, "Yeah, which by the way Chandler, I would like back one of these days." This is a very subtle reference to bestiality. Chandler immediately becomes defensive and remarks, "We used them as pillows when we went camping."

- In "The One Where Joey Tells Rachel" (8.16), Joey claims he is wearing a t-shirt that portrays Calvin doing Hobbes. This refers to the comic strip *Calvin and Hobbes*, featuring the imaginative world of a boy (Calvin) and his real-only-to-him tiger (Hobbes). After Rachel takes a peek at Joey's t-shirt, she comments, "Wow, I wouldn't think Hobbs would like that so much."

Pedophilia

- There is one crafty allusion to pedophilia. In "The One Where Joey Loses His Insurance" (6.04), Joey auditions for a TV commercial but an untreated hernia impacts his performance. In the segment he is paired with a little boy. To ease the abdominal pain, Joey places one hand down his pants to press on the protruding bulge in the groin area while reciting the line "Hey, Timmy, I've got a surprise for you," in a grisly voice.

Bloopers

- In "The One Where Chandler Crosses the Line" (4.07), Chandler apologizes for kissing Kathy and asks Joey what he can do to make it right with his friend. Matt LeBlanc then points to his crotch (implying a blow job).

- In "The One with the Late Thanksgiving" (10.08), Ross and Joey want to surprise Chandler with tickets to a Rangers hockey game. The guys enter Monica's apartment and Ross asks Chandler "Guess what Joey's got?" Joey is supposed to reveal the surprise tickets but instead Matt LeBlanc answers, "Gonorrhea!" This is a callback to "The One Where Underdog Gets Away" (1.09) where Joey is a poster child for VD (venereal disease).

- Later in that same episode, the gang is in the hall playing rock-paper-scissors. After Joey says "Ah, I win," (imitating a flame using his fingers), David Schwimmer looks at Joey's hands and asks, "What the f*ck is that?" On the next take, Ross properly asks, "What is that?" so Matt LeBlanc replies, "It's my f*cking fire."

- In "The One Where Chandler Gets Caught" (10.10), Monica and Chandler decide they should buy a home so she exclaims, "Oh my god. It's huge." Matthew Perry then looks at his crotch and says, "Thanks."

- In "The One with Princess Consuela" (10.14), Phoebe tells Mike that she changed her name to Princess Consuelo Banana [Kudrow then forgets her line and swears] f*ck. Paul Rudd doesn't miss a beat when adding the wisecrack, "You can't change your name to Banana F*cker."

Episode Structure

Typically, sitcoms follow the same episode structure by having a main plot with one or two secondary plots behind it. The *Friends* episode structure utilized three equally weighted storylines. The pilot episode signifies this structure: there is an A, B and C plot (Monica is dating a coworker, Rachel adjusts to singlehood, and Ross readapts to life without Carol). There is no plot that is featured more than the others.

***Friends* writers (from left): Bill Lawrence, Ira Ungerleider, Mike Sikowitz and Jeff Strauss**

In addition to having three equally weighted stories, the *Friends* episode structure had interwoven storylines. Although three separate plots played out for the six characters, their stories were intermingled. In other words, they all periodically interacted with one another despite being wrapped up in different, unrelated stories. There were a few exceptions, such as when Chandler was stuck in an ATM vestibule with model Jill Goodacre. His story was completely isolated from the other characters.

Having an ensemble cast with six principal players is a double-edged sword. The showrunners felt that using six equal characters, rather than emphasizing one or two, would allow for a "myriad of storylines and give the show legs." Of course, it's a Catch-22. Having only one headliner makes scriptwriting easier because there are fewer subplots. However, it also limits the stories because every major plot must revolve around the main protagonist. In contrast, an ensemble opens up an endless array of possible storylines because there are multiple characters with diverse backgrounds. The drawback, however, is trying to create a multitude of plots for every episode.

Having three coplots in nearly every episode made it very difficult for the *Friends* writers to generate fresh, original and exciting storylines each and every week. A single 24-episode season of *Friends* required 72 separate plots, each with its own introduction, development, conflict and resolution, as well as a wide array of jokes, bits and emotional moments. Thus, in most seasons of *Friends* the writers penned a clip show so they could devote their time to other more pressing projects. Although the clip shows were consistently rated the worst in the *Friends* catalog, the creators were willing to sacrifice one installment per year for the betterment of all the others.

Storylines

During the collaborative process in the writers room, ideas come and go, plots ebb and flow, and storylines wax and wane. There are changes made and those that should have been made. There are things that could have been, and things that never were. It happens to all television shows. It is the nature of the beast. *Friends* was no different.

According to David Crane, the hardest episodes to write were always "the first one and the last one of each season." Each summer the producers would outline the stories for the next season. Once the season started, they only worked a few episodes ahead but always kept an eye on the season-ending cliffhanger, but nothing was set in stone. Case in point: the third season finale was supposed to involve Pete (Jon Favreau) proposing marriage to Monica with her answer being kept a secret. However, shortly before the installment was produced, Favreau was fired from the series after objecting to his character being written as too nerdy. The entire marriage proposal cliffhanger with Favreau had to be scrapped. Thus, an alternate storyline was created where Chandler tries to prove to Monica that he is boyfriend material, and the cliffhanger focused on Ross choosing between Rachel and Bonnie (Christine Taylor). At this point in time, even the showrunners didn't know which woman he would pick so they ended the season on a single word, "Hi," but left the identity of the woman unknown to the audience.

Other season-ending finales were more definitive, especially as the series progressed. Season four was always going to be Ross' wedding (though, initially he was supposed to marry Chloe, not Emily), season six was slated as Chandler's proposal with a wedding the following year. Season eight had the birth of Rachel's baby, followed by Phoebe's marriage proposal (though the groom was up in the air), and, of course, season ten was the highly anticipated Ross–Rachel reunion for the series finale.

The most unexpected storyline modification involved Phoebe's wedding plans. Everyone, including Hank Azaria, believed that Phoebe and David would end up together. According to Azaria, he was under the impression that David was supposed to come back to the show after he was written off to Minsk. But then Paul Rudd entered the mix as a blind date for Phoebe, and his presence muddied the water.

Rudd was originally signed for only two episodes but the writers immediately recognized the chemistry he had with Lisa Kudrow so the writers kept coming up with more ideas for their characters. Rudd meshed well with the other costars and his fictional character was very likable, which is why many fans characterize him as the seventh friend. He appeared in 17 episodes.

Even the creators had no clue which way it would turn out for Phoebe. As they penned "The One in Barbados, Part 1" (9.23), her mate for life was undecided. Fans were split as well. The creators ultimately chose Mike (Rudd) because he was a better fit for her. "Once Paul Rudd came into the picture, I think he almost filled out another dimension of Phoebe, who was someone who wanted something more normal, conservative in a way," said Marta Kauffman.

Other story arcs sprouted out of nowhere during the course of the season. The idea for a relationship between Joey and Rachel was decided halfway through the eighth season. The creators did not want Ross and Rachel to get back together too soon, so while looking for a romantic impediment, a writer suggested Joey. The proposal was incorporated into season eight, but after the actors expressed concern that the storyline would make their characters unlikable, the arc was quickly wrapped up, until it resurfaced one last time in the final season.

With the addition of Emma in season nine, the creators had to figure out the number of storylines to devote to the infant. Her presence created a creative quandary: the creators did not want the show to revolve around a baby nor did they want to pretend she did not exist. They opted to feature Emma in a few episodes shortly after her birth and then only having her visibly present in later episodes (but uninvolved in the plots).

Of all the installments, the writers really enjoyed crafting bottle episodes. In episodic television, a bottle episode is produced cheaply and restricted in scope. In other words, there are no guest stars, two or fewer minor secondary characters, and no custom-made swing sets. *Friends* began using bottle episodes once per year starting in the third season. In addition to saving money, the showrunners quickly realized that fans preferred these episodes. "Somewhere around the fourth or fifth episode we started to figure out what made the show work best. The lesson we had to learn over and over again is it was always better to have them together than them with outside characters. The outside characters had to enter their world," Marta Kauffman elucidated.

Unused Script Ideas

The collaborative creative environment meant all the writers contributed ideas, good or bad, and everything was thrown into one giant hopper. As the ideas rolled in, they were saved for future use, if necessary. The writers room had a board of ideas—future use and never to be used. Some were kept simply because they were funny, such as the note "too many hats" which made them laugh every time they saw it. One of the unused ideas was labeled "Ross Sauce" but it never came to fruition.

There were numerous proposed plots but the most outlandish had the gang moving to Minnesota in the fifth season. In the projected storyline, Chandler is transferred for his job so the rest of the gang follows and they immediately discover a world of "cheap apartments, friendly neighbors and subzero temperatures." The relocation was supposed to last half a season. The concept was partially devised due to criticism that *Friends* did not accurately reflect the racial diversity of New York City. It was also a way to conceal Matthew Perry's substance abuse issues. He could be more easily written out of scripts if he relapsed. They did the same thing in season nine by sending him to Tulsa.

At the request of Walt Disney's CEO Michael Eisner, a script was written where the cast went to Disney World. In the plotline, Joey gets a summer job as a giant light bulb in the electrical parade. The gang schedules a visit but before they get there, Joey has a date with a woman who plays Cinderella in the parade. They go back to his place and have sex. Upon realizing it's midnight, she has to return the costume or they will dock her pay. She gathers up her clothing and leaves, but Joey doesn't know her name. In a play on Cinderella's glass slipper, the girl forgets her bra which is Joey's only clue to discovering her identity.

According to Kevin Bright, "That was the story we pitched to Disney, and that's where the story ended."

In the tenth season, there was going to be a story arc involving Ross and Rachel visiting Paris in preparation for her permanent move abroad. In the original script, Rachel resigns from Ralph Lauren after Ross agrees to help her move to Paris. "They go to Paris and have this big romantic time and that's when we see he's starting to fall in love with her again," David Crane revealed. This unproduced script was titled "The One Where Jetlag Wins" since they both end up falling asleep in their Paris hotel room after a long flight.

In season six, there was a proposal to have Rachel and Gunther become roommates. She had been booted out of Monica's apartment and needed a place to live. The story was finally scrapped because the arrangement seemed too contrived. Instead, the writers chose to write a joke about her rejecting the idea. In the added segment, Gunther asks Rachel if she is looking for a place to live and then tells her, "I was going to offer you my apartment." Rachel replies, "Why, where are you going?"

Although the network often censored jokes, bits and innuendos, they rarely censored entire plotlines, but it did happen at least once. NBC executive Don Ohlmeyer put his foot down to a storyline where Ross uses his ex-wife's menstrual pads for arch supports in his shoes and refuses to throw them out. "Overall, the network notes were almost nonexistent," David Crane stated, but this time "Don was uncomfortable with maxi pads."

The showrunners also rejected story proposals that failed to meet their minimum level of acceptability. One such storyline involved Phoebe being so enraptured with Chinese food that she attempts to marry it. This idea was resoundingly rejected. "I just find myself not caring," Kauffman declared, a response she regularly uttered to pitches she felt lacked an emotional through-line.

Although the cast had some leeway to refuse storylines, it rarely happened and only if they could convince the showrunners. Matthew Perry once objected to a plotline that too closely linked his character to being gay. In the script, Chandler went to an all-male strip club because it served great tuna melt sandwiches. Perry didn't find the idea funny and asked for it to be nixed.

The creators didn't always acquiesce to cast objections. In season ten, when the script called for Joey and Rachel to start dating, the entire cast confronted the show's producers to express their dissatisfaction. The top dogs refused to budge, claiming the story promoted an emotional storyline for Joey's character.

Script Changes

Although the creators encouraged a collaborative creative environment at all phases of the production process, once filming started, they became totalitarians who governed the soundstage with an iron fist. The script became the bible and changes were only allowed if the rulers so decreed. Thus, improvisation, ad-libbing, or any script deviations, whether planned or unintended, were strictly prohibited. "On the night of a show, they are staying pretty darn close to what is now scripted," Marta Kauffman asserted. "The cast definitely pitches jokes along the way during the course of the run-throughs and rehearsals but there is not a lot of ad-libbing. We're not very good with surprises."

Each episode was scripted for a reason. Every scene was about timing and cues so any improvisation could disrupt the symbiosis of the cast. Some big-name Hollywood stars that were unfamiliar with scripted television programs would often come close on their lines, so the writers would have to remind them, "No, you say exactly what is on the page. Nothing more. Nothing less."

There were a couple exceptions to their draconian rule. In "The One with the Blackout" (1.07), Cosimo Fusco (Paolo) improvised most of the Italian lines, including the romantic scene where he and Rachel are on the balcony looking up at the stars. Likewise, in "The One with the Stoned Guy" (1.15), former *SNL* star Jon Lovitz improvised several lines, such as the "tartlet" repetition, and the act of dropping Sugar-O's cereal into a bowl of milk to function as life preservers for gummy bears.

Of course, the costars had more leeway and often used one of their many scene takes to improvise a comedy bit, some of which made it into the episode. For example, in "The One Where Eddie Moves In" (2.17), the tag scene has the cast singing "Smelly Cat," but during one take the cast extemporized their screaming vocals which prompted all the scene extras to laugh and break character. The take should have been part of the year-end blooper reel but the editor liked the cut so it was included in the final edit.

Rachel and Monica (left) discussing condoms, and Joey (right) decorating with condoms

Other times, an unintended blunder was sufficiently humorous to be included in the episode. In "The One with Five Steaks and an Eggplant" (2.05), during the tag scene, Matt LeBlanc leaped for the phone, fell over the arm of the couch, and crashed into the counter before falling to the floor. The producers used this blooper segment because it was funnier than the scripted line.

Script changes also occurred during filming. Many times a joke flopped in front of the audience so the writers would huddle to brainstorm a better line. In "The One After Vegas" (6.01), Chandler's line: "I don't think they're as much dating as they are drunk," bombed during the first pass so after seven minutes of brainstorming, Matthew Perry came up with a better line: "I don't think they're as much dating as they are two bottles of vodka walking around in human form." Also in that episode, Rachel's line was "Ross, stop saying the word 'marriage.' Ross, stop, listen. If you don't get this annulled, I will." During a break, the writers huddled to discuss a better line and came up with: "Ross, this is not a marriage, it's the world's worst hangover." *Entertainment Weekly* called it the best line of the episode.

There were often times when the writers simply wanted to add a topper to punctuate the preceding one-liner. For example, in "The One Where Paul's the Man" (6.22), Ross and Elizabeth (Alexandra Holden) are at the cabin kissing on the couch before he abruptly pulls away. When she asks him what's wrong, he replies, "I'm just thinking about your father." During filming, the writers stopped production because they wanted another comeback to add to the joke. After a writers' huddle, they instructed Holden to respond, "Well, whatever works for you."

The showrunners also allowed the staff writers to try alternative jokes. On the night of filming, if a writer believed a different joke or bit would play better for the audience, the creators often took the time to shoot one more take of the scene to see if it worked. "We will talk about alternates that we will try," Kauffman stated. "If people don't believe in a certain joke, we will try an alternate joke." A good example is "The One with All the Cheesecakes" (7.11). Initially, David Crane was extremely resistant to the idea of having Joey eat cheese- cake off the hallway floor. "I remember David being like 'He's not a cartoon. He doesn't see giant hams in people's eyes. He's a human being. He doesn't walk around with a fork in his pocket,'" staff writer Shana Goldberg-Meehan stated. "But on the second take, he let us try it, and it got a really good reaction. He was like, 'You know what? I guess Joey's a human who does walk around with a fork in his pocket.' He let us keep the moment, even though it was probably a little bit larger than stuff we normally did."

The creators were writing perfectionists but they also had to appease the staff writers, studio and network executives, and the audience. The writers were easier to accommodate because it was usually a consensus that ruled the day. NBC executives were problematic but rarely stood in the way, though there were a few exceptions. The audience, on the other hand, was the best barometer. The writers trusted the audience to let them know if their words weren't quite good enough. "We knew we had to listen to the audience," said Marta Kauffman. "Their silence tells you a lot. Laughing in good and bad ways. Laughing at set- ups instead of jokes." David Crane concurred, adding: "You'll run a scene and you listen to the audience, and while you don't trust them entirely, still if we have a joke that we think is funny all week and nobody's laughing, maybe we're wrong. You have to have the courage to throw out things you've loved for a whole week."

Overall, the showrunners agreed that having multiple sources of feedback allowed them to craft the best possible shows. "We also felt everyone's opinion was valid," Crane declared. "There was no hierarchy. It made everything better, but longer too." The drive for perfection is a mixed blessing. "Sometimes we lost our energy because we took so much time trying to find a better joke when we should have just moved on," he regrettably acknowledged. But they took it one installment at a time. "We'd walk out after every episode and say, 'There's another one that didn't suck.' And we meant it. That's as far as we'd give ourselves."

Long Hours

The staff writers congregated around a massive desk on the seventh floor of a Warner Bros. Studios office building. They worked 14 to 16 hours every workday which once in a while stretched to 24 hours if an urgent deadline was approaching. On rare evenings they were able to leave the office early (i.e., 10:30pm). WB was their home away from home—at times a party place, other times a jail cell. There was no specified end to the workday; no set moment when they could punch out and head home. Ordering dinner at the office was a matter of course. All-nighters were a fairly standard occurrence. The last day of the work-week was widely known as Fraturday, since it usually did not end until they went home on Saturday morning.

The staff writers ate so many takeout meals at work that writer Ellen Kreamer thought the atmosphere in the writers room turned everyone into "a slightly fatter, greasier-looking version of themselves." In fact, years later the sound of a crinkling takeout bag would be enough to evoke momentary delight, transporting her back to those high-calorie days. "Our hours were crazy. There were so many mornings when we were still finishing the rewrites," David Crane recalled. It was never-ending rewrites. Each day they would get notes from the studio and network executives, but, according to Marta Kauffman, "It was *our* notes that killed us."

Writer Jeff Astrof once approached Crane about the long hours, stating that they were currently working 100% of the time and making a show that was 100%. But the staff was growing tired of seeing the sun rise over the Warner Bros. lot, so he wondered if they could cut back to 75% effort and make a show that was 90% excellent. Crane rejected the notion. "*Friends* had to be 100%, always."

The staff writers would entertain themselves with horseplay like tossing a small football back and forth for hours without letting it drop (inspiring "The One with the Ball," ep 5.21) or offering monetary inducements to eat outrageous foods, like an entire jar of garlic pickles (inspiring various wagers in numerous episodes, such as drinking the fat). They would play videogames to blow off steam or watch the latest installment of *The Osbournes*. Another fun activity was Taste Test Wednesdays where an assistant was sent to a local grocery store to purchase, for example, every brand of plain potato chips. The writers would try each variety and vote for their favorite, and then the best potato chip would be declared.

One late night, writer Shana Goldberg-Meehan entered the writers room, taking note of the roiling discontent, and told fellow writers Ellen Kreamer and Robert Carlock that they had 30 seconds to go "apeshit crazy" before they got back to work. Kreamer and Carlock jumped on tables and tore the room apart for precisely 30 seconds. Then it was business as usual.

It was also during the late nights or all-nighters when the conversation and banter in the writers room, often fueled by boredom or exhaustion, turned to its bawdiest and most puerile. This behavior resulted in three writers being sued for sexual harassment. They won the case but it exemplifies the raunchy atmosphere within the writers room.

Cocreator Marta Kauffman, having two young children at the time, was well aware of the relationship strains caused by working long hours. She feared having a story collapse during run-throughs because it meant another late night working on rewrites. Kauffman lived by one strict rule: she would not miss her children's bedtime two nights in a row. On late nights, she would drive home, put her children to bed, and then return to the office. On very late nights, she would drive home as the sun was coming up, shower, feed her children breakfast and get them dressed for school, and then head back to work.

Episode Titles

Seinfeld's use of simplistic episode titles inspired the *Friends* showrunners to adopt the format. *Seinfeld* cocreator Larry David advocated concise monikers (e.g., "The Library," "The Pen") so the writers could focus on script humor, not punning titles that no one would ever see. The *Friends* producers agreed with this philosophy but slightly modified the concept, utilizing more descriptive phrases, which was the brainchild of cocreator David Crane. He realized that when people discuss television shows, they often refer to installments by its content: "You always go, 'Oh, well, it's the one with the thing' ... so it was like, 'Let's just do that.' And then it stuck. It was easier and people remembered." He fittingly added, "It's not lazy, per se, but it's certainly efficient."

Director David Schwimmer with the creators (left) and writer Scott Silveri (right)

The showrunners realized that the episode title would not be featured in the opening credits so it would be unknown to most viewers. Although show titles were often listed in newspapers or entertainment periodicals, the creators believed that even die-hard fans were unlikely to remember such specifics when discussing episodic events the next day. People instinctively refer to installments by content, not title, so it made sense to designate titles accordingly. Consequently, nearly every episode begins with "The One with" or "The One Where" with only a few exceptions (e.g., "The One Hundredth," "The One After Vegas" and "The Last One").

Of course in the 2020s, installment titles are more commonly available and frequently utilized by viewers due to the widespread prevalence of DVR listings, daily newspaper and weekly magazine programming schedules, detailed onscreen cable and satellite guides, and multiple streaming services. None of these informational formats existed when *Friends* was originally produced.

Phoebe's Songs

Contrary to many reports that Lisa Kudrow wrote Phoebe's songs, in reality, the staff writers must be given all the credit for the lyrics. According to cocreator David Crane, "It's either written by whoever wrote that episode, or when we're in the room writing the show, someone will pitch out a lyric and everyone will sort of chime in." Kudrow did perform all 47 original songs on the show.

Phoebe's most famous song, "Smelly Cat," was conceived in 1995 by *Friends* staff writer Betsy Borns. She originally penned lyrics for "Smelly Dog" to memorialize a pungent pet she had once owned. "My dog was so smelly his name was Gouda, because he smelled like bad cheese," she explained. Borns ultimately decided a song about a foul-smelling cat would be more humorous. Adam Chase, another *Friends* staff writer, also contributed lyrics. In fact, everyone in the writers room had a part in formulating lyrics to the song.

The popular singalong debuted in "The One with the Baby on the Bus" (2.06). Kudrow composed the melody herself (as she did for all her character's original songs) and cowrote the music with Chrissie Hynde (lead singer of The Pretenders). Although Hynde used to get annoyed by fans asking her to perform "Smelly Cat" on stage, she has grown used to the popularity of it and considers the song to be "probably my biggest legacy now."

The tune became so popular that fans sent letters to the producers requesting them to release the track on an album. An updated and expanded version of the ditty, "Smelly Cat Medley," was eventually released on the soundtrack album *Friends Again* (1999), giving singing credit to Phoebe Buffay and the Hairballs. The track is a combination of "Smelly Cat" excerpts from various episodes and features vocals from Kudrow, Hynde, and The Pretenders. As a testament to the single's universal appeal, Kudrow even performed it live onstage with Taylor Swift at the Staples Center in Los Angeles in 2015. Midway through the song, Kudrow told Swift, "I'm sorry. That was good, but you have to really feel the lyrics."

The Portuguese quartet Gato Fedorento (Smelly Cat) had a self-titled television series that lasted nine years. The surreal comedy group is known for their subjective and absurd satire centering on the Portuguese language and the country's social reality. The group is composed of four comedians: José Diogo Quintela, Miguel Góis, Ricardo Araújo Pereira and Tiago Dores. When the quartet was choosing a name for the group, they purposely selected an appellation inspired by the song "Smelly Cat" which they first discovered on the *Friends* soundtrack.

Axing Matthew Perry

The first time Matthew Perry appeared on the cover of *People* magazine (September 25, 1995), he sent the issue to Dr. Web, one of his former high school teachers. Web once said that Perry would never amount to anything if he didn't stop joking all the time. Although Perry finally achieved fame with *Friends* in 1994, he was too young to cope with the perks of stardom so he turned to alcohol and drugs.

Perry's alcohol addiction began prior to *Friends* but it was never a serious problem until he began taking Vicodin, which precipitated a slow downward spiraling free fall. "I was on *Friends* from age 24 to 34," Perry methodically elucidated. "I was in the white-hot flame of fame. ... From an outsider's perspective, it would seem like I had it all. It was actually a very lonely time for me because I was suffering from alcoholism. It was going on before *Friends*, but it's a progressive disease. I wasn't a massive party guy. I wasn't a bull-in-a-china-shop kind of drinker."

By the show's third season (1996), he began losing significant weight and the following year, prior to the start of the show's fourth season, checked into the Hazelden rehab center in Minnesota to complete a 28-day inpatient program. "It was the scariest thing that's ever happened to me," Perry recalled. "You get a whole new respect for yourself and life when you go through something that difficult."

Perry openly admitted that he did not remember three years of the show, somewhere between the third and sixth seasons. "I was never high at work. I was painfully hungover. Then eventually things got so bad I couldn't hide it and everybody knew," he unabashedly acknowledged. The costars would be "forced to acclimate themselves to the sight of Perry shaking and sweating while trying to remember his lines." Perry was in trouble, but there was little his friends could do to help, other than to be supportive. Matt LeBlanc tried to intervene. "I tried to talk to him. There wasn't a response. ... They need to bottom out on their own," he said. Marta Kauffman also admitted it was "terrifying" watching someone she cared about be in "so much pain," and Lisa Kudrow stated the cast was "just hopelessly standing on the sidelines. We were hurting a lot."

Between 1997 and 2001, he was taking an "insane number of pills" (20 to 30 Vicodin per day) as well as drinking "probably a quart of vodka a day." But his addiction was steadfastly guarded. "The cast would never talk to outsiders about each other," said a production source. "When Matthew Perry really struggled with [drug and alcohol] addiction and got so sick, they closed ranks." It was during this time frame, specifically prior to season five, that the producers seriously considered transferring his character to Minnesota as a means of writing Perry out of scripts in case of another relapse.

On February 27, 2001, Perry again entered rehab for addiction to Vicodin, methadone, amphetamines and alcohol. While filming *Serving Sara* in Texas (during a production break from *Friends*), he suffered severe stomach pains and was advised to return to Los Angeles and check into Marina del Rey's Daniel Freeman Hospital. After this incident, the producers contemplated firing Perry. He obviously couldn't handle fame and his antics threatened to negatively impact the series. They decided to keep Perry because the entire seventh season of *Friends* hinged on his character's marriage to Monica.

Everyone felt the blowback from his hospital stay. The entire production schedule had to be reworked for several weeks. All of Chandler's storylines had to be cut with new scenes written, effectively relegating him to secondary character status, while the other characters' plotlines had to be modified to comport with the new script changes. Even filming catered to Perry's rehab schedule because he had very limited furlough times to visit the studio set and soundstage.

Another relapse in the summer of 2002 prompted the producers to change the direction of the show by having Perry's character transferred to Tulsa, Oklahoma. Chandler's move was the producers' creative way to cover for Perry's drug addiction. His absence from the daily activities of the gang allowed the writers to easily write Perry out of episodes in case he relapsed and entered another drug rehab program.

NBC Censors

Standards and practices is the policy used by television networks to justify censorship of television material. Throughout the series' run, the *Friends* producers had to negotiate with NBC's standards and practices team over a variety of issues, and the battle started on the first day of production for the pilot episode. NBC balked at the storyline where Monica sleeps with a guy on the first date and then fails to remember his name. Executives thought it was too racy for primetime television. The creators laughed at the hypocritical standards set by the network. When the sitcom started it was okay to say "penis" but taboo to utter "nipple." Three years later the word "penis" was banned and then it was later approved by season seven.

The struggle between artistic integrity and network censorship was a weekly headache. There was remarkable controversy related to "The One Where Dr. Ramoray Dies" (2.18). In the segment, Monica and Rachel discuss who gets the last condom but NBC forbade the characters from saying the word or showing the wrapper. Marta Kauffman exasperatedly proclaimed, "They're masturbating on *Seinfeld* and we can't show a condom wrapper." The creators were justifiably frustrated. The *Seinfeld* episode in question, "The Contest," which aired five months earlier, was the precipitating factor that commenced a moral conservative backlash aimed at network television.

Network censors became hypersensitive. "We went through a very difficult reactionary period. ... We couldn't talk about certain kinds of sex or show certain things," Kauffman explained. "The V-chip was being talked about constantly and it was just after the condom episode of *Seinfeld*. Suddenly we weren't allowed to show a condom wrapper." The V-chip is a technology that allows the blocking of programs based on its content ratings category. It is intended for use by parents to manage the television viewing of their children. According to Kauffman, the creators "tried to fight it tooth and nail."

In "The One with Barry & Mindy's Wedding" (2.24), the original script storyline had Joey auditioning for the part of an uncircumcised man so the gang helps him come up with ways he could look the part. Network censors felt this subplot was tasteless, and recommended changing it. The storyline was shelved for years and then resurrected in "The One with Ross and Monica's Cousin" (7.19) because network censors had finally softened restrictions on episode content.

NBC censors also influenced a scene in "The One Without the Ski Trip" (3.17). In the tag scene, Ross interrupts a lovemaking session between Carol and Susan but NBC forbade the writers from mentioning or describing the intimacy. To circumvent the policies, the writers wanted Carol to nonverbally communicate the message to Ross, but they could not devise a humorous way to do it. Luckily, Jane Sibbett (Carol) chimed in and suggested removing a pubic hair from her tongue. The writers loved it. It was the first time she pitched something that was really outrageous, and it actually made it into a scene.

The staff writers were always looking for ways to protest network censorship by subtly circumventing the rules. In numerous episodes the characters demonstrated an alternative means of using the swear finger—the pinky-side double fist bump. According to executive producer Kevin Bright, the writers created the hand gesture as an artful means of saying "F*ck you!" to network censors. The satirical gesture debuted in "The One with Joey's New Girlfriend" (4.05).

Another jab at the network occurred in "The One with the Worst Best Man Ever" (4.22). The producers discovered a clever way to sidestep the condom restriction by having Joey decorate his apartment with "balloons" that were in fact inflated condoms. The staff writers' passive-aggressive spitefulness is hilariously vindictive and exemplifies an adroit manner of outmaneuvering the network censors. This celebratory decoration was their retaliation for the condom ban imposed by NBC in "The One Where Dr. Ramoray Dies" (2.18).

Social Responsibility

Although *Friends* was an adult-oriented sitcom, the producers were cognizant of the age demographic of their audience which included adolescents. They understood the fictional characters were role models and that television influenced societal behavior. Toward that end, whenever sex was an integral part of the plot, condoms were either implied, present, or part of the conversation.

In "The One Where Dr. Ramoray Dies" (2.18), Rachel and Monica discuss who will get to use the last condom. The show's creators fought to include the condom wrapper but lost. "We felt so strongly that this was responsible television," Kauffman declared. "But we were never able to show that wrapper." Instead, viewers saw the girls fighting over a nondescript, unadorned cardboard box. "We could show the box, we could shake the box so you could hear the condom, but we couldn't say 'condom,'" Marta Kauffman frustratingly explained. Warren Littlefield, president of NBC Entertainment, remarked: "What could be more socially responsible than these characters practicing safe sex?"

Due to the controversial nature of the condom scene, this episode was the subject of multiple research studies on condom usage and efficacy. The conclusions were unanimous in showing that "The One Where Dr. Ramoray Dies" (2.18) affirmatively influenced teenage sexuality and behavior. Marta Kauffman "felt vindicated by that report" because the show was often criticized as being "overtly sexual" when she always believed the producers were "very, very responsible."

Directors

Executive producer Kevin Bright directed 54 *Friends* episodes. Each television season he was given first option to select the episodes he wanted to direct. He usually preferred the season opening and ending episodes, Thanksgiving, and the ones with the most appealing plots.

David Schwimmer directed 10 episodes of *Friends*. After graduating from Northwestern University in 1988, he and his fellow classmates founded Lookingglass Theatre Company in Chicago, which is where he developed a taste for directing. Once *Friends* became a success, Schwimmer found himself unable to pursue this passion on his own so he approached the creators for an opportunity to learn the craft. Even though he had no experience directing television sitcoms, David Crane respected Schwimmer for showing initiative and the other executive producers signed off on the proposal. His directorial debut was "The One on the Last Night" (6.06). After *Friends* retired, he directed a couple installments of the short-lived spinoff *Joey*.

Schwimmer commented on his experience behind the camera and fervidly proclaimed, "I love the collaborative nature of directing. The vision is coming from you, but you're incorporating talents and ideas from all these people. As an actor there's a great freedom, but the experience is much more isolated." He loved the chemistry with the other cast members so much that he always had new ideas and thoughts about expanding plots and subplots.

James Burrows directed the series pilot episode en route to a total of 15 episodes in the first four seasons. His stint ended earlier than anticipated because he clashed with Kevin Bright. The tension began with the pilot episode and the friction continued thereafter. Their contentious relationship was the reason Burrows was never asked to return after the fourth season. He went on to direct *Will & Grace* and *Mike & Molly*.

Friends never banked on one particular director to oversee the production of episodes. Some sitcoms preferred the consistency of having one production overlord with a certain vision and style, such as *How I Met Your Mother* using Pamela Fryman almost exclusively for all nine seasons. The *Friends* showrunners did not share the same philosophy. Directors were hired based on availability. It was never an issue of artistic style or technique. They were hired to do a basic job, not to create a cinematic masterpiece. Cocreator Kevin Bright summarized the role of a *Friends* director: "The job was to understand what the producers wanted, what the concept of that episode was, and not try to reinvent it or put your own touch on it." The creators believed it was the writing and acting that made the show, not the directing.

This limited creative role of the director made it possible for other, less experienced crew members, to have an opportunity to oversee episodes. The producers were very hospitable when it came to training aspiring directors. Besides David Schwimmer, the showrunners allowed a couple *Friends* crew members—technical coordinators Dana deVally and Roger Christiansen, and editor Stephen Prime—to get their feet wet in the industry. For deVally and Prime, *Friends* had the distinction of being their directorial debuts. Both crew members further pursued the profession with deVally directing 16 different series and Prime only three programs (he chose to focus on his original profession, editing). In addition to being a technical coordinator, Christiansen also worked as an associate director on *Friends* for 25 episodes, and continued the craft in the spinoff series *Joey* for 26 episodes. He went on to direct numerous shows, most notably 31 episodes of *Hannah Montana* from 2006 to 2009.

Wardrobe, Makeup & Fashion

Often overlooked or disregarded, wardrobe, makeup and fashion played a major role in the success of *Friends*. From the trendsetting styles to their glamorous visages, including all the storied hairstyles, these behind-the-scenes crew members were integral cogs in the situation comedy machine. Their artistry boosted audience interest and also helped sustain viewership, more so than any other noncritical element in the show's production.

Character Image

When devising the show's costumes for the pilot episode, *Friends* wardrobe designer Debra McGuire had numerous factors to consider, including the sets and the tone of the script. She wanted to create "an environment with the clothes that makes people who are watching want to be sitting on the couch with them and be in the room with them and be their friend." According to McGuire, "The subliminal aspect of the clothes is really, really important."

McGuire worked with the set decorator before mapping out character costumes. "We had this really great idea about color and excitement in the visual of the apartment," she ardently explained. "Color is played down because the sets are so vibrant. Monica's apartment has so many things in it. I want the characters to look soft," she further explained. The artist turned costume designer relied on the ageless color wheel that everyone learns as a child.

In the first few seasons, McGuire assigned color stories to each character to distinguish them and make them unique. "The original designs for the characters, I was thinking more in terms of color palette," she said. Each character had their own color palette and textures that were meticulously mapped to the mood board. In effect, the characters were given their own distinct "visual identities." The women in particular gravitated toward a great deal of color: "The female characters were distinguished by their preferred colors. Rachel went with greens and blues, Monica leaned toward red, black and gray, and Phoebe preferred yellows and purples, mixed patterns, skirts and unstructured pieces," McGuire detailed. "The male characters were more texture and styles: Ross was in tweeds, Joey leaned toward chenilles and textures, and Chandler had a vintage palette."

Although each character was uniquely attired, McGuire had to visualize the sextet as a unit so their wardrobe would complement one another. "In the beginning I was creating a palette of six people who needed to be together all the time. I was looking at them more as a palette than a fashion statement," she explained. "So if you put that all together ... it made a beautiful palette." She conceptualized their images like a painting rather than a fashion ensemble.

McGuire also strived to make sure the characters' clothes reflected what was happening in their lives. When they were unemployed or struggling financially they dressed one way but as their careers surged so did their wardrobes. This was most reflected in Rachel. "With [Rachel] working in a department store, I wanted to create a look that's not out there ... and to show off her body without being obnoxious," McGuire said. Since Rachel excelled in the fashion industry, it was important to have her sartorially stylish.

A final consideration was location. The sitcom was filmed in California but set in New York City, so the characters' wardrobes had to properly reflect the differences. "It was really important for me to get across that this was New York, not California," McGuire noted. "So for me, a New York palette is a basic of black, white, and gray."

Rachel

Clothes. Since Rachel was a JAP (Jewish-American Princess), McGuire gave her "lots of blues and greens and this warmer, fun palette." Rachel had a speedy transformation from spoiled, rich daddy's girl (in the pilot) to desolate working girl (in episode two). "It was not very expensive clothing but everything was darling and very Rachel—short skirts, schoolgirl looking." Rachel's look resonated with viewers at the time—especially those teeny crop tops.

Makeup. Although Rachel was the fashion focal point of the series, few fans realize her makeup was very subdued. "Her lip color was usually muted and a natural, neutral color," makeup artist Robin Siegel said. "Occasionally, I would put on a pale blue or pale lavender or pale green just to punch it up, or do some gray shadows but nothing that you'd ever really see on TV. It would just make her eyes pop out depending on the scene."

Hairstyle. Chris McMillan met Jennifer Aniston right after the series pilot. He did the touch-ups on her hair and created The Rachel haircut in the first season. The international obsession with the cut propelled him to stardom, which he parlayed into opening his own salon. He also witnessed her hairstyle evolution over the years. "Rachel kind of evolved from chunkier blonde to natural golden brown. Real subtle changes but if you look at it over the years, you notice there was definitely a change. And that's what I love about Jennifer. She is willing to go to those places and experiment." Stylist Jonathan Hanousek noted that after The Rachel hairstyle, Aniston "grew that out, and she just kept basically long layers for years and years, until she cut the bob." It was a bold cut that divided viewers. Aniston later commented that she did not like the bob cut, but she definitely preferred it to The Rachel, which she loathed.

Monica

Clothes. "Monica's palette early on was very New York typical," Debra McGuire stated. "I kept her very much in whites, off-white, burgundy, black, gray." In the 1990s, Monica's clothing was often overshadowed by Rachel's fashion-setting trends. According to McGuire, "She was the one character that was under the radar at the time. She was a little more New York, refined, classic than the others. And how interesting it is that that is the wardrobe that young people really resonate with. And I think a lot of it has to do with the fit, there was this oversized aspect to the 1990s clothes."

Makeup. "Monica's colors were the jewel tones," declared makeup artist Robin Siegel. "Sometimes she had bold lip colors, sometimes a soft lip color, her features are pretty vibrant with the dark hair and fair skin and the bright blue eyes. She photographs great, she looks great."

Hairstyle. Jonathan Hanousek often styled Courteney Cox's hair. "Of all the girls, her look changed the most over the last nine seasons. She took a little more chances," he said. "She went from that very blown-dry hair in the beginning to some softer looks, more wavy, a little bit longer. At one point she had cut it off chin length." Stylist Chris McMillan loved Cox's daring nature. "My favorite thing about Courteney is every few years she'll grow her bangs out, and then she'll say, 'Should I cut bangs?' And we'll cut bangs, and within a second she'll say, 'I hate my bangs. We got to grow them out,'" he recalled. "So we always make the mistake every three years, so she reminds me to this day, she'll say 'If I ever want bangs, talk me out of it.'"

There was only one instance where Cox's hairstyle was an issue with the producers. At the beginning of the fourth season, her hair contained streaks from a role in *Scream 2* and the style did not comport with Monica's image. The producers asked Cox to dye her hair to look the part of her character.

Phoebe

Clothes. Costumer Debra McGuire saw Phoebe as an opportunity to make a splash in color and express herself through jewelry and accessories. "Phoebe was a way to add color and texture to the palette," she remarked. "I'm bringing in a palette of florals and sheers and fabrics that move and things in her hair and lots of jewelry. I really wanted to bring in that element of flowy, feminine patterns." In fact, Phoebe was the only character to wear patterns. "Here was a character who could have some kind of bravado in jewelry and in expression with her hairstyles and accessories," McGuire added. "Just her overall vibe is so different than the others."

McGuire, a self-proclaimed ex-hippie, desired a modern bohemian, artistic energy for Phoebe. "I didn't want it to be sort of bringing back something; I wanted it to be reminiscent of bohemian life, but I wanted it to have a more contemporary feeling," she noted. "Phoebe was my Lower East Side vibe. ... I love that aesthetic of flowing, beautiful patterns."

Makeup. For Phoebe's more quirky characteristics, makeup artist Robin Siegel wanted to make a splash. "Her wardrobe was very, very colorful. I always use a rosy color or pink hued lip color on her, and brown shadows and liner on her eyes," she explained. "The idea was to have her look beautiful, and her clothing and her hairstyles reflected more of the quirkiness of her character."

Hairstyle. Stylist Jonathan Hanousek touched on changes with Phoebe over the years. "Phoebe was only wavy the first six or so episodes of the first season, and from then on you always saw her straight. Lisa has, actually, curly hair and she's a natural brunette. So she's got a lot of highlights to keep her that blonde shade," he recalled. "With Phoebe it was not so much about doing funky hairdos as it was about having pretty hair." Hanousek had other cast secrets: "A lot of people don't realize that Phoebe wore wigs on the show. Mostly because Lisa was doing movies when we weren't doing the show. So she would cut her hair or dye it a different color for the movies and we would have to keep Phoebe blonde and have this long blonde hair on the show. So we had wigs that we would use and nobody knew any better."

Ross

For the male leads, it was all about the clothes. Their hairstyles rarely changed, and when they did, the difference was negligible, such as growing it out or cutting it short, but nothing radical. The color never changed, other than a lighter shade or tint. Thus, the focal point for the guys was their wardrobe.

The head costume designer chose an attire for Ross that would fit with his occupation and higher educational level. In the beginning, Ross was very collegiate with patches on his elbows, and a flair of texture and tweeds and corduroy mixed in with his brown, beige, and rust colored clothing. According to Debra McGuire, "Ross, because he's a professor, I kept in a very sort of tweedy, J.Crew, Banana Republic, kind of classic professorial, but with a lot of fashion." Although it's a rather stereotypical fashion, it worked well for the character and the actor portraying him.

Joey

The *Friends* costumer was instrumental in sculpting Joey's image. As an unemployed actor, he was a sharp contrast to Ross and Chandler, the resident white-collar, working-class professionals. Joey was an actor and stereotypical lothario. In the pilot episode, Debra McGuire used this persona as the basis for his Fonzie-inspired style. "I wanted to use kind of an old leather jacket that had character, and what's interesting is I ended up buying an Armani leather blazer and kind of beating it up," she admitted. "We made it look like a poor man's choice, but really it wasn't." McGuire explained the laborious process: "I pulled hundreds of vintage leather jackets and this was the only one that was right. Sometimes finding something that's extremely expensive and deconstructing it is going to be more valuable visually, and vice versa. Sometimes the cheapest thing that you just find can work as something couture."

Chandler

In terms of menswear, the *Friends* wardrobe designer cited Chandler as being the most fun. "Chandler was the most creatively inspired. I created a lot of the garments for him," McGuire said. "He was the one character that made sense to bring in some inspiration from the past. I did that certainly with the girls a lot, but he was the only male character that I could sort of really play with that."

Of the three male protagonists, Chandler was the most eccentric. McGuire used this persona to construct a rather unique image, a throwback to a simpler time. "Chandler had a '40s movie star look," so in the beginning he wore "a lot of vintage clothes, tweeds, vintage ties. I did all those shirts with the racing stripes down the side," she casually revealed. "I was motivated by looks my dad wore in the 1940s—really interesting shirts, gabardine wool pants." Although Chandler's formal wardrobe remained vintage, it was filled with textures. "Through his job evolution he became very sophisticated," she recounted. "In his dressier clothes there was always that vintage kind of texture in the sports jackets and in the ties. He had a lot of Chanel sweaters and tweedy sweaters." The shirts and sweater vests quickly became synonymous with the character, and shortly thereafter companies began producing retro fashion, which was embraced by wardrobe designer Mary T. Quigley to outfit Charlie Harper for the sitcom *Two and a Half Men.*

Debra McGuire

Costume designer Debra McGuire (née Fine) was born in May 1952 in Cleveland, Ohio, to businessman Edward Fine (b. Oct. 1923), and homemaker Corrinne Fine (b. Aug. 1928), who both encouraged education and dreaming big. At age 7, she had one of her drawings published in a *Millie the Model* comic book, which triggered her desire to become a designer. With complete support from her parents, she enrolled in art classes at Cleveland Museum of Art, and had abundant exposure to art, fashion, films, etc.

With the Vietnam War raging in 1968, McGuire worked with inner-city schools making art to help make sense of the times. After high school she studied art at the University of Colorado, where she met a Tibetan Buddhist, Chogyam Trungpa, who became her spiritual teacher. In 1974, she graduated from the California College of Arts and Crafts in Oakland with a Bachelor of Fine Arts in painting with elementary and secondary teaching credentials. She taught art in numerous locations, including an Indian Reservation in Northern California, Mendocino College (at Trungpa's artist community), Ohlone College and UC–Berkeley. During these years, McGuire developed a love for meditation which she credits as the most important ingredient to her development as an artist. She also became engaged to and later married Robert Yohai.

After taking a goldsmithing class, McGuire decided to pursue a master's degree in metal arts at San Francisco State University. She later designed cinnabar art in her Oakland (CA) studio and had an art show in the Golden City. The gallery owner asked her to work in a different material so she did a series of necklaces in plexiglass and paper and paint. Someone from a department store saw the necklaces and asked her to design pieces for the shop. This began a 12-year career as a designer of Debra Fine Yohai Jewelry.

After her divorce, McGuire moved to New York City in 1980 and her jewelry designing career catapulted in the Big Apple and Providence, Rhode Island. She started throwing dinner parties that turned into "incredible soirees of artists, filmmakers, and designers," many of whom are still her friends. Within the next year her work was appearing on the covers of *Vogue* and *Harper's Bazaar*. Her jewelry was sold at upscale stores like I. Magnin and Bergdorf Goodman, and benefactors included Barbra Streisand, who commissioned McGuire to fashion her a "Queen Tut" necklace. The jewelry designer subsequently married William McGuire, and together they started a business making art deco–inspired jewelry.

McGuire traveled to Europe and Asia several times a year and on one of those trips she met Wendy Shankin, an American choreographer living in Paris. They became good friends and McGuire was invited to design costumes for Shankin's dance company, Calck Hook Dance Theatre. They did a performance in New York City at The Joyce and then the touring company ended up relocating to the Big Apple. Success gave McGuire the security and flexibility to dabble in other ventures so she started designing clothes. She created small private collections and then opened a hat company for a few years.

After a decade of success, the economy took a downturn and a lot of the department stores she had been working with went bankrupt, leaving vendors like her unpaid. It was 1990, and once again she was single but this time with a child. She contacted a friend, who happened to be the head of Warner Bros. Studios in California, and he asked her if she would be interested in coming out and working on a film. McGuire moved to Los Angeles and lived with her parents while working as a production assistant (intern) to the head designer for the Steve Martin film *My Blue Heaven*. Unsure whether she wanted to work in production design or costume design, McGuire spent considerable time observing the inner workings of the wardrobe department. She recalls thinking to herself, "People do this for a living?" She was hooked.

With a background in painting, McGuire was not particularly inclined to design clothing for a TV show. At the time, from a style perspective, television left a lot to be desired. "I never really liked the way people looked on television," McGuire recalled. "I was much more interested in the visual interest in a two-dimensional surface of a television." Nevertheless, her industry contacts led to more work, and at one point she designed costumes for 21 telefilms in one year. In 1993, she met Bright, Kauffman, and Crane and did both their shows, *Family Album* and *Couples*, which led to her being hired for *Friends*, and then her career blossomed. She was later hired by the trio for their other sitcoms, *Veronica's Closet* and *Jesse*, and became Jennifer Aniston's personal costumer for *The Morning Show*.

McGuire received the call to start working on *Friends* the very day she gave birth to her second child. "I literally was on the table with my legs open when the call came," she vividly remembered. "This was a Thursday, and I was like, 'Yeah, I'll be there Monday.' Saturday I interviewed people for my crew and Monday I was at work with my mother in tow and a 4-day-old baby in a basket." But, at the time, the television industry was not conducive to working moms. "The director asked me to leave the stage with my baby basket saying that a soundstage was no place for an infant," McGuire recollected. "Ours was not a kid-friendly environment until years later when our executive producer became pregnant, and our prop mistress and our actors. Then there were nurseries and nannies all over the stage."

Due to the instantaneous popularity of *Friends* and its image-altering fashion trends, McGuire wanted to capitalize on the opportunity so she tried to convince Warner Bros. to sponsor a clothing line. They declined. She then arranged numerous meetings with fashion executives from national retailers, such as Target, but no one was interested. She decided to do it on her own. In 1995, McGuire opened a custom couture atelier (studio) in Pacific Palisades (which relocated to Santa Monica in 2004), and four years later introduced a line of ready-to-wear clothing, available at Henri Bendel (McGuire also sold items at her Los Angeles boutique). Amazingly, she designed the entire 162-piece line over the two-month network hiatus. Prices ranged from $150 to $1,500. She also designed clothes for other TV shows, movies, and theatrical productions, such as *Fresh Off the Boat*, *New Girl*, *Superbad*, *Anchorman* and *Boston Marriage.*

McGuire is currently single with two adult children, Samuel Gavin (b. Jan. 1989), and Lily Ann (b. Apr. 1994). She has a regimented, disciplined life that doesn't involve much sleep, but remains committed to meditation, a practice she has maintained for nearly half a century. In her own words, "I'm afraid if I stop, everything will fall apart, and I'd suddenly look my age."

Wardrobe Process

Costume designer Debra McGuire was involved in the *Friends* series from start to finish. She set the gold standard for fashion, beginning with the pilot. When designing costumes for a television program, McGuire's creative process differs depending on the requirements of the job and the director vis-à-vis how much freedom she is allowed to exercise. In TV, for instance, it is often the opinions of studio and network executives that dictate wardrobe choices. This is the least creative process and it is simply a matter of exploring choices to present.

According to McGuire, the challenges inherent to her profession are actually gender neutral. "Men and women are basically the same challenge, one not being more difficult than the other," she noted. "The more an actor understands how important wardrobe is to developing a character, the better they are to work with." McGuire has all the patience in the world for an actor who is character driven but cannot tolerate ones who are ego driven.

Her creative process involves an original approach to fashion. "I come from a fine-art world, I'm a painter, so my perspective is a little bit different," McGuire confided. "Really, I'm not interested in fashion—I'm interested in creating something that no one's ever seen before, where we've got a two-dimensional surface, and how do we deal with that two-dimensional reality to make it something that's interesting that we haven't really seen." To her, coordinating wardrobe with the production designer and set decorator was a work of art. "My idea was to take six characters who were going to be next to each other, or in the same room, and how can I create something beautiful, like you do in a painting," she said. "I was more interested in color, shape, form and texture."

The show's creators wanted to keep the wardrobes as casual as possible and realistic to each character's economic standing in life, but McGuire did not agree. Thus, when Marta Kauffman said the characters should be hanging out in jeans, the head costumer pointedly objected. McGuire wanted to create something aspirational, and something fresh, yet still subtly reflecting the era and New York City. She also realized, "If we're going to make this aspirational, they have to look amazing." She then clarified her view: "I lived in Manhattan, and I never wore a pair of jeans. Nobody went to the Odeon [French bistro] at night in jeans. Nobody was, like, hanging out with friends and going to gallery openings in jeans. So I wanted it to be *that* New York, *that* world." Ultimately, McGuire's aspirational approach to apparel prevailed.

Of course, the importance of wardrobe must be tempered with nuance and subtlety. "It's important when you look at these characters [for] the clothing not to be too important because the writing is what it's about. The humor is what it's about. My job is to just support that and make it as visually interesting without distracting. And there's a very fine line there," she stated matter of fact. "I'm sure you watch a lot of television shows where that's not always the case. You want the clothes to be fabulous but you don't want them to consume the attention or pull the camera. So we're very conscious of that in the way that everything is put together." A fine example of distracting clothing can be seen in the hit sitcom *The Neighborhood* (2018-present). Nearly every fashion choice involves garish colors, off-putting patterns and obtrusive designs.

Lastly, McGuire touched on the fact that each storyline revolved around a wardrobe problem. "We had a wardrobe joke in every script. So not only did we have to get all these massive amounts of clothes, we had to sort of hyper-focus on what the wardrobe joke was for that week," McGuire delineated. From Ross' leather pants to Monica's boots to Joey wearing Chandler's entire wardrobe, *Friends* always featured clothes and accessories in some shape or form in every installment. "It was funny because the writers were killing us [with] ... scripts [that] ... were completely wardrobe centric," McGuire confided. When she confronted the writers, they said, "Well, we love you guys so much we just wanted to make sure we had storylines that included you."

Weekly Schedule

Most viewers believe a sitcom costumer has the easiest job in the world—randomly picking garments off the rack and handing them to the actors. Easy. But they would be mistaken. Actually, there is an incredible amount of work involved with six costars and numerous different time periods, not to mention guest stars, recurring actors, and scene extras. Everything must be coordinated, like choreographing a musical stage production. And each show had to be outfitted by a costume crew consisting of only five people.

Every week, the *Friends* design team was given the script for the upcoming episode, which could be filmed as soon as two days later. First, the costume crew read the parts for the various characters, noting each specific wardrobe need, and then they set off to local boutiques, department stores, thrift shops or designers to whip up enough outfits for the show (sometimes as many as nine outfits for each character per episode). The crew then fits and photographs each star in each costume change. Finally, a complete costume plan is submitted to the head costumer for approval. "I was a complete and utter control freak in the first couple of years of *Friends*—I had to choose buttons and socks," McGuire boldly admits. "But I found that once I relinquished a bit of that control to the people who work for me, they were happier, I was happier and I could do more. Everyone's better off for it."

According to McGuire's calculations, there were around 50 to 75 outfits needed per script, and that's not including guest stars or installments with flashbacks. "Do you think anyone watching the show understands what it takes to get from Monday to Thursday? Especially in shows like the Thanksgiving episode where there are multiple time periods and Phoebe's arms blow off as a Civil War nurse," McGuire rhetorically queried. "It's just sort of like whatever, it's a comedy, turn the TV on, turn the TV off. No one really cares, but it was a tremendous amount of work."

To put McGuire's job in perspective, just consider the clothing worn by Rachel alone. Six to nine outfits an episode, 24 episodes in a season, and 10 seasons equals nearly 2,000 costumes. Overall, McGuire produced over 13,000 outfits for the series. Her go-to designer labels—which she describes as the perfect mix of highbrow and high street—were t-shirts from Juicy Couture, Zooey and Michael Stars, and jeans from It-brands like Levi's, 7 For All Mankind, J Brand and Earl Jeans. As for Rachel in particular, she was dressed in Chaiken and Capone, Suss Cousins, Oilily, Workers for Freedom, Elspeth Gibson, DVF, Laundry and Michelle Mason. "This was a girl who knew how to rock high-waisted jeans and cargo pants," McGuire fittingly added.

In the early days, McGuire's workload burgeoned because very few of the costumes were off the rack. "For the first couple of years of *Friends*, I made so many of the clothes, and I wore myself out," she recalled rather dispiritedly. "When you make stuff, you have to have a muslin fitting, and then you do it in the right fabric, and then you have to have another fitting, and usually one more after that. It was hard enough to get them in for one fitting per costume, so trying to get them in for three ... it was like pulling teeth."

Each cast member was allotted only 15 minutes in wardrobe each week. Cast costume fittings were fast and furious. "They would run in on Wednesdays for a fitting and we had very little time before they needed to be back out," McGuire revealed. "Some of them didn't come in until Thursday and we had preshoot on Thursday and would film on Friday." Her frustration was discernable. "We were right up to the edge every single week." The primary reason for lightning-fast fittings was due to the female costars. "Those girls hated fittings," she declared. "They just wanted me to buy clothes from stores so it wouldn't be such a big deal."

Despite the show's trendsetting fashions, the cast never borrowed clothing from the wardrobe department. According to McGuire, the costars didn't want to be "seen as their character." The actors were more apt to request specific outfits to wear on the show. As *Friends* became more and more popular, the cast wanted to influence what their character wore. "Everything was so meticulously orchestrated from my perspective," McGuire confided. "I charted everything and did everything by color and they weren't really aware of what my system was. There were times when someone would say, 'I don't feel like wearing this, can I wear this?' And I'd be like, 'No, because it would throw us off the palette.'"

Memorable Costumes

McGuire can recall many memorable costumes that were worn by the cast during the show's decade run. Every piece of clothing worn on the show was housed in the Warner Bros. wardrobe department cage area where it was stored and cataloged. The girls' outfits were typically bought or specially designed by McGuire. Although websites claim to have official clothes from the show, nearly all such claims are false. However, every so often a piece of clothing is donated to a charity and auctioned.

The pink bridesmaid dresses worn in "The One with Barry & Mindy's Wedding" (2.24) were among the most haunting costumes. When designing the gowns, McGuire thought: "What would be the most hellacious outfit we could possibly put together?" In her mind she accomplished the task. "I mean, that bubblegum-pink color was horrible! We made all of it, and everything was bad: the taffeta was bad, the color was bad, the puffy sleeves were bad. It was exactly what I wanted." Much to her surprise, fans could not get enough of those dresses. "The intention was to be completely comedic," McGuire confessed. "You'd think you'd do a piece like that and would get messages saying that was really funny, but I got hundreds of emails from girls in the south who actually liked them." Nonetheless, McGuire still considers the gowns to be "one of the ugliest things I think I've ever made."

Distinctive wardrobe selections also appeared in "The One with the Prom Video" (2.14). The prom dresses were pulled from the Warner Bros. costume stock which is a huge warehouse full of period pieces from contemporary all the way back to the beginning of humankind. McGuire worked her magic to make the costumes as hideous as possible. "Monica's prom dress was really one of the ugliest things I think I've ever made, next to the [pink] bridesmaid dresses I made."

Other designs were simply gorgeous. In "The One with All the Kissing" (5.02), Rachel's strapless yellow dress with embroidered floral jacquard and high slit received more positive comments than any other garment worn on the show. Most of the inquiries were from fans looking to buy one. McGuire bought the dress from a boutique called Idol London but it has long since gone out of business so the only feasible option is to have it custom-made. "I got thousands of emails over the years just about that dress," she noted. "To this day, I get at least one email a week saying, 'My wife and I are watching *Friends* and I loved that dress—where can I find it?'" McGuire divulged. "I always write back and say 'That was 20 years ago!'"

During the first half of the series, McGuire designed practically all of the outfits and many remain her personal favorites, such as Monica's "burgundy suspender-type skirt" ("The One with Fake Monica," ep 1.21); Rachel's striped, boatneck button-down top that is accessorized with a man's tie ("The One Where Rachel Goes Back to Work," ep 9.11), and her short plaid miniskirt with knee-high socks ("The One Where the Monkey Gets Away," ep 1.19). The latter costume, often described as a "schoolgirl outfit," was not well received by Jennifer Aniston. She was hesitant to wear it and could not fathom how that could possibly be sexy. But, as McGuire recounts, "people went berserk over that outfit."

Clothing Evolution

It's interesting to note that the aesthetic McGuire created for the show, which has now become a benchmark for 1990s fashion, was in fact the very antithesis of what everyone was actually wearing at the time. "In 1994, when the show commenced, clothing was worn baggy and oversized. To make the characters' wardrobes different, I addressed that. The girls' clothes became more body-conscious, tighter, with bare midriffs. People didn't wear tight t-shirts then," she explained. "Fashion is all about understanding what works for you, rather than bending to be a part of the trend. And that's always the most important thing to remember."

Surprisingly, McGuire's trendsetting fashions conflicted with her idiosyncratic sartorial proclivities. "I'm a hippie who came of age in the '70s, and have worn Japanese designers for the last 35 years. My style is definitely a lot more avant-garde than any of the show's characters," she disclosed. Being a mother, it also conflicted with her maternal instincts. "I was raising a young daughter and didn't really want her to be wearing those little t-shirts. I had to really have a consciousness about it at all times, because I know that I was setting things for young people [even though] it's not necessarily what I believed was appropriate," she confessed.

As the head costumer, McGuire did not want the characters to have stagnant clothing styles over the years so their wardrobe was constantly evolving as she acquired new fashion ideas from around the globe. As part of the evolutionary process, she admits her fashion sense changed after the show had been on the air for a few years. "It wasn't until around the third season that I lightened up on my palette and allowed fashion to come into play," she shared. The clothes did get tighter, and she credits Juicy Couture for the inspiration. "I had met the girls that owned Juicy, and they started making these t-shirts that were body-conscious," McGuire recalled. "So then it became this era of tighter t-shirts, shorter sleeves —belly-baring in some instances." The final years of the show were couture (clothes made to fit a client's specific requirements and measurements) but the fashion was more elegant.

In the first couple years, McGuire insisted on making about 75% of the show's wardrobe in order to create the look she desired. "But by the third year, I loosened up a little bit," she said. "Then I allowed characters' palettes to overlap." By the sixth season, *Friends* was a megahit and the characters were fully developed so it was no longer necessary to use attire to define them. Thus, McGuire began mixing and matching designers like J.Crew, Calvin Klein, Laundry by Shelli Segal, D&G, Miu Miu, Katayone Adeli, Catherine and Petro Zillia. She started dialing back on designing—doing only 30% of the girls' wardrobes—partially because it was becoming harder and harder to get the girls to come in for fittings, but also due to the fashion industry starting to become very interested in labels. "Everyone's focus started being more on brands than on looking unique, and by the fifth or sixth season, I was like, 'Whatever,'" she recounted rather disapprovingly. "I'd already made my mark, I'd already created these characters, and I basically let fashion in for the sake of fashion." It wasn't as exciting, but McGuire made sure she still controlled the image of the characters.

Part of the image control involved buying designer pieces rather than borrowing them. McGuire wanted the flexibility to alter the garments to comport with her singular artistic vision. "Let's say I bought a Dolce & Gabbana. I wasn't committed to keeping the arms on the dress, you know what I mean? So that's why I didn't take anything for free. People were always offering to give us clothes. Never, never. I was not interested because it was about our vision, not theirs," she emphatically insisted. "I wasn't gonna let other designers design my show."

McGuire also added her own unique touch to the show by incorporating pieces from her personal wardrobe collection, such as the hot-pink faux fur jacket ("The One That Could Have Been, Part 1," ep 6.15), the embroidered bridesmaids jackets for Phoebe's wedding ("The One with Phoebe's Wedding," ep 10.12), many of Rachel's monochrome outfits, and most of Chandler's retro shirts.

It always fascinates McGuire to assess fashion over time. When *Friends* first came out, Rachel was all the rage—her hair, her style, her fashion. In the 2020s, the sartorial focus shifted to Monica. "It always used to be Rachel's wardrobe people would ask about. Now it is Monica's," said McGuire rather astonishingly. "That is so funny to me because I never heard a word about her high-waisted pants and cropped t-shirts at the time. She was a working chef and her wardrobe was more straightforward and realistic." McGuire is wily enough to understand the forces behind the changeover. "Fashion is cyclical. It's all about common sense and what the eye gets tired of seeing, be it colors, shapes or silhouettes."

Of course, Rachel remains a sartorial influence. "I don't think Rachel's fan base ever waned. Kids today discover the show when they hit their teenage years, and connect with it like it has gone on air now. Millennials are pretty conscious about wastefulness, and would much rather wear a great vintage piece; high-waisted jeans are vintage, so are crop tops and oversized jackets—1990s pieces fly out of second-hand stores. Young people are seeing these looks for the first time and they still look new," the famed designer surmised. She still receives close to five emails every week about Rachel's wardrobe.

Rachel

In the beginning, "Rachel's palette was primarily kind of greens and blues, and in terms of the pieces themselves, they were a little bit more refined," Debra McGuire stated. "And then there is an evolution of when these choices become hers, not just something you could buy at Bergdorf Goodman. [She's] someone who has so much and then has no value of what she has, and then sort of takes on a reality of having to value the things that she gets because she's the one making the money to get them."

Once Rachel started earning money by working in the coffeehouse, she began wearing a memorable series of tiny skirts and printed aprons. "We loved making all of those tops and all the aprons and all the accouterments for her looking adorable in that space, and her kind of being in control of her look in that space, because she would have [been]," McGuire indicated. "And then as we evolve and she gets jobs and starts to work at Ralph Lauren, then the level of sophistication kind of starts to change."

For better or worse, Rachel's look resonated with viewers at the time, especially those teeny crop tops. She wore more body-conscious styles and exposed midriffs, which set a look for a new wave of girls and young women. McGuire chose to infuse Rachel's wardrobe with multiple designer labels because she wanted Rachel to be able to look alluring and sexy but preferred a wardrobe that a working woman in her 20s might enjoy.

According to a 2021 study by Money.co.uk—analyzing Google data compiled over a 12-month period (March 2020 to February 2021)—Rachel Green was the television character that most influenced societal wardrobes. Despite the show ending nearly two decades ago, she easily beat Madi Peritz (No. 2), from *Euphoria*, a series that debuted on HBO in 2019. In addition, the number of searches for "Rachel Green Aesthetics" was eight times that of the same period in 2017, and the number of online searches for "Rachel Green Costumes" was reported to have increased by 58%. This is another example of the timeless nature of her fashion. Not surprisingly, Rachel's signature style, such as pleated miniskirts, bellybutton-baring tees, trumpet sleeve tops and a tomboy style with printed camp shirts, blazers, 501 jeans and denim overalls, are currently being worn by the young and influential cast of *Euphoria*.

Monica

Monica went through numerous different career changes, "but she stayed pretty clean," McGuire declared. "I kept her in this black-white-gray-burgundy world for a long time, and then she became a chef and that suited her really well." In the overall scheme, Monica's wardrobe did not actually deviate from its original design. "It's a funny thought, but even after all these years, it would be the same! I'd probably do something very close to what she originally wore on the show even if it were happening today," McGuire concluded.

Phoebe

Artsy Phoebe was the most visually interesting of the group. She wore a lot of colorful florals, sheers and fabrics, hair barrettes, and abundant jewelry. Following season four, her wardrobe was invigorated after McGuire met with British designers and investigated international showrooms. "There was a company called Idol London that I really resonated with at the time and bought lots of amazing things for Phoebe," she recalls. But McGuire made sure the character stayed true to her original profile as the years progressed. In season ten, though, Phoebe had one sartorial evolution, albeit ever so slightly. "The One Where Rachel's Sister Babysits" (10.05) is the last episode where Phoebe wears jewelry on all her fingers. Mike's marriage proposal changes her. She removes all her ornaments and only wears an engagement or wedding ring for the rest of the series. It is meant to symbolize the evolution of the character from flaky spiritualist to mature traditionalist.

Ross

As a college professor, Ross wore academically appropriate clothing—jackets with elbow patches, tweeds and corduroy. This basic framework never changed over the course of the series. His occupation stayed basically the same, moving from museum paleontologist to NYU professor. During nonworking hours he wore mostly button-down shirts (occasionally over a tee) and sweaters. Ross' basic palette stayed the same over time. Debra McGuire's favorite Ross clothing moment was his leather pants in "The One with All the Resolutions" (5.11). She fondly recalls the moment: "The leather pants, that was huge, you know? And having to rehearse, and getting it right—couldn't get 'em off, couldn't get 'em on! Had to act in 'em! Oh my God, that was hysterical."

Joey

In the pilot episode, Joey was wearing a leather jacket to accentuate his cool persona as a lothario. In the following installments, his character changed to be friendlier and more approachable; he was dressed in soft sweaters to make him huggable, a sharp contrast to his macho persona. His signature style was defined by texture, gray chenille sweaters, and flannel shirts. "I kept him in a very tactile, soft palette as well as texture," McGuire stated. Over the years, from episode two until the finale, his style stayed relatively consistent.

Chandler

In the first season, Chandler sported a lot of 1940s shirts with racing stripes down the sides, vintage ties, and ample tweeds. Afterwards, he wore more business attire to coincide with his office promotion and modern casual attire (1990s shirts and sweaters). His attire was purposely made excessively baggy in seasons three through six due to Matthew Perry's severe weight loss related to his drug addiction. During those years he sported garments two sizes too big for his frame and frequently wore layers, like vests and jackets, though his vogue remained unaffected. The final seasons followed the same sartorial style but more couture.

Makeup

The makeup for each character was not haphazardly applied; it was always coordinated with other preproduction departments, most notably wardrobe. "We also collaborated with Debra McGuire, who's the costume designer, just to find out what they're wearing. And that always made a difference in how much makeup, how little makeup," recalled Robin Siegel, the *Friends* head makeup artist. "There was always a basic look that everybody has but we would change maybe lip colors depending on if they were dressed up or dressed down for the scene."

Very few television viewers realize there is a difference between onscreen and offscreen makeup. "Makeup for TV can be a little stronger than in everyday life and it will still appear to be natural," Siegel explained. Obviously, the true goal was to appear natural. "Their look was meant to be just beautiful, natural, something. A look that people could relate to, that didn't look too overly made up, but didn't look totally nude. They definitely were modern women and they had some makeup on."

The makeup process for television is rather hectic. The head makeup artist described the weekly procedure:

> "On a sitcom, we're there usually only two days a week: the prep day and the shooting day. When an actor comes in and sits down, I usually start out with some skin care. Sometimes I do an undry treatment that just refreshes and revitalizes under the eyes. Also I like the skin care part because it's a way to begin to touch somebody because I'm right in their face. And it's also beneficial for the skin. I actually think that skin care is almost more important than makeup. If their skin's in good condition, the makeup looks amazing."

Siegel further expounded:

> "I usually begin with eye makeup first. I do the eye makeup. Whatever's called for that day, some eye shadow, some liner around the eyes, mascara, eyebrows. And then I'll clean the face again, reapply some moisturizer, if I feel like it needs it, and then go for the foundation, cheek color, and the lips are last." A typical makeup session lasts about an hour (less for men and more for women).

In April 2021, Money.co.uk reported that *Friends* was No. 3 on their list of "shows that influence our makeup," and more specifically, the three female leads were the main source for beauty inspiration. The sitcom drew 99,880 annual online searches, though the number is dwarfed by the latest sensation, *Euphoria*, with 2,018,670. Nevertheless, the timeless sitcom remains a force in the $382 billion cosmetic industry. In 2020, Revolution Beauty released their own collection based on the series, featuring eye-shadow palettes, lipsticks, lip gloss and more.

Hairstyles

According to David Crane, the producers did not get involved in the actors' decisions to change their hairstyles. "Generally, if the actors' haircuts change, it's because they want to do it. They will usually run it by us. I can't think of any time we ever said 'Don't,'" he said. "The only time it matters is if we're shooting out of sequence and we need some continuity." Although they never forbade a hairstyle, the producers still had control over what appeared onscreen. For example, during the 1999 summer hiatus (prior to season six), Lisa Kudrow donned a short bob for a role in the movie *Hanging Up*. When she came back to work on the *Friends* set in August, the producers didn't feel it was a suitable cut for her character so she was asked to wear a wig for the entire year.

The female leads seemed to change their hairstyles annually but the most iconic cut was dubbed The Rachel. It debuted in the first season, in "The One with the Butt" (1.06), and lasted until the end of the second season. Set stylist Jonathan Hanousek explained the peculiar cut: "Basically, it's a razor cut with lots of layers; longer layers on the top and lots of movement. The great thing about that haircut is that it looks good on almost anybody, almost any face shape. I think that the reason it became such a huge phenomenon was the fact that all these women all over the country who were running around saying 'I want this haircut' actually looked good in it."

Jennifer Aniston loathed the cut because it was impossible to style on her own—she had to rely on her hairstylist to do it for her. "Looking back—honestly, even during that time—I couldn't do it on my own. I needed Chris [McMillan] attached to my hip. Left to my own devices, I am not skilled with a hairbrush and blow dryer." She said she would rather shave her head than get that haircut again. The hairstyling was equally time consuming for the on-set stylists. Consequently, in many episodes Rachel had her hair pinned up because there was not enough time to get it right. "I was not a fan of The Rachel. I think it was the ugliest haircut I've ever seen," Aniston honestly and openly confessed. "That was kind of cringey for me."

Amazingly, the *Friends* reunion special sparked a revival of The Rachel cut. Once HBO released teasers in May 2021, a new generation of fans flocked to hair salons requesting the quintessential style. Just weeks after the teaser first aired, demand for The Rachel hairstyle skyrocketed by 179%.

The Rachel

The hairstyle is defined by precise highlights, freshly cut layers, tons of volume, and a perfect little flip at the ends. It became a 1990s sensation rivaling actress Farrah Fawcett's feathered layers a generation earlier. Most leading ladies of the decade—including such stars as Tyra Banks, Meg Ryan and Mariah Carey—sported some variation of The Rachel at one point in their careers.

Women worldwide brought Rachel's photo to their stylists. Aniston's longtime stylist Chris McMillan created the cut using a razor instead of shears for the choppy, layered look, and colorist Michael Canalé brought out the cut with signature highlights around her face. McMillan later admitted he was high on marijuana at the time of her appointment and had accidentally buzzed her hair with a razor. To correct the mishap, he extemporized, but in the process unwittingly created one of the most recognizable hairstyles ever.

Photographer Robert Trachtenberg called the legendary look "a gigantic presence in pop culture." As Rachel's hairstyle evolved, women continued looking to her for inspiration. Los Angeles hairdressers in the mid-1990s reported that as many as 40% of their clients were requesting The Rachel. An estimated 11 million women in the UK sported the style. In a profession backlash, hairdressers across the US began refusing to do the cut and style for their clients.

Despite Aniston's angst toward The Rachel cut, she and McMillan have remained close friends ever since. While he attends all of her dinner parties, he's also her go-to man on set (he works with her on *The Morning Show*) and at photo shoots. In 2018, Aniston presented McMillan with *InStyle*'s Hairstylist of the Year award. Reflecting on their nearly 25 years of friendship, she said, "You're one of the most passionate and kind human beings that I've had the good fortune of getting to know and I get to call you my family. I feel blessed every day for that."

Fashion

It is undeniable that *Friends* set the tone for fashion in basically every way possible, whether it be hairstyles, clothing, footwear or accessories. When hairstyles were undefined, *Friends* offered The Rachel. When clothing was baggy, *Friends* gravitated toward couture. When accessories were passé, *Friends* made them chic. The series defined style and fashion for the 1990s, and since fashion is cyclical, the élan has taken center stage in the 2020s.

Friends head costumer Debra McGuire created the unique vogue for each character. In the early seasons of the series, none of the characters paraded designer apparel like Gucci boots or Chanel Boy bags, which lent credibility to the sextet and made the series relatable. They had impeccable fashion from comfy to classy and streetwear to runway; every one of the characters in every episode had exemplary styling. Thus, each *Friends* season provides a perfect time capsule of its era, sartorially speaking.

Rachel has excellent officewear, co-ords, classic separates and a splash of athleisure. Monica rocks the timeless monochrome, minimalism and plaid, but also colorful dresses, sweaters, heeled boots and slim-fit jeans. And Phoebe's bohemian sensibility gravitates to oversized knitwear, colorful blouses and skirts, chunky boots and excessive hair and hand accessories.

Denim

Denim has been a wardrobe essential in basically every decade but it played a special role in the 1990s, and *Friends* was a major source of inspiration. While Monica amazed in mom jeans and slashed denim jackets, and Phoebe gravitated toward embroidered denim vests, Rachel invoked a signature style incorporating both looks while adding countless variations such as short dungarees and sleeveless tops. Denim vests and jackets have also gained traction in the 2020s as consumers shop for denim with handcrafted qualities and utilitarian designs.

Bohemian Style

Phoebe was the original thrift and upcycle queen. She wore recycled necklaces, DIY fringed jackets and patched denim before it became a part of the conscious fashion culture. It was a mixture of bohemian and grunge. Phoebe had a unique sense of fashion that few women could have pulled off but thanks to her being whimsical and self-confident, she managed to own the style.

Flowing skirts and peasant blouses were all the rage in the early 2000s. While people are quick to give credit for this 1960s revival to fashion icons like Sienna Miller or Mary-Kate Olsen, proper recognition belongs to Phoebe and the popularity of *Friends*. In fact, she remains the inspiration for igniting some of the boho chic trends nearly three decades later.

Plaid

Rachel was known to experiment with fashion, and one of her most incomparable looks was the schoolgirl style, featuring a plaid miniskirt with knee-high socks. The ensemble was designed by costumer Debra McGuire and is one of her favorite outfits in the series. The style is often compared to Cher Horowitz, the lead character in the 1995 feature film *Clueless* starring Alicia Silverstone. However, Rachel started the trend since she debuted the look over four months before the film premiered.

Capri Pants

In 1961, Mary Tyler Moore debuted as Laura Petrie on *The Dick Van Dyke Show* and her predilection for cropped trousers made a bold fashion statement. She had to fight to keep her capris, a common sense sartorial measure that inspired female viewers everywhere. The revolutionary choice sparked plenty of studio and sponsor trepidation, most notably their concern about "under cupping"—that is, how formfitting the pants were on her derriere. Despite the objections, she remained committed to her ideals. She believed the portrayal of women wearing "little flowered frocks with high heels" while vacuuming was antiquated. No woman would ever do that.

Over three decades later, the series *Friends* led the resurgence of capris. As early as the fifth episode, "The One with the East German Laundry Detergent" (1.05), Rachel sported the close-fitting calf-length tapered trousers and continued the look through the rest of the decade, despite the obvious "under cupping" she exhibited.

Slip Dress

All the *Friends* leading ladies flaunted slip dresses throughout the decade. At the time, only models like Kate Moss and rocker chicks like Courtney Love dared the vogue. But then Rachel came along and made it accessible to the masses. It was definitely one of the sexiest trends of the decade, and Rachel wasn't afraid to show it off, especially with the bold, sultry sleepwear she wore when meeting her boyfriend's parents in "The One with Rachel's New Dress" (4.18). Another illustration occurs in "The One with Ross's Wedding, Part 1" (4.23) where all the fashionistas agree that her brown, slinky summer slip dress and casual platform flip-flops is one of the best outfits from the series. In contrast, Monica was less likely to slink into a slip dress, but her most stunning use of the style was in "The One After Ross Says Rachel" (5.01). The garb has seen a resurgence in the 2020s.

Leather

Ross looked good in leather pants. Although he did not start the trend—which is often credited to Uncle Jesse (played by John Stamos) in *Full House*—Ross definitely kept the vogue alive. The fashion was previously confined to rockers like Jon Bon Jovi and silver screen heartthrobs like Hugh Grant, but the 1990s TV stars made it mainstream.

Leather jackets became popular in the 1900s but didn't soar until 1957 when Jimmy Stewart wore one in the movie *Night Passage*. By the 1970s the masses became heavily influenced by celebrities and commenced sporting the look. Since then, the outerwear has become a fashion that never goes out of style. Nearly every member of the *Friends* gang wore leather jackets as part of their sartorial ensemble. It was a very popular design at the time, and the series certainly progressed the trend into the next millennium.

Tied Button-Down Shirt

All the girls get credit for this fashion statement, though Rachel is usually given the most accolades. The style was predominate in the first season of the show. It's a look that seems effortlessly thrown together but mostly because the costars always look good in the apparel. Tying the bottom of a button-down shirt has made its way back into fashion, but it is a totally quintessential 1990s look.

Crop Top

One of the coolest outfit ideas from the 1990s is probably the cropped shirt. The fashion is simple yet ever so cute. Monica and Rachel popularized the look in the show. The *Friends* sartorial trend is still fashionable today and probably will not disappear anytime in the near future.

Androgynous Style

Simply put, androgynous style refers to clothing and accessories that fall outside the typical "female or male" gender norms. Two common examples of this include men wearing skirts and women wearing ties. Monica is most associated with androgynous attire—men's button-down shirts with jeans and white sneakers. It is the ultimate Gen-Z fashion uniform of today. Her checked shirt will never go out of style. As a career businesswoman, Rachel was known to wear ties, though it was often with a feminine top. In recent years, women have sported ties with business suits, quite similar to the three-piece vested suits worn by men for nearly five centuries.

Modern Athleisure

Athleisure is a hybrid of workout clothes and loungewear, including yoga pants and sneakers, which makes for super versatile pieces that can go from the gym to the couch and even to the workplace. Rachel and Monica's sporty style was always on point. Rachel preferred boxy t-shirts, joggers and baseball caps. Monica was all about the sports bra and bicycle shorts. Their gym and on-field fashion can easily pass as the contemporary street style of today.

Monochromatic

Monochromatic colors are all the colors of a single hue. The color schemes are derived from a single base hue and extended using its shades, tones and tints. Tints are achieved by adding white, and shades and tones are achieved by adding a darker color, such as gray or black. Although Monica's wardrobe consisted predominantly of color and prints, there were a handful of classic monochrome moments that will never go out of style. For example, in "The One Where Ross and Rachel...You Know" (2.15), she is dressed in stunning formal attire, an all-black outfit accented with a white vest. Rachel also gravitated toward monochromatic colors, especially for work, like in "The One with the Tiny T-Shirt" (3.19) where she wears a periwinkle button-up jacket with a maxi skirt.

Minimalism

Minimalist fashion is defined by one major principle: simplicity. Streamlined shapes, monochromatic colors and unadorned garments can easily create a beautiful combined look. Monica's minimalist clothing choices—from casual to party dresses—effuse a cool, casual, and calm vibe. An excellent illustration is Monica's minimalist slate-gray mini with black pantyhose and complementary accessories in "The One with Phoebe's Dad" (2.09).

Coordinates

Rachel's expert officewear style offers a vast array of skirt and trouser suits. A classic example occurs in "The One with the Flashback" (3.06) where she sports a purple power suit during the flashback scenes in the local tavern. Women's power suits of the 1990s are in fashion today as the catwalks flaunt matching colors and boxy shapes.

Sheer Tops

See-through garments, especially those made with lace-like materials, never go out of style. It gives a sexy, chic touch to the whole look, while at the same time remaining classy. Whether it's a dress, shirt, or blouse, Rachel was always a trendsetter. In "The One Where Rachel Tells Ross" (8.03), she rocks a black sleeveless sheer fabric top with ruffle details and matching decorative tie over a coordinate halter. Sheer tops are reminiscent of the 1980s punk style from London. The look is one that keeps coming back in various guises season after season.

Structured Blouses & Puffy Sleeves

Rachel's outfits are always a lovely cross between trendy and feminine. She wore more fitted blouses in the late 1990s, which is aptly exemplified in "The One with the Soap Opera Party" (9.20). Structured blouses and corsets are making a huge comeback, and great when paired with jeans to feel a little less refined.

Neutral Separates

As Rachel navigated the new world as a working mother, her style evolved to match it. She displayed more neutral separates that had a soft power—simultaneously romantic and no-nonsense. There is a perfect illustration of this attire in "The One with the Cake" (10.04). Neutral separates remain a popular choice since they are stylish and versatile pieces that double as officewear and weekend attire.

Gingham

Rachel channels the gingham school dress perfectly in "The One with the Thumb" (1.03) and Phoebe slays the vogue in "The One with Phoebe's Husband" (2.04). Picnic prints still remain strong in the 2020s. In the fashion world, gingham (like polka dots and florals) rolls around every summer. Thus, it is always a good idea to invest in the print; invariably it will be omnipresent in summers to come.

Sleeveless Turtleneck

The sleeveless turtleneck (aka high-neck tank) is a breezy, versatile summer staple with a relaxed fit. Monica occasionally wore the attire but Rachel epitomized the style. As the resident *Friends* fashionista, Rachel blazed the fashion in at least six separate episodes.

V-Neck Sweaters

One trend the 1990s conquered was the V-neck sweater. From Rachel's solid-colored cashmere versions to Chandler's preppy sweater vests, V-necks took center stage in the late 1990s, on the small screen and off. Wearing the trendy look in the summer is also more than acceptable, though a very deep V-neck is somewhat out of fashion.

Boots

Each of the female leads sported boots but Monica was the sartorial star of the bunch, covering the gamut from ankle and biker to mid-calf and knee-high. She was such a boot lover that an episode was specifically devoted to her footwear. In "The One with Monica's Boots" (8.10) she wears the ever elegant Stuart Weitzman Gentry leather boots.

Accessories

Friends reintroduced fashion accessories and made them accessible to the masses. It all started with fun, playful hair accessories (clips, scrunchies, slides, barrettes, headbands, bows, etc.) that epitomized Phoebe's vogue. She was rarely seen without a few accessories adorning her locks. While some designs may scream tween, overall hair accessories are still big business and their impact is often underappreciated. "The One Where Rachel's Sister Babysits" (10.05) is a good example of Phoebe's use of hair accessories.

From the moment the *Friends* leading ladies latched their first Y necklace, the jewelry turned into a nationwide bestseller. Although Jennifer Aniston is often credited for starting the Y necklace craze in the 1990s, it was actually Courteney Cox who donned the accessory almost exclusively in the first season. The jewelry received a huge boost in "The One Where Chandler Can't Remember Which Sister" (3.11) when Rachel was hired as an assistant to a fashion buyer at Bloomingdale's. Her office was filled with accessories from real-life fashion designers.

The man purse was first popularized in *Seinfeld* (ep "The Reverse Peephole") where Jerry Seinfeld uses the European carryall to store his girlfriend's purse contents. Of course, his man purse was markedly smaller, like a typical woman's purse; it was not big and bulky like Joey's satchel. The fashion accessory, once relegated to bike messengers, was a craze in the 1990s so some fashionistas credit Joey for popularizing the man purse (or satchel) and making it more accessible to the public.

Title Sequence

A title (or opening) sequence is the method by which television programs present their title, as well as the cast and key production members, by utilizing conceptual visuals and sound. It establishes the setting and tone of the program. The 1960s ushered in snappy instrumentals linked to title sequences (e.g., *I Dream of Jeannie*) while others added catchy theme songs to summarize the show's premise (e.g., *Gilligan's Island*). In the 1970s, title sequences capitalized on theme songs that were released as Top-40 popular singles, such as *Happy Days* and *Welcome Back, Kotter*. This trend continued through the 1980s (e.g., *The Greatest American Hero* and *Cheers*) and by the 1990s television title sequences were consuming up to 90 seconds of the show's total runtime, e.g., *Twin Peaks* (90 seconds) and *Family Matters* (80 seconds). Unlike other sitcoms that did not have a title sequence, most notably *Seinfeld*, a lengthy intro slashed valuable time from episode stories. In the world of sitcoms, first-run episodes typically time out at 22 minutes so a 90-second title sequence effectively consumes 7% of the show. This is an enormous waste of valuable time for soapy sitcoms like *Friends* that need every second to tell their stories.

In 1993, *Frasier* set a new standard for truncated television title sequences. The speedy 35-second intro sent a wake-up call to producers from coast to coast. The *Friends* creators liked the idea because it didn't give viewers a chance to tune out, turn the channel, or get up to do something else, and it gave their program additional dialogue. Thus, they chose to start the series with a 45-second intro and then shortened it to 35 seconds by season six.

The trend to shorten title sequence runtime continued into the early 2010s where most new programs had intros that maxed out around 30 seconds, and the movement reached its pinnacle by the next decade when many of the new television shows were doing the bare minimum, having title sequences lasting around 6 seconds or so. Some programs began adopting title-only openings with no title sequence, opting for a title card bearing the show's name and perhaps a creator credit. The remaining cast and production credits were superimposed over the first few minutes of the program, much like numerous theatrical films. An illustrative example is the sitcom *Ghosts* (2021-present) which has only a title card and no creator credit.

Early Ideas

After the pilot episode was shot and edited, the *Friends* producers contemplated adding a title sequence to the show. Since it was a pilot episode and few are picked up, they opted for a simplistic, inexpensive opener. "We basically sat [the cast] at the coffee shop and shot a bunch of footage of them playing cards," Kevin Bright explained. But then Warner Bros. President Les Moonves told the showrunners, "there's not gonna be a title sequence. NBC doesn't want one, don't waste your time." So the idea was dropped.

Bright submitted the final edited cut of the pilot episode to NBC on Tuesday, May 10. After network executives screened the show, the overall feeling was that the show was out of touch with the real world. NBC returned the pilot edit with one note from executive Don Ohlmeyer: "The opening is too slow" and then he sternly threatened, "[If] you don't cut some of the dialogue and pace it up, you're not on the air." He wanted it changed and returned to him within five hours.

The showrunners were nonplussed. They loved the opening. They thought it was perfect and didn't want to change it. To comply with the network's request, Moonves recommended adding installment clips. It was already past the deadline to submit the final edit so Bright asked for one hour to throw something together. He decided a theme song was needed and told the music editor to cut 45 seconds of "Shiny Happy People" by R.E.M., but only repeat the chorus, no verses. The crafty executive producer then spliced together a 90-second title sequence using pulls (clips) from the pilot episode and then overlaid it with the infectious ditty. Everything else remained intact. He delivered the cut to NBC at 1am (four hours past the deadline). After viewing the new edit, Ohlmeyer said, "Now it's right." The creators later admitted, "We didn't cut anything, but it started with energy. ... We didn't have to change a single word."

Although NBC loved the new version, the producers were unable to license the tune for the series so they decided to write an original theme song. Once that decision was made, they all agreed to create an original title sequence.

Locations

The executive producers kicked around several ideas for the title sequence. The original concept involved filming on a rooftop in Los Angeles. They envisioned a location having a scenic view resembling New York City with abundant lights as a backdrop, towering buildings in the distance, and apartment rooftops down below, something that would transport viewers to the fictional setting.

The showrunners hired a title sequence company called Three Headed Monster. Graphic designer Deborah Naysee partnered with the company and was commissioned to create the *Friends* logo. She received payment for the design but didn't get another dime for its future use and international recognition. (FYI: There are six dots in the *Friends* logo. One for each friend.)

Once the team delved into the details of the project, they realized there were too many variables that could go wrong, especially the weather (wind, rain, cloud cover, etc.), and it was just too expensive, so Marta Kauffman nixed the idea. Warner Bros. suggested using their ranch (i.e., small movie studio), which had a park setting with a fountain and a row of European-style apartment buildings as a backdrop. After checking out the location, Kevin Bright adored the setting because it resembled a park in the Village.

As the trio brainstormed ideas, they all agreed they wanted to do something with the building's windows, like add interior lighting, and considered using the fountain but were not sure in what manner. They went back to Three Headed Monsters and told them what they found. Together the team worked out the details—lighting the building, adding a sky-line backdrop, having the cast in and out of the fountain, and adding props, such as a sofa and floor lamp. By the time it all came together, it was early September and the series was set to debut in a couple weeks, so all the parties involved had to act quickly to schedule a location shoot.

Fountain

The showrunners loved the WB ranch fountain because it reminded them of Pulitzer Fountain in New York City, which is an outdoor fountain located in Manhattan's Grand Army Plaza. It is aptly named after newspaper publisher Joseph Pulitzer who bequeathed $50,000 for the creation of the fountain. Pulitzer Fountain was erected in 1916 to honor Pomona, a Roman goddess of abundance and wealth. A *Friends* location scout confirmed the similarity when he was sent to photograph celebrated images of the city. The Warner Bros. fountain was constructed on the Warner Bros. studio lot in 1934 on Park Boulevard, presumably depicting a Boston thoroughfare.

Although the WB fountain is an original, some New Yorkers claim the fountain looks similar to Cherry Hill fountain in Central Park. In fact, New York City tour guides have been known to make claims that the Cherry Hill fountain was actually used in the *Friends* title sequence. In reality, the fountains do not even remotely resemble one another. It is a tour guide ruse. They have made similar claims about the fountains in Washington Square Park, Lincoln Center, and Central Park's Bethesda Terrace. All such assertions are false.

In 2019, the WB ranch was sold so the fountain was excavated and moved to the main Warner Bros. studio. It is located just off Midwest Street and part of the studio's Hollywood Tour. Although the backdrop is different, it is the original *Friends* fountain.

Some fans are shocked to learn the *Friends* fountain is not original to the series. Astute movie aficionados can spot the fixture in other Hollywood productions, such as the movie *Hocus Pocus* (1993), which is set in Salem, Massachusetts. *Friends*, of course, takes place in New York, yet both productions use the same fountain to represent different locales. In the movie, Max, Allison and Dani celebrate in a nearby park and the *Friends* fountain is in the background behind Allison and Dani.

Friends' 1994 title sequence (left) and Jay-Z' 2017 parody music video "Moonlight" (right)

Filming

The title sequence was shot in early September 1994, just weeks before the pilot aired on September 22nd. Filming began at 10pm on a very cold California evening. The night began with promotional photos of the cast, as well as filming segments on the orange couch and around the fountain. Since Jennifer Aniston was not officially a cast member, she was asked to excuse herself from some of the shots. "When we were shooting the first grouping of cast photos in front of that fountain, I was asked to step out of a bunch because they didn't know if I was going to be still playing Rachel," she stated. At the time, her contract with _Muddling Through_ had not been resolved so NBC had to hedge its bets by excluding her in case a different actor needed to take her place.

After several hours, and numerous promotional shots, the cast began imbibing alcohol to facilitate a party atmosphere. "As they got later into the evening, they had more fun with the back and forth," set decorator Greg Grande revealed. "They were just happy to hang out and have a few cocktails." Soon they loosened up and agreed to jump in the water. "I don't want to say who started it, but one of them did and they ended up inside the fountain," he cautiously confessed. "And that was some of the best footage. It was kind of an impromptu, wonderful moment."

The idea of dancing in the water fountain came from a staff member at Three Headed Monster. The writers came up with a few bits for the cast to perform in the fountain but most of the physical activities were extemporized. "To my best recollection, that wasn't a scripted thing," recalled Grande. "It was more impromptu." The cast had to dance without the benefit of music and were asked to lip-sync to a song that had not been written. They were given the title to the theme song, "I'll Be There for You," and told to repeatedly utter those five words. After the final edit, Jennifer Aniston is the only cast member visibly lip-syncing in the opening credits. This version is only available in the pilot episode (though a couple double-length episodes replay the original title sequence which shows her mouthing the words).

The costars were not enamored with the idea of performing in the fountain. According to Jennifer Aniston, "We felt it was a little ... I don't know ... dancing in a pond? A fountain felt sort of odd." She indicated the only reason they did it was because they "were told to." Courteney Cox confirmed the miserable experience. "Somebody thought that would just be really fun, and let me tell you what happens—it's not fun to be dancing in a fountain for hours and hours," she insisted. Although the water was heated through a pump, by the end of the night, the actors were soaking wet, freezing, and miserable. Everyone had pruney fingers. The entire shoot lasted four hours.

Final Edit

A series editor pared the hours of fountain frivolity into 45 seconds of playful, youthful rambunctiousness. The twinkling lights of the Manhattan skyline were matted in postproduction. The showrunners expected this version to be the official intro for the entire series' run. They never expected to do another title sequence nor did they expect to modify the final edit. But then again, they forgot who they were dealing with—their network nemesis, NBC West Coast President Don Ohlmeyer.

The original title sequence aired with the pilot episode on September 22, 1994. After its broadcast, Ohlmeyer informed the creators that he wanted the title sequence axed because, in his opinion, it said to the audience, "We're young, we're hip, we're dancing in a fountain and you can't dance with us." He wanted to go with the title sequence that was submitted in May which only contained pulls (episode clips) from the show, and no irrelevant footage; he wanted it to be like the title sequence for _Laverne & Shirley_.

The original *Friends* title sequence (left), and the alternate title sequence (right)

Executive producer Kevin Bright began pondering some type of compromise. He did not want all the time, effort and expense that went into producing the title sequence to go to waste. He spoke with the editor who suggested using the title sequence as a wraparound and then inserting episodic clips which could function as a series recap. And that's what Bright did. Clips were added but part of the original title sequence remained intact. He was pleased with the final result, and praised Ohlmeyer for making such a fuss because it was one of the few positive contributions the NBC executive made to the show.

Bright was responsible for all future edits to the title sequence. He changed the episode clips twice each television season. Once for the first 12 episodes, and then one more time for the final 12.

Alternate Title Sequence

The *Friends* title sequence was reshot once, for the sixth season's double-length episode "The One That Could Have Been" (6.15, 6.16). This is the only installment with an entirely different title sequence. The producers decided to recreate the iconic fountain scene to give the impression that "this is the way life really went for the characters." Each character is portrayed in their alternate reality persona with clips from nonexistent episodes.

At the beginning of the title sequence, as Monica sits on the couch, the sofa is rigged to rise on the opposite end to illustrate her immense heaviness. However, since Courteney Cox is quite petite in real life, Matthew Perry offers a little assistance by removing his weight from the arm rest and lifting his end of the couch to ensure it elevates.

The decorative Tiffany firefly floor lamp next to the couch is not the original fixture used in the 1994 version. *Friends* property master Marjorie Coster-Praytor was unable to locate the original in the Warner Bros. property warehouse because it had been nearly four years since the lamp was last used. She had no other choice but to substitute the original with a somewhat comparable replica.

Other than the floor lamp, there was one other change from the original title sequence. "The only thing we really couldn't do was light up all the buildings like we did before," Kevin Bright admitted. A green screen was set up behind the fountain and city lights were added in postproduction.

The alternate title sequence was shot immediately after the crew finished filming "The One That Could Have Been." Courteney Cox was already in the fat suit and didn't need any costume or makeup preparation for the fountain shoot. The cast and crew remained on the Warner Bros. ranch shooting until one in the morning.

This is the only installment in season six where the theme song isn't cut. It rolls for 45 seconds compared to the reduced 35-second version that was prevalent throughout the last half of the series.

Theme Song

After the pilot episode was shot and a preliminary title sequence was hastily thrown together for NBC executives, the desired theme song was "Shiny Happy People" by R.E.M. because it captured the spirit and essence of the show. The producers tried to acquire the licensing rights but the band's lead singer, Michael Stipe, declined the offer. He made it clear how much he disliked the song and apparently didn't want it attached to a TV show where it would play week after week. The producers were adamant on having an opening theme song so they set out to create an original tune. Their ideal song had to be something fun with a catchy hook, upbeat rhythm, and addictive lyrics.

The desire for a theme song was a product of the creators' upbringing. They were raised in an era where TV show theme songs dominated the airwaves. Programs in the late 1960s through the 1980s featured cheery intros with intoxicating hooks that often became top-40 hit singles. The most classic examples include *The Jeffersons*, *The Golden Girls* and *Three's Company*. David Crane confessed that he grew up watching *Gilligan's Island* and *The Brady Bunch* and wanted to continue that theme song tradition for *Friends*. The producers are proud their ditty made its mark before television theme songs faded from the industry. "We were one of the last real theme songs," Crane stated. "Today you barely get a three-second musical sting, so I feel lucky—like we got in just in time."

Writer

Since R.E.M. refused permission to use "Shiny Happy People," the producers needed to come up with a new title theme song. Marta Kauffman passed along the pilot episode to her husband, musician Michael Skloff, and tasked him with writing a theme for the show since he had written a good instrumental for *Dream On*. Kevin Bright told Skloff that he wanted a vibe like a Beatles or CCR song; something recognizable like "I'll Feel Fine" by The Beatles.

While driving through the city en route to picking up his 5-year-old daughter, Skloff turned on the radio, and coincidentally, "Paperback Writer" by The Beatles was cued. He immediately felt that this song encapsulated the essence of the show. When Skloff got home he immediately began writing the music, focusing on spirited 1960s pop songs from artists like The Beatles and The Monkees. In his mind, "the song should sound like the feeling of waking up on a Saturday morning with a smile on your face."

Although Skloff's natural forte is writing music, not lyrics, he pieced together five words to accompany his melody. The show was about friendship, and being a friend meant being there for each other. He came up with one line that he thought was pretty good and likely to serve as the chorus: "I'll be there for you."

Skloff sat down and recorded a very rudimentary demo, which merely consisted of an instrumental with the chorus repeated. "We recorded this 45-second version and I heard it and I knew immediately it was a hit song. There was just no question in my mind," Kevin Bright proudly touted. He recommended using the services of his friend, lyricist Allie Willis, who penned the Earth, Wind & Fire hits "September" (#8, 1978) and "Boogie Wonderland" (#6, 1979), the Pet Shop Boys/Dusty Springfield duet "What Have I Done to Deserve This?" (#2, 1987), the Pointer Sisters single "Neutron Dance" (#6, 1984), and many others. She accepted the challenge and wrote the lyrics. Willis jokingly referred to this title theme as "the whitest song I ever wrote." In 1995 she received an Emmy Award nomination for "I'll Be There for You." Willis died in December 2019 at age 72.

Performer

With the joint collaboration of Skloff and Willis, the *Friends* creators finally had a song. They just needed someone to perform it. Executive producer Kevin Bright did not want a jingle writer performing the theme song so Skloff was commissioned to locate a recording artist. Unfortunately, as he discovered, most bands will not perform a song they did not write. Twice he approached R.E.M. lead singer Michael Stipe—once to perform the song as a solo artist and once as part of a duet with his good friend Natalie Merchant, lead singer of 10,000 Maniacs—but both times he declined. Next, Skloff contacted the band They Might Be Giants but, again, the answer was no. (Curiously, six years later TMBG contributed the single "Boss of Me" as the theme song for the sitcom *Malcolm in the Middle.*)

Despite all the rejections, Allie Willis' publisher finally came through by suggesting The Rembrandts. The band was an intriguing option. They had a Beatles-like sound that Kevin Bright desired, and were relatively unknown, having only one modest hit: "Just the Way It Is, Baby" (#14, 1991). Bright contacted their manager, and the duo (Danny Wilde and Phil Solem) agreed to give it a try. Bright wanted a melody and tempo similar to R.E.M.'s 1987 single "It's The End of the World as We Know It (And I Feel Fine)" so he sent the song along with a tape of the pilot episode. The band was asked to expand the song into a full-length record but they were reluctant because it didn't really represent their musical style at the time. (Ironically, three months later their record label refused to release the band's album without a full-length version of the *Friends* theme on it.)

On Thursday, September 15, 1994, the band members sat down with Skloff because he was responsible for the music and the vibe of the show. Band member Danny Wilde stated, "All they had was a 30-second verse and a chorus, so we tweaked the lyrics a little bit, Phil [Solem] came up with the signature riff at the start of the song, and we went back a few days later and recorded the verse and the chorus." Ideas were pitched and hashed out to make sure all the parts worked while Willis continually faxed lyrics for them to try. At the end of the day, they had a rough draft. The entire process took three days. The final version was heavily influenced by The Beatles—especially evocative of the "I Feel Fine" guitar riff— and highly reminiscent of The Monkees' "Pleasant Valley Sunday."

In the original demo, Skloff used processed drum sounds to provide a drum fill at one particular moment in the song. In the final cut it was taken out. When Bright heard the final cut, he immediately called and asked, "Where's that drum fill?" Skloff had replaced it with an improvisation by the band's drummer. Unbeknownst to Skloff, Bright had already edited the title sequence, and used the four beats of the drum fill to make four rapid visual cuts. Without the fill, his video didn't quite work. Skloff was sent back into the studio to record some new drum hits when someone suggested filling the musical space with a series of hand claps. There were no better suggestions so Skloff, along with Bright, Kauffman, and Crane, stood behind a microphone and clapped along with the song. The most memorable sequence of one of the most fabled television theme songs had just been recorded.

Solem and Wilde never fathomed the song's distinctive hand claps. They initially had lyrics in mind. "But we'd hammered back a couple of beers, were getting loopy and decided to finish the next day. The following afternoon, they played us what we'd done, but had added claps. I went, 'Okay. That's the hook!'" Wilde wanted to know who thought of that because the clapping was the best part. As he recalled, before pausing and putting his face in his hands, "Oh my god. All they had to do was go (clap, clap, clap, clap). And it was like, 'Take 25!'" Wilde clapped four, not five times when he recounted that story. He was happy to clarify that it is indeed four claps, then a kick drum comes in and plays one, which even confused some of the cast members. Courteney Cox was on *Jimmy Kimmel Live!* and even she got it wrong, clapping five times, not four.

Once the theme song was completed, the band asked to remain anonymous. "In those days, it was uncool for a band like ours to be involved in television," Solem explained. Of course, circumstances quickly changed and they were forced to attach their name to the project.

Full-Length Single

Hammering out a series theme song in three days was not the end of the story for "I'll Be There for You," it was just the beginning. Shortly after *Friends* debuted with its peppy, spirited intro, Charlie Quinn, the program director at Nashville radio station Y107 (WYHY), looped the original 45-second ditty a few times, thereby turning it into a nice three-minute pop song. "It got a crazy amount of requests. The phone lines started blowing up and all the sister stations started playing it and it went national," recalled band member Danny Wilde.

Although The Rembrandts' studio album was finished and 100,000 advance copies had already shipped nationwide to radio stations, executives at their record company label, East West Records, got wind of the hoopla surrounding the looped version and demanded the band finish the song to include a cut on the album or it would not be released.

Solem and Wilde wrote and recorded the full-length cut themselves, but Warner Bros. felt it wasn't perky enough so David Crane and Marta Kauffman were summoned to help write the final version. "Here's what was really crazy: At that point, the producers got in on the writing. So we all just sat around, tossing ideas around," Solem said. "There was a lot of interaction. It was, like, seven people!" Still, the recording duo wanted to make the song fit their album concept. "There was a version that we did with a different second verse and a completely different bridge," he indicated. "We tried to make it more like what the rest of the songs on our album were and they didn't like it because it kind of went a little dark. It never got put out, but there's some secret copy floating around."

The band resented their record label for insisting that the *Friends* theme song be a part of the album. The original LP had already been finished and the bubblegum pop song did not fit their concept. The duo was forced to accede or abandon their project. After finishing a full-length version of the tune, a new album was reissued, and all the other CDs, vinyls and cassettes were destroyed. Despite their angst, the pair are somewhat thankful since the snappy single sold a lot of albums. "It's like Styrofoam—non-biodegradable," said singer Danny Wilde of the song. "It will be around forever."

In 1995, "I'll Be There for You" was the most played single on the radio but the band refused to release it as a single because they did not write it. Nevertheless, it soared to No. 17 on the US Billboard Hot 100 chart based solely on radio airplay and became the song of the summer. It topped three US charts: Adult Contemporary, Mainstream Top 40 and Hot 100 Airplay (for eight weeks). It also topped three Canadian charts: Adult Contemporary, Top Singles (weekly), and Top Singles (year-end charts 1995). The theme song was also a huge hit across the Atlantic on singles charts in the UK (No. 3), Ireland (No. 3) and Scotland (No. 1).

Legacy

Friends debuted at a time when networks were beginning to eliminate theme songs from the opening credits but the popularity of "I'll Be There for You" and its endless radio airplay and music video broadcasts helped reverse the trend.

Two decades after that fateful week in the recording studio, rockers Solem and Wilde, to celebrate the *Friends* 20th anniversary, sang "I'll Be There for You" at a Central Perk pop-up in New York with James Michael Tyler (Gunther) joining them on vocals. This started a lasting friendship between Solem and Tyler. "*Friends* was the theme, but we became real friends, which was a sweet surprise," Solem declared. But the musician has not seen the core cast of *Friends* since the band performed "IBTFY" at a 2016 event honoring director James Burrows.

Despite the song's immense popularity, the *Friends* cast did not really warm up to the theme pop hit. Even so, Jennifer Aniston and Courteney Cox belted out the track on June 7, 2018, at American Film Institute's 46th Annual Lifetime Achievement Award ceremony honoring George Clooney.

In 2017, *Paste* magazine had the *Friends* title sequence, which includes the hit song "I'll Be There for You," ranked No. 59 in its list of The 75 Best TV Title Sequences of All Time. In contrast, *Blender* magazine in 2004 ranked the song No. 15 on its listing of The 50 Worst Songs Ever. In 2019, the song was streamed on average 96,000 times and downloaded 85 times every week.

Music Video

The "I'll Be There for You" music video wasn't shot until spring 1995 primarily due to the director's inability to coordinate the schedules of all six costars. "It kept getting postponed and postponed and postponed because the cast members couldn't all get together," Rembrandts member Danny Wilde revealed. The video short took three days to shoot on *Saturday Night Live*'s Rockefeller Center stage (Studio 8H), which was concealed with a white backdrop. The set was filled with snacks, such as M&M's, crudités, and cigarettes (everyone except David Schwimmer smoked at the time).

Originally, the music video was highly scripted. "There was a scene that the director had specifically written where the cast was going to be trying to get into one of our shows, as if they would do that," Phil Solem joked self-deprecatingly. "They were going to get into one of our shows and apparently, they were going to bring this frozen fish and use it to, like, knock us out." When the band met the *Friends* cast in Aniston's New York hotel room shortly before the video production meeting, the cast did not like the script, especially the fish prop.

***Friends* music video (left) and the band posing with cast (right)**

"We all guffawed," said Solem. "I think David Schwimmer said, 'I'm not sure I like the idea of someone hitting somebody with a fish. We don't need violence.' We started throwing around ideas and none of the script made it in. Danny and I played the song and went along with whatever they made up." The cast controlled the content but violence was never the real sticking point because in the final video cut Schwimmer and Matt LeBlanc forcibly remove the keyboardist from his duet bench, and Courteney Cox uses a drumstick to knock out the drummer so she can play the instrument.

The final cut became a simple video of the band and cast performing the song onstage. The first video script called for Marcel to portray the director, but with the capuchin's film career in high gear (*Outbreak* and NBC's *Virus*), David Schwimmer and Jennifer Aniston received the parts instead.

The Rembrandts did not give any of the *Friends* costars tutorials on how to fake their musical skills, but they acknowledged that Courteney Cox took her time behind the drum kit very seriously. The drummer hired for the shoot was trying to give her lessons, but she said, "Pfft. I can do this." Matthew Perry, however, landed on the other end of the spectrum. With a guitar strapped to his hips, he was loudly screaming, "You guys, we're rock and roll stars!" not realizing all the while the instrument had come unplugged. After the video shoot, Solem concluded that Jennifer Aniston and Lisa Kudrow were the most fun, while Matthew Perry was the one they ended up with at the hotel bar (big surprise).

The pop success that followed has been described by Solem as "the golden albatross—it flew, just not in the way we expected." Suddenly on tour, the pair barely recognized their audience; the stands were now packed with mothers and daughters hungry for "IBTFY." Tiring of fans yelling "*Friends!*" throughout their set, they began opening with the theme song. "Then we watched half the audience file out," Solem said. "But over time it opened doors. We've got a whole pile of friends that came to us because of *Friends*."

Regrettably, the fanfare took a toll on Solem. The heightened media attention sapped the rock star. There were endless 4am interviews, too few days off, and the strain weakened his voice. "My vocal parts were way up in the stratosphere, so my voice would burn out and there was no day off to recover. It's beyond embarrassing when you go to sing a high part and sound like a fraud." Having that, coupled with sleep deprivation, Solem gave up and quit the band in 1997. He and Wilde later reunited, releasing new material on *Lost Together* (2001) and *Via Satellite* (2019).

Pilot Debut

When *Friends* debuted on September 22, 1994, the creators' mindset was not focused on long-term prosperity; they were just hoping their comedy wouldn't get canceled. The trio was still reeling from the prior television season where their sitcom series (*Family Album*) was canceled after six episodes so their only aspiration was to get to seven. Of course, after the rating numbers remained relatively high, NBC immediately ordered the remaining 11 installments to make it a full season with 24 episodes.

Although the six costars were relatively unknown to the public, Courteney Cox had the most acting success at the time. Consequently, NBC capitalized on her television popularity and name recognition to promote the upcoming comedy in media publications and press releases. After all the anticipated hype and hoopla, the series premiere was met with a lukewarm reception.

Reviews

The *Friends* premiere received numerous negative reviews from notable sources. *People* gave it a D+ rating and *Variety* claimed the show "touts promiscuity." *Time* magazine was particularly scathing, with Richard Zoglin writing: "In *Friends* the crowd is always around to share their latest personal woes or offer a shoulder to cry on. But who would want advice from these dysfunctional morons, with their obsessive pop-culture references?" *Washington Post* reviewer Tom Shales loathed the show: "Another ghastly creation from professional panderers Marta Kauffman and David Crane, the witless duo who do *Dream On* for HBO. *Friends* is more a scripted talk show than a sitcom. You keep waiting for Sally Jessy or some other cluck to interrupt the jabbering."

On the flipside, there were a few complimentary assessments. *Los Angeles Daily News* reviewer Ray Richmond called the series "one of the brighter comedies of the new season" while a *Los Angeles Times* reviewer lauded it as "flat-out the best comedy series of the new season." Other remarks compared it to NBC's top sitcom. *Cleveland Plain Dealer* critiquer Tom Feran said the series hinged "vaguely and less successfully on the hanging-out style of *Seinfeld*" and Ann Hodges of the *Houston Chronicle* called it "the new *Seinfeld* wannabe, but it will never be as funny as *Seinfeld*."

Critics also assessed the individual actors. *Chicago Sun-Times* reviewer Ginny Holbert claimed Joey and Rachel's characteristics were underdeveloped, while *Los Angeles Daily News* critic Ray Richmond commended the cast as a "likeable, youth ensemble" with "good chemistry." Robert Bianco of *USA Today* called Schwimmer "terrific" and praised the female leads, but claimed Perry's role was "undefined" and LeBlanc was "relying too much on the same brain-dead stud routine that was already tired the last two times he tried it."

Ratings

The *Friends* debut had 21.5 million viewers and was the 15th-most-watched program of the week. It was sandwiched between *Mad About You* (No. 14, 23.2 million) and *Seinfeld* (No. 2, 32.8 million). Overall, *Friends* had a strong outing for a new show and fared quite well in holding the lead-in audience, only dropping 1.7 million viewers. Although not really wowed by the numbers, NBC was particularly disappointed in its most anticipated sitcom, *Madman of the People* starring Dabney Coleman, which secured the best timeslot in NBC's schedule, following *Seinfeld*. *Madman* ended the week at No. 13 with 22.7 million watchers. In other words, it failed to hold the attention of over 10 million viewers, which ultimately dampened the series premiere numbers for the network's new hospital drama *ER* (No. 12, 23 million).

The pilot episode features a runaway bride (left), and a duplicitous coworker (right)

Premiere Facts

The ages of the cast when the series premiered (youngest to oldest): Perry (25), Aniston (25), LeBlanc (27), Schwimmer (27), Cox (30), and Kudrow (31).

When Cox received her first paycheck, she bought a brand new $80,000 silver Porsche Carrera. One of the first things Matt LeBlanc did with his newfound wealth was buy a home for his mother. He worshiped his mother like a good Italian boy. She even saved DIY home projects for him to complete when he visited. "I'm still a mummy's boy. I always wanted her to be proud of me," he unabashedly admitted. "Even now she calls me up before I do a talk show to say, 'Now, whatever you do, Matt, just don't be nervous.'"

Cast Collegiality

Many television castmates claim to be close both on and off set, but for *Friends*, it was actually true. Shortly after the series debuted, Matt LeBlanc declared, "These people have now become my friends and it's really nice—you see them at work and everybody gets along really well." But it did not start that way.

First Impressions

On the first day of production, Matt LeBlanc appeared on set dressed in character. He was wearing leather jeans and a plain white t-shirt, much like Fonzie from *Happy Days*, Instinctively, the cast's first impression was to presume he *was* just like his character. When Schwimmer first met LeBlanc he was skeptical and immediately thought his costar was "Joe cool stud" and hated him on sight.

Jennifer Aniston had a different impression—she was scared of LeBlanc. She took one look at his résumé, character profile, and greaser attire, and immediately assumed he was a bad boy. LeBlanc, a 27-year-old Italian from Newton, Massachusetts, had a blue-collar background having been raised by his father, a mechanic, and his mother, a circuit board assembler. His acting credits included cool-guy roles in Bon Jovi and Tom Petty music videos, and his onscreen persona was typically a lothario. He had a well-known modeling gig with Levi's, and appeared in popular television commercials for Coca-Cola and Heinz. Aniston initially wrote him off as being a macho, egotistical dude. "I was scared of that type of guy," she boldly confessed. Of course, this negative perception faded fast. According to Aniston, "He thinks it's very funny now. And actually, he can sit down and comfort me just like Courteney or Lisa could."

Naturally, once the actors settled into their jobs and got to know one another, they quickly became close friends. And this friendship put everyone at ease so they could hone their craft. They would bounce ideas off of each other, ask for advice, accept criticism, and make each other laugh. "That was the lightning in the bottle because they captured that joy of being friends, and that playfulness, and it was magic," Jane Sibbett (Carol) recalled.

Forging Friendships

Director James Burrows was instrumental in forging friendships among the castmates. "It's really important for me that the cast bond," he stated. "You knew from the instant we shot the pilot how electrifying the six of them were together." The cast had a similar sentiment. "We would all hang out playing poker and bonding because I think we all understood that the point of the show was that we were family and best friends," Kudrow expounded. "We needed to hang out, get to know each other, and bond as quickly as possible, because that's the only way that the show was going to work."

To facilitate cast collegiality, Burrows offered the sextet use of his much larger dressing room as a venue to hang out together. He knew the cast would have a hard time bonding in their smaller dressing rooms because there was not enough space for everyone to assemble together. Thus, it made sense to use his deluxe accommodations as the meeting place for the cast.

Friends production began in Stage 5, which is one of the smallest soundstages on the Warner Bros. studio lot (14,850 sq. ft., 110'x135' and 35' high). It is so small that the cast dressing rooms are located under the audience bleachers. The following season, after the production team moved to the more expansive Stage 24 (21,600 sq. ft., 160'x135' and 35' high), the cast inherited upgraded accommodations. Then Courteney Cox's dressing room became the new student union for the gang. Since her space was always the cleanest, she became hostess to all the group's gatherings.

Female leads bonding (left) and cast members joking around during a rehearsal break (right)

The cast immediately gelled and became like family. Their friendship was genuine. In fact, the costars yearned to be close to one another. "The cast was so close that they had all their dressing rooms moved to one end of the soundstage upstairs," a production source said. Their isolated quarters became a place for the costars to hang out, gossip, and banter in a cordial way.

Las Vegas Trip

In mid-September 1994, after the cast had filmed a handful of episodes, but before the show premiered, series director James Burrows called Warner Bros. President Les Moonves and requested to borrow the corporate jet to take the *Friends* cast to Las Vegas. Burrows wanted to give the cast a well-deserved break and nurture the camaraderie that was swiftly blossoming between them. He hoped their respect for each other could turn into genuine love and affection, and that those genuine feelings would be visible onscreen in their work. "Ensemble casts are a tricky thing," he opined. "The audience needs to believe that there are strong bonds between the characters." Thus, Burrows became the first to champion cast unification.

Moonves agreed to the request, and the septet boarded a plane for Nevada, screening the *Friends* pilot on the short flight. Burrows took them to dinner at Wolfgang Puck's Spago restaurant at Caesar's Palace (now located in Bellagio), and as they dug into their entrees, he told them that this would be their last shot at anonymity: "Your life is going to change. The six of you will never be able to do this again." The actors looked at him, bewildered. He explained, "Once the show comes on the air, you guys will never be able to go anywhere without being hounded." The gang was hesitant to believe him. "We had no clue what he was talking about ... and sure enough, that was the last time we were able to [do that]," Aniston recalled.

After the meal, Burrows asked if they wanted to gamble. No one had enough money to cut loose, so Burrows spotted them the cash, and they wrote checks to cover their gambling expenses. LeBlanc was in for $500, and the others staked $200. Burrows later regretted not saving their checks as mementos.

Intervention

By the second season, the female costars were earning a reputation for being late to the set though Jennifer Aniston was by far the worst offender. When the problem persisted, in the fall of 1996, David Schwimmer rallied the cast to assemble an intervention to address her tardiness. The male leads were extremely frustrated having to wait for the girls to arrive on set practically every workday, but it particularly miffed Schwimmer, who took the lead in confronting Aniston. "The boys did an intervention with me about my tardiness," Aniston confessed. "David did it. Very kindly. The day my alarm didn't ring." The intervention was somewhat serious but presented in a loving, largely joking manner: "You've had bad luck getting to work," Kudrow diplomatically proclaimed. In Aniston's defense, she felt pressure having to come to work "hair and makeup ready."

Friendship On Set

Most fans are surprised to discover that the cast of *Friends* was a tight-knit alliance that behaved as a family—they fought, shared intimate secrets, hugged, loved one another, hung out together, and supported each other. "We're still pretty much in shock every day that we come to work and we just realized how well we get along and no one gets on anyone's nerves and no one gets picked on more than the other," Aniston remarked in the early days of the show.

Shortly after the series debuted, the cast was beaming about their closeness. "It's pretty amazing, I mean I think we're all really sort of taken aback by it because to us, down here, it just seems we're all just sort of a theater group," LeBlanc revealed. "We're a really tight ensemble, we get along really well. It's just a real productive environment and a great time." Aniston further expounded: "We fell in love with each other and wanted to hang out."

Throughout the 10 seasons, the three female costars spent considerable time together during rehearsal and production breaks, and their indisputable love for one another was apparent. While working on "The One Where Underdog Gets Away" (1.09), Jane Sibbett (Carol) recalled seeing the trio together splashing in a puddle near the soundstage when no one else was around. "They were just falling around laughing with one another," she fondly spoke. "The love this group had for one other was extraordinary." Sibbett felt like she was privy to a privileged moment.

In fact, the female costars congregated for lunch every workday, and enjoyed the same entree—the Jennifer Salad—a Cobb salad of sorts. Courteney Cox explained: "We always had the same thing—a Cobb salad. But it wasn't really a Cobb salad. It was a Cobb salad that Jennifer doctored up with turkey bacon and garbanzo beans and I don't know what."

One excellent example of cast jocularity and collegiality occurred after a couple seasons together. Courteney Cox and Matthew Perry made a bet to name the movie known for the famous line "Chicks cannot hold their smoke, that's what it is." Perry adamantly declared the quote was from *Weird Science*, but Cox confidently asserted *The Breakfast Club*. Crew members became involved in the debate and the costars kept raising the stakes. The pair realized Judd Nelson was on Stage 29 doing *Suddenly Susan* so they ran over there and found out that yes, indeed, it was *The Breakfast Club*. As payment for their wager, Perry was obliged to be Cox's man slave for five months.

The most important unifying ingredient was the lack of professional envy. That was the consensus among guest stars and crew members. Cosimo Fusco (Paolo) observed, "They were all very normal. All of them had a great human side. They were very humble." Mitchell Whitfield (Barry) confirmed this assessment and interjected, "There was no ego on set." And that never changed as the waves of success came crashing down upon them. All the pitfalls of fame and success never affected their attitude, behavior or demeanor. "In season two there was a change in everything. You'd notice it in the cars they would drive, or they'd talk about buying this or that. There was wealth coming in," Fusco recalled. "But as people? They didn't change. Not with me." Even more astonishing is the fact that the actors were very supportive of one another. Christina Pickles (Judy Geller) witnessed the extraordinary team work: "They were a united group. They would watch each other's work. If someone had a scene they weren't in, the others would watch it and laugh. It's very unusual to be so supportive of each other on set."

Friendship Off Set

The cast was cognizant of the importance of being friends in real life in order to make the show work. "I think it was unspoken but we instinctively felt like we need to be friends, we need to get along, we need to connect," Lisa Kudrow opined. But friendship cannot be forced to work. If the bond is weak, it will inevitably break. That never occurred with the cast of *Friends*.

The sextet spent considerable time together outside the studio. They played poker and games (Scrabble was a favorite), met for lunch during filming hiatuses, partied as a group, hit the clubs together, and the girls often went shopping as a singular unit. "I think we were genuinely having the time of our lives," Schwimmer confided. The cast would jointly celebrate after filming wrapped on Friday nights and continue bonding on weekends. They even vacationed together. For example, during a production break, the three male leads headed to London for a getaway in 1996.

For the first few years, the cast would hang out at each other's homes and watch the first-run broadcast of their series. Matt LeBlanc described their episodic screenings as "a comedy within a comedy." He detailed a typical Thursday night: "Actors, when they watch themselves are a little insecure," he remarked, noting that the group tended to compliment each other ad nauseam, e.g., "You were great," "No, that's terrible, you were great," and "No, come on, you both were great." But none of that mattered. It was spending time with one another that counted.

Kathleen Turner (left) and Tom Selleck (right) thought the cast was unwelcoming

Matt LeBlanc confirmed the cast unity. "It's corny but we really were all there for each other emotionally. We had 10 years to sit around in a big studio without windows and talk about our personal lives," he reflectively reminisced. "I was the Bear, the big brother figure. I'd always be saying, 'Who said what to you? Do I need to go and beat someone up?'"

David Schwimmer concurred about the tight-knit ensemble. "We spent an enormous amount of time together those first several years. We wouldn't want to leave each other," he asserted. "There was something very bonding about how scary the whole experience was. We had the other five, like a very protective cocoon." Lisa Kudrow had a similar point of view: "We spent 10 years together, almost every day. ... We all went through something significant together, and that's a strong bond. As you get older, you realize, oh, you don't have that with just about everybody."

Of course, like all types of relationships, there were rough patches so they worked hard to maintain their friendship. "It wasn't like we were in college together. We were on a giant f*cking television show together. Everybody worked really hard," LeBlanc ardently asserted. "We really spent a lot of time if someone's feelings got hurt. 'Oh, let's drop everything and fix that. And I'm sorry.' Rule number one: Get along. Everyone knew the importance of getting along the whole way through." Lisa Kudrow interjected, "I worked harder on these relationships than I did on my marriage."

Cast Clique

The cast became such a tight-knit clan it often appeared from an outsider's perspective that they didn't want anyone penetrating their bubble. This view was especially prevalent among older guest stars who felt ostracized by the *Friends* cast. Kathleen Turner (Helena Handbasket aka Charles Bing) and Tom Selleck (Richard Burke) were the most outspoken about their frigid encounters with the youngsters. "The *Friends* actors were such a clique— but I don't think my experience with them was unique," Turner said. "I think it was simply that they were such a tight little group that nobody from the outside mattered." Although Selleck once claimed the *Friends* set "was a great place to work," he complained that sometimes he felt left out by the cast because of their close bond, specifically referencing being excluded from the cast's preshow huddle where the sextet privately shared a moment to wish each other luck with their performance. A *Friends* production worker noted that since the cast and guest stars' dressing rooms were on opposite ends of the soundstage, the TV stars "rarely talked to them."

In contrast, recurring regulars, including older actors such as Elliott Gould, Christina Pickles and Marlo Thomas, felt welcomed by the cast at all times. But this may be related to their presence in the hit series during its formative years. "It's not always easy to walk into a show that has already been established and where everyone has their characters, and they're a tight-knit family. Sometimes it's not roomy enough for a new person to come in," Thomas indicated, confirming the claims made by Turner and Selleck.

Notwithstanding the older day players, the cast clique always dissolved around younger recurring regulars and guest stars—they were wholeheartedly embraced by the sextet. Jane Sibbett (Carol) was part of the series since the ninth episode and claimed to have been part of the clique and felt the camaraderie. Freddie Prinze Jr. and Reese Witherspoon equally confirmed the welcoming nature of the cast. Lauren Tom (Julie) stated: "I thought it was really incredible that they would include someone who just had a recurring part in their little tight-knit group. It was lovely." From most accounts, the costars were very friendly and supportive and willing to share advice during production.

Pranks & Banter

The cast's unifying fellowship was apparent on set each and every week of production from the table read through pickups. Christina Pickles (Judy Geller) called them a "united group" and mentioned that their closeness was evident from their pranks and banter. Paget Brewster, who played Joey and Chandler's girlfriend Kathy, remembered how they'd poke fun of each other. "If someone made a joke and it didn't work, they'd all turn on the person and be like: 'You blew it, Lisa!'" she said. "They would bust each other's balls." There are too many examples to list but a few memorable on-set antics stand out.

- In "The One with the Soap Opera Party" (9.20), Joey enters Monica's apartment and opens his robe. In an outtake, Matt LeBlanc opened his robe to expose his boxer shorts, and covering the genitalia area was a headshot of David Schwimmer.

- In "The One Where Ross Moves In" (5.07), Joey and Ross are playing Cowboys and Indians. Schwimmer and LeBlanc played a prank by exiting the fort and pulling up their zippers just as Matthew Perry waltzed into their abode to witness the act (implying they were having sex in the fort).

- In "The One with the Truth About London" (7.16) Schwimmer pranked Jennifer Aniston by pretending to fall down the stairs during a scene (he actually screamed and then tossed a life-size dummy to land in front of her). Aniston shrieked, completely mortified, and then sprinted to offer assistance. After discovering the ruse, she was justifiably outraged.

- In "The One with the Secret Closet" (8.14), Schwimmer ran past the hospital waiting room causing Aniston to burst out laughing. In the next take, she and LeBlanc purposely hid to confuse their costar. It worked. Schwimmer calmly walked into the waiting room, looked around and didn't see his castmates, so he continued down the corridor. He actually thought he missed his mark again. Later, when he forgot his line, Aniston jestingly shouted, "You just suck! What happened to you? You used to be able to act!" It's a fine example of cast solidarity on the set.

Often their playful banter made it into scripts. For example, in real life, while one of the cast members was discussing a boring subject, the others would pretend to fall asleep. The writers witnessed this humorous behavior so they added it to a couple scripts, namely, "The One with the Butt" (1.06), "The One Where They're Up All Night" (7.12) and "The One with the Soap Opera Party" (9.20).

One thing was certain: if they were joking on set, Matthew Perry always had to have the last laugh. According to actress Paget Brewster, "If it was the end of the scene, he would consistently pitch something. They'd make fun of him for literally always wanting to have the last laugh." Perry later admitted his compulsion for attention. "To me, I felt like I was going to die if they didn't laugh," he honestly confessed. "And it's not healthy, for sure. But I would sometimes say a line and they wouldn't laugh and I would sweat and just go into convulsions. If I didn't get the laugh I was supposed to get, I would freak out."

Backstage Drama

The *Friends* cast was less frequently in the rag magazines than cast members in most other successful shows, such as *Roseanne*. Sure, the cast fought with each other, yelled, walked off the stage, became upset at the producers and director, but it was all kept under wraps. They resolved their issues onstage, not in the media. The best illustration involved Matthew Perry's addiction. The entire cast and crew knew his condition for years but it never made it into the tabloids.

Tight lips also pertained to the executive producers. They were all low-key and stayed private, consumed by their work, not the backstage drama. Each show occupied 60 to 80 hours of their workweek. The time spent at the studio had the greatest impact in their lives, not the press or soundstage hysteria.

So in a nutshell, the cast argued occasionally but for the most part they got along just fine. They helped each other and became close friends. Their celebrity status did not impact their performance or their relationships. No one person became a star above the others, and they all shared the experience together, as a group.

No-Sex Pact

Shortly after the series premiered, rumors began circulating that the cast entered a no-sex pact. In other words, the cast allegedly vowed to abstain from sleeping with one another for the duration of the series. The informal agreement was purportedly made to maintain cast unity. The cast denied this rumor for decades but in 2021 the guys claimed there was a pact, but the girls said no. In separate interviews, Lisa Kudrow and David Schwimmer admitted that, if there was a pact, it was definitely broken a few times. Of course, Kudrow was married during most of the series and never partook in any of the casual dalliances, but Aniston was linked to all three male leads at one point or another. In 2021 she and Schwimmer admitted to a mutual crush during the first couple seasons but denied acting on it. After hearing the revelation, LeBlanc quickly interjected a fake cough while saying "Bullshit." The producers also thought the pair were a romantic couple. "We all thought something might have been going on because they were just so good together," Kevin Bright said.

Schwimmer commented on the crush: "At some point, we were both crushing hard on each other," he reported, "but it was like two ships passing because one of us was always in a relationship, and we never crossed that boundary. We respected that." Aniston further expounded on the mutual crush. "We were in relationships and it was always never the right time and it wouldn't have worked," she proclaimed. "The beauty of that was that whatever feelings we had we just literally channeled everything into Ross and Rachel, and I think that's maybe why it resonated the way it did." When pressed further whether they consummated the relationship, she added: "No, we never, on my life. And Courteney and Lisa would know if it did [happen] because they would've heard about it. They can vouch for me." Cox interjected, "It's true." Aniston then closed the subject by declaring, "I would proudly say I banged Schwimmer if that happened. But no."

The concept of a no-sex pact was even incorporated into an episode of *Friends*. In "The One with Ross and Monica's Cousin" (7.19), Monica claims she and Chandler made a "no-sex pact" (a pact to abstain from sex until after the wedding). This dialogue was scripted because of media rumors that the *Friends* cast made a similar pact with each other once the series took off. The writers thought it would be a comical way to satirize the media gossip.

Continued Friendship

Aniston and Cox remained very close friends after the show ended, and are best buds to this day. Kudrow is still friends with both but not as close as the other two. They see each other often but not on a regular basis, and stay connected using a group text chain. They regularly partake in Cox's Sunday dinners, as well as Aniston's pool parties, and often meet for dinner at their favorite West Hollywood spots like Sunset Tower and Craig's.

After the series ended, the cast members often supported one another by guest starring in each other's television series. Everyone except Aniston appeared in an episode of Lisa Kudrow's webseries *Web Therapy*. Aniston popped in for Cox's drama *Dirt*, and Aniston, Perry and Kudrow guest starred in Cox's sitcom *Cougar Town*. Cox showed up in Perry's short-lived sitcom *Go On*.

Matt LeBlanc and Matthew Perry remained very close after *Friends* but few of the cast members remained close to David Schwimmer. None of the guys were invited to Aniston's 2015 wedding to Justin Theroux, though partly due to it being an intimate gathering with only 75 guests.

In a rare cast get-together, the entire cast met for dinner at Cox's house on October 5, 2019. In Aniston's Instagram post, the group photo inadvertently captured lines of cocaine in the background. It was the first gathering of all six costars since the series finale wrap party over 15 years earlier.

Character Development

"You set out to do things, and then actors come in and they breathe life into it,
and it's not quite what you imagined it was going to be."
—Marta Kauffman

The original pilot concept had four costars and two secondary characters. Chandler and Phoebe were meant to interject humor whenever necessary but they were not to be integral to the storyline. This fact is evident in the pilot episode where the three main stories revolve around Monica, Rachel and Ross. However, after casting the actors and watching them in rehearsals and run-throughs, the pair became an essential part of the ensemble cast. The producers realized that the actors brought to the show "so much more than comedic relief," including excellent cast chemistry, so their characters' roles were expanded and written with more meaningful stories. Phoebe's first major storyline occurred in "The One with the Thumb" (1.03) while Chandler's came into play a couple episodes later in "The One with the East German Laundry Detergent" (1.05).

According to Marta Kauffman, "The characters were definitely loosely based on friends, [and] relatives of ours. [The show] was based on us and our experiences. We knew those people." However, after casting the costars, the creators rewrote the pilot script to adapt to the actors' personalities. The duo did not want to force the actors to play their designated roles as written, they wanted to fashion the dialogue to comport with the special qualities and characteristics of each actor. These character profile adjustments occurred throughout the first season as the writers learned about each actor and their idiosyncrasies.

Rachel

The final casting of Jennifer Aniston did not change the manner in which the Rachel character was originally scripted. Aniston's deft portrayal made the character believable and likable so no adjustments were necessary. Rachel's cataclysmic transformation from JAP (Jewish-American Princess) to working-class gal was always meant to occur in the pilot episode. After working as a waitress for over two years, she slowly eased her way into the fashion industry and then climbed the corporate ladder. In romantic relationships, she had crushes and flings, dated younger and older men, and had a tumultuous elongated on-off love affair with Ross.

Monica

Cocreator Marta Kauffman was the primary inspiration for Monica. "I see myself closest to Monica," she confided. "A little neurotic, very perfectionist, a little competitive, a little control freak." David Crane confirmed the assessment: "Marta has a lot of Monica in her." Their primary commonality was their OCD tendencies. "I have a lot of Monica in me, in terms of everything having to be a certain way," Kauffman revealed, including "putting the top on the pen until it clicks." This OCD behavior was spotlighted in "The One with Two Parties" (2.22) where Monica chastises partygoers: "I've noticed that some of you are just placing them on. You wanna push the caps until you hear them click." The staff writers purposely added this pet peeve to the script because Kauffman, too, was equally obsessed with pen-cap protocol. Kauffman added: "I'm the one who has the pencils at perfect angles. Color coding? My favorite thing in the world. I do that with characters. They're all color coded." Naturally, Monica's profile incorporated this neurotic tendency.

In the original pilot script, Monica was the queen of the one-night stand but NBC's top brass compelled a script rewrite to make her appear less promiscuous. In the revised draft, Monica became more invested in the relationship so her character profile changed to her being frustrated by the dating scene. She was worn out by an endless stream of dates. "She feels like if she has to eat another Caesar salad, she's going to die," Kauffman stated. This attribute was based on Marta Kauffman's string of failed romances while she was attending Brandeis University and during her early years in New York. She felt the same way until she began dating her future husband, Michael Skloff.

The casting of Courteney Cox dramatically transformed the character she portrayed. Monica was original conceived as "darker and edgier and snarkier." She was not maternal, nurturing or caring. She loved short-term relationships with men and never intended to marry. The original Monica character was much more cynical, wisecracking and tough. The producers doubted Cox was right for the role because she had a warmth about her, but it turned out she could pull off the harshness of her character because of her warmth.

During Cox's audition, the creators realized that "Courteney brought a whole bunch of other colors to it." Based on her delivery, the producers rewrote the character to comport with Cox's acting style. Monica became more neurotic, maternal, caring, obsessive and less sexually energized, though she remained sarcastic and tough. For example, Cox was the resident on-set den mother, offering healing words for every wound and a bandage for every scrape (another characteristic based on Kauffman). Aniston confirmed this fact, stating that her costar was "the mother of the group." Monica was also initially penned as a working-class woman in an "upper-crust sphere" but with Cox's rendition, the character was made to be more middle-class and suburban. The creators decided that Cox's portrayal of the character was "a lovelier place to go."

In the early episodes, the writers felt the Monica role was too limiting. They privately called her The Riddler because all she seemed to do was ask questions to set up jokes for everyone else. Kauffman promptly called a meeting and asked writers to come up with a list of adjectives that might describe Monica. Mike Sikowitz raised his hand and offered, "She's inquisitive?" Then one day after rehearsal the Monica character changed and became better defined.

Adam Chase and one or two other writers were hanging out on set, and they noticed Cox straightening the furniture in her pretend apartment after everyone else had left. He realized that they had stumbled on a breakthrough. They brought their accidental discovery back to the writers room, and Monica, who had previously been very opaque as a character, suddenly became substantially clearer. The idea of concentrating on Monica and Rachel as roommates, and playing up Rachel's slovenliness against Monica's obsession for order, gave Monica's character colors she had been lacking. Alexa Junge saw it as an ideal opportunity to place her stamp on the character. As a self-proclaimed type-A personality, Junge seized the moment by transplanting her traits into the Monica character to further develop her persona.

Thus, the new take on Monica as an obsessive-compulsive neat freak blazed a path for her character which allowed the writers to move her away from The Riddler status. The idea that she had OCD-like tendencies opened up dozens of potential storylines that had not been available to the writers. Once again, Marta Kauffman was a source of inspiration for many of Monica's idiosyncrasies.

Although Monica was acquiring nuances to her profile, Cox's portrayal still seemed a bit stifled. "It wasn't until we did the first Thanksgiving episode that we realized how much fun Monica's neuroses are," Kauffman noted. Originally, Monica did not have the intensity that later defined her character, but that sequence where she freaked out about the meal being ruined gave the writers new insight into her character.

Marta Kauffman may have been the model for the Monica character, but Courteney Cox could have been her twin. "I don't think they know how close they got it," declared Dorothy "Dottie" Pickett, Cox's sister. "The character's neat, capable, controlling." Cox then chimed in "And a little sarcastic." She then acknowledged the similarities to her character: "I'm very similar to her. ... I'm not as clean as Monica, but I am neat," she confided. "OK, I am a neat freak," Cox finally proclaimed. "I don't use a lint brush or anything, and I don't iron, but I could easily pick lint off of someone else."

In reference to the television character she portrays, Cox stated, "She's obsessive, the one who has to be perfect and please everybody. I'm so similar to her it's frightening." Cox is also very competitive like Monica. The actress even confessed that she would be annoyed pretty badly from time to time by her character. She imagined that Monica was a funny character, but admitted she would never get excited about a label maker like Monica would. The actor went on to say, "You can't help that I've become Monica a little, and Monica has become me a little." She objectively concluded, "So I'm like Monica. Big whoop."

In the pilot, Joey was a greaser (left); his image received a makeover in the second episode (right)

Monica's maternal tendencies also paralleled Cox's life. Deep down Cox wanted to take care of her friends and guide them to the right decisions. She was the one who went around the set telling everyone precisely what car phone model to purchase. She was the one who knew how long it might take to rehearse a scene or the length of time for one of her costars to go through makeup. She was the one who could sketch a minute-by-minute plan for the next day's work, factoring in every detail of her five costars' schedules. She was the one who would clean her costars' dressing rooms when they got too messy. Monica was not Courteney Cox, but there were elements of Cox's personality that were heightened and exaggerated for the purposes of creating Monica. Marta Kauffman astutely surmised Cox, "Let's face it, she's adorable and intelligent and really together. She *is* Monica."

Cox confessed that she incorporated some of her older sisters' idiosyncrasies into her portrayal of the character, but credits one person in particular for helping her mold her character—Matthew Perry. He helped her the most in developing Monica's personality into the character that ultimately appeared onscreen.

Phoebe

The original series pitch described Phoebe as "sweet, flaky, a waif, a hippie." According to Marta Kauffman, Phoebe "sees the good in everyone, which is a nice way of saying she's indiscriminate. One week she can be in love with a Japanese businessman, the next a street mime, the next a 53-year-old butcher." The character was originally written as a "serial monogamist," the kind of person who "doesn't date, but just moves in with guys." Phoebe did not have her own apartment—"she owns what she can fit in her backpack." The pilot episode would eventually tone down her love life while retaining her musical stylings and flakiness.

Phoebe's ditziness and fantastical spirituality is modeled after Marta Kauffman. "I'm not as ethereal as Phoebe but I have the tendency toward the weird stuff, the spirits and that side of life," Kauffman stated. "I really wanted to bring that New Age character in. It meant a lot to me because it seemed like it's part of what's going on in the world these days." Lisa Kudrow then transformed the character to the one we know today, though her portrayal, surprisingly, was partially inspired by costar Jennifer Aniston. At the time, Aniston was into spiritual and New Age subjects, and Kudrow found her costar's interest in the concepts enlightening.

Kudrow also developed a unique twist on Phoebe's tragic life story. She chose not to focus on the tragedy her character endured. Instead, she reconfigured Phoebe's backstory by creating a character who had a laid-back attitude about all the trauma she endured. In Kudrow's mind, Phoebe was so clueless about her trauma that it was funny.

Phoebe's uplifting outlook on life was channeled from one of Kudrow's Vassar College friends who always had a positive attitude, even when her world was in disarray. Kudrow decided that Phoebe needed the same positive attitude: "I thought that would be funny if she thought, 'I'm normal like everybody else, I have the same experiences as everybody else has. Mother commits suicide, dad's in jail.' And then it's all not a big deal. That to me is what formed the whole character."

Although masterful at portraying a ditzy blonde, Kudrow confessed that she struggled portraying her character during the third season of *Friends*. "I feel like shit, I tricked them. At the audition, I was the only one who could cope with the audition process and that's how I got it, I think. So I had to work hard at being Phoebe, you know. I had played dumb girls but it wasn't really me," she confided. "I was struggling so much. I remember Matt LeBlanc going, 'What's going on with you?' And I said, 'I don't think I have it. I don't know what I'm doing.' And he went, 'You're her, relax, you got it. You've been doing this f*cking character for three years. You're working too hard, that's your problem. You don't need to work this hard, relax.' He was right." She snapped out of her funk and went on to earn six Emmy nominations for her role as Phoebe, winning one award.

Ross

Basically, the Ross character was written specifically for David Schwimmer so the first season's scripts already incorporated many of his idiosyncrasies. Thus, the writers did not need to tweak the character to comport with the actor's personality. It was Schwimmer who tweaked the character by giving Ross his trademark visage.

In the original pilot pitch to NBC and first draft of the script, there was no mention of a particular hairstyle for Ross. The distinctive cut was sheer happenstance. While living in Chicago, Schwimmer was performing in the production *The Master and Margarita*, where he portrayed Pontius Pilate. In order to appear temporally authentic, he sported a buzz cut for the role. When Schwimmer was cast as Ross, the pilot filming was less than two months later. His hair grew out a little but not enough to style differently. Thus, Ross debuted with very short hair. For continuity, Schwimmer purposely kept the same basic style throughout the series.

Ross' job was never intended to be integral to his character. In fact, the showrunners' original pilot concept listed him as "A paleontologist. Not that it matters." His occupation may have forever remained inconsequential but NBC insisted that the showrunners begin emphasizing workplace activities of the characters to broaden the settings for the series. Consequently, Ross has numerous scenes working in a museum and college classroom.

Joey

Initially, the casting search for the Joey character focused on finding a leading-man type. David Crane was taken aback to find that this approach led Joey to feel more boring than they had expected him to be. None of the actors properly conveyed the charm they had in mind. As it stood, Crane felt as if Joey did not belong in this particular circle of friends. "The part of Joey was much more limited in the pilot than what it ultimately became in the series," Kevin Bright stated. "If any of our characters fell into an area of being stereotypical, probably Joey was the only one." Marta Kauffman divulged, "It took us longer to figure out his character."

Joey was initially envisioned as a city slicker from Chicago and self-involved jerk. After LeBlanc was cast, Crane and Kauffman began to rethink the role. Joey would now come from an outer-borough with a working-class demeanor. Since LeBlanc had charisma and charm, he was not suited to be conceited so this characteristic was downplayed in the pilot episode.

After the series was picked up, LeBlanc informed the producers that his character did not make sense because the other characters would never befriend a vainglorious cretin. The creators agreed so Joey transitioned from being egocentric to a simpleton. According to David Crane, Joey's transformation was "incremental."

The evolution of Joey's persona must be credited to Matt LeBlanc, James Burrows and a crew member. The former planted the seed and the latter two made the idea blossom. When Matt LeBlanc first auditioned for the role of Joey, he put a "different spin" on the character, playing Joey as rather dimwitted. The writers did not originally like his rendition but then during production week director James Burrows asked the creators to have Joey "dumbed up a bit." Despite the initial hesitancy of the creators, while shooting the pilot David Crane was finally convinced to make a change after someone stated, "Matt plays dumb really well." The writers quickly realized this take on the character would be a major source of comedy. However, since the creative team did not embrace the character shift until after the pilot episode was shot, astute fans will notice that Joey is not addlepated in the first episode.

LeBlanc played the vacuous role so convincingly that many of his friends assumed he was extraordinarily witless in real life. "People will speak slowly to me sometimes. And they always ask me if I'm all right, because I'm much more low-key and reserved than my character in *Friends*," he disclosed. "They think that I'm depressed, or I'm sad, or upset—but I'm just not amped up to go out in front of an audience and do a TV show. That's not who I am."

David Crane had this observation of Joey: "I don't want to use the word 'dumb,' but there are things where Joey is not the sharpest tool in the shed." Matt LeBlanc defended his sitcom character: "For me, he was always just incorrect. He had his own sort of parallel universe stream of logic." For the writers, the problem became where to draw the line and "what's too dumb for Joey." Nearly every episode they debated jokes pertaining to Joey's dumbness to determine whether his level of obtuseness was going too far. For example, in "The One with the List" (2.08), Joey made the following comment, "I have two words for you: threesome." The writers actually debated whether the dialogue was too dumb for Joey.

In the initial concept, Joey was also a perpetual horndog and stereotypical womanizer with an overflowing black book of sexual conquests. In fact, he propositioned Rachel, who was still in her wedding dress after leaving her fiancé at the altar. Once again, LeBlanc questioned the actual believability of his character: "I remember standing back and being as objective as I could about Joey and thinking, 'This thing could go a long time. Does my character fit if it goes a long time?' Because in the beginning I was hitting on the girls all the time." LeBlanc worried that, as a one-dimensional creep, Joey would soon wear out his welcome with the other characters and with the viewers. So he went to the creators and said, "Could it be that Joey thinks of these girls as little sisters, and wants to go to bed with every other girl but these three? Then I'd buy that they're friends. Otherwise, I just don't think they'd even talk to him if he hits on them every single time."

The creators agreed and LeBlanc's character went in a different direction. Joey was retooled to be a funnier and warmer character within his group of friends, and ultimately became a better fit. He became an older, protective brother of the girls, though he was still a lothario. "What became apparent after we started the series was Matt's great diversity as an actor," Bright stated. "He was an actor that showed he was really able to display heart. And the focus of Joey later on in the series is how much heart this guy had."

Finally, the initial pilot concept had Joey and Monica as the show's central romantic couple. After casting the actors, LeBlanc and Cox had chemistry, but it was not romantic in nature. This created a quandary for the creators during the first week of pilot production, but then David Schwimmer and Jennifer Aniston filled the void by displaying pure romantic chemistry during rehearsals. Moreover, having Joey and Monica as a couple would have required a major character shift for both characters: he would have to abandon his lothario ways and she could no longer be the queen of the one-night stand (which was her character profile at the time). Their preconceived romance would have irreparably changed the overall group dynamic.

Chandler

While fleshing out character personas by incorporating the actors' personalities, the creators invited each costar to lunch on separate days. Although few intimate gatherings harvest bountiful inspiration, one meeting proved quite fruitful. In fact, the creators were able to assemble most of Chandler's profile directly from Matthew Perry's personality, proclivities and quirks.

During their informal assemblage, the creators told Matthew Perry to simply be himself. And he was. He was brutally honest. Perry confided that he was "just awful with women"—that he had really bad relationships and was scared to ask women on dates. Then he added a pitch: "That's the kind of character you haven't seen before." He continued, "I also am not comfortable with any silence at all. I have to break any awkward moment, or any silences, with a joke." Once again, in pitch mode, his follow-up comment was: "What better character for a sitcom is that? It's a built-in excuse for him to be funny."

The head writers also made note of the unusual manner is which Perry spoke—how he emphasized certain words in his speech pattern. As Jennifer Aniston remarked, "He has this way of speaking, using questions like 'Could this *be* any more this or that?'" This vocal tic was ultimately used in an early episode and then became a recurring gag throughout the series. For example, in "The One Where No One is Ready" (3.02), Joey mimics Chandler by proclaiming, "Look at me! I'm Chandler! Could I *be* wearing any more clothes?" This was exactly how Matthew Perry spoke in real life. So the staff writers crafted a storyline in "The One with the Ick Factor" (1.22) where everybody in his office makes fun of him because of the manner in which he speaks.

Marta Kauffman commented on Perry's unique manner of speech, "That's all him. That is his genius." She noted that he always tried to make the script his own because he did not want to do specific lines that are all repeated a million times. That was something Perry did so well. "It became a signature for him," she revealed. "We used to do this thing where if we really, really wanted him to emphasize a certain word, we would have to underline the other word. He always found a way to twist what we had written to make it his—in the best way." For example, in "The One with All the Poker" (1.18), Ross is pining for Rachel at the coffee shop so Chandler offers his signature catchphrase delivery: "Could you *want* her more?" However, the original script called for Perry to emphasize the word "her" but he chose to stress the prior word.

The showrunners also took notice that Perry was quite sarcastic. This too became part of Chandler's persona. As the character once remarked, "I'm not great at the advice. Can I interest you in a sarcastic comment?" This epitomized Matthew Perry.

Although the actor and character were not clones or facsimiles, Perry did acknowledge the similarities, but then added, "These characters are slightly exaggerated, slightly more entertaining versions of ourselves." He added. "I know Chandler is similar to me. But if you watched my whole life for a week, there would be many more boring parts."

One characteristic that was written in reverse related to Perry's comedic humor. The cast and crew were constantly laughing at his jokes but in the episodes it was written for his friends to remain stoic toward his wisecracks. The purpose was to frustrate Chandler and make him feel insecure, which fit the character's traits.

Chandler's sexual orientation was also an issue during the formative days of developing the pilot. David Crane considered writing the character as gay, but once Perry took the job, Crane acknowledged, "I don't think we ever considered making Chandler gay." But that didn't stop fans from questioning his sexual orientation. When Lisa Kudrow first heard Matthew Perry read Chandler's dialogue, she was surprised because she, like many other people, had assumed his character was gay. Hordes of fans believed his sexual proclivity would eventually become an episode plot. However, in 1997, the idea was put to rest when David Crane asserted: "No, Chandler isn't gay. Nor will he be gay."

One final character change involved Chandler's level of nerdiness. According to Marta Kauffman, "Chandler started out as a computer geek who liked *Star Trek*" but this characterization did not fit the type of character that Matthew Perry seemed adept at portraying. Thus, after casting Perry, this characteristic was excised from Chandler's profile.

Love Interests

In nearly every television series, from pilot concept to series finale, the script writers contemplate a scenario where the main characters hook up, date and break up, or develop a lasting romantic relationship. *Friends* was no different. However, the journey of the sextet took an unexpected trajectory with a myriad of scenarios, contrived pairings, intended and unintended couplings, and many unexpected consequences.

Joey—Monica

When Marta Kauffman and David Crane pitched the pilot, the original concept had Joey and Monica hooking up in the first season. Since these characters were the most sexual, it only seemed natural they would couple. Joey, the perpetual horndog, is beguiled, and then possibly tamed, by the alluring vixen, Monica. In this initial version, Joey was a ladies' man with a big-city attitude.

The creative strategy was to establish sexual tension between the characters. Lothario Joey thinks he's God's gift to women, but Monica unequivocally rebukes his advances. They quickly become foils for each other, arguing about whether men are intimidated by women with strong personalities or whether such a woman is a bitch. (Kauffman once vowed that she would never use the word "bitch" on the show, yet the term actually appeared in the original pitch document and was mentioned over a dozen times in episodes.)

After casting Matt LeBlanc and Courteney Cox, numerous changes occurred to their respective characters which made a romantic pairing infeasible: Joey was no longer a city slicker and Monica became less sexual, and Joey turned into a big brother to his female friends and Monica morphed into a den mother to the gang. The showrunners decided the characters no longer worked as a romantic couple. Kauffman thought the idea of Joey and Monica made sense on paper, but once Cox and LeBlanc were cast, it no longer did. Plus, the actors lacked onscreen romantic chemistry so the sexual pairing of their characters would have never worked.

Nevertheless, at the end of season four, the creators revisited the idea of pairing Joey and Monica. They sketched a story arc for season five where the two neighbors become the central romantic couple for the series. The Chandler–Monica hookup at the end of season four was meant to be a one-night stand. However, the audience reacted so enthusiastically to the coupling that the creators decided to test the waters with this unintended romance. When their romance proved to be wholeheartedly accepted by audiences, the Joey–Monica hitching was nixed for good.

Joey and Monica (left) as the primary romantic couple, not Ross and Rachel (right)

Ross—Rachel

Prior to rehearsing the pilot episode, the creators never fathomed a romance between Ross and Rachel. After the first rehearsal, Kauffman and Crane knew the characters were destined for love so they quickly sketched an unrequited love scenario and crafted dialogue to set the wheels in motion. The characters became the quintessential will-they–won't-they couple on television. The showrunners described the pairing as "an indescribable mixture of attraction and loathing and tenderness and brutishness." This unintentional plot twist became the primary thematic focus for most of the first season. "Once storylines start to work, the show takes over and tells you what to write," Kauffman disclosed.

Sexual tension is great for ratings but once it becomes a thematic issue, it must be resolved—either they become a romantic couple or face eternal banishment to the friend zone. To the astonishment of the staff writers, the creators were able to tease viewers with the unrequited-love story for an entire year. But in the following season a resolution was imperative so Ross and Rachel became a couple. Kevin Bright explained the writers room dilemma: "We were well aware the audience wanted to keep them together but when we got them together—when the first kiss happened—we go, 'Wow, the air has kind of gone out of the balloon.' There wasn't that sexual tension anymore." Thereafter, the primary concern was whether their relationship would stagnate. Director James Burrows explained why the couple had to break up in season three: "It's the same as Sam and Diane [from *Cheers*]. They flirted for a lot longer, but you have to shake it up. ... If you don't fight, and if you don't get angry, you have no place to go."

The initial relationship breakup was supposed to be Rachel dumping Ross, but then during discussions in the writers room, the pros-and-cons list came about as an easy way out. The pair promptly reunited only to break up for good in the third season due to Ross' jealousy. Although the lovebirds remained apart for over half a decade, the writers often hinted that the couple may reunite—by adding dialogue or innuendos where one or the other exhibited romantic feelings—just to keep the audience invested in the relationship. Naturally, in the finale, the creators reunited the fictional soul mates.

Joey—Rachel

Friends fans may remember that a possible romance between Joey and Rachel had its inception in season eight. He developed feelings for her that she did not reciprocate. The romance was resurrected at the end of the ninth season and carried over into the tenth because the writers needed a romantic barrier to delay the inevitable Ross–Rachel reunion that was scheduled for the series finale. The writers revisited the controversial liaison more for convenience than anything else because it only involved establishing a story to make Rachel reconsider her feelings for Joey. There was no need for a long arc to establish a love barrier to keep Rachel and Ross apart.

Immediately after reading the script for the first episode of season ten, Matt LeBlanc did not want to do the story. "It's wrong. It's like I want to be with my sister," he kept uttering. Kevin Bright recalled the tumultuous time: "He was very firmly against it, saying that he's Ross' friend, and that the type of friend that Joey is would never go and take someone else's girlfriend." The executive producer added, it took "a lot" to convince LeBlanc to agree to the storyline. Even writer Scott Silveri commented that it "did feel more like a brother-sister relationship."

LeBlanc publicly proclaimed his displeasure with the script: "It felt wildly inappropriate. That's how close we all were to the character." His costars agreed and the sextet confronted the creators to voice their objections. The group stated, "We're really concerned about this. It doesn't feel right. We have a problem with it." The creators replied: "Yes, it's absolutely wrong. That's why we have to do it. You can't just keep spinning the same plates. You have to go places where you're not expected to go."

Although many fans perceived the unconventional romance as signaling the moment *Friends* jumped the shark, the showrunners defended the decision. "We liked it," Marta Kauffman said. "It felt real. That's what happens in groups of friends and it was vulnerable for both of them." She was speaking from experience because she did the same thing in the early 1980s when Michael Skloff was part of her circle of friends in New York. Their hookup resulted in a 31-year marriage and three children (they divorced in 2016).

Besides, the fact that it felt so wrong to so many viewers is what made it feel right to the creators. "It was wrong in a really cool way," David Crane enthused. "You get to see them come to that realization, and it let Joey show some emotional colors that he hadn't up to that point. We liked it because it was dangerous. We knew people would go, 'You can't do that!' and that was one of the selling points for us."

Privately, Crane reassured the cast that although the relationship was controversial, it was never meant to be a long-term thing. Publicly, he played up the polarizing relationship. He wanted to capitalize on the intense conflagration of public opinion to further fuel a firestorm of controversy to increase publicity for the show. "The Joey–Rachel thing I know is controversial. I love it. I love it because it's wrong, and we knew going in, this is wrong. And that happens in life," Crane said. "There is the relationship that shouldn't be. Even though you love someone, that's not who you're going to be with."

Realistically, Crane thought the story would provide a good roadblock for the inevitable Ross–Rachel reunion. Deep down the creators always knew the Joey–Rachel relationship was doomed, after all, Rachel and Ross had a child together, but the writing team hoped to resolve the contrived coupling in a "really interesting, moving and compelling way." But, in hindsight, Crane did acknowledge that the plot was rather sad. "Once it actually started it was heartbreaking because it couldn't go anywhere," he professed. "It was always going to be Ross and Rachel."

Chandler—Monica

The first hint of a possible Chandler–Monica romance occurred in "The One Where Ross Finds Out" (2.07) where she functions as his personal fitness instructor. According to the staff writers, this storyline illuminated the onscreen chemistry between Courteney Cox and Matthew Perry. "There was a real fun dynamic between the two of them," writer Scott Silveri stated. "So even as early as that, [the writers] said, 'Oh, they're kind of special together. If we're ever looking for another relationship, that's something to file away.'" Which is exactly what the writers did for an entire year.

The notion of pairing Monica and Chandler was seriously pitched in the writers room in season three. According to Silveri, everyone got really excited about the idea, but his writing partner, Shana Goldberg-Meehan, thought it was too soon in the show's life to introduce another romantic couple. "She was the one who said, 'I just feel like at this point it would feel a little desperate,'" Silveri recalled. "We had gotten excited about the stories we could tell, but once she said that, we were all shamed and ran away. It became clear it was too early to explore something like that." Another reason the writers put a pin in the idea was its closeness in proximity to the Ross–Rachel debacle. "There was a little bit of relationship ennui among us writers," Silveri said. "We'd already done a lot of drama between Ross and Rachel. And nobody wanted it to become the 'Get Together and Break Up' show."

Although the writers didn't officially unite the couple, they did hint at the possibility of a romance in the near future. At the end of season three, in "The One at the Beach" (3.25), Monica laments the thought of never finding another boyfriend so Chandler comforts her by stating, "If worst comes to worst, I'll be your boyfriend." This set up a storyline where he tries to prove he is boyfriend material but she adamantly resists his efforts.

As the creative team got together in the summer of 1997 to map out stories for season four, the writers decided that bringing Monica and Chandler together would be, according to Silveri, "a great goal for the end of the season." They just needed to figure out how. As the creative team plodded through the season, the sting of the Ross–Rachel "break" was fading so the timing objections seemed to vanish. Plus, the logic of another coupling was starting to grow stronger, at least in the minds of some of the staff writers. "The thinking was, if the show's going to be entertaining for years to come, it can't simply rest on this one relationship [Ross and Rachel]," Silveri said. "So it follows that if another pair got together, that would be fun and provide more story. And it's organic: If you get six friends together, all around the same age, there's gonna be a little mixing and matching as time goes on. It felt real."

Monica and Chandler's one-night stand (left) becomes a lifetime commitment (right)

The Monica–Chandler romance began with subtle foreshadowing in "The One with the Free Porn" (4.17). Very few viewers ever noticed that, in one of the scenes, Chandler and Monica are cuddling on a club chair, even though they are not dating and the entire couch is unoccupied. This was intentionally choreographed to presage the couple hooking up in London six weeks later. It was a baited line cast by the writers and now all they had to do was reel in the audience.

"The goal from the get-go was to treat Monica and Chandler's hookup as a surprise, a jolt in the second half of the hour-long episode to add some energy and fun," Scott Silveri stated. "The only real debate was around just how we'd get Monica and Chandler there that morning [and] how many crumbs to drop to lead the audience and the characters to the moment, all in hopes that [it] ... wouldn't feel unmotivated and false." In an early scene at the rehearsal dinner, Monica is depressed about not having a boyfriend and being mistaken as Ross' mother, so Chandler comforts her by saying, "Who wouldn't want you?" Silveri quickly added, "[We were] basically shooting for the spot between 'This stinks, that never would have happened!' and 'This stinks, I saw that coming!'" Basically, the writers were looking for an audience reaction that could be characterized as "That is surprising, but also very satisfying and organic. It might not stink!"

During filming, the producers had a sense of how viewers would react to the hookup because all three London audiences responded the same. "The first time, I was huddled around a monitor, watching [the two actors] perform. And when Monica popped up from beneath the sheets, there was just this explosion from the audience. It was a combination of a laugh, gasp, cry and shriek. They were just blown away by it. It was so intense," Silveri recalled. "For the second or third takes, instead of watching the monitors, I just turned around and watched the audience." The crowd screamed for 27 seconds, forcing the actors to hold their marks before delivering the next line. "It was a wonderful stroke of luck that we came up with doing it as a surprise—not seeing them get together, just revealing them together," Kauffman fondly recalls. Today, of course, the scene would have been filmed on a closed set because audience members would be tweeting the epochal event the very second it was performed. "Before the dawn of social media, you could keep secrets," Silveri stated. "We didn't have to worry about it."

Monica and Chandler's hookup in London was never supposed to be a long-term thing. Originally, it was going to be a humorous mistake. But the British studio audience reaction prompted the creators to reconsider their position. "We were stunned. So that's when we sort of went, 'Huh, guess this is going in a different direction,'" Kauffman commented.

Despite the rollicking reaction from the London audience, the creators were tentative about keeping Monica and Chandler as a couple. "The fear was that we'd jump the shark," David Crane revealed. So they played it cool. "We really did not think it would go on," said Kauffman. "We thought it might go on for a few episodes." They decided to monitor fan and media reaction to the coupling for the first few months of the fifth season. "We didn't want to invest too much too quickly because sometimes in a sitcom you put people together and it takes energy out of the show, and it kind of relieves sexual tension in a certain way," said Kevin Bright, speaking quite reserved. "So we wanted to see gradually how it would go with Monica and Chandler. The period of them keeping it a secret allowed us to see how much does the audience really love this."

The writers knew they could not copy the Ross–Rachel romance so they pulled a page from George Costanza's playbook and did the opposite. According to writer Scott Silveri, the reactionary approach to relationship breakups was metaphorically applied to TV sitcom production. "If someone's too high drama, you look for someone stable," he insisted. "And so with Monica and Chandler, we decided to roll out in a way that was a reaction to the last big relationship [the show] had." Since Ross and Rachel's relationship fizzled in a blaze of bitter and cantankerous glory, the showrunners made a conscious decision to present it incongruously for Monica and Chandler's relationship. "All of their fights would be light and breezy, and never have the edge that Ross and Rachel's did," Crane elucidated, "principally, to make them feel different from each another." So the mandated order was to introduce the Monica–Chandler dalliance in a way that would be "not too heavy, not too soap opera, but also something surprising."

"Monica and Chandler were the first couple to really make an impact on the show since Ross and Rachel," Bright recalled. "We were very careful with them to protect them because we felt with Ross and Rachel sometimes we played the cards too early and broke them up and put them together and all that stuff too quickly." The creators wanted to do everything right this time. "We wanted to take our time with Chandler and Monica, and not make any commitments," he said.

Even after the Monica–Chandler romance was accepted by the public, it was never the creators' intention to have them remain a couple until the end of the series. Courteney Cox and Matthew Perry were trepidatious about the aftermath of the tryst. Similar to the other costars, they were protective of their alter egos and kept questioning the writers: "Is this the right thing to do?" They were not concerned about a rendezvous, they worried about the ramifications of a romance. Fortunately, fans loved the couple, and David Crane further noted, "They were so great together, and it kept giving us stories. It was the gift that kept on giving." Nevertheless, the showrunners took their time to slowly develop the romance. "The road to marriage would be one that would take some time and that hopefully we would enjoy that as much as we enjoyed them getting together," Bright surmised. Many of the staff writers believe this pairing rejuvenated the show as a diversion from the Ross–Rachel roller coaster romance. "Without Monica and Chandler, it ends three years earlier," Silveri definitely declared.

Joey—Phoebe

Although the showrunners never considered a romance between Joey and Phoebe, they found the notion intriguing. Toward the end of the series, Matt LeBlanc and Lisa Kudrow pitched the idea that their characters had been having casual sex the entire time. In his proposal to the creators, he stated, "We'd go back and shoot all the historical scenes and just before a moment that everyone recognizes, there's Joey and Phoebe coming out of a broom closet together." Crane and Kauffman swiftly rejected the idea.

Many fans of the show were desperate to see the pair become an item but the producers felt it did not "fit the tone of the show." The producers opined that they would like to believe Joey and Phoebe were hooking up offscreen throughout the entire course of the show, but not enough to do an episode on it. Besides, recreating the earlier scenes would reflect the actors' age differences and create numerous other continuity concerns (e.g., weight gain, hairstyle changes and dental work).

Although the idea was rejected, the writers offered a consolation by occasionally adding dialogue to intimate a possible dalliance between the pair. For example, in "The One Where Rachel Tells Ross" (8.03), Joey makes the following sexual proposition to Phoebe: "Monica and Chandler are married. Ross and Rachel are having a baby. Maybe you and I should do something." She replies in a sultry voice: "All in good time my love. All in good time." This is one of many allusions to a potential liaison between the friends.

Teaser Relationships

As season three rolled around, the creators projected a midseason Ross–Rachel breakup but they also wanted to keep an eye on the next romantic relationship. Thus, they penned "The One with the Flashback" (3.06) to monitor how audiences would respond to certain romantic couplings, namely ones that had not previously been linked (i.e., Monica–Joey, Rachel–Chandler, Phoebe–Ross, and Monica–Chandler). The hope was to pair Rachel and Chandler, which is the reason for the tag scene teaser. But audiences didn't react positively to the coupling so the idea was shelved. Based on the audience's response, the only pairing that seemed plausible was Monica and Chandler. The producers pondered the idea and then waited for the right time for a hookup, which didn't arise until the season four finale.

Other Romances

According to Kevin Bright, when he would cast love interests for the protagonists, the goal was to "generate an interesting story and great comedy" but he cautioned "until it gets started, until you see how the audience responds to it, you're not really sure." He clarified, "There have been times where we thought we were embarking on an arc of a love interest but decided that maybe one episode was a better way to go." A good example involved Paget Brewster. Although she appeared in six episodes in season four, the creators originally plotted her story arc to extend longer but decided to shorten it because they felt she lacked good chemistry with Matt LeBlanc.

In other instances, a story arc was truncated because of unanticipated circumstances such as an actress' pregnancy. This happened to Helen Baxendale (Emily) which prompted her earlier-than-expected exit. The Ross–Emily relationship was supposed to extend into season five but Baxendale's real-life pregnancy precipitated a condensed story arc where her character has a whirlwind romance, expedited wedding, and swift breakup, all within less than half a television season. Story arcs can also end early because an actor is fired or quits. For example, Jon Favreau was dismissed for objecting to the way his character was written as a lovable loser, and Reese Witherspoon quit after two installments because live audience performances scared her.

Occasionally, a story arc is extended because the producers love what the actor brings to the series. A classic example is Maggie Wheeler as Janice. She was supposed to appear in one episode and be summarily dumped by Chandler, but audiences loved her nasally voice, vexing laugh, and addicting catchphrase. She appeared in all 10 seasons for a total of 19 episodes. Another illustration is model Elle Macpherson. She joined the cast for a five-episode story arc as Joey's roommate, Janine Lecroix. The producers invited her to guest star in more episodes, but she declined the offer. She was living in London at the time and didn't want to travel such a great distance for each appearance. A third illustration is Tom Selleck as Richard Burke, Monica's older love interest. He was supposed to be in 3 episodes but the producers kept extending his recurring role which amounted to 10 episodes over four seasons.

Pregnancy Issues

When the series was first pitched to NBC, the creators never fathomed having to write pregnancy issues into their scripts. But as events arose, they opted for unconventional childbirths. The writers wanted to remind the world that there is no right way to live our lives—having a baby is a deeply personal decision and it is different for everyone.

The first pregnancy arose in October 1997 when Lisa Kudrow informed the producers of her condition. At the time, about one-third of the installments for season four were already filmed and a few more plots were projected. Thus, the first allusion to a pregnancy was not revealed until January 8, 1998, in "The One with Phoebe's Uterus" (4.11), where Frank Jr. asks his half sister to be a surrogate.

Since Phoebe was not romantically involved with a man, the staff writers did not want to introduce a love interest who would immediately impregnate her, nor did they want an unplanned pregnancy to end with a baby being added to their milieu. The creators chose surrogacy for her half brother and giving birth to triplets because neither had been done on television before.

Since Lisa Kudrow was four months pregnant when the surrogacy storyline was first filmed, her condition had to be concealed until her fictional girth caught up to her real-life girth. Once the pregnancies were in sync, though, almost immediately, Kudrow had to start wearing padding to account for the added weight of carrying triplets. (Only one episode was shot without padding.)

The next pregnancy issue was contrived, not based on an actress becoming pregnant. It involved Rachel's unplanned, out-of-wedlock pregnancy that dominated the eighth season. The story arc was devised solely to offer the creators a grand event (giving birth) for the season finale, as well as offering hope to viewers that Rachel and Ross may reunite in the future since they shared a unifying bond, Baby Emma.

The final pregnancy focused on child adoption. At the end of season nine, Monica and Chandler experience infertility so they decide to adopt. Ironically, one month into filming the tenth season, Courtney Cox became pregnant in real life. This created a new dilemma. The showrunners could not logically incorporate her pregnancy into the series, as they did Kudrow's, because it was already established her character could not conceive a child. The producers opted to hide Cox's pregnancy. Her condition was disguised using props and baggy costumes along with special lighting and camera blocking. Despite utilizing these gimmicks, her pregnancy bump was quite visible, especially in the finale.

Episode Production

Workweek

A typical sitcom season lasts eight months so all 22 episodes are taped in 34 weeks. (When *Friends* first aired, a typical television season was 24 episodes.) Besides the winter holiday break, the production team is constantly hurried to produce nearly an episode per week while working on other scripts for future episodes. A typical workday had the cast appearing by 9 or 10 each morning, and staying until 5 or 6 in the evening. The writers, on the other hand, were on a completely different schedule. They would arrive earlier in the morning (8-9am) and often stay late into the evening (10-11pm). Depending on the script changes and number of rewrites, they could stay most of the night, each and every day of the workweek. Moreover, if they were working on a new episode, their hours would often extend into the weekend.

Monday

On Monday, a new script was distributed to the actors for a table read where the cast vocalized the text while the director, writers, producers, and executives from the studio and network observed and took notes. The weekly table read had 25 to 30 people in attendance. Someone would usually function as a stand-in for guest actors during this embryonic stage of episodic production. In the afternoon, various head honchos discussed the table read and offered notes (changes to the script). This could be a very tense meeting in the struggle between artistic integrity and network conservatism.

The showrunners also held a production meeting to coordinate all the departments. The producers discussed everything from wardrobe and makeup to props and set design. Each department received a script to prepare for filming at the end of the week. For example, the wardrobe department received a script so they could begin working on costumes for the actors. The makeup department needed to plan hairstyles and makeup to coordinate with the costumes. The construction department used the script to build sets for the various scenes. Everyone had to be on the same page so it could all come together by Friday night.

Executive producer Kevin Bright toured the set to make sure everything was in place for the next day's rehearsal. The actors memorized the lines and worked on their delivery. The writers room was the usual hub of activity as they continued to rewrite the script so a fresh copy could be distributed on Tuesday morning.

Tuesday

The second workday of the week involved actor rehearsal. Kevin Bright would start the day by meeting with the cast and crew to be sure everyone was in sync by summarizing the previous installment. Then the actors performed the scenes and made changes to how they wanted to deliver their lines. The staff writers watched, scripts in hand, hanging on every line of dialogue. If some of the jokes weren't funny or a scene wasn't working, they would be looking at another long night of rewriting. The cast and director began to work on physical comedy bits.

Tuesday was also the first day of camera blocking, which involves organizing all the actors' movements in relation to the camera. It's like choreographing a dance or ballet. All the elements on set (actors, extras, vehicles, crew, equipment, etc.) should move in perfect harmony. In order to keep the camera dollies from crashing into each another, the camera assistant placed numbered tape marks on the stage floor to designate where the cameras needed to be located in every scene. Stand-ins were used to coordinate the placement of actors on the stage.

Wednesday

Day 3 entailed a cast rehearsal where the actors offered advice on upgrading the script material. Later in the afternoon, the cast performed a quick run-through for the writers who would then spend the evening rewriting the script. This was the time Marta Kauffman was most actively involved with the cast and their stage presence. She frequently observed their interactions and worked with the actors on their stage presence and delivery. The cast enjoyed sharing ideas with her but the female leads were tentative at first.

During the first season, she observed the cast and noticed the male actors were more willing to pitch ideas than the women. If the guys thought a particular joke wasn't clicking, they would mess around and make each other laugh until they had something they liked. Marta Kauffman believed the female performers were still fearful of embracing their inner comedian. Of course, this changed as the series progressed. In future seasons the female leads were equally involved in the comedy as their male counterparts.

Wednesday occasionally involved fittings but only for specially designed costumes or in preparation for a Thursday afternoon preshoot. The director finalized camera blocking and made arrangements for any upcoming preshoot.

Thursday

During the fourth day of production, the actors memorized a modified script and had a full-fledged run-through where the entire script was rehearsed as if filming the show. This was also a time for any last-minute changes to the script dialogue or insertion of physical comedy into the scenes. The actors continued to work on timing and delivery to improve scenes or bits. The wardrobe department would arrange fittings for the cast to make sure the costumes fit properly.

Thursday was also the time for shooting on location or filming scenes that required substantial costume changes or makeup work. These scenes were shot without a studio audience. A few notable examples include all animal scenes, most flashback episodes (the costume changes and makeup adjustments were very time consuming), the beach episode where Ross' girlfriend Bonnie shaved her head (affixing a skull cap takes hours), and all scenes involving VCR playback images (the director wanted the segments to appear as if filmed in the past).

Friday

The final day of the workweek was a live performance and audience taping. Since the cast would be working well into the evening, or sometimes the early morning hours, they did not arrive on set until the afternoon. They partook in a casual run-through with minor adjustments to the final script, had dinner (typically on set), went through wardrobe and makeup, and then made any last-minute preparations before their live studio audience performance. Each 22-minute episode took more than five hours to film—twice the length of most sitcom tapings—mainly due to the numerous takes and script rewrites. Filming involved multiple takes per scene (usually three but it could be a dozen) with several scene breaks for wardrobe, makeup and set changes, each of which typically lasted 15 to 20 minutes. During breaks, the male leads would play videogames (*Super Mario Bros.* and *Mario Kart 64* were their favorites) and the female leads would hang out in Cox's dressing room to talk.

Cast jitters were especially evident in early installments. According to Christina Pickles (Judy Geller), "At the beginning of *Friends*, Matt LeBlanc was anxious. Every time he did something he would look for approval to the director, the producers or the writers, if they were around. There would be a look of, 'Am I doing this right?'" Jennifer Aniston admitted to experiencing "opening night jitters" with each live performance, while Matthew Perry confided that taping was much more traumatic for him. He had a constant fear of failure which haunted him during every performance.

Director James Burrows worked blazingly fast when filming scenes to get a loose, witty, exuberant version of the script on film. As the one true sitcom veteran among the creative team, he was concerned about wearing out the jokes. Burrows believed that doing too many takes of the same segment resulted in diminished returns. He had been trained in theater and lived by the motto: if you wanted to see a second take, you should buy a second ticket. Despite his efficiency, the production process was slow. It was not uncommon for audience members to slowly trickle out of the bleachers before filming wrapped.

Since filming nights were lengthy and time consuming, when *Friends* produced double-length episodes, they were always filmed over a two-week time frame. The producers did this for a variety of reasons: (1) there were more sets involved and the stage could not hold them all at once so changing sets would take longer than usual, (2) not all the sets could be built in time, (3) it would be too much for the cast to learn all the lines, and (4) a 10-hour shoot would be unbearable for the cast, crew and spectators.

Filming Episodes

The first season was shot on Stage 5 at Warner Bros. Studios in Burbank, California. At the start of the second season, production moved to the expansive Stage 24 (later renamed "The *Friends* Stage" following the series finale), taking over the soundstage that previously housed *Full House*. Stage 24 is purportedly haunted. It is one of the oldest stages on the Warner Bros. lot and rumors of late night "occurrences" have been circulating for years.

Since the beginning of the show, the main players had duplicate names—Matts and Davids—so the crew assigned nicknames to avoid confusion. Matthew Perry was referred to as Matthew or Matty, while Matt LeBlanc was simply known as LeBlanc. David Crane was called David while David Schwimmer's appellation was Schwim.

Before filming each episode, the six costars assembled in a private room for a backstage huddle; no one else was present and no cameras were allowed. Schwimmer commenced the tradition and would always say, "All right, have a good show, love you, love you, love you, love you," as they all shared a group hug before heading onstage. One episode was special for Lisa Kudrow. Prior to filming "The One with All the Wedding Dresses" (4.20) the gang said, "Have a great show, love you—love you, little Julian!" Kudrow was touched her fetus was included in the huddle.

The preshow huddle was skipped only once, in "The One Where No One's Ready" (3.02), due to production delays that held up the start of the shoot. "We were like, 'We're taking too long, and the audience has been waiting—let's just go,'" remembers Kudrow of that fateful decision. Shortly after filming began, Matt LeBlanc separated his shoulder and had to be taken to the hospital. Thereafter, they vowed never to skip a huddle.

On a typical night of filming, 500 tickets were issued but only 300 fans were seated for the show. The bleachers were elevated above the stage so the audience could see the sets and actors without the cameras and production crew blocking their view. Prior to filming and during set changes, a large black curtain with the *Friends* logo covered the stage. It was raised after the cast was introduced, and for the start of each scene.

After four hours of waiting in line, attendees were ushered into the studio. In the first half of the series, the show started production at 6pm (the typical start time for sitcoms), which made each session extend into the early morning hours. If any of the studio audience members became exhausted, the crew would search for "fresh" bodies to take their place. This elongated filming process began to take its toll on the cast. Around the fifth or sixth year they stood united to confront the showrunners and insist on a change. Thereafter, the audience was seated at 3pm and ushered out of the studio by 9pm.

During the sitcom's fledgling years, there was little fanfare or big-budget production as part of the audience experience. As the series grew in ratings success, so did the perks and entertainment hoopla. The producers hired stand-up comedian Jim Bentley to warm up the audience before each episode taping and during filming breaks. His duties also included meeting celebrities and dignitaries, and providing an appropriate cast introduction. As the series became more popular, especially after season one, the studio audience experience was enhanced significantly.

In the first season, the audience energy was good. By the time the *Friends* team filmed the second year it was like a circus. Kevin Bright dubbed it "Club *Friends*" because there was a "pinch of Beatle-mania in it." Supervising producer Todd Stevens commented on the "excitement and energy," and likened it to a concert. By the second season the audience experience included various contests, singers, and free giveaways (hacky sacks, frisbees, cups, etc.). The producers even ordered pizza twice a night for the attendees. That's a total of 85 pizzas to feed 300 fans. Craft services prepared dinner for the cast and crew, which occasionally included sushi, and then the entire production team snacked on pizza at the end of the night.

As Bentley entertained the crowd during production breaks, the sets were changed and redressed, and the cast had makeup adjustments as well as costume changes—basically, whatever was necessary to get ready for the next scene. Most of the time the audience never noticed the bustling activity on the soundstage because it occurred behind a massive black curtain. Of course, on rare occasions the delay could last up to an hour, which made it very difficult to keep the audience engaged. The best illustration was "The One with Monica and Chandler's Wedding, Part 2" (7.24). It involved bridal formalwear with impeccable makeup for not only the three female costars, but also three female guest stars.

The studio audience was occasionally reminded to limit applause during the first cued entrance of guest stars, primarily Tom Selleck's guest appearances. During some audience interruptions, the editors were forced to shorten the laughter or insert a laugh track. In other instances, the applause was cut so the next line could be delivered promptly. On the other hand, sometimes the audience was inexplicably silent. There were times when the audience was in a foul mood (due to world events or a prior emotional scene) so the scene had to be reshot the following week or the filmed footage was replayed for a different studio audience to capture their applause and laughter. But it wasn't always fun and laughter. The dramatic segments often had the audience speechless. According to Marta Kauffman, "There are moments when you can hear a pin drop; they were so invested in the conflict and the romance."

After the audience departed, the cast would work an hour or two on pickups (reshooting scenes), which wrapped typically around 11pm. The cast and crew would often hang out to discuss the show, and then the sextet would depart to Il Sole in West Hollywood.

Despite the very long production day, the cast and creative team loved performing for a studio audience. Live performances galvanized the cast. Matthew Perry stated, "Our energy grows with every audience. It was like a real-time rehearsal in front of the most loyal fans." Jennifer Aniston claimed it was one of her "most energizing experiences to date" and she loved the "energy of an audience" that accompanies every taping. To her, the excitement from a live performance was so much more intense than movie or single-camera filming. Each cast member reiterated the benefit of having immediate audience feedback to gauge their performance and increase their energy level.

"A sitcom is as close to live theater as television can get," Kevin Bright aptly assessed. "The actors play to the audience, and their feedback is crucial." Schwimmer concurred, "It's like putting on a one-act play every week." Matt LeBlanc stressed the importance: "It's very important. It's like a test to see if the material works, if the jokes work, if the story tracks, if the audience is with [us], if we've given them enough exposition along with jokes."

The writers also loved live audience performances because they were able to test jokes. "Usually, you do television in a vacuum, and you have to depend on your own instinct or the opinions of a small group of people who are heavily invested," Kevin Bright stated. "But when you go in front of a live audience, and a joke flies, and you don't hear any laughter, you can tell yourself all you want that it's funny, but you'd better go change that joke. It's like walking a tightrope." Marta Kauffman called the audience "a wonderful barometer," and then stated: "The audience is gonna tell you what's working and what's not working. Things that crack us up, they sometimes don't get. Sometimes they get the setup and then you don't even need the joke."

Every scene was filmed several times with a surprising amount of rewriting between takes. If the audience didn't react to a joke while filming, the writers would huddle together, discuss ideas, and then try a new bit for the crowd. Each episode may encompass up to a dozen pitched dialogue changes on the night of filming. For example, in "The One After Vegas" (6.01), during Ross and Rachel's argument in Monica's apartment, Rachel's original line was "Ross, stop saying the word 'marriage.' Ross, stop, listen. If you don't get this annulled, I will." During a break, the writers huddled to discuss a better line and came up with: "Ross, this is not a marriage, it's the world's worst hangover." *Entertainment Weekly* called it the best line of the episode. "Some of the best jokes we've had on the show were just pitched out on the stage," David Crane proclaimed. "And sometimes you need radical solutions. We've had whole scenes that have just flat out died."

Rewriting scripts during filming is a novel concept in television, and it really impressed Matthew Perry. "The changing as we go is a really good testament to just how smart the executive producers are," he stated. "I've done a lot of shows in the past where it's a kind of tyrannical, don't touch the words, and it's just not the way to do a show. If a joke doesn't work, you just see this whole group of smart people just get in this huddle and then they come out and they tell you a joke."

This novel approach to interactive filming made *Friends* unique, though credit must be given to the showrunners for being diplomatic and democratic. If they didn't see the humor in a joke but the writers did, they would often defer to the majority. Similarly, if there was a question as to whether the audience understood a joke or inference, the audience would be polled during a filming break. For instance, in "The One After Vegas" (6.01), Phoebe states, "It's not like you're married everywhere," implying she was once married in Vegas. The staff writers were worried the audience would not understand the inference so they took a vox pop (poll) of the crowd during a filming break. It was this type of immediate feedback that helped improve the show. (And, yes, they understood the implication.)

Friends was shot on 35 mm film, which uses the 16:9 widescreen format (but television screens in the 1990s used 4:3 format which cropped the sides). Three to four cameras were typically used to tape an episode, which totaled up to 12 hours of footage and 30,000 feet of film (i.e., over five miles), which had to be edited to 22 minutes. Most episodes, on average, had 52 takes, 14 scenes and seven rewrites. It took 366,000 watts of electricity to light all the sets for one night of filming. That is the equivalent electrical power for 34 homes for an entire year. The show spent $1,700 a week on globes (light bulbs).

One thing that changed over the seasons was the position of the cameras. In season one, Burrows positioned them more intimately. The cameras were moved into the sets to get closer angles when filming the actors. As the series grew and different directors oversaw the projects, the cameras moved back as though to accommodate the size of the stars.

Although the series is set in New York City, not one scene of *Friends* was ever shot in the Big Apple. Kevin Bright felt that filming outside the studio made episodes less funny, even when shooting on the studio lot outside the soundstage. Some people thought that the season five finale was filmed on location in Las Vegas, but the episode was actually taped on Stage 24 at Warner Bros. Studios. The crew had to dismantle the Central Perk set to construct a Caesar's Palace casino replica.

Although a vast majority of the show was filmed in front of a live studio audience, some scenes were kept under wraps to prevent spoilers. As a general rule, all the season-ending cliffhangers were filmed without the benefit of an audience, such as the season four finale, "The One with Ross's Wedding, Part 2" (4.24), where Ross accidentally utters Rachel's name while delivering his wedding vows to Emily.

Animal Filming

All the animals used on the show were hired from Benay's Bird and Animal Rentals in Woodland Hills, California. In business since 1982, Benay's has over 100 trained bird and animal actors. Their employees were always on set to function as animal wranglers during filming.

Since the show's animals could not be trained to perform on cue, the director often let the cameras roll—with the actors improvising their lines and actions—hoping to get a good usable shot. Although the cast had a general framework of dialogue and comedy bits, they had to ad-lib based on the actions of the animals. "The beautiful thing about Marcel is that the director let the cameras roll and the actors were good about playing to whatever the monkey decided to do, which was some of the best footage that was not rehearsed," Greg Grande revealed. "We always ended up with the unexpected take that would work, it was just magic."

Shooting animal scenes was difficult and extremely time consuming. The animals were often uncooperative or unruly. On one occasion, Rachel was trying to explain a TV show to Marcel and the monkey simply wouldn't sit still, climbing over the couch and knocking over popcorn. In another scene, Marcel was supposed to pick up a bra, but ended up throwing it at Jennifer Aniston instead.

The cast had several issues with the simian. First, no one liked the manner in which Marcel responded to orders; yelling was all that worked but it drove everyone crazy. Second, David Schwimmer despised working with the monkey because it always missed its mark. "I love animals, and I love primates," he adamantly proclaimed. "Here was my problem: the monkey was obviously trained, and had to hit its mark. What inevitably began to happen is that we would all have choreographed bits timed out, and it would get messed up because the monkey didn't do its job right. We were about to do something really funny, but the monkey didn't hit its mark, so we'd have to start again." But, Marcel's trainer, Mike Morris, claims it was the other way around—that Schwimmer threw off the timing of the monkey.

Third, Schwimmer didn't like the unsanitariness of working with a primate. "When the monkey was resting and waiting for us to roll, it would sit on my shoulder," Schwimmer recalled. "The trainer would come up and give the monkey live grubs to eat. So the monkey would be sitting on my shoulder, take some grubs, break them in half, eat it and then [pat my head]. I had monkey grubby hands all over."

Finally, the simian had a tendency to disappear on set. Everyone would have to take a break for 5 to 10 minutes until the monkey was located. It happened quite frequently. In the aptly title episode, "The One Where the Monkey Gets Away" (1.19), the capuchin evaded handlers and disappeared. With a soundstage that soared four stories before ascending to rafters, there was a great deal of ground to cover. It took the crew 30 minutes and a lot of mealworms to lure the simian down to the ground.

Filming at Leo Carrillo State Park (left) and Vasquez Rocks State Park (right)

As the production issues continued to mount, Marcel was expeditiously written out of the series. Most fans never liked the addition of Marcel to the series. Although he was not dropped due to audience discontent, his removal inspired the television term "dropping the monkey," which was coined to describe a cast change that drastically improves or even saves a series.

In contrast, the chick and duck were easier to deal with than the monkey. They rarely evaded handlers and were used more as props to set up comedy bits. Unlike the capuchin, which was highly trained, the chick and duck were untrainable, so their usefulness to the series was quite limited. They could not be integral to the plotlines like Marcel. However, the chick and duck were easy to work with during production which explains their periodic presence on the show for over three years.

Baby Filming

All segments with infants are preshot for the benefit of the babies. First, preshooting allows for more precise filming because the director focuses the camera solely on the infant. "Anything that we need for the comedy or the acting on the show, we can do later on after the babies are gone," Kevin Bright stated. Since newborns can only be used in 90-second intervals due to the intense heat from stage lighting, the crew must work swiftly. Second, it is warmer. When a studio audience is present the soundstage temperature is set in the 60s to keep the crowd comfortable. Under these conditions, an infant is more susceptible to illness. Finally, it is much quieter. Live shows are too loud for the infants' fragile eardrums. Moreover, actors tend to speak softly around newborns which makes their dialogue difficult to capture with boom mics. Using dolls allowed everyone on the stage to speak clearly and enunciate their words.

Filming with infants and toddlers usually required hiring twins for the role. "We always have to have, at the very least, twins when we use babies," Marta Kauffman said. "Babies go through phases where they get fussy, they don't want to be held. We had to just make sure we always had quiet babies."

In "The One Hundredth" (5.03), Phoebe's childbirth scene uses triplets. The director wanted to make the birth real, yet keep it comedic, so there is no umbilical cord or other technical aspects of birth. The babies are covered with grape jelly to represent birthing fluid. When the babies turned 1 year old, the producers hired quadruplets, hoping only one infant would be uncooperative during the shoot.

The triplets were played by the Cimoch quadruplets (one girl, three boys: Alexandria, Paul, Justin and Cole). Since Phoebe had two girls and a boy (Leslie, Chandler and Frank Jr. Jr.), at least one of the boy quadruplets had to play a girl. This was quite noticeable in a couple episodes. A good illustration occurs in "The One with Joey's Porsche" (6.05) where male genitalia is visible on baby girl Chandler during a couple different camera angles.

Catering

Set-dressing food and prop food were often used to represent real food, especially when it was decorative in nature for a sequence. For example, in "The One with the Truth About London" (7.16), Joey is seen picking up a chicken leg with his fork but he never actually eats it. The reason is that the entire table is filled with set-dressing food that is inedible.

Real food was used in all episodes that involved the actors eating. Caterers specializing in on-camera food were hired to cook the meal. It was warmed in ovens on the soundstage, and then the prop department would set the plates and table. The actors actually ate the food so it had to be edible; their facial expressions must relate to the scene, not to the taste of the food. The meals were prepared to the liking of each actor. Naturally, if an actor had special dietary requests or restrictions, those were honored as well. Kevin Bright noted that "Matt LeBlanc eats everything off of his plate each take."

Catered food was usually reserved for holiday episodes because the cost of the service was prohibitive. Catering was never haphazardly used. A tremendous amount of food was prepared for holiday episodes. Every time a scene was reset for the next take, all the food on the table was replaced. Kevin Bright joked, "Usually there is enough food to feed a small army." After the show, the unused leftovers were given to a homeless shelter.

Location Shooting

The *Friends* production team rarely filmed outside the studio. They preferred performing in front of an audience because it elevated the energy of the cast. Thus, the crew only went beyond their comfort zone when it was absolutely necessary, either to save production costs or when an exterior setting could not be replicated on the soundstage. It mostly occurred in season one because *Friends* was filmed on Stage 5 which had no space for a street scene. In the second season, when the show moved to Stage 24, the producers built a permanent street outside Central Perk so most "outside" scenes could be filmed on the soundstage.

Warner Bros. Studios

Most of the location shooting occurred during the first season of *Friends* because the soundstage was too small to accommodate city street filming. The showrunners turned to Warner Bros. Studios in Burbank, California, which offered a new universe with business and residential thoroughfares on one of the many backlots. Studios like Warner Bros. are experts in using the same location over and over. By utilizing slight cosmetic alterations or different camera angles, viewers rarely realize the director is using the same sets over and over.

The most frequent location shoot involved Hennessy Street which was prominently featured for Marcel's movie. The cemetery scene for Nana's funeral was filmed on Blondie Street. When Ross and Rachel search for Marcel, they are traversing Brownstone Street. Phoebe's estranged dad lived on Midwest Residential Street, which was also the location for the Geller residence in "The One with the Prom Video" (2.14). French Street has a park so it was used for Ross' rugby match. Joey's WWI feature film premiere was filmed on New York Street, and Elizabeth tossing a water balloon from her dorm window was shot on Embassy Courtyard.

Paramount Studios

The *Friends* crew ventured beyond the WB lot only a couple times. When the producers felt the studio's business and residential streets were inadequate, they looked for other locations to meet their needs. Of course, on-location shooting is expensive so only once did they actually pay to reserve time to film on another studio's lot. In "The One with the Baby on the Bus" (2.06), one segment had the guys riding a bus for an extended time and then chasing it. This was too much outdoor activity for the much smaller WB Studio lot so the crew filmed the scene at Paramount Studios in Los Angeles, specifically Brooklyn Street.

Real World Filming

There were two memorable segments filmed outside the confines of the studio lots: (1) Joey's big hole at the beach and the jellyfish incident were filmed at Leo Carrillo State Park along the Pacific Coast Highway near Malibu, California; and (2) Joey's movie *Shutter Speed* was filmed just north of Los Angeles at Vasquez Rocks State Park in Agua Dulce, California, in the stunning Sierra Pelona Mountains. The latter park location was used in numerous films and TV shows, such as *Austin Powers: International Man of Mystery* (1997), *Star Trek V: The Final Frontier* (1989), and the *Star Trek* TV series (often referred to as Gorn Rock by many Trekkies). The only other real-world location shoot was London for the double-length episode.

London Filming

Nearly a year prior to filming the London episode, during the summer hiatus of 1997, the *Friends* producers were contacted by Channel 4, the British first-run broadcaster of the series, with a proposal to film an episode in London. The showrunners loved the idea but needed a believable storyline to justify the entire gang traveling abroad. When they decided on a wedding for Ross, they made his girlfriend a London resident visiting New York for two weeks, which commences a tornadic romance. The creators had already planned on Ross marrying the hot copy girl (Chloe) for the season-ending finale, so the narrative only needed to be tweaked a little to have it apply to Emily.

A couple weeks before leaving for England, the crew filmed all the apartment scenes in Los Angeles on Stage 24. Each department packed their equipment, and the entire cast and some of the crew boarded a plane to arrive in London in time to start episode production on Monday, March 30, 1998. The two-part episode was filmed in front of a live studio audience at Fountain Studios in Wembley over a two-week period—part one the first week and part two the following week. All interior scenes, e.g., restaurant, Waltham's residence, reception hall and hotel rooms, were filmed at Fountain Studios.

The London episode was shot in three pieces: on the sets in Los Angeles, on the streets of London, and on a Wembley soundstage in front of an audience of 500 doting fans. They lined up for six to seven hours in the rain for a chance to see a live taping. Unlike shooting in Los Angeles, where each scene is filmed multiple times, one after the other, and rewrites occur between each take, in London, the entire episode played out for one audience, from beginning to end. The crowd's response was documented for each scene, and then rewrites occurred before the next audience arrived. The cast performed the entire show again, with the writers taking notes and rewriting the scenes afterwards, and then they did it all over again one last time.

In the episode, the *Friends* characters stay at London Marriott, which was the actual hotel used by the cast and crew while filming in England. This was part of a lucrative paid promotion. The accommodations were free in exchange for promoting the hotel throughout the double-length episode.

Most of the location shooting featured scenes with Chandler and Joey: London Marriott, Grosvenor Square, Trinity Place, Westminster Abbey, London Bridge, Big Ben, Buckingham Palace, and the open-top bus as it crosses Tower Bridge. The outdoor shots were based on convenience and proximity, which included combining locations as much as possible. For example, after Joey and Chandler visited Westminster Abbey, the crew simply moved to the other side of the landmark to film a spot with British royalty.

When selecting a celebrity cameo, the showrunners went through a long list of famous British people, but they preferred royalty because it is something unique to their culture. Luckily, Sarah Ferguson (Fergie) was available and willing to do it. Kevin Bright thought she was hysterical. She agreed to the cameo because her daughters, Eugenie and Beatrice, were obsessed with *Friends*. Although "coaxed into the appearance by her daughters," it actually helped relieve some of the animosity toward her in Britain. "At a time when Fergie-bashing had become a national pastime, *Friends* was a welcome relief," the Duchess of York exclaimed. The showrunners wanted to film her segment in front of Buckingham Palace but the Palace administration prohibits filming of the royal residences unless it is for a documentary or news story without exception, including former in-laws (Fergie).

Bright had the responsibility of assembling a production crew. He insisted on using his cameramen for the shoot. "We flew our entire camera crew over to London because that was the one part of doing the show that we really couldn't expect British cameramen to step into and have our short hand," he noted. "Most of the lighting crew, and the set crew, and the prop crew were British crew. The way the two crews went together was all kind of seamless. It's like we've been working together for years."

Despite enjoying the trip to London, afterwards, David Crane vowed they would "never, ever do that again." He explained his adamancy: "We could have shot three-quarters of the show in LA. We didn't have to shoot as much as we did in London, but we thought, 'How cool would it be to shoot it in front of a British audience and do it just like we do it?' It was cool but it was also so complicated and exhausting."

The British media was frenetic. "We were on every morning show, every evening show, there was a *Friends* watch on the radio all the time, press conferences," Bright declared. "It was really crazy the amount of attention there. It was like The Beatles in reverse but without quite as much screaming."

A radio station was constantly announcing where the film crew would be next so fans could race to the location and watch. Over 1,000 people showed up, screaming "We love you" during the filming. Local security then recommended that the only way to appease the hysterical crowd was to have the cast come over, greet the fans, and take some pictures. It worked. After a brief interaction, the crowd dispersed.

The exterior establishing shot for Ross and Emily's wedding was St. John's Church in Wapping (east London). Set designers erected a false exterior to resemble a construction site. The church interior was a studio-constructed set.

The street vendor segment was shot in Trinity Place just outside the Tower of London. Millionaire Richard Branson offered 75 first-class tickets for the cast and crew via Virgin Atlantic airline to film an episode in London, provided he could be a guest on the show. He was given the part of a souvenir salesman who cajoles Joey into purchasing a Union Jack hat.

Channel 4 commissioned a behind-the-scenes program, *The One Where Johnny Makes Friends*, hosted by British television personality Johnny Vaughan, which featured comical interviews with the six costars. The program was broadcast on May 6, 1998. A tie-in book, *Making Friends in the UK,* was published by Channel 4 Books in November 1998. It was bundled into a gift pack entitled "The One with the Whole London Wedding" with an uncut version of the episode.

The episode received good critical feedback in the US on its first broadcast, and is often cited as one of the series' best episodes; however, many British viewers regarded it as an ill-informed and patronizing caricature of the UK and its people, causing the installment to be unofficially labeled "The One Where They Insult the English."

Postproduction

After filming wrapped each week, the exposed film was rushed to a lab to be developed overnight. It was then returned to the *Friends* office to be reviewed by the editor, usually Stephen Prime. On Monday morning he would sync all four cameras to play simultaneously on his machine. Then he started cutting the show together, slicing and dicing 30,000 feet of film and 12 hours of footage down to roughly 30 minutes. He chose the best cuts for scenes and then adjusted the sound, laughter, and any other audio issues.

After three days of editing, Kevin Bright and Marta Kauffman screened the first run-through. They discussed their likes, dislikes, suggested changes, different ways to view it, wide angles, better cuts, different angles, etc. Bright and Prime then worked jointly on the changes. After the modifications were complete, the biggest challenge was getting the show down to exactly 22 minutes.

After editing, the installment was passed to a number of technical experts where every frame of film and every second of audio was carefully examined and polished. Here, sound effects were added in a process known as foley—the reproduction of everyday sound effects that are added to films, videos, and other media to enhance audio quality. The reproduced sounds, named after sound effects artist Jack Foley, can be anything from the swishing of clothing and the clomp of footsteps to squeaky doors and breaking glass.

The next step in the process was music editorial. A music editor screened the show to determine the places where music was necessary. "Each show is not scored" (using original compositions), explains Merelyn Davis, a music editor for *Friends*. "A bulk of music is given to the editors by the composer every year, about four or five new batches a year. And those are then—in the parlance of the industry—tracked." It is her job to search and locate the most appropriate music for each episode. "Here we make sure that the music fits both the mood, the situation, and fits physically. Music editing is cutting to make fit," Davis added. "It is really amazing how long it takes us to do a show with 20 cues, three seconds each. In sitcoms, it's like, boom boom boom, every week, and everybody is doing their job and it all comes together at the mix."

The mix aka audio mixing, is a process where all the different sound elements—laughs, dialogue, special effects, foley and music—are combined by engineers. Their job is to set the proper volume levels for each track and filter out unwanted noise and hiss. "It takes four to five hours to complete a half-hour sitcom," noted engineer Charlie McDaniel. "So we're kind of known as the triage of mixing in half-hour sitcoms."

From start to finish, an episode takes five to seven weeks. Three or four weeks to plot the story and write the script. One week on the soundstage to rehearse, block cameras, and film in front of an audience. And one or two weeks in editing and postproduction. It is then submitted to the network where programming executives decide the order of airing and the date of broadcast.

Series Music

Kevin Bright was the primary advocate for incorporating popular songs into the series. "We always wanted music to be an important part of *Friends*," he said. "We just wanted the musical taste of the characters to be reflected in the music in the show." But the creators also wanted to use master recordings of popular songs, not cheaper cover versions that were often used by shows airing in the 1990s. Although master recordings cost significantly more, it was worth it to Bright. Since Warner Bros. paid the licensing fee, executives had to approve the expenditure, which they did, provided the privilege wasn't overused. The use of master recordings started in the pilot episode with Jackson Browne's "Sky Blue and Black" (it played during the scene where Ross and Rachel peer out separate windows into night). Of course, it wasn't a popular Browne track so it was cheaper to license than one of his hit songs, but nonetheless, it was an original recording.

There were several memorable moments where music played an integral part to a scene. In "The One Where Ross Finds Out" (2.07), the showrunners wanted to use U2's "With or Without You" as background music for Ross and Rachel's first romantic kiss but the series' production team didn't have enough time to secure the necessary licensing rights. Instead, they used stock music from a recording industry catalog to simulate the song. Naturally, the rights to the U2 ballad were secured the following week so it was then used as a radio dedication.

In "The One with the Monkey" (1.10), the first party song was "Shiny Happy People" by R.E.M. It was the original choice as the *Friends* theme song but the group's lead singer refused to grant permission for its use. The record label, however, did allow a single-use license.

An R.E.M. single was used in another installment as well. In "The One with Two Parts, Part 2" (1.17), the first song played at Phoebe's birthday party was "What's the Frequency, Kenneth?" Kevin Bright often included the band's songs in a variety of episodes because he was particularly fond of the Athens, Georgia, quartet.

Finally, in the *Friends* series finale, after Ross discovers he went to the wrong airport and Rachel boards the plane for Paris, the production song is "Yellow Ledbetter" by Pearl Jam, which is often the band's final encore song. As of 2019, it was used 337 times in the final encore position. The series creators' chose the single to symbolize the final encore of the Ross–Rachel relationship. It was the first time the band licensed a song for a television show.

Production Costs

In 1993, a typical sitcom cost $500,000 per episode to produce. At the time, *Cheers* set the record as the most expensive sitcom at $3 million per installment. For the next half decade, *Seinfeld* assumed the throne as industry leader with its skyrocketing production budget. By series end (1997-98), each *Seinfeld* episode cost $5 million, whereas the average sitcom budget barely topped $1 million. The production costs for *Friends* didn't escalate to astronomical numbers until the next millennium.

In the seventh and eighth seasons of *Friends*, the actors' salaries accounted for $4.5 million of the production budget per episode. At this point, *Friends* surpassed the milestone set by *Seinfeld*. When it was confirmed that *Friends* would return for a ninth season, their exorbitant salaries propelled the weekly production expenditure to $7 million.

After year-long speculation that the ninth season would be the series' last, NBC inked a deal in late December 2002 to bring back *Friends* for a tenth and final season. NBC agreed to pay $10 million to Warner Bros. for the production of each episode, the highest price in television history for a 30-minute series. Although NBC was unable to cover this cost with advertising revenue, the series was integral to its Thursday night schedule, which brought higher ratings and profits to the other television programs.

Even though *Friends* was immensely successful and extremely profitable, it was also outrageously expensive to produce. When comparing the 30-minute sitcom to a 60-minute drama, *Friends* was No. 3 overall, with *ER* topping the list at $13 million per episode during its 1998-99 season. Sitcoms are often much cheaper to produce than dramas for a myriad of reasons, such as fewer sets, a smaller cast and fewer day players. With each *Friends* star earning $1 million per episode, 60% of the weekly production cost went directly toward the actors' paychecks. Had the series not been canceled in 2004, it is most probable that NBC could not have afforded another round of production talks.

Advertising

After relocating to Thursday night, *Seinfeld* averaged nearly 30 million viewers and in 1995 commanded $390,000 per 30-second commercial, the highest advertising rate in TV history at that time. The following year it continued its revenue-breaking pace at $550,000 per ad and generated $9 million in advertising revenue per 22-minute episode, or nearly $200 million per year. NBC only paid Castle Rock Entertainment $46 million annually for licensing fees, salaries and production costs (far more than any other sitcom at the time), thereby netting $150 million. After the cast signed their record-setting contracts in 1997, advertising rates increased to $575,000 per 30-second commercial and Castle Rock was paid $3.5 million per episode, which reduced NBC's profit by $30 million.

In 2002, *Friends* averaged 22 million viewers and a 30-second spot sold for $450,000. Oddly, during the final season, its advertising rates only increased slightly, to $455,700 per ad, yet *Friends* remained the most expensive program for advertisers. NBC's *ER* was the second-most-expensive show for advertisers, at $438,514, with CBS' *Survivor* close behind. Other than NBC's hit sitcom *Will & Grace* ($376,617), no other series topped the $300,000 mark.

Product Endorsement

Of all the programs produced in the history of television, including corporate-sponsored shows in the 1950s, *Friends* is one of the most notorious sitcoms for its egregiously blatant use of product placement and brand integration. Product placement is a practice in which manufacturers of goods or providers of a service gain exposure for their wares by paying for it to be featured in films, television programs, music videos or streaming video on demand. Although the product is visible, it is often not the primary focus, since it needs to fit almost seamlessly into the context of a scene or story.

Brand integration, on the other hand, is defined as a special type of placement in which the product or service is central to the program's plotline. The brand is interwoven within the script—calling out specific product functions or showcasing unique features—and the product is exposed onscreen to a high degree. This rarely occurs without significant payment to the production company, or a lucrative media buy (advertising) with the network. It is an effective tool to offset exorbitant production costs. As *Friends* became more expensive to produce each year, the lure of corporate incentives sufficiently enticed the producers to sell out the show for some quick corporate cash.

Product placement is expensive. Brand integration is exorbitant. Numerous factors are weighed when setting a price for either service—single placement versus comprehensive program, product visibility (handled, mentioned, or background image), show popularity, estimated number of viewers, competitive product category (food versus cars), etc. In other words, in a scripted network TV show, a single background placement for a food item may cost as little as $60,000, whereas a comprehensive program can easily exceed $1 million. Moreover, in addition to a placement, the network may demand a $1 million advertising buy-in. Thus, in *Friends*, a Rold Gold pretzel bag in the background is at the lower end of the fee schedule, while the Porsche plot used extensive brand integration so the cost was somewhere in the lower seven figures.

Product Placement

During its inaugural season, *Friends* was wildly popular but companies were unsure about its staying power or impact on the public so brand names were rarely sponsored. The few sponsors they did have, such as Nike and Bass shoes, paid a small fee for the product placements. As part of the fair use doctrine of the trademark law, the producers were able to stock the cupboards with brand-name products without providing compensation to the companies. However, when the product was prominently displayed—where characters wear or feature brands or the product logos was accentuated—the entertainment industry often paid a licensing fee or obscured the logo.

Warner Bros., the production company for *Friends*, was able to make some inroads into product placement with a few companies and then slowly expanded promotions in future years. "The One with the Thumb" (1.03) was the first episode of obvious product placement. In the scene, Rachel and Joey enter Central Perk with Nike cleats flung over their shoulders and purposely positioned for a clean camera angle. Nike would remain a major sponsor throughout the series' run.

"The One with the Birth" (1.23) was the first installment to flagrantly flaunt a product. Although previous episodes had the characters carrying paper bags to advertise D'Agostino Supermarkets and Bloomingdale's department store, this installment purposely positioned bottles of 409 cleaner on the janitor closet shelf to be overtly visible from different camera angles with a strategically positioned spotlight to illuminate the product.

This level of obtrusive product placement continued over the course of the following four seasons, but the producers' greed resurfaced and hit its peak in season six, which is replete with corporate sponsorship. *Friends* is often designated the poster child for blatant product placement and brand integration in a TV program. The producers wear a scarlet letter for their shameless avarice.

Of course, in their defense, product placement is an effective way to defray production costs. It was not invented by the *Friends* producers. Product placement started as early as the 1890s, though the first successful venture was the 1982 movie *E.T. the Extraterrestrial* using Reese's Pieces. The Mars candy company was initially contacted to feature M&M's but declined. So The Hershey Company was contacted and asked if it wanted to put money behind a tie-in promotion of the film and the candy. Hershey's liked the movie, put up $1 million, and sales of Reese's Pieces skyrocketed 70% the month after the film's release. Two months later, more than 800 movie theaters carried Reese's Pieces, though none had done so before.

Although the list of product placement sponsors is voluminous, here is a sampling of the most noteworthy brands that appeared in *Friends*: Oreo, Coca-Cola, Budweiser, Instant Lunch, KFC Bucket, Ben & Jerry's ice cream, Hotel London Marriott, Operation, Ray Ban sunglasses, Bloomingdale's Little Brown Bag, Macy's, Farmland Skim Plus Milk, Scrabble, Zabar's, Victoria's Secret, and Ray Bari Pizza.

Product Displacement

This is the opposite of product placement. It involves removing a trademark by blurring or partially concealing the logo. Concealment often entails using tape or a marker to cover part or all of a logo, a practice commonly called "greeking," which is considerably less costly than using a computer to blur or pixelate a logo. Other times, the show's art department will create a fictional brand, something that is very close to the national brand packaging and logo it is mimicking, but just different enough to sidestep any trademark infringement. There are also numerous prop companies specializing in fictitious knockoff brands, such as The Earl Hays Press.

Product displacement is used for three specific reasons. First, a trademark owner may require a licensing fee for prominently displaying its logo. Fair use aside, obtaining a license can be a lengthy and expensive proposition. On the other hand, a legal battle over its use is often lengthier and much more expensive.

Second, commercial networks do not want companies to get free advertising. They want corporations to pay for any promotions. Oftentimes, there may be a conflict of interest. For instance, a network may have several advertisers paying to promote their product so it may lose sponsors by giving competitors preferential treatment with free endorsements. Besides, the network may have an exclusive agreement with one manufacturer which prohibits them from using competitor products in shows carrying their advertisements.

Lastly, the trademark owner may object to its logo being displayed, particularly when a product is portrayed in a negative light. For example, news reports may feature interviewees wearing clothing with pixelated logos. This is a legal precaution. If one of those people say or do something potentially embarrassing, the media outlet could face backlash from the trademark owner of that clothing logo. Likewise, *Friends* avoided negative associations with brand names. In "The One with Joey's Porsche" (6.05), Chandler offers Phoebe's triplets a toy named Krog, a fictional action figure. It is actually a modified He-Man action figure from *Masters of the Universe*. The art department repainted the toy and added curly horns and accessories, such as a sonic blaster. The producers couldn't get permission to use a brand-name action figure because of the episode's negative portrayal of the children's toy as being unsafe.

In sum, displaying trademarked logos is allowed, especially in creative works such as films or TV shows. It is protected as fair use. Nevertheless, studios, production companies and networks often err on the side of extreme caution. Fundamentally, it's a balancing act. Executives must weigh the fair use doctrine which offers free advertising versus requiring companies to pay for their product placement.

In the early years of *Friends*, the producers could not afford licensing fees for brand-name products but it still wanted to project an image that the series was a real, legitimate show, so they instructed their art department to modify national brand packaging images to circumvent the trademark laws. The first incident occurred in "The One with the Thumb" (1.03) where Monica is eating from a tub of ice cream that is clearly Häagen-Dazs from the label design. Label-masking continued as a matter of course in *Friends* through the third season. In "The One with the Giant Poking Device" (3.08), a juice carton for Minute Maid is visible but the "d" was obscured. Ironically, by the fourth season *Friends* could afford to pay licensing fees, but now corporations were paying for product placements or donating their merchandise for use on the show as free publicity.

There is one noteworthy example. In "The One Where Chandler Can't Remember Which Sister" (3.11), Rachel is hired as an assistant to a fashion buyer at Bloomingdale's. Her nice office had to be dressed with accessories, so the producers hired Hollywood International Placements to provide merchandise and set dressing. The designer products included Echo scarves, costume jewelry from Carolee and Christian Lacroix, Alain Mikli eyewear, Michael Anthony fine jewelry, Bonjour belts, Mark Cross handbags, Movado watches, Fossil and Joe Boxer. Each fashion designer company paid a large sum to have their products displayed in her office.

Brand Integration

The first incident of brand integration occurred in the second season of *Friends*. Iranian fragrance designer Bijan Pakzad, inventor of Bijan cologne, paid seven figures to promote his product in "The One with the Breast Milk" (2.02). In the episode, Joey is a department store cologne spritzer hawking Bijan for Men in an epic battle against Todd, the Hombre Man.

Another instance of brand integration occurred in "The One with the List" (2.08) where Chandler flaunts his new laptop computer, a Compaq Contura 4/25cx with a color screen, 12 megabytes of RAM, 500-megabyte hard drive and a 28K modem. Believe it or not, it was very high end in 1995 when the installment first aired. Now, over 25 years later, mid-end laptops have over 1,000 times more RAM and disk space, and 2,000 to 20,000 faster data connections.

In anticipation for the London wedding, Toblerone was heavily promoted in a couple episodes of *Friends* at the end of season four. The most egregious incident occurred in "The One with the Free Porn" (4.17). Toblerone is a Swiss chocolate bar brand owned by the US confectionery company Mondelēz International, Inc., formerly Kraft Foods. It is produced in Bern, Switzerland, and well known for its distinctive shape (a series of joined triangular prisms). The producers were paid well for the advertising plug.

The *Friends* production company was paid to promote Boddingtons beer in "The One with All the Kissing" (5.02). At the time, Boddingtons Brewery was only a regional brewery in England, but following its brand integration in *Friends*, the brewery earned international recognition and beverage sales spiked. Its beer brands are now owned by the global brewer Anheuser-Busch InBev.

Season six was a banner year in the producers' efforts to shamelessly sell out the series for lucrative corporate side deals with Porsche, Ralph Lauren and Pottery Barn. In "The One with Joey's Porsche" (6.05), besides featuring the latest 996-generation Porsche 911 Carrera Cabriolet Convertible Metallic Sports Car, there was flagrant brand integration in dialogue, attire, and accessories (e.g., jacket, t-shirt, cap, fanny pack, pants and keychain), not to mention the German car manufacturer shelling out dough to have its brand name featured in an episode title. Porsche continued its sponsorship in other episodes but limited its reach to product placement, not brand integration.

Ralph Lauren was the most frequent source of brand integration for the *Friends* series. The UK-based clothing company, known for its classic Polo shirts, also designed outfits for the wedding ceremony of Priyanka Chopra and Nick Jonas. *Friends* helped boost sales and company recognition, and fashion designer Ralph Lauren had a cameo in one episode. The company's conspicuous promotion commenced in "The One with Ross's Teeth" (6.08) and continued through the final season of the show.

The most egregious act of brand integration occurred in "The One with the Apothecary Table" (6.11). Pottery Barn, a US-based home furnishing store, showcased products from the store, in what many describe as a 22-minute advertisement for the retail chain. In fact, the episode title was purposely named after one of the high-end retailer's furnishings. The not-so-subtle brand integration had the desired effect—viewers purchased the apothecary table in droves. *Entertainment Weekly* ranked this installment No. 1 on their Best Product Placements roundup for television shows. The brand's name is mentioned 18 times. Even the company logo is affixed to a store window.

The precise financial arrangement between Pottery Barn and Warner Bros. has never been disclosed, though WB executive Peter Roth claimed the deal was necessary to "offset the high cost of production." Pottery Barn donated pieces for the episode but denied paying for any promotion. Patrick Connolly of Williams Sonoma said it is "the gift that keeps on giving" because "the phones light up with catalog requests every time it airs in syndication."

The apothecary table was, in fact, a real item available in Pottery Barn stores at the time. Series set decorator Greg Grande went to the store and asked if he could use it for an episode. They gave him carte blanche to shop for anything he wanted. A fair amount of the small pieces in Phoebe's apartment, including the ornamental birdcage, partition wall and small tchotchkes (trinkets) were from Pottery Barn, as well as the larger items such as the Sahara desk (on wall by kitchen) and Parker console table (on back living room wall).

Crossover Marketing

Another creative promotional strategy implemented by the *Friends* production team was crossover marketing. It's a cheap but effective way to advertise a series through promotion within a different but highly successful show. It is basically free advertising to target tens of millions of viewers. Since fans like the show, and it is promoting another series, a sizable share of viewers will tune in the associated program. That is exactly what *Friends* did for the serial *Days of Our Lives*.

The *Friends* producers struck a deal with NBC to promote its struggling daytime soap opera *Days of Our Lives*. "Years ago when we were deciding that [Joey] would be on a soap, NBC came to us and said, 'Please, have it be *Days of Our Lives*,'" Marta Kauffman recalled. The showrunners were quite hesitant because *Friends* is set in New York and *DOOL* films in California. "We wanted it to be *One Life to Live* which does shoot in New York, but they said no, they really would like us to use *Days of Our Lives*."

NBC also liked the idea that *Days of Our Lives* starred John Aniston (as Victor Kiriakis), the father of *Friends* costar Jennifer Aniston. The familial link between the two shows was an added benefit. The promotional ploy worked. After Joey debuted on *Days of Our Lives*, the ratings dramatically improved for the real-life soap opera. *Friends*' crossover promotion elevated the serial from No. 6 to No. 2 in the ranking of top daytime television dramas and increased its viewership by half a million.

Emotional Serial

Sure, *Friends* was not entirely unique at the time it first aired. There were other sitcoms focusing on the travails of twentysomethings. And yes, *Friends* copied several conceptual constructs from *Seinfeld* such as three equally weighted interwoven storylines, no moral lessons, and no political or social causes to tout. The *Friends* creators even capitalized on the sexual tension of its main characters using a trick developed a dozen years prior in *Cheers* with Sam and Diane.

But one unique, distinguishing characteristic of *Friends* was its use of sentiment and comedy in a soap opera format. Other sitcoms had emotional elements, in fact they were filled with episodes mixing sentiment and comedy, but they often hinged on social causes, personal tragedies or moral lessons to be learned. *Friends* focused on the soap opera of life; the smaller things in our existence that are important and permeate the very being of everyone at one point or another. After a few episodes, NBC President Warren Littlefield noticed the emotional resonance of the scripts. "I thought, this is a Shakespearean soap opera," he said. "It's a drama that's really, really funny, and with a complex architecture."

It was unlike any other sitcom on TV. Critics repeatedly compared it to *Seinfeld*, but in this respect, *Friends* was unparalleled. "*Seinfeld* lived to be funny but not to feel," Littlefield noted. David Crane had the same belief: "That's why we were always surprised when people compared us to *Seinfeld*." It was the emotional element that brought people back, time and time again. "In between all the jokes, there was this emotional thread," Matt LeBlanc said. He then added, "You cared about these people. You were invested in these relationships. You can't get enough of these people. ... That emotional through-line threaded the whole season." The soap opera format enthralled audiences and kept them interested. "It was so surprising to us how invested the audience was in these characters, how desperately they wanted them to be happy, how putting them together made some kind of weird sense," said Marta Kauffman.

Cheers was known to have emotional moments but it paled in comparison to *Friends*. Kauffman and Crane were masterful in their intricate infusion of sentimentality and humor on a repeated basis. In that respect, *Friends* was incomparable. No sitcom comes close to that level of emotional resonance.

Recurring Regulars

The journey to stardom was a long and winding path for some of the recurring actors who appeared on *Friends*. For others it was a matter of network politics. And still others it was luck, chance or happenstance. The most colorful path to fame involved James Michael Tyler, though most fans know him as Gunther. In his slow climb to pop culture icon status, the once down-and-out actor became a multimillionaire over the course of a decade.

James Michael Tyler (Gunther)

Other than the six series costars, James Michael Tyler (Gunther) appeared in the most installments. He portrayed Gunther in nearly every Central Perk scene, which totals over 200 episodes, but his visage appears in only 178, although a vast majority are simply his physical presence as a background extra, not actually delivering dialogue. The day before shooting the second episode of *Friends*, the producers realized they needed someone who could convincingly operate the coffee shop machinery and play the bit part of a barista. Assistant director Joel Wang knew that Tyler worked as a barista and could convincingly operate the espresso machine so he called the actor and said, "Hey, do you want to come on and be in the background in a coffee shop?"

When *Friends* debuted in 1994, Tyler already had four years' experience working as a professional barista at Bourgeois Pig, a Hollywood coffee shop. Since his role on *Friends* as the Central Perk manager was relatively inconsequential, basically a glorified extra, the struggling actor debated whether to accept the job because his barista job paid more. His girlfriend, Barbara Chadsey, convinced him to work both jobs, so he kept his "real" job for another four years until he became a recurring regular on the series which required his presence on set all weeklong.

For the first 32 episodes, Tyler did not have a character name or speaking part. He was merely referred to as "Coffee Guy" on the show's call sheet. Everything changed one day when Marta Kauffman asked if he had acting experience. Tyler recalled the conversation: "I said, 'Yeah, I have a Master of Fine Arts in acting, actually. I've done a lot of stage, theater stuff, and things like that.' And she said, 'That's really good to know,' and then walked away. The next week, I came in and she said, 'Your name is Gunther.' I said, 'Excuse me? What?' And she said, 'Your name is Gunther now.' I still didn't get it. Then, she said, 'Oh, that's your character name. And you get to say, 'Yeah' today. So, we're giving you a line.'" That one line changed his life. Gunther quickly became an integral part of the series.

After one and a half seasons, the showrunners eventually recognized the talent in Tyler. "James was a genuinely kind, sweet man," they noted, and it caught their attention. "When he started as an extra on *Friends*, his unique spirit caught our eye and we knew we had to make him a character. He made Gunther's unrequited love incredibly relatable." Thereafter, Tyler helped mold the character to what we know today. His ever presence in Central Perk and quirky charm have some fans calling him the seventh friend.

Despite being a bit player, Tyler transformed his fictional character (Gunther) into a perennial fan favorite. His trademark bleached white hair and puppy dog crush on Rachel captivated audiences, and he turned what could have been a forgettable role into a rather legendary part. When asked about his unexpected success, Tyler joked, "I honestly always thought my masters in fine arts would get me further in the acting world than knowing how to work an espresso machine."

Born a natural brunet, Tyler was not required to dye his hair white for the job. As he proclaimed, it was just "a happy coincidence." His friend, an aspiring hairdresser, wanted to practice bleaching hair so Tyler volunteered, and the resulting white locks became his signature look. Naturally, the next morning he received a call to shoot the first season of

Friends. Since he was originally hired as a background extra, it didn't seem like a big deal, but once he was promoted to barista, which was a visible role, he had to maintain the look. Tyler acknowledged the upkeep was brutal. He had to bleach his locks every week for 10 years. The set hairstylist bleached it at first but Tyler eventually decided to do it himself, performing the ritual the night before filming each episode. He stopped dyeing his hair after taping the series finale.

The quintessential hairstyle even made it into an episode script. In "The Last One, Part 1" (10.17), Rachel remarked "When I'm in a cafe, having coffee, or I see a man with hair brighter than the sun, I'll think of you." Tyler bantered about his trademark cut, "I wanted to be The Gunther. You know, they had The Rachel. I always wondered why The Gunther never took off."

Despite his rise to fame, James Michael Tyler still fraternized behind the scenes with the other extras. He was a cat lover, and actually adopted a feline he found on the set of *Friends.* He named it Cubby and kept it for years.

After *Friends,* Tyler did not have much luck making it as a bona fide actor in Hollywood. He blamed typecasting. He decided to take a break from acting to focus on writing scripts and producing music. In 2006, he was part of a failed TV pilot called "Nobody's Watching" in which two TV megafans try to start their own sitcom with Warner Bros. In the unaired cameo role, he played himself, discovered by the would-be series' stars on a replica set of Central Perk on the studio lot.

In 2012, he appeared as himself in Matt LeBlanc's series *Episodes,* where he poked fun at the fact that he was the only former *Friends* star that LeBlanc could get to appear on his faux show. In the scene Tyler quipped, "You know, you're like the only one I don't keep in touch with … I still see Schwimmer, and Courteney and I text all the time. … I housesit for Jennifer when she's in New York." But in reality, Tyler's had almost no contact with the cast since the show ended.

Tyler entered the webseries industry in 2010 with a show called *Keeping Up with the Downs* and three years later appeared in *Modern Music.* In 2020, he worked on two short films, *The Gesture and the Word* and the independent horror film *Processing.* He also hosted a webseries of author interviews for Expanded Books. Ironically, Tyler auditioned for a lot of day-player roles where the casting call indicated, "we're looking for a Gunther from *Friends* type character," but he honestly admitted, "I would never get them."

Tyler was often recruited by Warner Bros. studio to help promote *Friends.* He appeared as Gunther as a cohost voice-over in the *Friends* trivia game for PS2, PC and Xbox, and the DVD game *Friends*: Scene It? Tyler was part of the grand openings of Central Perk replica pop-ups in London and New York, and the inaugural UK FriendsFest in 2015. Though often excluded from *Friends* reunion gatherings, he did appear remotely in *Friends: The Reunion* in May 2021.

James Michael Tyler was born in Greenwood, Mississippi, on May 28, 1962, and named after his uncle. He was the youngest of five children. At 10 years of age, he lost his father, and the following year his mother died. After spending a year living with relatives, he moved to Anderson, South Carolina, to be with his sister. After graduating high school in 1980, Tyler studied at Anderson College, where he earned a two-year associate degree, and then transferred to Clemson University, where his love of acting blossomed as a member of the student theater group The Clemson Players. Despite graduating in 1984 with a Bachelor of Science in geology, Tyler decided to pursue acting so he enrolled in a graduate program for theatre and film at the University of Georgia where he was granted a Master of Fine Arts in performance in 1987. He found the Atlanta acting scene rather limited so the following year he moved to Los Angeles looking for better opportunities. There, he immediately found work as a production assistant on the war-drama feature *Fat Man and Little Boy* (1989). He also worked in the industry as an assistant film editor but paid the bills working as a barista at Bourgeois Pig, a Hollywood Hills coffee shop that first opened in 1989.

The actor had his share of personal issues. Tyler married Barbara Chadsey, a personal trainer, in 1995, they separated in 2003 and divorced in 2014. Shortly thereafter he started dating Jennifer Carno, a script coordinator and production assistant, who admits that she had no idea he was famous when they initially met. Their first public appearance together was FriendsFest in 2015 and they married April 8, 2017.

In September 2018, Tyler was diagnosed with prostate cancer. The cancer mutated and he suffered fractures in his bones, and tumors up and down his spine. It advanced to stage 4 and led to paraplegia (paralysis of the lower body). In June 2021, he made his condition public. "My goal this past year was to see my 59th birthday. I did that," he said. "My goal now is to help save at least one life." His public pronouncement was to encourage early detection, which he failed to do. With the dire diagnosis, Tyler acknowledged his mortality, having stated, "Eventually, you know, it's gonna probably get me." He succumbed to the disease on October 24, 2021.

Marcel

Ross' pet capuchin was played by two females, Katie and Monkey. The duo later starred in films and TV shows such as *Bruce Almighty* (2003) and *30 Rock*, and had a modeling gig with Kendall Jenner. Katie also became the mascot for the Los Angeles Angels team and costarred with Barry Keoghan in the short-lived FX series on Hulu *Y: The Last Man* (2021).

Early in the first season of *Friends*, writers Adam Chase and Ira Ungerleider suggested a storyline where Ross adopts a pet so he would appear more saucy and Mediterranean. Ideas were batted around and the writers settled on two options: monkey or iguana. Their colleague, writer Jeff Strauss, had been a biology major in college and considered becoming a veterinarian. He felt strongly that Ross getting a pet monkey would be a major mistake. Strauss launched into a diatribe about a monkey being a terrible pet. They were not cute little people that could be deployed at will to inject charm into a storyline. Monkeys spent most of their time masturbating, enjoyed throwing their feces to express dissatisfaction, and what appeared to be a smile was actually a hostile glare. The showrunners ignored his objection.

David Schwimmer did not enjoy working with the monkeys. "The trainers won't let me bond with it. They're really, really possessive," he claimed. "It's like, 'Land on your marks, do your job, don't touch or bond with the monkey.' It's a bummer." But if he had to choose between them, Monkey would win because she was much calmer than Katie, which made filming easier. In 1995, he remarked: "I hate the monkey. I wish it were dead," and then in 2021 reiterated his discontent by stating: "It was time for Marcel to f*ck off!"

One of Marcel's trainers, Mike Morris, thought it was "despicable" for Schwimmer to be speaking ill of Marcel when one of the capuchins, Monkey, had passed away of cancer in 2020. "Schwimmer was fine with the monkeys for the first couple of episodes and happy to be there," Morris said. "But people would laugh at the monkey and I think he got jealous because it wasn't him getting the laughs. He seemed to get a little bitter about them being there after that. And of course the monkeys didn't like working with him after he turned on them." He added: "My colleague who also worked on the show says that people would laugh at the monkey and throw Schwimmer off. He's not the kind of actor who can improvise."

Another trainer, Nerissa Pulitzer, said of her charge: "If Marcel were human, she'd be Meryl Streep." Simian actors are mercurial, prone to unpredictable rages, and extremely untrustworthy as a performers. In fact, Courteney Cox stated that the monkeys scared her. "Marcel was just a pain in the ass. It's hard to love an animal when it's such an idiot," said costumer Debra McGuire. "He was an obnoxious monkey, just not very likable." Some of the other cast members, on the other hand, did not have problems with Marcel—Jennifer Aniston said that she "loved" the monkey and Matt LeBlanc indicated that he "got along great with it." Marcel was written out of the show after eight appearances. The writers even added a comedy bit several years later where Ross commented, "Remember when I had a monkey? What was I thinking?"

Paul Rudd (Mike)

Paul Rudd debuted in "The One with the Pediatrician" (9.03). Casting director Leslie Litt recalled the difficult process finding the right actor to portray Mike Hannigan. "We had a casting session for that role but no one was quite it. Paul agreed to do a one-time meet and read with Lisa [Kudrow]. All I wrote on my notes was 'dreamy.'" He was promptly cast as Phoebe's new love interest. Rudd was originally signed for two episodes but his chemistry with Lisa Kudrow was undeniable so the writers kept coming up with more ideas for his character. Rudd was a very likable actor and meshed well with the other costars, which is why many fans view him to be the seventh friend. He appeared in 17 episodes.

Although Rudd had a recurring role on *Friends* for nearly two years, he thought his first day on set was going to be his last. Jennifer Aniston had broken her toe and was using a Segway for mobility. The cast was marveling at her scooter, and Matt LeBlanc even gave it a try. Rudd's test drive was not so smooth. "I spun around and rolled it right over Jennifer's foot!" he said. "The producers' look of panic was as if to say, 'Is it too late to fire him? Has his character been established yet?' I felt awful. Such an inauspicious start." Fortunately, he didn't re-break her toe or cause any other injury, though Aniston was not amused.

For the longest time, the creators weren't sure which love interest to choose for Phoebe; it was a toss-up between Mike and David (Hank Azaria). Ultimately, they settled on Mike because his character felt more real. He was a good fit for Phoebe. Although he depicted a memorable character, Rudd never felt like he stood out on the show. "In something like *Friends*, the show was about them. I was only in it for just a blip. I felt, 'I'm like a prop on this show. It's not about Mike Hannigan.' But there's a very interesting feeling to be a part of something that has that kind of profound impact on pop culture."

In recent years, Rudd is most recognized as the titular character (Scott Lang) from the *Ant-Man* movies. After earning a Bachelor of Arts in theater from the University of Kansas, he studied at the American Academy of Dramatic Arts, with fellow actor Matthew Lillard, while also working as a deejay at bar mitzvahs. After graduation, he had a variety of odd jobs, such as glazing hams at the Holiday Ham Company in Overland Park, Kansas. In November 2021, he was chosen as *People* magazine's Sexiest Man Alive.

Maggie Wheeler (Janice)

Actor Maggie Wheeler (née Jakobson) married sculptor Daniel Borden Wheeler in 1990. During her first decade in Hollywood she earned numerous parts, but her breakout role ended inauspiciously—she was axed from Ellen DeGeneres' sitcom *These Friends of Mine* (aka *Ellen*) following its first season in 1994. "I was one of the first of many people to get fired as they retooled that show," she stated. "And then the *Friends* episode came across my desk—in those days across my fax machine—and I looked at that part and I knew exactly what I wanted to do with it."

When she first auditioned for the role of Janice, the script made no mention of how to portray the character. "It just said, 'Fast-talking New Yorker,'" she recollected. "But then I just looked at the rhythm of the language, ... and she says: 'Here I got your socks. Mix and match. Moose and squirrel,' and I could just hear her; I heard her speak in my head. I thought, 'Okay, that's what I'm gonna do.'"

Janice premiered in "The One with the East German Laundry Detergent" (1.05). Her first words in the series, coincidentally, would later became her signature catchphrase ("Oh my God"). However, she had not yet perfected the trademark delivery and did not speak in her signature whiny, nasally voice. As the segment progressed, she went in and out of her delivery before committing to the voice we all know and expect. Wheeler claimed she didn't have sufficient time to mold the character with only one week of rehearsals.

But she did have enough time to properly formulate Janice's vexing laugh. "I was a little worried—because I hadn't been on the set yet, and I wanted to be able to do a good job—so I thought, okay, this character needs to be able to laugh," Wheeler explained. "He's [actor Matthew Perry's] probably going to crack me up and I need to be able to cover, so I created the laugh." But it was more by accident than preconceived. As she further expounded, "the laugh happened organically in the first rehearsal."

In real life, Wheeler doesn't sound anything like Janice. Her nasally whine is based on voices she heard growing up in the Big Apple, where her father worked on the New York Stock Exchange and her mother, an architecture and design writer, served as a Museum of Modern Art trustee. Irrespective of those influences, her voice was derived primarily from Fran Drescher, who played a similar-sounding character in the title role of the sitcom *The Nanny* (1993-99).

Maggie Wheeler was only supposed to appear in one episode but her intoxicating laugh and vexing voice resonated with audiences. She became such a fan favorite that the show's producers continued inviting her back to boost ratings but always kept her appearances secret. They wanted her unexpected entrance to electrify the crowd so they could capture the uproarious applause on tape. "It was sort of a rock star moment," she fondly recalls. "They would keep me hidden—I could barely come down to get a donut. I had to stay in my dressing room until the last moment and then they'd secretly move me from behind the set to the right spot and they'd keep a black screen so the audience couldn't see me until I made my first entrance. I will never have anything like that again. It was incredible." She appeared in 19 episodes.

Tom Selleck (Richard)

The role of Dr. Richard Burke was not specifically written for Tom Selleck. After the writers plotted a story arc involving an older love interest, who also happened to be a friend of the family, they needed to find a skilled actor "appealing enough that you believe the relationship." David Crane explained the process: "We asked around to see if there were any guest star–type actors who were interested and we heard that Tom was interested and we were thrilled. That's perfect. That's exactly what you want. He's sexy and smart, and you can believe, even though there's a significant age difference, she would be into him."

Despite being a seasoned actor, Selleck was required to do a screen test with Courteney Cox before he was offered the role. "And the minute we put them together, there was this wonderful chemistry," Crane exclaimed. Selleck was actually warned by colleagues to avoid doing the show because it would appear like he was "crawling back to television." But he decided to do it anyway. "I liked the show and I liked Courteney, because I did a screen test with her for [the 1992 flick] *Folks!*" He added, "It kind of scared me, so I took the job."

The producers never expected the Monica–Richard coupling to be a serious relationship. It just happened. "With Courteney and Tom Selleck, if I'm not mistaken, there was no sense that was going to become a relationship with a capital 'R,'" writer Scott Silveri stated. "And then they had such good chemistry, the producers and the writers at the time decided to explore it a little more."

Selleck originally signed a three-episode commitment but during a table read he was asked to do more. Selleck recounted, "They said, 'Hey can you do a few more?' So then I did more. And I quickly realized, 'Wow, this is a big deal.'" He was so popular that every time he appeared onstage, his first cued entrance received a standing ovation from the audience. It's a nice ego boost, but terrible for actor timing and postproduction editing. The footage was always unusable so the crew had to reshoot the scene after the audience departed.

In Selleck's final guest starring role on the sitcom, "The One with the Proposal" (6.24, 6.25), he had final say on the script. Before the producers inked one line of dialogue, they contacted him to make sure he was available and then pitched the plot to get his approval. "Tom has very strong opinions about the material so we wanted to make sure that he was happy with what we were doing before we went into it," David Crane admitted. "With our finales, we try to clear it with everybody before we get into it. When it's a major story point, all six of them want to know where are we going, and what are we doing, and where is it leading and what do I do in it."

For his role as Dr. Richard Burke, Tom Selleck was nominated for a Primetime Emmy Award for Outstanding Guest Actor in a Comedy Series. He appeared in 10 episodes.

Sheldon Twins (Emma)

The first twins to portray Emma were Elizabeth and Genevieve Davidson in season nine. The pair were replaced by Alexandra and Athina Conley, beginning with "The One Where Rachel Goes Back to Work" (9.11). Then starting with "The One in Barbados, Part 1" (9.23), Emma was played by twins Noelle and Cali Sheldon.

The female costars loved filming scenes with the Sheldon twins because they could play with the babies backstage during breaks. Gretchen Carpenter, mother to the twins, stated that the feeling was mutual. "Everyone was really, really nice to Noelle and Cali, and treated them like little princesses on the set," she declared. "[*Friends*] filmed before a live audience, and Cali and Noelle would come out, and they would be waving and engaging with the live audience. It was a lot of fun."

The Sheldon twins were featured in "The One with the Cake" (10.04), where Chandler and Monica videotape a segment bashing Emma for sleeping because it caused them to miss their romantic vacation. Chandler says, "Hi, Emma. It's the year 2020. Are you still enjoying your nap?" In honor of Emma's 18th birthday in 2020, Noelle Sheldon (Emma) posted a message on Instagram poking fun at this episodic video message: "Just woke up from the best nap of all time, happy 2020!!"

The twins' final appearance was in "The One Where Estelle Dies" (10.15). Since 2004, the twins have performed in college films, local stage work, and the 2007 drama pilot, *Life*. With nearly a dozen acting credits, their prime role was the 2019 thriller *Us*, which earned more than 10 times its original $20 million budget.

Cole Sprouse (Ben)

Over the course of the series, Ben Geller was played by four different actors: Michael Gunderson (season two), twins Thomas and John Christopher Allen (seasons three through five), and Cole Sprouse (seasons six through eight). Sprouse's twin brother, Dylan, was not part of the series. The Sprouse twins began acting when they were 8 months old.

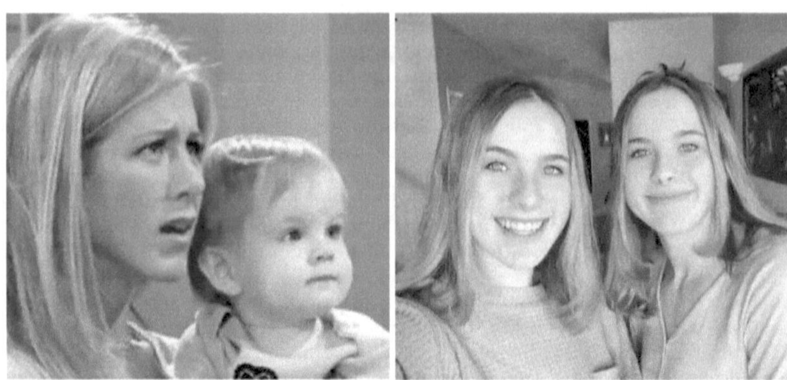

Cali and Noelle Sheldon as Emma in 2003 and taking a selfie in 2021 (age 18)

"The One That Could Have Been, Part 1" (6.15) marked the series debut of Cole Mitchell Sprouse as Ross' son, Ben. Sprouse was cast after a solid performance in *Big Daddy* (1999) starring Adam Sandler. Since the character Ben was getting older in the show, the creators needed "a genuine actor who could handle the comedy and go in front of an audience" since it is often extraordinarily difficult for kids to perform properly and not be distracted by the circus atmosphere of a live studio performance.

The precocious child actor often flaunted his memorization skills by correcting the cast during filming. In "The One with the Holiday Armadillo" (7.10), David Schwimmer forgot his lines so the youthful actor reminded his scene partner what to say next, and then quipped, "Man, I know all of his lines." Schwimmer took it in stride and even offered a high-five to the future star. Similarly, in "The One with the Truth About London" (7.16), Sprouse did the same thing, but this time to Jennifer Aniston. She was not amused especially after he ended the corrective dialogue with a dismissive hand-wave.

Ironically, Sprouse often forgot his lines while filming scenes with Aniston, but he had a very good excuse—puppy love. "I'm pretty sure I fell in love with Jennifer Aniston, which the whole world had at that point," he honestly admitted. "I was infatuated. I was speechless. I'd get all bubbly and forget my lines and completely blank. It was so difficult." His crush was rather noticeable, too. "I was teased a little bit by the crew, because they saw it, and I would just forget [my lines] and be looking at her."

Sprouse's favorite *Friends* episode is "The One with the Holiday Armadillo" (7.10). "I was infatuated with the costumes, and the practical effects that they had," he explained. "That was probably my most memorable thing to shoot." Surprisingly, his last appearance was in "The One Where Joey Dates Rachel" (8.12), over two years prior to the series finale.

Triplets

The baby triplets were played by the Cimoch quadruplets (three boys, one girl): Justin, Paul, Cole and Alexandria). Since Phoebe gave birth to two girls and a boy, at least one of the boy quadruplets always had to play a girl. Alexandria Cimoch was featured in "The One with Joey's Porsche" (6.05), as the baby being fed by Chandler. She hasn't given up acting entirely having appeared in a production of the musical *Hair.* In 2021, Cimoch graduated from the University of Wisconsin–La Crosse with a Bachelor of Arts in communication and media studies and musical theater, and works as a marketing and public relations intern for Skylight Music Theatre in Milwaukee. Interestingly, her parents had twin girls after the quadruplets.

The toddler triplets were portrayed by Sierra Marcoux (Chandler), Dante Pastula (Frank Jr. Jr.), and Allisyn Ashley Arm (Leslie). The first two had only a couple acting credits, and nothing since 2007. The latter (aka Allisyn Snyder) is by far the most successful actor. She starred opposite Demi Lovato in *Sonny with a Chance* and also joined the series spinoff *So Random!* Currently, she stars in the webseries *Astrid Clover* (which she created) and costars in *A.P. Bio.*

Elle Fanning (*Super 8, Maleficent*) auditioned to portray one of the triplets, but took the rejection hard. "I auditioned for it but I didn't get it and I was like, 'I'm boycotting the show, I'm never watching this again,'" she emphatically stated. A few months later her older sister Dakota was cast for the show but that did not sway Elle to change her position: "Then my sister was on it, and I refused to watch the episode. I was like, 'I am not watching this!'"

Then and now: Cole Sprouse (Ben) (left) and Dakota Fanning (Mackenzie) (right)

Elliott Gould (Jack Geller)

Besides James Michael Tyler (Gunther) and the six costars, only two actors physically appeared in all 10 seasons of the show: Elliott Gould and Christina Pickles, who portrayed Jack and Judy Geller. (Maggie Wheeler played Janice in all 10 seasons but one year she had an uncredited voice role.) Ironically, Gould was instructed by his agent to reject the *Friends* role because it didn't pay enough money. He accepted the part anyway because he wanted to work with director James Burrows.

Although Gould was a beloved actor on set, there was one incident that had him in hot water. In "The One with Ross's Wedding, Part 2" (4.24), the series' producers took extreme measures to ensure the ending would remain a secret. They briefed the entire cast not to give anything away, and even evacuated the studio audience before filming the last scene. However, after returning from London, Gould appeared on *The Rosie O'Donnell Show* and revealed Ross' bride. The executive producers were furious. Lisa Kudrow tried to do damage control by falsely claiming they had filmed three alternate endings, hoping to cast doubt on Gould's revelation.

At one time, Kevin Bright pitched the idea of killing off the Jack Geller character and having Ross honor his father's request for a burial at sea. At the time, Bright was going through a family crisis with his father (Jackie) who was in declining health and in need of caretaking from his son. "I was going through in my life at the time of the role-reversal that you go through with parents—the realization that you're the baby and they take care of you and then you rebirth and you start taking care of them, and the realization your parents aren't immortal," he solemnly confided. His story pitch was resoundingly rejected. "Nobody wanted to kill off Elliott Gould," he added.

Throughout the series, Elliott Gould (Jack Geller) and Christina Pickles (Judy Geller) felt like parent figures to the six costars. And the pair were amazed how often they would get recognized by old and new fans. In fact, many preteens would approach the TV parents quoting lines from the show. Elliott Gould's favorite episode is "The One Where Ross Got High" (6.09).

Guest Actors

The sheer number of famous guest stars who appeared in *Friends* is mind-blowing, and covers the gamut. There were full-fledged movie stars (e.g., Gary Oldman, Susan Sarandon, Bruce Willis, Brad Pitt, Julia Roberts, Sean Penn), excellent silver screen performers (e.g., David Arquette, Charlie Sheen, Dakota Fanning, Winona Ryder), and bona fide television stars (e.g., Christina Applegate, Tom Selleck, Helen Hunt, Jason Alexander).

Other guest stars included soon-to-be-famous actors (such as Hank Azaria, Anna Faris, Ben Stiller, George Clooney and Kristin Davis), well-liked musicians (Chrissie Hynde and Chris Isaak), famous models (Elle Macpherson and Jill Goodacre), businessmen (Richard Branson and Ralph Lauren), British stars (Jennifer Saunders, Olivia Williams and June Whitfield), and even royalty (Sarah Ferguson).

When *Friends* debuted, it did not have a large budget to sign big-name stars, which was fine because the creators were content with their ensemble. However, halfway through the first season the network began pressuring them to track down a celebrity to feature during February sweeps week. "Of course, you always get some pressure from the network and the studio to get some name guest stars on your show to try to create events, and help during sweeps periods and ratings, and holidays and such," Kevin Bright explained. "[The goal is] getting an established great actor to enhance a good role in your show and to turn it into something special."

Movie Stars

When *Friends* debuted in 1994, movie stars made a point of never appearing on the small screen outside of talk shows or *Saturday Night Live*. "We have a hard time getting guest stars. We're not sure why ... but [it's] difficult for us," Marta Kauffman recalled. But the early success of *Friends*, a blockbuster extravaganza following the Super Bowl, and exorbitant guest star salaries created the perfect storm to change television history. "We were aware that getting some of the names we got was special and unique at the time," Marta Kauffman stated. "TV was looked down upon, so it felt like a real coup." Thereafter, other shows continued the trend. "You'd see shows like *Will & Grace* and you'd go, 'Oh my God, there's Cher!' It was just this cavalcade of stars," David Crane noted. "But when we were first starting out it was pretty shocking."

According to Crane, the creators never actively pursued A-list cameos even though later seasons featured superstars like Brad Pitt, Winona Ryder and Sean Penn. "We would just write parts, and then casting people would come back and say, 'So-and-so really wants to do the show,' and we'd be amazed. It was never like, 'We have to get so-and-so for this!' If anything, we felt like 'We have this incredibly famous person guest starring on the show. Are we giving them enough to do?' Our heart was always with the six principals, and that's who always got the best of the writing."

Signing a guest star also required a lot of time and effort. "When it comes to guest stars it generally has to do with how big the part is and how juicy a part is," Crane explained. "If it's just gonna be the nice guy who Phoebe's dating and she gets to be funny around him but his part is not that interesting, then you don't want to go after a name actor because they'll be very, very frustrated." The role has to have enough substance. "It can't just be a few lines here and there. It has to be part of a main story," Kevin Bright added. "It has to be a part that gives them something to do on television that they normally wouldn't be able to do in a movie."

Brad Pitt (left) and Bruce Willis (right) had memorable guest-starring roles

Brad Pitt

At the time the episode aired, Brad Pitt was married to Jennifer Aniston. He frequently visited her at the studio during rehearsals before and after his guest role, but stayed out of sight on filming night to avoid being a distraction. During one of his visits, the producers asked him to appear for a special episode. He happily agreed because the cameo offered a platform to promote his latest film, *Spy Game*, in 2001.

Surprisingly, before he was approached for a role, Pitt was a longtime fan of the show. "It's a happy show," the actor said. "It comes on and it makes me happy. It's always been that way since its first incarnation, before I met my wife [Aniston]." While promoting the episode, NBC made no mention of him and blurred his face in television spots, teasing the public about a high-profile guest star. However, trade publications reported that Pitt would appear that season, and most media outlets correctly predicted he was the mystery guest star.

For his role as Rachel's high school nemesis, Will Colbert, Brad Pitt was nominated for a Primetime Emmy Award for Outstanding Guest Actor in a Comedy Series.

Bruce Willis

One night during production on the film *The Whole Nine Yards* (2000), Bruce Willis and Matthew Perry were partying when they made a bet: if the movie topped the box office on its opening weekend, Willis would appear on *Friends* and donate his salary to charity. And that is precisely what happened. Willis ultimately appeared in three episodes so he donated his paychecks to five different charities chosen by Perry: The American Foundation for AIDS Research, AIDS Project Los Angeles, the Elizabeth Glaser Pediatric AIDS Foundation, the Rape Treatment Center, and UCLA Unicamp (a summer camp for underprivileged children).

Although *People* magazine Star Spotlight 2000 reported that Willis agreed to a guest stint on *Friends* because he and Perry "thought it would be fun," he also told *Wired* in a videotaped interview that "I was on *Friends* because I lost a bet to Matthew Perry." The truth is a combination of both reports. The actors discussed a role on *Friends*, and Willis thought it would be fun, so that's why he made the bet.

Bruce Willis won a Primetime Emmy Award for Outstanding Guest Actor in a Comedy Series for his three-episode performance.

Gary Oldman

Matt LeBlanc helped secure Gary Oldman to guest star in the double-length episode "The One with Chandler and Monica's Wedding" (7.23, 7.24). They worked together on the film *Lost in Space* (1998) and discussed having Oldman appear on the hit sitcom. When he finally agreed, the executive producers wasted no time crafting a memorable role for him but waited until the season seven finale to cast him because they wanted a big-name star as a promotional gimmick to boost ratings.

Even though Gary Oldman appears in both installments, all his scenes were filmed in one week because he had other filming commitments. Oldman's early stage departure was actually beneficial for filming because the soundstage could not hold all the sets. Once his scenes were shot, the movie set was torn down to make room for the wedding sets. On the downside, the director had to make sure he had every shot he needed because there would be no pickups after filming wrapped. Oldman's performance was then edited to make it appear as if he was present for both weeks of production.

Prior to *Friends*, Oldman had never appeared in a TV sitcom so he was rather offended when the writers talked to him and offered notes to improve his performance. "He was very confused by that and wondered why we were being so disrespectful of the director," Marta

Kauffman recalled. This exemplifies the difference between television and feature films. It is commonplace to give notes in small-screen productions but anathema on the silver screen sets.

Gary Oldman received a Primetime Emmy Award nomination for Outstanding Guest Actor in a Comedy Series for his portrayal of Richard Crosby.

Julia Roberts

Prior to agreeing to appear on *Friends*, Julia Roberts asked Matthew Perry to write her a paper on quantum physics. He obliged. He went to the library, researched the topic, and faxed it to her the next day. The two obviously knew each other in the past and this was more a flirtatious game—Perry was hitting on her and she was playing coy. They exchanged numerous private letters via fax. "There was a lot of flirting over faxing. She was giving him these questionnaires like, 'Why should I go out with you?' And everyone in the writers room helped him explain to her why," writer Alexa Junge discretely detailed. "He could do pretty well without us, but there was no question we were on Team Matthew and trying to make it happen for him."

The actors began dating during production week. Writer Jeff Astrof was a little offended by the budding romance. "I remember standing with her on the sidelines. She kept saying, 'Chandler's so funny!' And I'm like, 'I wrote every one of those lines!'" he exclaimed. "I felt like Cyrano [de Bergerac]," he added. "Like, 'Chandler is going to date Julia Roberts and I'm going to go home to my horrible girlfriend.' That's my memory of that episode."

Julia Roberts filmed her scenes from January 6-8, 1996. Members of the *Friends* crew and studio audience commented on the authentic intensity of their onscreen kisses. After filming wrapped, the pair continued their romance offscreen and were seen on a number of dates in the first half of 1996. Their romance lasted about six months.

Danny DeVito

The original script called for a stripper that was "the oldest performer on the planet or the world's most unlikely stripper," basically, someone that nobody would want at their bachelorette party. Danny DeVito was the first person approached for the role of an old, washed-up stripper. The 4'9 actor had no problem with all the jokes being made at his expense. When he first entered the apartment, the audience went crazy. They loved it. His wife (Rhea Perlman) was present for the taping and she was howling, and their son Jacob, who was friends with Marta Kauffman's daughter Hannah, was laughing hysterically.

DeVito came up with the dance performance himself, which was then polished by Robin Antin, founder of the modern burlesque troupe The Pussycat Dolls. She has also worked with Paris Hilton, Anastacia, Pink, The Offspring and No Doubt. Antin worked with DeVito for four days during rehearsal. According to director Kevin Bright, the editing room made DeVito a better dancer. He had issues tearing off his clothes because the Velcro wouldn't rip, and also getting the sleeve between his legs. Although the audience loved the bloopers, the mishaps delayed filming.

Danny DeVito was nominated for an Emmy Award for Outstanding Guest Actor in a Comedy Series for his performance in this episode.

Kathleen Turner

When formulating the fictional Charles Bing character, the creators initially considered introducing him as the best female impersonator ever, by casting a woman to play the part. Their ideal actress was supposed to capture the essence of female performer icons like Liza Minnelli, but none of the actresses felt right portraying a man who was playing a woman. "Then the focus shifted to finding really good actresses who might be great in the part, and that's when we ended up with Kathleen Turner," said David Crane.

The idea of casting Turner just popped into their heads, and she was perfect. Turner was cast for the role due to her deep, gritty voice and large frame which authenticates her portrayal of a transvestite. According to Turner, she was in San Francisco to appear in a one-woman show based on actress Tallulah Bankhead when David Crane came backstage and stated, "You have to play Chandler's dad," she recalled. After he made the pitch, she thought to herself: "A woman playing a man playing a woman. I haven't done that. So I said yes." Curiously, NBC received more complaints about her portrayal of a transvestite than it did for airing a lesbian wedding.

Turner appeared in a three-installment arc, but refused to reprise the role due to a bad experience on set. While younger guest stars quickly bonded with the cast, Turner slammed the sextet for being unwelcoming: "I'll be quite honest ... I didn't feel very welcomed by the cast," she proclaimed. "I remember I was wearing this difficult sequined gown, and my high heels were absolutely killing me. I found it odd that none of the actors thought to offer me a seat. Finally, it was one of the older crew members that said, 'Get Miss Turner a chair.'"

Robin Williams—Billy Crystal

The appearance of the comedic duo was unscripted. Robin Williams and Billy Crystal were working on the Warner Bros. lot and visited Stage 24 to watch the filming of a *Friends* episode. Executive producer Kevin Bright knew Crystal so he asked the comedians if they would be up for an impromptu cameo (they agreed). The writers quickly sketched an outline for the opening scene in which Tomas (Williams) discovers his wife is having an affair with Tim (Crystal).

Nearly all of the coffeehouse dialogue was ad-libbed. Although Williams and Crystal are polished comedians, their improvisation required four filming takes to get it in the can. The impromptu cold opening was not meant to be included in any particular episode so it was purposely withheld to correspond with the premiere of the comedians' feature film *Father's Day*, which opened on May 9, 1997, the day after this episode aired. It was the producers' way of thanking the duo for their cameo. Lisa Kudrow would later costar with Crystal in the 2001 film *Analyze This*.

Brooke Shields

In a rare move for a silver screen star, Brooke Shields agreed to appear before reading the script. She was enthusiastic about her appearance but the gig was not without drama. Tennis star Andre Agassi was dating Shields at the time and visited Stage 24 to watch her live studio performance. After witnessing an intimate scene where she kisses Joey, licks his hand, nibbles on his fingers, and giggles like an insane person, Agassi stormed the set and berated Shields, leaving her in tears. He drove to his home in Las Vegas and "systematically smashed and destroyed every single trophy he had won, including Wimbledon and the US Open," according to Shields. Despite his violent temper, she married him the following year but they divorced two years later.

Shields' performance impressed NBC executives so much that she was offered her own sitcom, *Suddenly Susan*, for the network's 1996 fall lineup. The series lasted four years (93 episodes).

Susan Sarandon

When casting the character Cecilia Monroe, the showrunners wanted an experienced actress with "credibility, comedy and drama." Someone who could give a great performance reminiscent of Susan Lucci in *All My Children*, and the first person that came to mind was Susan Sarandon. She agreed to the role because she, her husband (Tim Robbins), and all three of their children were big fans of the show. The entire family was on set to watch her performance live.

The primary reason for casting Susan Sarandon was to create an advertising gimmick for sweeps week. "This was sweeps so we knew we wanted some special things, and we very often will look at a role and say, 'Is this big enough to offer to someone big?'" recalled Marta Kauffman. "This one was, and once we knew it was [Susan Sarandon], we probably made it bigger."

Director Kevin Bright felt uncomfortable having Tim Robbins present during the taping of the episode. "It's intimidating to have her Academy Award–nominated husband director standing behind me while we were shooting the scenes. It was hard not to want to feel like every once in a while I should turn and say, 'Is that okay? Was that good for you?' Actually, I did it once." (The one incident in question was the soap opera segment where Dr. Drake Ramoray and Jessica Lockhart kiss.)

Freddie Prinze Jr.

After another famous movie star canceled at the last minute, Freddie Prinze Jr. received a call from his agent asking if he wanted to be on *Friends*. He jumped at the offer but was shocked when his agent stated, "Yeah, it shoots tomorrow." He had less than 24 hours to learn a musical instrument and memorize his lines. On set, he was "totally nervous" until David Schwimmer offered comforting words and said, "You'll have a ton of fun, don't worry about a thing." Prinze was given four hours of professional lessons on the recorder. He did not play the instrument during the live performance for the studio audience; he was simply doing the proper fingering technique. A professional musician was subsequently hired to record the music which was added in postproduction.

Billy Crystal (left) and Robin Williams (right) take time to pose with the *Friends* cast

Television Stars

Although numerous famous movie stars appeared in *Friends*, there were also a couple noteworthy television stars who brought their Hollywood swagger to the sitcom.

Jon Lovitz

The first legitimate celebrity to appear in *Friends* was Jon Lovitz. Midway through the first season, NBC wanted the *Friends* producers to feature a big-name star for February sweeps week. Fortunately, Lisa Kudrow and Courteney Cox both knew a comedian to fill the role. Kudrow knew Jon Lovitz from childhood—he is best friends with her older brother David—and Cox met him on the set of *Mr. Destiny* in 1988. Lovitz agreed to appear because he thought Kudrow's parents would get a kick out of seeing them on TV together.

Lovitz is best known as a *Saturday Night Live* regular from 1985 to 1990, though he did appear in 19 movies prior to his audition for *Friends*. The audience's exuberant reaction to his cued entrance illustrates his immense popularity at the time. Although he was hired to bring a little star power and sashay to the sitcom, he thought it was the other way around. "They treated it like I did them a favor, but by the time it came out, they were doing me a favor," he stated. The *Friends* appearance actually helped his career surge. He became more popular than ever. Lovitz reprised the role in "The One with the Blind Dates" (9.14).

Christina Applegate

Prior to her first appearance in "The One with Rachel's Other Sister" (9.08), Christina Applegate already knew most of the cast. She met Matthew Perry in 1988 while making the telefilm *Dance 'Til Dawn* (they played teenage lovers), knew Courteney Cox and Lisa Kudrow since the late 1980s, and worked with Matt LeBlanc in 1991 on two shows, *Married... with Children* and *Top of the Heap*. Although she didn't know Jennifer Aniston, she dated Brad Pitt in 1989, and he, of course, ended up marrying Aniston in 2000.

Applegate also knew the show's executive producers. They all worked with her when she starred in the TV series *Jesse* (1998-2000). Thus, when it came time to cast the part of Amy Green, the showrunners instantly thought of her. Marta Kauffman had nothing but praise for the guest star. "This was, as far as I'm concerned, the best bits of casting we ever did," she stated. Applegate had two *Friends* appearances and both earned her an Emmy Award nomination for Outstanding Guest Actress in a Comedy Series (she won once).

Jason Alexander

Marta Kauffman invited Jason Alexander to appear on the show because she is good friends with him and his wife Daena Title. Kauffman and Alexander first met in 1985 when he costarred in *Personals*, an off-Broadway play written by her and David Crane. The famed *Seinfeld* costar guest starred in "The One Where Rosita Dies" (7.13), although he was also referenced in another episode, "The One with the Sonogram at the End" (1.02), where the dental receptionist announces that Jason Greenspan is gagging. The actor's birth name is Jay Greenspan, and his stage name is Jason Alexander. The allusion is a portmanteau of the monikers.

Hugh Laurie (left) and Olivia Williams (right) guest starred in the London episode

British Actors

When the *Friends* crew traveled to London to film "The One with Ross's Wedding" (4.23, 4.24), the showrunners hired numerous British actors for supporting roles, such as June Whitfield as the housekeeper, Jennifer Saunders as Emily's stepmother (Andrea Waltham), Olivia Williams as a bridesmaid (Felicity), and Hugh Laurie as the impertinent passenger sitting next to Rachel on the plane.

At the time this episode aired, June Whitfield and Jennifer Saunders were costarring in the British series *Absolutely Fabulous* (1992-2012) where they played mother and daughter. Unfortunately, in the *Friends* installment they did not share screen time. Olivia Williams became famous the following year with her role in *The Sixth Sense* (1999). Hugh Laurie is best known as Dr. Gregory House in the medical drama *House* (2004-12). He recalled his agent calling and asking if he would be interested in a small part that required him to sit next to Jennifer Aniston. According to Laurie, it was the "easiest decision in the world."

Acting Anxiety

Although the *Friends* cast was acclimated to filming in front of a live studio audience, guest actors were rarely prepared for the multi-camera format and mass audience hysteria. Most movie stars were more accustomed to single-camera shooting without an audience. Inevitably, many seemingly composed, infallible actors were visibly nervous and scared to appear onstage. Debra McGuire noticed the impact on movie stars: "I have to say, these six actors are so brilliant in terms of everything—their timing and their physical humor. You really noticed it when guest stars came in—and guest stars could be really famous movie actors—and they would be blown away, and feel very intimidated."

The producers also witnessed the phenomenon. "Any guest star that's been on the show has commented that it's kind of an intimidating process," cocreator Kevin Bright explained. "It's mainly because we all know what we're doing so well, the actors are so on their game in terms of how quickly they can memorize a line and get off script, and how many changes come during the week, how many changes happen live during the course of the show." He also noted that when actors perform for feature films, there's a lot of waiting-around time to study lines and process script changes, but on *Friends*, they don't get that luxury. On the *Friends* set, actors were fed lines on the spot and had to make it work without thinking or rehearsing.

Charlie Sheen

In "The One with the Chicken Pox" (2.23), director Michael Lembeck wanted the studio audience to be surprised by the appearance of a real-life movie star, so he purposely staged a special guest star entrance. Unfortunately, Charlie Sheen missed his cue because he was so nervous. His legs were shaking uncontrollably so his brother, Emilio Estevez, had to be taken out of the audience to calm him down, rub his back, and encourage him to return to the stage.

Sarah Ferguson

Sarah Ferguson (Fergie, the Duchess of York) agreed to appear in a celebrity cameo for the two-part London installment. Most people would expect a person holding a position of royalty to be at ease with public appearances. But that was not the case with Fergie. The royal celebrity admitted that she was "extremely nervous" during the filming of her segment so Matt LeBlanc kept running lines with her to calm her down, and Matthew Perry stayed behind to offer support.

Sarah Ferguson (left) and Helen Baxendale in a wedding gown (right)

Reese Witherspoon

When it was time to cast Jill Green (Rachel's sister), the creators immediately pursued Witherspoon. "We were obviously big fans of her. Anybody who saw her in *Election* would just say, 'Oh my God, yes, get her!'" said David Crane. And Witherspoon wanted to appear because she was a huge *Friends* fan. "I would not stop watching *Friends*," she said. "They were my friends and there was no taking me away from my friends."

According to Witherspoon, the first scene was magical. "The most exciting [moment] was that I got to be in a scene where I'm in the apartment and Joey walks in and he goes 'Hey, how you doin'?'" she recalled. "This was like this iconic line and I was so excited! And to watch a famous character say his famous line, I mean, come on." Witherspoon felt like she "won the lottery" when she was cast as Rachel's sister.

Despite Witherspoon's long list of accomplishments, she was ill-prepared for working in front of a live studio audience which left her overwrought with stage fright. "I completely forgot something very crucial—that I had never been on television ever before in my entire life and I never really had been in front of a live audience before ever in my entire life. I panicked. I totally froze. It became immediately clear to me that I had no idea what I was doing and I was completely out of my league." Thankfully, Jennifer Aniston stepped in to quell Witherspoon's nerves and from there the pair became fast friends.

Witherspoon was supposed to have a six-episode story arc but quit after two. Numerous sources claim she didn't reprise her role because she and Aniston clashed on set. This is furthest from the truth. The pair became good friends from day one and remain close. In fact, they costar in the Apple series *The Morning Show*. She has stated, "Aniston is a very strong and welcome presence in my life." Witherspoon declined the *Friends* offer because she didn't enjoy live audience performances. She openly admitted to being "scared and too nervous."

Tom Selleck

Like many prominent guest stars on the show, Tom Selleck was no stranger to having butterflies in his stomach before performances. When reflecting upon his time on *Friends*, the legendary actor was a bit overwhelmed. "I hadn't done a three-camera live show since *Taxi*," he confessed. "It scared me a little. But that's the price you pay for opportunity."

Brad Pitt

Despite being a Hollywood A-list star, even Brad Pitt was fallible. While filming in front of a studio audience, he actually botched the opening line during his first cued entrance: "I flubbed my first line. We had to stop and start again," he admitted.

Paget Brewster (left) and Richard Branson (right) experienced anxiety on the set

Susan Sarandon

Matt LeBlanc was "very, very nervous to be working with Susan Sarandon," said Marta Kauffman. "He was terrified about it. He kept feeling like he would never live up to things, and then he ended up having to calm her down." She, too, was very nervous to appear on the show. Sarandon later stated, "Matt LeBlanc was so sweet and patient that we actually did work past the panic to a place where we enjoyed ourselves."

Paget Brewster

Prior to *Friends*, Brewster had only one acting credit so she was terrified her first day on the set. She was intimidated because the cast was so famous and it was the biggest show in the country. Brewster ended up hiding in her dressing room. "It was my first real acting job. I remember so little because I was so scared," she recalled.

Richard Branson

Understandably, UK businessman Richard Branson is not an actor so his nervousness was justifiable. On the day of his cameo, he came to the set immediately after an important meeting with the Prime Minister of Israel and didn't have time to learn his lines, which may explain his troubled performance. In fact, his poor performance became one of the biggest challenges of the London shoot because he could not credibly deliver his dialogue without assistance. Kevin Bright admitted that Branson "was very nervous that day" but "ended up coming out great in the editing room." Viewers can observe Branson's nervousness as he visibly rocks back and forth on his feet and constantly fidgets.

Disappointing Guest Stars

Despite all the accolades that some actors receive for their performances on the silver screen, there are times when they fail to replicate the rendition for a television guest star appearance or they are not as famous as the producers had expected. This happened a few times in *Friends*. Either the actors gave subpar performances or the audiences didn't know who they were.

Jonathan Silverman

Jonathan Silverman had feature film success with *Brighton Beach Memoirs* (1986) and *Weekend at Bernie's* (1989) so the *Friends* producers thought they had a legitimate movie star with ratings swagger. He appeared in "The One with the Birth" (1.23), but his first cued entrance was rather inauspicious—the audience was surprisingly muted. Unlike other big-name stars like Tom Selleck who was always greeted with a standing ovation, Silverman, on the other hand, was a dud, which shocked the *Friends* creative team. A few months later, he became more recognizable to the television viewing public when he starred in the sitcom *The Single Guy*, which aired from 1995 to 1997.

Charlie Sheen

When the *Friends* producers booked actor Charlie Sheen to appear in "The One with the Chicken Pox" (2.23), they thought they snagged a superstar due to his silver screen fame in *Wall Street* (1986), *Major League* (1989) and *Hot Shots!* (1991). Apparently too much time had lapsed because his special guest star reveal was met with little fanfare. Sheen was not yet a household name, and didn't become a television star until he replaced Michael J. Fox in *Spin City* in 2000. Of course, he is best remembered as Charlie Harper in *Two and a Half Men* from 2003 to 2011.

Possible guest stars (from left): Justin Timberlake, Owen Wilson, Justin Theroux and Sting

Chris Isaak

With Chris Isaak on board for the star-studded Super Bowl episode, i.e., "The One After the Superbowl" (2.12, 2.13), the producers thought they secured a musician with massive star power due to his hit single "Wicked Game" in 1991. Thus, for his first cued entrance, he was instructed to pause for a roar of applause from the audience. When he entered as instructed, the musician was met with dead silence—the audience had no idea who he was. The showrunners, to this day, consider Isaak to be the biggest casting "miscalculation."

Sean Penn

Two-time Oscar winner Sean Penn appeared in two episodes in season eight. He was offered the role after one of his many visits to the *Friends* set. The actor often observed the rehearsals with his two children, Dylan and Hopper, because they were fans of the show. Director Kevin Bright wasn't a fan of Sean Penn's cameo. Of all the guest stars, Bright said that Penn was the least successful because "there was a little deer in the headlight effect." Matthew Perry disagreed, claiming that the dramatic actor was "really funny," though Perry did admit to feeling intimidated while working with such a star.

Jennifer Grey

When Jennifer Grey made her first cued entrance, the audience was dead silent—no one recognized her. Although she achieved stardom with her breakout performance in *Dirty Dancing* (1987), she had been absent from the spotlight for eight years and underwent two rhinoplasty procedures before appearing in *Friends*. Surgery in 1989 corrected her hook nose but then she underwent a cosmetic procedure in 1995 which severely distorted her visage. "I went into the operating room a celebrity and came out anonymous," she stated. "It was the nose job from hell. I'll always be this once-famous actress nobody recognizes because of a nose job."

"The One with the Evil Orthodontist" (1.20) was Jennifer Grey's only guest starring role in a *Friends* episode before she was replaced by Jana Marie Hupp in "The One with Barry & Mindy's Wedding" (2.24). Although many sources have reported that Grey refused to return because of failed rhinoplasty or negative script references to her fictional *Friends* character (Mindy), the truth is that she had scheduling conflicts due to multiple movie commitments.

John Stamos

When the sitcom series *Full House* debuted in 1987, John Stamos became an instant heartthrob to millions of female fans. His popularity as a sex symbol was stratospheric and he will be forever remembered for the catchphrase "Have Mercy!" But less than a decade after the show left the airwaves, Stamos seemed like a ghost from Christmas past after no one in the *Friends* studio audience reacted to his first cued entrance in "The One with the Donor" (9.22). Critics claim the *Full House* star didn't resonate with the crowd because he lacked relevance due to the age disparity between him and the studio audience.

Guest Star Wish List

In every television program, whether it be sitcom, drama or reality, there is always a story about the one that got away. *Friends* is no different. There were several possible stars that nearly made it onscreen, but in the end, the gig fell through for various reasons.

Justin Timberlake

The singer, songwriter, actor, and record producer expressed interest in appearing on the show and even partook in a meeting with the show's producers to seal the deal. Marta Kauffman acknowledged his interest: "We got a call that Justin Timberlake wanted to do the show." The meeting went well so the creative team pondered possible story scenarios to incorporate the teen idol, but, as David Crane later revealed, "We didn't have a good part for him." Kauffman regretted revealing this missed opportunity to her children. "My kids were furious," she said. "They wanted to kill me."

Owen Wilson

During the time period when *Friends* originally aired, Owen Wilson was at the height of his popularity—leading man of numerous feature film comedies and famed member of the Frat Pack, which consisted of Owen Wilson, Luke Wilson, Ben Stiller, Vince Vaughn, Steve Carell, Will Ferrell and Jack Black. Wilson's stardom attracted the attention of the *Friends* producers who discussed featuring the comedian on *Friends*. He would have been a ratings boon, but then a staff writer read an interview where Wilson admitted that his "biggest fault was giving writers a hard time." The *Friends* creative team weighed the pros and cons of signing a major Hollywood star, and decided to withhold making an offer because they did not want to deal with any unnecessary drama on the set.

Justin Theroux

Justin Theroux's acting debut was in *I Shot Andy Warhol* (1996). He made a few other movies before he was afforded the opportunity to audition for an episode of *Friends*. Since he was riding high on recent feature film success, the future husband to Jennifer Aniston purposely skipped the audition because he wanted to sleep in that day.

Tom Hanks

Multi-award-winning actor Tom Hanks was scheduled to appear in "The One with the Male Nanny" (9.06) as Sandy, the male nanny, but canceled at the last minute due to a delay while filming a movie. Known for his comedic and dramatic roles, Hanks is one of the most popular and recognizable film stars worldwide, and regarded as an American cultural icon. His films have grossed more than \$4.9 billion in North America and more than \$10 billion worldwide, making him the fourth-highest-grossing actor in North America. In the end, the *Friends* role was ultimately awarded to Freddie Prinze Jr.

Sting

The former frontman of The Police was booked to have a brief cameo in "The One with Monica's Boots" (8.10), but canceled at the last minute so his wife Trudie Styler filled in on his behalf. He claims he never agreed to appear, just his wife, and that he was on tour at the time of filming. In truth, Sting agreed to appear otherwise the producers wouldn't have scrambled to replace him and then hastily thrown together a plot involving his wife.

Due to Sting's abrupt cancellation, the writers purposely added a jab at the rocker by having his wife claim he is unavailable for a meeting with Phoebe and Ben because he has a concert, to which Phoebe cynically replies: "Concert. Yeah. That does put us in ... quite a pickle."

Paul McCartney

Casting director Leslie Litt revealed that Paul McCartney almost had a role in the show. He was projected to play Emily's father in the two-part London episode. "I went through his manager and gave him all the details," Litt said. "One day, someone in the office brought me a faxed letter written to me by Paul himself!" She continued, "He thanked me for my interest and said how flattered he was, but it was a very busy time for him." The role was awarded to Scottish actor Tom Conti.

Stand-Ins, Body Doubles & Extras

Stand-ins, body doubles and extras are vital components to any television program or movie project but these actors never receive recognition. They are barely noticed and easily forgotten. However, some well-known actors got their starts as stand-ins or extras, and then went on to achieve success and even stardom. One perfect example is actress Audra Lindley (Phoebe's grandmother). She started as a stand-in and then went on to costar in *Three's Company* and its spinoff, *The Ropers*. Another illustration is James Michael Tyler (Gunther). He parlayed an insignificant extra job into a multimillion-dollar recurring role.

Stand-Ins

Most stand-ins start their career as background or scene extras (aka extras). As their title aptly states, their job is to "stand-in" for a big-name actor so the crew can set lighting and boom mics and the director can determine camera blocking. Stand-ins typically do not appear on camera. However, *Friends* was the exception to the rule; the directors often gave bit parts to the stand-ins.

As of July 1, 2020, stand-ins for feature films and many television programs working under a SAG-AFTRA contract make $209 for eight hours. Stand-ins under a Legacy AFTRA contract make $215 for eight hours.

Kim Harris

As the stand-in for Jennifer Aniston, Kim Harris appeared in many *Friends* episodes, often without speaking lines, i.e., an uncredited performer. Her most memorable episodic appearances were in "The One with Phoebe's Ex-Partner" (3.14) as the actress starring in the Cat Fresh cat litter commercial, "The One Where Joey Loses His Insurance" (6.04) as the youthful casting director for Joey's first audition, "The One with the Cheap Wedding Dress" (7.17) as the bridal boutique owner, and "The One with the Donor" (9.22) as the Bloomingdale's department store employee who spritzes Phoebe with men's cologne.

Harris was ever so subtly referenced in two magna doodle messages in "The One with Chandler's Work Laugh" (5.12). The first message reads: "Joey, Call Kim" with a smiley face. Later in the episode it reads "J—Kim called Again!" This was written by crew member Scott E. Bruza, a set dresser and artist who had paintings displayed in Central Perk. He and Harris met on set and later married. She quit acting in 2005 to assist him with set construction projects. Harris appeared in one episode of *Joey* and functioned as Jennifer Aniston's stand-in for the movie *The Good Girl* (2002).

Joe Everett Michaels

As the stand-in for Matthew Perry, Joe Everett Michaels had three episode appearances: "The One Where Joey Loses His Insurance" (6.04) as the casting director for Joey's third audition for the part of dying man, "The One with Chandler's Dad" (7.22) as the audience member from Bakersfield, and "The One in Barbados, Part 1" (9.23) as a waiter carrying a tray of hors d'oeuvres. Although relatively unknown in the acting world, Michaels carved a solid career as a theater producer in Los Angeles.

Heather Sims

The stand-in for Lisa Kudrow was Heather Sims. She had very few appearances in the series, though her most notable roles were in "The One with the Baby Shower" (8.20) as a guest at Phoebe's birthday party, "The One Where Rachel Goes Back to Work" (9.11) as an extra in a soap opera restaurant scene, and "The One with the Soap Opera Party" (9.20) as Jan Rogers, the voice on Joey's answering machine. Sims later appeared in two episodes of *Cougar Town*. She has only four acting credits on her résumé.

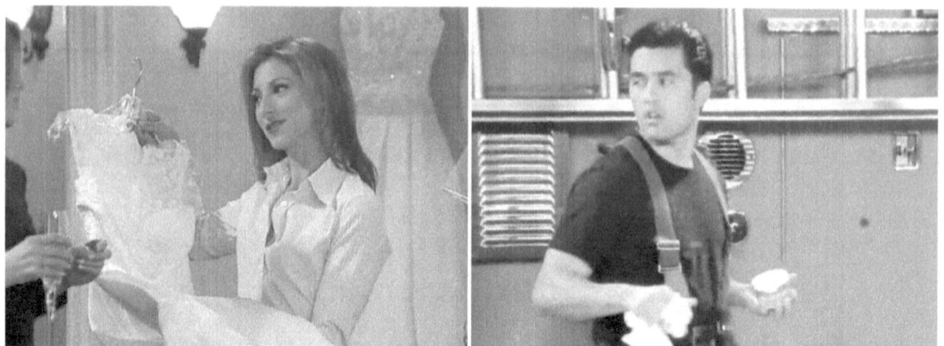

Two of the most frequent on-camera stand-ins: Kim Harris and Douglas Looper

Lisa Calderon

Lisa Calderon (aka Lisa Avery) was the stand-in for Courteney Cox in 193 episodes from "The One with Russ" (2.10) up to "The Last One, Part 2" (10.18). She had several indelible appearances: "The One with Rachel's Sister" (6.13) as the nude body double for Courteney Cox, "The One That Could Have Been, Part 2" (6.16) as Phoebe's coworker, and "The One with the Baby Shower" (8.20) as Erin, the casting director at Joey's *Bamboozled* audition. Calderon was adored by the actors and made a career as a stand-in, working on most of the projects for Courteney Cox and Matt LeBlanc, such as *Cougar Town, Dirt, Joey* and *Man with a Plan.*

Douglas Looper

Matt LeBlanc's stand-in was Douglas Looper, who often appeared in *Friends* episodes. His most memorable roles include "The One with the Breast Milk" (2.02) as the first Saks customer that Joey tries to spritz, "The One with Ross's Thing" (3.23) as a fireman, "The One with All the Thanksgivings" (5.08) as a hospital paramedic and injured soldier, "The One Where Chandler Can't Cry" (6.14) as the vampire in Ursula's porn movie, and "The One Where Rachel Has a Baby, Part 1" (8.23) as the husband wheeling his pregnant wife into Rachel's hospital room. Looper only had two other minor acting credits, and nothing since 2005.

Body Doubles

In filmmaking, a body double is a person who substitutes in a scene for another actor but their face is not shown on camera. Productions that operate under Screen Actors Guild guidelines have standard rates for on-camera talent: A full-body body double earns $795 for a full shift, while a parts model (e.g., hand model) typically gets a rate of $445. A model who's willing to do a nude scene may net double pay.

Lisa Kudrow's real-life sister, Helene Marla Sherman, worked as Kudrow's body double, but only in episodes involving Ursula. Kudrow spoke all the lines for both characters, while Sherman functioned as a body double opposite her sister. For example, when Ursula spoke, the frame often showed the back of Phoebe's head (which was Sherman).

A body double was needed for the twins' scenes to match eye lines and for the over-the-shoulder shots where Sherman was only seen from behind. In scenes where both fictional characters appeared in the frame, the director used two techniques. In closeups, Kudrow shot one angle (Phoebe talking to Ursula) and then the other camera angle (Ursula talking to Phoebe), and then the two takes were spliced together in postproduction. In wide-angle shots, both sisters appeared onscreen but it was filmed from a distance to conceal their physical differences since Kudrow and Sherman are not twins in real life.

Lisa Kudrow did not really enjoy filming scenes with her sister. "Lisa really did not have a good time doing them. She did not like acting with a double, and in a way she might have made it more difficult for herself because her double was her actual sister," said director Kevin Bright. "I think feeling the [stress] she put her sister into by being the double was more in her head at the time, so those scenes were a little bit tricky to shoot. But it ended up being a lot of fun when you put it together." Kudrow acknowledged the discomfort she felt working with her sister and insisted those scenes were the most difficult to perform. The producers registered her complaints and decided to axe Ursula from the show.

Helene Sherman with Lisa Kudrow (left), husband David (center), and working as a sculptor (right)

Extras

Being an extra is a great part-time job for retirees, college students and anyone else with a highly flexible schedule. Extras can earn anywhere from minimum wage (nonunion) to more than $50 per hour (union). The standard pay usually increases with greater role visibility, performing something extraordinary (e.g., swimming, ice skating, playing golf, riding motorcycles), or having to bring a costume or prop (e.g., tennis racket, golf clubs). A common workday in the industry can last 10 to 15 hours. The union standard pay rate is about $200 a day.

Each *Friends* installment enlisted anywhere from 35 to 50 extras. Many were used in multiple episodes. For example, Andre Lachaumette appeared in three episodes: "The One with the Screamer" (3.22) as a theater after-party guest, "The One After Ross Says Rachel" (5.01) as a wedding reception guest, and "The One with Ross's Inappropriate Song" (9.07) as Tom, a friend of Mike Hannigan's parents. Since extras are paid for a full day, they were often used in multiple scenes. There are two notable illustrations. In "The One Where Paul's the Man" (6.22), the same extras are visible in five different scenes, even though a sizable amount of time had lapsed between scenes. Similarly, in "The Last One, Part 2" (10.18), the same woman (wearing a scarf) and young man (in a black shirt) are visible in two airport scenes, even though both scenes take place in different airports.

There were several celebrities who were invited to be scene extras in *Friends*, such as Australian Olympic swimmer Ian Thorpe, British television host Ben Shephard, and British journalist Sarfraz Manzoor. One of the most popular *Friends* extras played the part of Ugly Naked Guy. Since Ugly Naked Guy is an uncredited role, many fans mistakenly believe he was portrayed by Michael Hagerty (Mr. Treeger). He was actually played by Jon Haugen who first applied for the role through Central Casting. According to Kaufman, casting an actor to personify the usually unseen character was easy. "Surprisingly, there are people who want to play Ugly Naked Guy. They do. It's just [shot] from the back, they don't have any lines, it wasn't an audition—it was just about, physically, what do we imagine?"

Ugly Naked Guy was merely an extrapolation of a man that many of the staff writers observed living across from their apartments in the past (especially those who lived in New York). Coincidentally, the *Friends* staff received a letter from a woman who grew up in the building used to represent Ugly Naked Guy's tenement, and she confided that "there was, in fact, an authentic Ugly Naked Guy living across from her," and then rhetorically asked, "How did you know?" When Ugly Naked Guy started gaining a cult following, Warner Bros. requested that he keep his identity secret from the public. "They wanted everybody to have a guess who I was," Haugen said. Regarding his time on *Friends*, he added, "It was the best time in my life. I was the man."

In the series finale, the Central Perk scene is filled with background extras that include family, friends and colleagues of the executive producers. At the round table behind the orange couch (from left) is the creators' agent Nancy Josephson, their unidentified lawyer, Lisa Kudrow's husband (Michel Stern), and David Crane's life partner, Jeffrey Klarik. As Ross and Phoebe get into the taxicab, Marta Kauffman's cousins are scene extras in the background. As Ross and Phoebe first arrive at the airport, the individuals standing by the payphones are Colleen Mahan, Eric Goldberg and Missy Krehbiel, the assistants to Marta Kauffman, Kevin Bright and David Crane, respectively. In the next airport scene, where Rachel is standing in the ticket line, the background extras include Kevin Bright's kids (Zachary and Justin), casting director Leslie Litt, and Marta Kauffman's Pilates instructor. As Rachel reaches the ticket counter, the blonde woman seated behind her is NBC publicist Barbara Brogliatti.

Ugly Naked Guy (left) played by Jon Haugen (center), and Lisa Calderon as Cox's stand-in (right)

Even the writers were known to sit in front of the camera for a quick cameo. They were often part of large group settings, such as sporting events or airplane cabins. Occasionally they appeared in scenes as featured extras, but it was never a speaking part. The executive producers popped up in several segments playing theater and feature film producers.

Shoutouts

The *Friends* writers were known for adding the names of friends and family members to scripts as a subtle shoutout and acknowledgment to the ones they love. Marta Kauffman was most likely to add names to the scripts, such as ex-boyfriends (e.g., Danny Arshack, Billy Dreskin), childhood friend (Kathy Karabetsos), nanny (Rebecca Holt), friends (e.g., Deb Franzblau, Rona Oberman, Adam Ritter) and godchild (Avery Michelle). David Crane made numerous references to his life partner, Jeffrey Klarik.

Other *Friends* staff writers named characters after their friends and relatives. In "The One with the Baby on the Bus" (2.06), writer Betsy Borns named the character Stephanie, played by Chrissie Hynde, after her sister, and Markel's tavern after her boyfriend's father. In "The One After the Superbowl, Part 1" (2.12), Dean Lipson (Zoo Owner) is named after a mutual friend of writers Jeff Astrof and Mike Sikowitz.

The showrunners also tossed in a few references to their college years. Emily Waltham's surname was based on the city where the creators attended college. Brandeis University is a private college located in Waltham, Massachusetts, just on the outskirts of Boston. In the pilot episode, Monica compares her special feelings to how Rachel felt when dating Tony Demarco. The character was named after a World Welterweight Champion from the North End neighborhood in Boston. The creators learned about the boxing legend while attending Brandeis. In "The One with the Blackout" (1.07), Chandler is trapped in an ATM vestibule at Emerson Bank. This bank is named after Emerson College in Boston, Massachusetts, which is executive producer Kevin Bright's alma mater.

The neighborhood around Central Perk usually had businesses named after people or companies that were near and dear to the hearts of the executive producers. For example, Dot's Spot restaurant and Dottie & Herman's bodega were named after Marta Kauffman's parents, Jeffrey's Flowers is a tribute to David Crane's life partner, Jeffrey Klarik, and Free Being Records is homage to a record store that Kevin Bright frequented as a youth.

Sets, Props & Dressings

A set is the enclosure in which a scene is shot. It is normally constructed on a studio backlot or soundstage and includes scenery, props and dressings. A prop is anything an actor touches or handles. Dressing entails decorating a particular set with wall hangings, knickknacks, curtains, and furniture; filling shelves; and generally making the environment look real and lived-in.

Friends art director John Shaffner designed the sets and selected the layouts and color schemes, while set decorator Greg Grande located items for the sets. Kai Blomberg, Quent Schierenberg and Greg Bruza made up the set dressing department. They assembled the sets every week, and redressed Joey and Monica's apartments and Central Perk when those "permanent" sets were torn down to make room for other expansive sets that were required for the season-ending finales (e.g., casino, Monica and Chandler's wedding, hospital and resort hotel).

Many of the sets were built and then stored for future use. *Friends* had a huge storage bay on the Warner Bros. lot. Rather than building a new set each time, the crew used sets interchangeably, adding different dressings, lighting, etc., to create a distinctive mood and environment. Thus, they could get three or four unique restaurants over a number of years using the same set.

Set decorators spend a lot of time reading design and fashion magazines and shopping —scouring the studio warehouses, flea markets, swap meets, and secondhand stores—to locate items for the set, though they also buy from antique stores and rent from Hollywood prop houses. Decorating the sets during the first season was especially challenging due to the sitcom's limited production budget. For example, in "The Pilot" (1.01), which only had two sets, Monica's apartment and Central Perk, the decorating bill was around $60,000. A comparable sitcom pilot today costs at least five times that amount. During season one, the *Friends* weekly budget was minuscule (around $3,000) but it swelled to nearly $20,000 in its final season. In comparison, other hit comedy shows like *Dharma & Greg* and *Ellen* were substantially less, $12,000 and $6,000, respectively, at the height of their popularity.

One goal of the set designer was to keep the look and feel of the show fresh. "One thing that we always tried to do was keep it alive over 10 years so that it didn't become frozen in time," John Shaffner pointed out. Thus, he liked to regularly change the set dressing. For instance, in Monica's apartment there was a modern chair with an ottoman near Rachel's bedroom, which were eventually replaced, and for a while Monica amassed Bose stereos. Though few fans would notice such subtle changes, Shaffner did. He kept a keen eye on the evolution of the set over the years.

If the script called for an actor to touch an object, *Friends* property master Marjorie Coster-Praytor had to locate the prop and specialize it for the character, whether a box, briefcase or coffee cup. For example, in "The One with the Dollhouse" (3.20), Phoebe built a dollhouse out of shoeboxes so the prop department had to construct six identical replicas and only had three days to do it. As part of her duties, Coster-Praytor rummaged antique stores, knickknack shops, supermarkets and even garage sales in order to locate the props required for each weekly show.

Coster-Praytor also photographed and cataloged every prop and set dressing that was ever used in *Friends* so a duplicate set could be reproduced years later. However, since many items were rented from prop houses, occasionally the original items were unavailable because someone purchased them for personal use or another show had the item on loan. That happened numerous times, most notably with the Tiffany firefly floor lamp from the title sequence and first two seasons of *Friends*. When it came time to locate the lamp for the alternate universe episode four years later, the lamp was no longer available so a similar substitute was used instead.

Monica's apartment building (left) and the inconsistently shaped balcony sets (right)

Despite all the iconic props and set dressings used in the show, the crew behind the scenes never received credit nor reaped any reward. Set decorator Greg Grande proclaimed: "It is really crazy and it's awesome to think that I put such a fingerprint on that show—and it's really sad that I can't get any piece of the action! Somebody owes me, for God's sake!" He actually tried to partner with Warner Bros. to capitalize on the show's popularity. "It's funny because I did pitch them a whole furniture line after the show but they didn't want it," he recalled. Ironically, 20 years later Warner Bros. partnered with Bloomingdale's and Pottery Barn to create *Friends*-inspired furniture pieces. Once again, Grande did not get a piece of the action.

Monica's Apartment

Of all the sets he designed, John Shaffner was most proud of the primary apartments (Monica's and Joey's) because he had all of the interior doors connecting to the main room —it forced all activities to be centered in that location. Shaffner described it as a "classic theatrical technique to create comedy and farce." He and fellow designer Joe Stewart lived together on West 14th Street in Manhattan in the late 1970s which became the inspiration for Monica's apartment. It was a sixth-floor walk-up but the bathroom was just outside the bedroom. Shaffner used his old abode as the template for Monica's and Joey's apartments, but moved the bathroom into a better location for filming.

Monica's bathroom was originally designed so the back wall could be removed to allow a camera to film the apartment from a different angle. Kevin Bright liked the idea but opted for an opposite angle which required shooting from the living room wall. Consequently, the bathroom became mostly a fake room and was reduced in size. However, as the years went on, and when it was necessary to the script, the crew built a separate bathroom set, which was slightly larger than the original design.

Shaffner designed every aspect of the apartment, from windows and wall colors to floor plan and furniture. "To be able to envision all of this, one needs to get familiar with the tone of the series, with its humor, and with the director's ambitions," he declared. "The simple way to define my job would be to say that I breathe life into a project. I create a frame, an environment."

Typically, sitcoms use neutral pigments for walls so the actors will pop out more. When *Friends* was in its infancy, Shaffner initially painted Monica's apartment white. The series' producers, though, did not like the color. They didn't want it to look like every other sitcom; they wanted an apartment that "reflected the sensibility of these twentysomethings." When Shaffner suggested purple, it made everyone apprehensive, until he repainted the set. Then the splash of color was fully embraced. The producers immediately requested a lot of bright colors, which Shaffner accommodated with blue kitchen cabinets, amaranth (deep purple) bathroom, and rose bedroom. The showrunners wanted color to pop out everywhere—walls, blankets, clothing, etc.

Shaffner liked the purple color because it went so well with everyone's skin tones. "Blue is good, but blue is more gender neutral, and the purple did give that atmosphere of being a little more feminine," he said. Not only that, it also suited a range of hair colors, which was useful on a show that revolved around characters with a pretty broad brunet spectrum. Shaffner also believed the purple color helped "establish the show's identity" by setting it apart from other programs, and it encouraged viewers to "stay tuned" instead of changing the channel. Just the sight of Monica's apartment was enough to lift people's moods and get them ready to laugh along with the sitcom. If Shaffner had been given the opportunity to repaint the apartment for the show's 25th anniversary, he would have painted it light gray because that was the fashionable shade at the time.

The large balcony window was installed at the suggestion of director James Burrows. Originally there was supposed to be two regular-size windows, but he thought an oversize window would provide a better view of the background. Burrows wanted something more distinctive than ordinary windows so Shaffner suggested a skylight and offered alternatives. And so the floor-to-ceiling skylight balcony window was born. According to Shaffner, this was the only note he was given regarding the apartment design.

Burrows requested one addition to the set—the wooden beam archway separating the kitchen-dining area and living room. It was present in many apartment scenes, especially in the early years. Other directors found the beam obtrusive so it became a signature of Burrows. As an inside joke, whenever he returned to the series to direct an episode the crew would install the beam. In "The One Where Rachel Goes Back to Work" (9.11), the archway was reinstalled for director Gary Halverson, but the structure had to be rebuilt because the original beam was misplaced after five years in storage. Since Burrows had not directed an installment since the fourth season, the archway got lost in the Warner Bros. property warehouse. Fittingly, in the *Friends* reunion in May 2021, the beam was installed in Monica's apartment as a nostalgic remembrance for the cast.

Shaffner explained that the beam was installed in the pilot episode to connote that the residents, at some time, had taken down the wall between the kitchen and living room, a common practice in New York apartment buildings because "landlords don't bother to come see what you've done." Shaffner also incorporated appliances and electronics that were fully functional, such as the television and refrigerator. The apartment realism, however, caused many soundstage visitors to forget it was just a set. There came a time when visitors (e.g., friends, family and executives) had to be reminded that the on-set bathroom did not have functional plumbing.

The view outside Monica's kitchen window changed several times during the series. In the first season, the window backdrop was a painting from the 1940s created by a company called JC Backings. It was a necessary addition to the set because the art department did not have sufficient funding to purchase something nicer. In the second season, after the production moved from Stage 5 to Stage 24, Shaffner noted, "We had a lot more room and a lot more money." He opted to build a miniature apartment building about 10 feet away from the window with bricks at about five-eighths the real size. This edifice was large enough that it was also visible through the window in the apartment building hallway set.

Few *Friends* fans realize the bedroom doors were false (fake) entries. The Central Perk set was actually positioned behind the doors. The bedroom sets were only assembled as needed for a scene. Similarly, the secret hallway closet was initially a walk-in closet but after the sitcom moved to Stage 24 at the start of the second season, it also became a false entry. The closet door was actually a backstage passageway used by the crew.

There has been considerable debate whether Monica could afford her apartment. As of 2024, the 1,500-square-foot, two-bedroom with balcony in West Village, Manhattan, was worth over $4.2 million and would cost at least $14,000 a month to rent. According to the Geller siblings, however, the apartment was supposedly their grandmother's rent-controlled apartment—a New York law since 1971 where the original tenants can only be charged a certain amount for rent. Thus, if true, Monica's rent-controlled abode would be affordable on a chef's salary. Moreover, Shaffner believed Monica's place would be more reasonably priced because it was an upper-level residence—"you got a bigger apartment for less money if you're willing to climb six flights of stairs." In his opinion, he estimates that a comparable apartment in 1994 would cost between $1,000 and $1,400 a month to rent.

The producers acknowledged that the apartments depicted in the show were larger than a normal New York apartment, but it was necessary because they needed adequate space for filming. "In the reality of life in New York for people of this age, yes, they are rather large apartments," Kevin Bright conceded. "But in the process of making a TV show, the space has to be big enough for cameras, lighting, and for the audience to be able to see what's going on."

Monica's apartment: kitchen and living room

The *Friends* set decorator, Greg Grande, had never been to the Big Apple so Shaffner explained to him that New York residents often sniffed around the wealthy apartments on bin night, hoping to find usable discarded furnishings. Grande utilized this tidbit as part of Monica's profile, and reasoned that she may have done the same to furnish her apartment. He described the decor as an "eclectic taste with a flea market, whimsical, and anything-goes style." The apartment was decorated with a "thrifted inspiration" and the mismatched chairs that surrounded the kitchen table were regularly swapped out over the 10 seasons. "Monica really couldn't afford a matched set of dining table chairs, but it was meant to be that the character had a really good eye and was really meticulous and creative," he said, "so her Sundays were spent in New York in these parking lot swap meets and she did a lot of mixing and matching."

Although Monica's apartment was decorated like she spent her nights dumpster diving for furnishings, the set decorator did not use the same furniture-acquiring method when it came time to decorate the set. Shaffner suggested using the Warner Bros. massive property warehouse (which he jokingly referred to as Worn Out Brothers, due to its plethora of old furnishings), and in the process, Grande found a ton of very useful artifacts to create an eclectic milieu.

The primary reason for Monica having a thrifty approach to home decorating was the limited production budget for the pilot episode and during the first season. Grande had to be creative and resourceful, which translated into her having rather spartan household furnishings. In fact, during the entire first season, Monica's apartment didn't have curtains to cover the windows. By the second season, though, with an expanded budget, he was able to add curtains, furniture and props to make the apartment look "a little more colorful, a little richer." Of all the items Grande curated for the apartment, one item stands out as his favorite. "There's one wood carving that's kind of tucked down her hallway," he said. "It's kind of an old piece of wood that a guy's carved into with his finger pointing up in the air. That was a really classic find."

Most fans have noticed the apartment numbers changed but many do not know the reason behind the switch. At the show's inception, Joey's apartment was #4 and Monica's #5. In "The One Where Underdog Gets Away" (1.09), the designation changed to #19 and #20, respectively. The change occurred rather organically. David Crane was sitting on the set one day and realized the cast always looked downward to peer into Ugly Naked Guy's apartment. Since numbers 4 and 5 corresponded to a lower level, and Monica and Joey's apartments were on an upper floor, they had to make a numerical change for continuity.

Even the hallway between the apartments has a history. In the beginning, Warner Bros. was eager to cut production costs any way it could. Originally there wasn't going to be a hallway between the apartments. However, set designer John Shaffner pointed out that since Joey and Monica live across the hall from each other, the adjoining hallway may as well be a permanent feature. The size of the hallway changed as well. In season one, it was three feet wider than in later seasons. The move from Stage 5 to Stage 24 in season two facilitated the need for a smaller hallway because the Central Perk neighborhood street set was enormous.

Real-Life Apartment

One of the things that amused the *Friends* set designer was the establishing shot used to represent the building exterior for Monica and Joey's apartments. During preliminary set design discussions for the pilot, John Shaffner was told the creators only wanted general shots of New York. "I went to New York and came back with an armful of pictures of the tops of the sixth-floor buildings with [mullion] windows like that," he noted. But then, while editing the pilot, Kevin Bright needed a transitional establishing shot to the apartment, so a random building facade was expeditiously chosen. "They found a building that had arched windows all the way across the top floor," Shaffner said. "And I'm like, 'We don't have any arched windows.' And they said, 'Oh, well, their apartment is in the back. That's just the building.'" Shaffner went back to New York to find a comparable tenement. "I couldn't find any building with huge, street-facing windows like the one Monica's apartment has," he said. "That's okay," said a production executive at Warner Bros. "It's not like anybody's going to obsess over this sort of thing."

Some critics of the show accuse the set designer of giving Monica's apartment the kind of balcony and window design that did not exist in New York. Shaffner defended the design as an accurate depiction of the city, after all, he used to live there in the 1970s. He decided to prove those naysayers wrong. He went on a mission to find that balcony in New York and took "a million" pictures to prove he didn't make it up. He successfully accomplished the task and quelled the nitpicking critics.

The real-life address for the apartment building used in the exterior establishing shots is 90 Bedford St. in Manhattan's West Village, on the corner of Bedford and Grove Streets. Since Ugly Naked Guy lived across the street, his address is 19 Grove St. While the sitcom never filmed scenes in New York City, the building is a bucket list landmark for any *Friends* fanatic. (FYI: The invitation to Ross' wedding was mailed to Monica's apartment which was listed as 545 Grove St., Apt. #20, New York, NY 10001, which is a fake address to avoid any potential lawsuits.)

The ground floor of the apartment building is not Central Perk, it is a restaurant named The Little Owl. Its cheeseburger has been named the best in New York though it also serves spicy Mediterranean cuisine. The eatery remains open for business and still attracts a lot of *Friends* fans, many of whom are disappointed it is not decorated like a coffeehouse.

Peephole Picture Frame

According to set designer John Shaffner, when he lived in a New York City apartment, he always had something hanging on the door. His door usually had a peg for scarves or an umbrella, or maybe a chalkboard, so he wanted something similar for Monica's tenement. Contrary to popular belief, the archetypal golden picture frame was not a mirror.

Set decorator Greg Grande found the picture frame accessory at the Rose Bowl Swap Meet. "I'd bought this yellowish-gold papier-mâché picture frame at a craft fair intending to use it on a side table," he stated. While dressing the set for the pilot episode, crew member Ricky Parker bumped the table and broke the glass. "I took the backing off and tried it over the peephole," Grande declared. His boss, Shaffner, fondly recalled the day: "I remember so clearly. He waved at me and he said, 'Come over here.' I came over, and he said, 'What do you think about this?' He held up the little yellow picture frame, and held it over the peep hole. First of all, the color against the purple was spectacular. And I loved that it was so whimsical and fun, and it's a picture frame, for the peephole through which you see your friends. So it's like a picture of all your friends! I just thought it was the most marvelous thing. I took one look and said, 'Glue it on!'" The producers thought it was a good fit for the eclectic, bohemian vibe of the apartment. "It actually was as simple as that," Grande stated. "Kind of a funny mistake."

Old-Fashioned Doorbell

The hall entry door to Monica's apartment has a round, golden antique twist doorbell modeled after the Victorian style which operated much like a bicycle bell. Early doorbells on record in the Victorian Era used a twist handle, like turning a key. When the visitor turned the handle, it caused a tiny hammer or clapper to strike a bell on the inside of the door. A rapid trill or ringing sound was produced. Although the bell was never used in the series—Monica's door was almost always unlocked or visitors knocked—it is kind of cool to know the set decorator took the time to add antique accessories to the legendary set.

French Poster

The poster above the television in Monica's apartment is Aux Buttes Chaumont: Jouets et Objets Pour Étrennes (toys and gifts for New Year's) by French artist Jules Chéret (1836–1932). The 1885 poster is promoting toys at a department store near Paris' Parc des Buttes-Chaumont. It conveys the image: "We are très chic ... We have joie de vivre!" (We are very stylish. We have joy of living). Chéret started producing advertisements in the 1870s and his work helped to move art out of the gallery and into the streets. He is known as the father of the modern poster.

Posters in Monica's bedroom: 1980 Winter Olympics and 1920s Portuguese wine

The Aux Buttes Chaumont (French poster) covered a large hole that was cut in the wall so a camera could shoot a different angle into the abode. The special effects team designed a device to mechanically elevate the poster to expose the opening whenever the camera was needed. Therefore, whenever the director wanted to film from the perspective of the French poster, a simple flip of a switch would raise the poster for a clear shot.

The French poster wasn't the original artwork selected for that living space. In the pilot episode, set decorator Greg Grande originally hung an old 1900s tapestry that he retrieved from the Warner Bros. drapery department. After studio and network executives did their final walk through, they objected to the rug because it was too religious. "I had to scramble a little bit and that's how I ended up starting to flip through my research books of circus and French posters from the early 1900s. I found that image, took it, and reproduced it for a poster," Grande said. "It fit the apartment's feminine, eclectic style, and it was believable for Monica because it was good design on a budget."

Olympic Poster

The flower poster hanging above Monica's bed is Mikhail Avvakumov and Olga Volkova's *You Are Welcome!* artwork design for the 1980 Olympic Games in Moscow. The US actually boycotted the Games to protest the Soviet Union's invasion of Afghanistan, which led to 65 nations refusing to participate. A large part of the Olympics promotion featured the Soviet Union welcoming different nations to Moscow. Thus, its slogan, You Are Welcome! written in different languages, is somewhat ironic.

Portos Ramos-Pinto Poster

Monica's bedroom has a 1920 Portos Ramos-Pinto poster on a side wall. The vino print illustrator is René Vincent and it advertises the famous port wine by featuring two lovers in profile leaning into one another with only a famous glass of the irresistible Porto Ramos between their lips. An anxious cupid awaits below with bow in hand, using the delicious drink as his arrow. This vintage image is still very much associated with the company to the present date. It is also Vincent's most recognized work as an artist.

In 1880, artist and merchant Adriano Ramos Pinto opened a wine house on the banks of Vila Nova de Gaïa facing the city of Porto, Portugal. Casa Ramos Pinto rapidly became widely known for its innovative and enterprising strategy. Associated with quality bottled wines, it started operating on the Brazilian market in the early 20th century and quickly became responsible for half of the wine exported to South America, while also retaining its generations of loyal customers in Portugal and Europe.

Fleur-de-lis

A wall hanging in Monica's bedroom features a fleur-de-lis (lily flower). The image has been used by French royalty and throughout history to represent Catholic saints of France, e.g., the Virgin Mary and St. Joseph. The symbol is deeply ingrained in Louisiana's history. It is seen in architecture, the state flag, and the NFL helmet for the Saints, but originally it was once used to mark slaves.

Refrigerator

Monica's apartment had three different refrigerator models. In the first six episodes it was a 1950s Westinghouse with a mid-range teal accent. The original fridge broke and had to be replaced so the set decorator purchased a similar model, a 1953 Westinghouse, to keep the eclectic vintage style of the set. In season four, Monica's kitchen was redecorated so another refrigerator was installed, a vintage 1950s International Harvester rounded top with mid-range copper-colored decorative strip.

Regardless of the refrigerator make or model, it was not meant to be set dressing or an insignificant prop. It was entirely pragmatic. In fact, the refrigerator was fully functional and housed cold beverages for the cast and crew. It's one of the rare instances on television where an actor is actually given a cold beverage out of the refrigerator during filming. Joey's fridge, on the other hand, was usually left empty unless it was needed for a specific interior shot.

Excelsior Poster

In nearly every shot of Rachel's bedroom, there is an Excelsior sewing machine poster. The inscription at the top is "La machine a coudre parfaite" (the perfect sewing machine). Although Rachel has no sewing skills, the set decorator chose it simply for aesthetics—he liked to use foreign prints as wall hangings.

Maina Poster

Inside Monica's apartment, to the left of the hallway door, is a print often overlooked, though it is present in nearly every episode of the series. Maïna La Voyante (Maina the Clairvoyant) is a vintage theater exhibition poster from 1920 by artist Louis Galice that was used to promote a magic stage act. In 1924, it was made into a French silent film drama.

Michelangelo Chest

One obscure furnishing, often present, though frequently moved around the apartment, was a unique decorative chest inscribed with an original poem entitled *On Dante Alighieri* by Michelangelo Buonarroti (aka Michelangelo). The transcription is "From heaven his spirit came, and robed in clay, the realms of justice and of mercy trod, then rose a living man to gaze on God." Michelangelo was an Italian sculptor, painter, architect and poet. Several scholars claim he is the greatest artist of all time. He is most known for the David sculpture and painting the ceiling of the Sistine Chapel.

Joey's Apartment

While Monica's apartment was splattered in color (purple, amaranth and rose), Joey's apartment was a stark contrast with a drab earth-tone palette. "For the boys' apartment, in the first season, I said, everything in this apartment is going to be brown," Shaffner stated. "So we had brown carpet on a brown floor with brown drapes and a brown sofa and tan walls, and the boys were scared of color. Then they kinda got over it and got their yellow sofa, and started to jazz it up a bit as they got more secure in their manhood."

During the first season, Joey's apartment was not a frequently used set. As such, it was sparsely furnished primarily because the show could not afford two fully furnished abodes. "We wanted it to look a little barren and like they didn't really care," explained Grande. The second season had a larger budget so more furnishings were incorporated, but since the guys weren't making money, their apartment incorporated lower-quality furniture. As the set-decorating budget continued to grow over the years so did Joey's tenement possessions; his residence became cluttered with knickknacks and other obscure, esoteric furnishings, such as a life-size mannequin.

Laurel and Hardy Poster

Although the guys' apartment was spartan, the set decorator still had to cover the walls with something. Since Joey was an actor, Greg Grande gravitated toward movie posters. The most memorable poster was the movie still of Laurel and Hardy in bed. In the scene, Stan has a toothache so he ties a handkerchief around his jaw with a knot atop his head like rabbit ears. It is from their 1928 movie *Leave 'em Laughing*.

The set decorator intentionally chose the monochromatic poster of Laurel and Hardy to symbolize the close relationship between Joey and Chandler. The comedic duo dominated Hollywood cinema from 1921 to 1951 but their offscreen friendship was equally remarkable as they both supported one another and remained a vital presence in each other's lives. In fact, when Hardy died in 1957, Laurel became so lost that he refused to act in movies.

Movie Posters

In the early years of the series, Joey's living room often featured old-time movie posters. One such representation was for the feature film *Grand Jury Secrets* (1939). In the movie, a newspaper reporter gets involved with shady stock promoters when he eavesdrops on a jury room session. The poster appeared throughout the first three seasons.

Chandler's bedroom contained a couple noteworthy movie posters. The first was for the 1938 feature film *Reformatory.* In the movie, the inmates at a juvenile detention institution plan a mass breakout, despite the attempts of a new superintendent to bring in a more liberal regime. The print is visible throughout the first two seasons of *Friends.* The other poster is *It's a Wonderful Life* (1946) starring James Stewart. In the classic holiday film, an angel is sent from Heaven to help a desperately frustrated businessman by showing him what life would have been like had he never existed. Since Chandler's bedroom was rarely featured, the poster is only visible in two episodes during the first two seasons.

Joey's bedroom was also decorated with feature film memorabilia. One wall frequently displayed an Alfred Hitchcock poster, which promotes the famed director, not one of his movies. Since Joey was a self-proclaimed fan of Al Pacino, the set decorator made sure to feature a print from the screen legend's epic film *Scarface* (1983). Fittingly, in the spinoff series *Joey*, the *Scarface* poster followed Joey to Los Angeles.

Recliners

One of the guys' prized possessions was a set of matching recliners. The black leather loungers debuted in "The One Where Ross and Rachel...You Know" (2.15). Eighteen months later, the burglary storyline in "The One with the Cat" (4.02) was purposely written so the set decorator could replace the black recliners. According to Mikel Neiers, the director of photography, the black chairs were like black holes for lighting on Joey's apartment set. "The black in the original chairs would absorb more light than the objects near them on the set, making them more difficult to set lights for," explained series producer Todd Stevens. "Apparently the crew tried to make them work, but ultimately they had to be replaced."

The *Friends* staff writers loved brainstorming possible replacement recliners. "In one of the meetings they started talking about, 'Oh, wouldn't it be funny if there was an arm that lifted up and they had cold storage for the beer?'" said Grande. "So I got two Barcaloungers from the company and I found leather and reupholstered both of them to match." The new recliner, the La-Z-Boy E-cliner 3000, was a modified version of the La-Z-Boy Oasis (or Cool Chair). According to Grande, "I looked for the most obnoxious ones I could find." FYI: The E-cliner 3000 brand name is fictitious (though La-Z-Boy has a model called the Explorer e-cliner).

Due to the popularity of *Friends*, and the masterful addition of one-of-a-kind props, set decorator Greg Grande has been credited for generating interest among thirtysomethings for the lounge chair. He even appeared on the Home Shopping Network in 2000 to hawk the recliner, and noted, "It's selling incredibly well so it's not just for men over 50 anymore." His appearance was a success, as the network sold a lot of recliners.

Pat the Dog

The molded-plastic greyhound statue made its debut in "The One Where Eddie Moves In" (2.17). Tons of internet sources claim Pat the dog was owned by Jennifer Aniston—a good luck gift from a friend on the first day of shooting *Friends.* In reality, set designer Greg Grande purchased the storied prop for Joey's new apartment. "The only note I got was 'Give it a little Italian flair,'" he said, referencing Joey's heritage. "I went to a store called Italy 2000 and saw this dog. It had a '70s flavor and was too funny." Thereafter, the piece took on a life of its own, being referenced and featured in multiple episodes. In fact, during the closing scene of the series finale, Grande, playing a mover, can be seen wheeling the statue out the entry door.

Grand Prix Poster

Joey's bedroom often displayed a 1954 Grand Prix poster. The Danish print celebrates the 1954 double victory by Mercedes-Benz cars (driven by Juan Manuel Fangio and Karl Kling) during the French Grand Prix (later Formula 1). The English translation: "Fights in fierce battle against international competition, a superior double victory in Grand Prix of France 1954. If Mercedes-Benz wins, however, the winner is you as a cohort in a Mercedes-Benz, a car in which all race experiences are renewed."

Le Matin Poster

Throughout the series' run, Joey's living room featured the French poster *Les Mystères de New-York* (1915) presumable created by artist Charles Tickon. The feature was written by Pierre Decourcelle, though it is a re-edited version of three chapters from the American serial *The Exploits of Elaine* (1914). The French series screened weekly in theaters between

December 1915 and May 1916, and Decourcelle's written version of the story was printed in the French newspaper *Le Matin*. It was one of the first cross-promotional campaigns.

Guinness Poster

On the bathroom door of Joey's apartment is the advertising poster My Goodness My Guinness (c. 1939). It was a staple in the apartment for most of the series' run. The print illustrator, John Gilroy (1898–1985), began working for Guinness in 1928. His work was so popular that he continued producing whimsical advert posters well into the 1960s, until the brewery moved away from its fun and playful campaigns and transitioned towards more mature and serious themes. Gilroy's work is still quite popular to this day and Guinness continues to profit from it—selling merchandise, vintage posters, and even a wide range of collectible cans.

Boxing Kangaroo Poster

Throughout the first eight years of the show, the decor in Joey's apartment featured the 1933 Кенгуру-Боксер (Boxing Kangaroo) print, advertising a boxing match between animal trainer Vladimir Durov Jr. and a kangaroo. The bottom text reads "Vladimir Durov Junior" and the logo by the kangaroo's shoulder is GOMET—the Soviet State Department's Ministry of Enlightenment that was created for the regulation of musicals, theaters and circuses. The Durovs were a family of performers who brought renown and prestige to the Russian circus, and their descendants still perform today.

Bieres de Chartres Poster

The 1920s Bieres de Chartres (Chartres Beers) poster is barely visible hanging to the left of Joey's bedroom door, however, when Joey and Chandler moved into Monica's abode, it hung on the secret hallway closet door. Created by obscure artist AK Girenel, the poster depicts a waiter drinking the beer he is supposed to be delivering to a patron. Chartres is a commune and capital of the Eure-et-Loir department in France. It is located about 56 miles (90 km) southwest of Paris. The historic city is famous worldwide for its Gothic cathedral, mostly constructed between 1193 and 1250.

Hugsy

The stuffed toy made its first appearance in "The One with the Inappropriate Sister" (5.10) where it can be seen sitting on a barstool beneath the dartboard in Joey's apartment. Curiously, Hugsy was plain and unaccessorized—he wore a red scarf but no vest or goggles.

Hugsy was prominently featured in "The One Where Everybody Finds Out" (5.14). While walking on set, the stuffed toy caught the attention of writer Alexa Junge, who decided to incorporate the penguin pal into a script. Hugsy "guest starred" in other TV shows as well, such as *Boy Meets World*, *Everybody Loves Raymond*, *8 Simple Rules* and *Spin City*. It was a gag prop—the TV version of Where's Waldo? but with Hugsy. The popular bedtime toy pal later showed up in the spinoff series *Joey*.

Soviet Poster

Chandler's bedroom wall included a 1940s Soviet Union vintage aviation art poster with a fleet of red planes soaring over a city with the propaganda slogan "Long live the strong aviation of the socialist country!" It was visible only once, and very briefly, in "The One with the Boobies" (1.13). After Rachel sees Joey naked in the shower, Chandler runs out of his bedroom to inquire about all the commotion. As he opens the door, the poster is fleetingly evident.

Ross' Apartment

Throughout most of the series, Ross' apartment featured the print *Russian Thinker* by A. Lebedinsky and S. Shukhman, two relatively unknown artists. It depicts a young man studying with the text: "To build you need to know, to know you have to learn." The 1958 print was made during key Soviet events: launch of the Sputnik satellite (1957) and its first manned orbital flight (1961).

In the last two years of the series, Ross' apartment prominently displayed a large giclée (ZHē'klā) print entitled *Questions and Answers* by artist Jeff Schaller from Downingtown, Pennsylvania. It has a giraffe from the neck up with an all-white man and boy sketching overlaid and For Sale at the bottom. Giclée is a special technology for fine art or photograph reproduction using a high-quality inkjet printer to make individual copies.

Two of the most recognized French posters in Monica's apartment

Ross' desk contains a phrenology bust. Phrenology is a pseudoscience which involves measuring the bumps on the skull to predict mental traits. Developed by German physician Franz Gall in 1796, the discipline was influential in psychiatry and psychology during the 19th century. Gall's premise that character, thoughts, and emotions are located in specific areas of the brain was an important historical advancement toward neuropsychology.

In the pilot episode, there is a *Speed Racer* poster on the dining room wall in Ross' new apartment. David Crane and Kevin Bright were avid fans of the animated series when they were kids. *Speed Racer* (aka *Mach GoGoGo*) is a Japanese comic about automobile racing. *Mach GoGoGo* was originally serialized in print in 1966 and adapted into anime with 52 episodes that aired from April 1967 to March 1968. Selected chapters were released in the 1990s under the title *Speed Racer Classics*. The television series itself is an early example of an anime becoming a successful franchise in the United States, spawning multiple spin-offs in both print and broadcast media. *Friends* incorporated numerous allusions to the show (jokes, posters, t-shirts, etc.), even though many viewers may not know the cartoon or its characters. According to Kevin Bright, "If it rings a bell with all of us who work on the show, that's what we use as our barometer."

Hidden Nudity

Most *Friends* fans are astonished to discover the hidden nudity scattered throughout the various sets. Spotting nudity in the series has turned into an adult version of Where's Waldo? For example, during Lamaze class in "The One with Two Parts, Part 1" (1.16), there is a picture of a seemingly nude child taped to the side of the TV. Also, when the girls are performing the ex-boyfriend cleansing ritual in "The One with the Candy Hearts" (1.14), Rachel's t-shirt has an image of a topless woman pulling up thigh-high stockings.

The most egregious example occurs in "The One with the 'Cuffs" (4.03) where Joanna's office contains a secret nude photograph. In the wooden cabinet with glass doors, on the second shelf from the top, there is a framed photo of a topless woman. The picture is visible after Chandler retrieves his pants from an office wall hook and utters the words "I'll make something up."

In several episodes, such as "The One Where Phoebe Runs" (6.07), on the side wall in Phoebe's apartment living room is a poster of a woman wearing a red top and holding a parasol while lounging in a canoe with her top partially undone, exposing one breast and nipple. It is a very risqué advertisement for The Great Eastern Dispensary LTD (c. 1930s). Starting in the 1920s, this Shanghai enterprise began making medicines and advertising its products, propelling it to become one of the most famous and influential dispensaries at the time.

In a deleted scene from "The One with the Nap Partners" (7.06), Chandler is watching *The Bikini Car Wash Company* (1992), a sex comedy about a group of young women who sport bikinis while washing vehicles to help a local business owner. The movie clip shown in the episode features a topless woman—her bikini top lacks adequate coverage as she scrubs a car window with her soapy breasts. The segment is included in the uncut DVD version of the episode.

Posters in Joey's apartment

Easter Egg Hunt

In the early years of the show, the *Friends* crew had a little rag doll they used to hide in and around some of the sets as their own personal Easter egg hunt. They hid the toy in the freezer of Monica's refrigerator or in little nooks and crannies around the permanent sets, i.e., Monica and Joey's apartments and Central Perk. In later years, the crew became more creative by rigging the set dressing or hiding other objects in unusual places as a personal challenge to their coworkers.

There were several notable examples. In "The One with Chandler in a Box" (4.08), when Joey enters Central Perk and asks Gunther if he's seen Chandler, the glass pastry dome has a russet potato in it. In "The One with Rachel's New Dress" (4.18), Joshua's parents' condominium has a bust on a side table in the corner of the living room. There are several scene cuts where the eyes of the bust are glowing red, but only when Joshua and Rachel are in the same frame. Finally, in season ten, there is an M&M collectible (a yellow peanut M&M seated on club chair) in Joey's oven. The oven proved to be a good hiding place. The toy remained hidden in the appliance for the rest of the series.

Gladys

Phoebe's 3-D artwork (Gladys) was created by an independent artist. It was not created specifically for the show. Set decorator Greg Grande bought it at a flea market because he thought it "would be really funny as artwork for Phoebe's apartment wall."

Gladys debuted in "The One with Phoebe's Dad" (2.09), hanging on a living room side wall in Phoebe's grandmother's apartment. After the set was struck (dismantled), the piece was stored in the Warner Bros. property warehouse. When the artwork was retrieved a year later, the left hand had become severed and could not be located. The set decorator liked the imperfection because it made the piece "eclectic" which was a good fit for Phoebe's eccentric persona.

Gladys was specifically featured in "The One with Ross's Grant" (10.06). After the script was penned, the art department was instructed to create Glynnis, a comparably creepy 3-D artwork. The crew members loved this installment because it allowed the team to create a comparably creepy 3-D piece.

Few fans realize that Gladys occasionally sported different-colored hair and clothing. At times she had blonde hair or a blue dress but in most episodes it was black hair and a red dress. The set decorator occasionally changed Gladys' hair and dress colors to comport with the tone or mood of a scene.

Magna Doodle

The doodle board was usually attached to the back of Joey's entry door and often was adorned with cartoon drawings or important messages. The magna doodle became a fun accessory for fans to track, hoping to gain insight into each episode plotline. After it was introduced in season three, nearly every episode had at least one new drawing.

The magna doodle was first introduced in "The One with the Hypnosis Tape" (3.18) on the wall next to the entry door in Joey's apartment. The left column had a grocery list "Buy Milk Eggs Bread" and the right had a note, "Joey call your dad." In the early episodes, the message board had no assigned artist, so occasionally it was left blank or unchanged. Since no one was assigned artistic duties, anyone with an inclination could leave their mark. The early artists were both cast and crew, such as producer Todd Stevens, gaffer (electrician) Paul Swain, and leadperson (head set dresser) Scott Bruza. Swain started the ritual as a prank but the producers liked it. In the fourth season he was officially designated as the doodle board artist.

Typically, the magna doodle featured random drawings. There was no hidden meaning behind the sketches. Every so often the drawing corresponded to a writer's special request as it related to the storyline, such as Emma's birthday greeting in "The One with the Cake" (10.04). Other times it was an inside joke for the crew. For example, Swain once drove his truck into a ditch. The following week he sketched a truck stuck on a mound of dirt with two guys, one in front of the vehicle and the other in back, and the word "Oops!" across the top. It seems like whenever the crew went hunting, to the beach, or attended hockey games, their adventures were memorialized with drawings. Swain usually crafted the drawings for preshoots or a couple hours before audience filming started, though he often changed the doodles during filming breaks or pickups (filming scenes after the audience departs).

The magna doodle quickly became a way for the show's producers and cast members to send messages to their friends or fans. It often depicted funny lines or jokes, and at times featured really cool drawings. For a long time after the 9/11 terrorist attack, the doodle board was a way to convey heartfelt thank you messages to first responders in New York. Other times, Swain liked to show off his artistic skills by sketching deep-sea diving or outer space images, two of his favorite interests.

Over the course of the series there were two magna doodle drawing boards. The first one wore out so the prop master searched for an exact replica to match the original and found it on eBay. During the series' run, the magna doodle appeared in 108 episodes with 117 original messages or drawings. It was left blank five times, twice there were duplicate notes, and once the board was absent from the apartment (Swain forgot to return it to the set after sketching a drawing for the show).

New York Landmarks

The exterior shot for Chandler's office is the Solow Building, near Bergdorf Goodman and the Plaza Hotel. The 1974 building has 50 floors (49 floors above ground level), and is featured in *Sex and the City* (1998-2004), *Superman* (1978), *Zoolander* (2001) (headquarters of Mugatu fashion empire) and *Cloverfield* (2008) (as monster bait). The building address is 9 W. 57th St., which became the namesake for the Nine West shoe store chain.

When looking at several of the establishing shots of Chandler's office building, viewers often mistake the hotel on the right (Plaza Hotel) as the Tipton Hotel, the main setting for *The Suite Life of Zack & Cody*. In reality, the exterior shots of the fictional Tipton Hotel were the Fairmont Copley Plaza in Boston and the Vancouver Hotel in British Columbia.

The Plaza Hotel is mentioned and featured in several episodes as the setting for special events. Built in 1907, using the popular French Chateau style of the time, it was originally a residential building for the wealthiest New Yorkers, which explains its perfect downtown location (near Central Park, museums, etc.). The interior decor was made to suit the most luxurious residents of the 20th century with gold, marble and crystal details. The famous hotel appears in numerous New York–based movies, e.g., *The Great Gatsby* (2013), *Eloise at the Plaza* (2003), *Serendipity* (2001), *Sleepless in Seattle* (1993), *Home Alone 2: Lost in New York* (1992) and *Moonstruck* (1987).

Ross worked at two museums: Museum of Prehistoric History and Museum of Natural History, both of which are fictional employers. The establishing shot used to represent the museums is actually the Alexander Hamilton United States Custom House at 1 Bowling Green, Manhattan, New York, built in 1907.

The Trump Building at 40 Wall St. is featured in several transition clips, such as "The One with All the Cheesecakes" (7.11) when Ross and Monica attend Frannie's wedding. It's a 927-foot-tall (283 m) neo-Gothic skyscraper between Nassau and William streets in the Financial District of Manhattan. The building was erected from 1929 to 1930, and was first known as the Bank of Manhattan Trust Building.

Pete Becker's office building uses an establishing shot for the Brown Brothers Harriman high-rise, located at 140 Broadway in Lower Manhattan. The building's foreground artwork features Isamu Noguchi's *Red Cube* sculpture which is not actually a cube, but a distorted shape seemingly stretched along its vertical axis. His other famous work, Sunken Garden, is situated in the open plaza in front of the Chase Manhattan Bank building. The base of the garden is set one story below street level in a circular space cut out from the plaza.

NYC landmarks (left to right): Washington Square Arch, Jefferson Market Library, Cooper Union and St. Paul's Chapel

A frequent scene transition clip features Washington Square Arch. It is a marble Roman triumphal arch in Washington Square Park, in the trendy Greenwich Village neighborhood of Lower Manhattan. Designed by architect Stanford White in 1892, it commemorates the centennial of George Washington's 1789 inauguration as President of the United States, and forms the southern terminus of Fifth Avenue. It is constructed using white Tuckahoe marble to imitate a Roman Triumphal Arch. The Arch stands 77 feet (23 m) high, the piers are 30 feet (9.1 m) apart and the opening is 47 feet (14 m) high. The iconography centers on images of war and peace.

In "The One with Ross's Grant" (10.06), a transitional clip spotlights Jefferson Market Library fka Jefferson Market Courthouse, a National Historic Landmark located at 425 Avenue of the Americas in Greenwich Village. Built from 1874 to 1877, the *AIA Guide to New York City* calls the building "A mock Neuschwansteinian assemblage ... of leaded glass, steeply sloping roofs, gables, pinnacles, Venetian Gothic embellishments, and an intricate tower and clock; one of the City's most remarkable buildings."

A transition clip in "The One with the Ballroom Dancing" (4.04) focuses attention on St. Paul's Chapel, an Episcopal parish for Trinity Church, located at 209 Broadway. Built in 1766, it is the oldest surviving church building in Manhattan, and one of the nation's finest examples of Late Georgian church architecture. When St. Paul's Chapel was left unscathed after the September 11, 2001 terrorist attack and collapse of the World Trade Center right behind it, the chapel was subsequently nicknamed "The Little Chapel That Stood."

In "The One with Phoebe's Ex-Partner" (3.14), the establishing shot for Rachel's fashion lecture is The Cooper Union Building, a private college in the East Village neighborhood of Manhattan since 1859. The cube artwork, *Alamo*, was installed in 1967. It was named by the artist's wife because its scale and mass reminded her of Alamo Mission in San Antonio, Texas.

Moondance Diner

In "The One with Two Parties" (2.22), Monica regrettably accepts a waitstaff position at the Moondance Diner. This was a real restaurant in the SoHo neighborhood of Manhattan, located at 80 6th Ave. between Canal and Grand streets. The eatery was featured in *Spider-Man* (2002) (where Kirsten Dunst's character worked), *Sex and the City*, *Miami Vice*, and even the children's show *Reading Rainbow*.

The diner opened in 1933 as Holland Tunnel Diner. It seated 34 people, with six tables and 10 counter stools. Like most diners of its vintage, it was built elsewhere and hauled to its site. The restaurant was roughly 36 feet by 16 feet. The establishment evolved into a 1950s-themed diner and by the 1990s it was a major tourist attraction. The Moondance Diner closed in 2007 to make room for the ModernHaus SoHo hotel which opened in 2010.

In mid-2007, the eatery was donated by Extell Development Company to the American Diner Museum in Providence, Rhode Island, which put it up for sale on its website before the structure was moved. In August, the diner was purchased from the museum for $7,500 by Vince and Cheryl Pierce and transported 2,400 miles (3,900 km) on the back of a semi-trailer truck to La Barge, Wyoming, at a cost of $40,000. That winter it suffered significant weather-related damage, but reopened in March 2008 and immediately made *USA Today*'s list of 51 "great burger joints." Unfortunately, after a decline in trade due to a downturn in the local Wyoming gas-drilling industry, the diner permanently closed in March 2012.

The crew hid a potato in the pastry dome (left) and an M&M collectible in the oven (right)

Central Perk

The *Friends* coffeehouse setting was inspired by Insomnia Cafe, a coffee shop located at 7286 Beverly Blvd. in Los Angeles, California. Kauffman was driving to work one day when she passed a funky beatnik cafe. This seemingly innocuous locale inspired her to cowrite the *Friends* pilot episode using a coffee shop as the primary setting. Since she and David Crane had been feeling nostalgic about their younger days in New York, they decided their sitcom would take place in a Manhattan coffeehouse.

Design

Once a New York coffee shop became the primary location for the sitcom pilot, Crane and Kauffman had the daunting task of figuring out exactly what the set should look like. After much consideration, they agreed on a warm, cozy environment with natural wood, brick walls and tattered furnishings where customers would feel free to kick back and put their feet up on the furniture. This was the basic ambiance of Insomnia Cafe.

The idea behind Central Perk was to have it feel like a comfortable, casual living room, a nice hangout space, and "not your typical generic coffee shop with the computers." When the creators outlined their design to set decorator Greg Grande, the first place that came to mind for him was Insomnia Cafe, the same coffeehouse that inspired Kauffman. He called it "one of the first interesting coffee shops in LA," and "the inspiration for eclectic, old, classic pieces of furniture." Grande used it as the model for the set. He wanted to make the gang's go-to haunt comfy but different from the apartment sets. "We went with repurposed, old-school pieces and a palette of rich earth tones," Grande explained.

Set designer John Shaffner indicated that the "coffeehouse had a bit of a bohemian feel to it, from the '50s, with Phoebe playing music in there." Meanwhile, Grande emphasized the decor: "Nothing really matched, but there was collectible artwork on the wall so I took that and kind of drove that point in." Together, they transformed Central Perk into such a quintessential part of *Friends* that Grande called it the "seventh character on the show."

One interesting design note: the coffee shop floor plan was specifically designed to shift focus on Rachel for her grand entrance in the pilot episode. The doors were intentionally positioned diagonally to showcase her entrance through the double doors wearing a white bridal gown. According to the producers, that one segment was the linchpin of the episode. Everything hinged on her dramatic entrance. And the cafe's door placement accentuated her importance because "everybody had to physically turn and look at Rachel, making her the focus of the scene."

Inspirations

The basic floor plan for Central Perk is relatively insipid, so the *Friends* art director was searching for a signature design to be the focal point of the cafe. For inspiration, he went back to his days in New York where one local restaurant came to mind. "The coffeehouse came about because there was a little restaurant that we used to all go down to on West Fourth Street in Manhattan, and it had a door in the corner," Shaffner said. "So we went to Kevin and Margaret and David and when we showed them the model and I said, 'We want to do a little corner door like the restaurant that we used to go to,' and they remembered it as well. It was called Arnold's Turtle." The eatery was located at 51 Bank St. in New York's West Village. Unfortunately, it no longer exists.

The Central Perk design was really an amalgamation of many coffee shops and cafes that David Crane, Marta Kauffman, Kevin Bright and John Shaffner experienced in their youth, especially while living in New York in the 1970s and 1980s. The gang often visited

Café Manhattan at 35 W. 45th St. in midtown Manhattan, which inspired the real wood bar that was added to the Central Perk set.

The showrunners were also inspired by Cholmondeley's (aka Chum's), a coffee shop and lounge in Usen Castle at Brandeis University, their alma mater. The name Cholmondeley was inspired by Ralph Norman's Black and Tan Coonhound. In 1950, Norman became the first campus photographer. Chum's decor is rather impersonal, but it does have sofas, club chairs, pub tables and mismatched furniture, and boasts a lengthy history of prominently displaying the artwork of local artists and featuring musical guests, the most famous being Tracy Chapman, J. Geils Band, Joan Baez, and the first American performance of Genesis. Obviously, *Friends* incorporated many aspects of Chum's decor as well as its traditions of prominently displaying artwork on the back wall and having musical guests perform for its patrons.

Coffee Shop Location

The exact location of Central Perk was never revealed in the series. Many fans assumed the coffee shop was on the first floor of the main apartment building, primarily because some of the characters referred to it as being "downstairs," and Joey once mentioned that Central Perk was exactly 97 steps away from his apartment. Of course, his math is slightly skewed since a typical apartment building has 18 steps between each floor, which in Joey's case would total 108 staircase steps from his sixth-floor abode. Both inferences reinforce the theory that Central Perk in on the lower level. However, the exterior establishing shot of the apartment building has the ground floor occupied by a restaurant with red awnings, not a coffeehouse with red-white-gray striped awnings. So, in effect, no one really knows where Central Perk is actually located in the fictional universe.

Interior Decor

During the series' decade run, set decorator Greg Grande and his crew often updated the decor of the coffee shop (e.g., reupholstered chairs and barstools, replaced the orange sofa, and updated the menu chalkboard). They also switched out the flowers, wall art, and posters every three to four episodes. However, in the first season, the decor never changed because the sitcom's production budget did not allow for expenditures on unnecessary set dressings.

Central Perk was dismantled four times over the course of the series' run in order to build other sets, i.e., casino, hospital, Barbados resort, and airport (in the finale), and it was gutted and redressed once, for Monica and Chandler's wedding. As with all sets facing demolition, according to *Friends* construction foreman Dan Kelley, the entire structure was thoroughly photographed to document the location of every prop and dressing, so when it came time to rebuild and redress the set, the tedious, time-consuming process was much easier to accomplish.

Burnt-Orange Sofa

The iconic velvet burnt-orange, tufted mohair couch from the early 1900s was found by *Friends* set decorator Greg Grande in the basement of the massive Warner Bros. property warehouse. "Literally in the back corner, shoved under another piece, was this sofa with beautiful carved wood," he recalled. According to set designer John Shaffner, the low-slung design encouraged a slouchy, home-away-from-home posture. It seemed perfect for Central Perk.

Most *Friends* fans are astonished to discover that the storied furniture piece was not originally part of the pilot set. Shaffner had chosen a beige-tone couch but during the first walk through, NBC executives told the producers to replace the sofa (they preferred a less repellent shade). The davenport had to be swapped out before rehearsal the next day and Grande did not have time (or money) to shop for something better. His decorating budget was so restricted that he often saved money and cut costs by relying on used and discarded items to furnish the sets. "The first thing I did was scour the Warner Bros. prop house," Grande explained. Deep in the basement he found a gem but it was tattered and torn. He didn't have many options so he cleaned it up as best he could and placed it on the set.

During rehearsal the next day, the studio and network executives objected to the sofa. The burnt-orange pigment was acceptable but its bedraggled condition was deplorable. "I remember explicitly, there were network and studio notes because there was a rip in the back of the sofa and it was a little tattered on the arms," Grande recalled. Director James Burrows confronted the executives and defended the couch as being "absolutely believable and real." The parties ultimately compromised—Grande had to conceal the biggest rip with a tapestry throw, sew the fringe, and mend the smaller tears.

After the series was picked up for the fall television schedule, Grande found the same fabric in Europe and reupholstered the couch. Then he put a piece of plywood under the cushions to keep the actors from sinking too deeply and slouching. Eventually, he had a second couch made. The original can still be seen on the Warner Bros. studio tour.

No one knows the early history of the celebrated burnt-orange sofa, but Grande has his theories. "It was probably used in an old movie," he speculated. But its past doesn't seem to matter to doting fans. "We refurbished it and gave it new life. Over the years we've had a lot of calls from people wanting to know where to buy the couch."

Artwork

Due to the limited budget for set dressing, the Central Perk interior remained relatively intact during the first season. This included the artwork. Initially, series set decorator Greg Grande envisioned swapping the flowers, wall art and posters every three or four episodes to mimic a real neighborhood coffee shop. His plans had to be put on hold for a year until the decorating budget was expanded. Once the show became a steady success, he was able to do everything he envisioned.

In the early years of the show, Grande met with local and regional artists to procure pieces for the Central Perk wall, but as the show grew in popularity, artists from around the world were clamoring to have their work featured in the show. By series end, the sitcom showcased pieces from local, national and international artists, and Grande even hired a few to create original pieces for the show. *Friends* actually advanced the careers of many previously unknown artists. All the artwork was displayed for free. The artists didn't have to pay a dime for having 20 to 30 million people ogling their creations every week.

Most of the paintings were from the pop art genre, comparable to the works of Andy Warhol, Roy Lichtenstein, Jean-Michel Basquiat or Keith Haring, while others resembled adaptations of other famous pieces. There were three talented artists in particular that were Grande's favorites: pop artist Burton Morris, Cajun artist George Rodrigue and pop art encaustic painter Jeff Schaller.

Burton Morris

The most popular and oft-used artist made it onto the show by accident. "It was sort of a fluke," explained pop artist Burton Morris. "David Schwimmer wore a t-shirt of mine in an episode. I called Warner Bros., showed some of my work to one of the producers and now I'm known as the *Friends* artist." Soon Warner Bros., Jennifer Aniston and Oprah Winfrey added his pieces to their collections. "It helped my career take off and blossom," said Morris, who was thereafter commissioned to design art for the Olympics. "I was very fortunate to be part of television history." The Pittsburgh native became the most prolific art contributor to the show. Over a dozen of Burton's original pop art paintings and designs were displayed in more than 70 episodes of *Friends*, including such works as *Coffee Break* (steaming cup of coffee), *Lady Liberty*, *King Kong*, *Uncle Sam* and *Jump Toast*.

The artist's meteoric fame began with a t-shirt. In "The One with the Thumb" (1.03), as the guys enter Central Perk after a softball game, Ross is wearing a Big Hitter t-shirt that features the artwork of Morris. "It was of a baseball player—that was actually a Pittsburgh Pirate, without the 'P,'" Morris said. The pop art garment was part of a line he was selling at the time. When his sister moved to California, she took some shirts with her and one ended up in the hands of a production worker on *Friends*. When Schwimmer saw the design, he asked the guy, "Hey, can I wear that shirt? I think it is a great shirt for this scene."

The artist was unaware that his artwork appeared on the hit series until he received a phone call from his sister. "I will never forget the moment in 1994 when my sister called me from California, saying she was watching a new television show called *Friends*, and that one of the actors was wearing a t-shirt with my artwork of a big hitter baseball player," he endearingly recalled. He then placed a phone call to Warner Bros. Studios. After speaking to Kevin Bright on the phone, Morris was invited to the set of *Friends* if he should ever be in LA. Coincidentally, he had been planning a trip to Southern California just two weeks later, so he stopped by the set. After that, he was flown to the studio for a meet and greet. "I got to meet all the actors and hang out with everyone," said Morris. "We were all the same age, and they were all brand new, so I didn't know who any of them were." Bright asked if he could hang some of Morris' art in the background of sets and the talented artist jumped at the opportunity to get national exposure for his work.

Central Perk paintings created by pop artist Burton Morris

Morris' *Jump Toast* pop art painting debuted in "The One with the Race Car Bed" (3.07). "The first piece of mine was a big toaster painting that was in Central Perk and currently it resides in the Heinz History Center in Pittsburgh," Morris stated. "In every season, one by one they started using more of my work. It wasn't on every episode, but every season they would change it up, so they might have a piece on for three to four episodes, then change to something else."

The international exposure from having his artwork appear on *Friends* inspired Morris to design neckties, which were released in October 1996. He partnered with Pittsburgh's clothier Charles Spiegel and their collaboration became a very popular accessory worn by Chandler (though Gunther also sported a few ties). The *Friends* producers even purchased Perrier water to feature in the show because the bottle labels were designed by Morris at the request of the carbonated water company.

Morris calls the longevity of the show's reach as a "mix of luck and good fortune" since "no one would have known this show would still be lasting and reaching new generations." As a result, people who weren't even born when the show debuted are discovering *Friends* for the first time and seeing Morris' work prominently displayed.

Born in 1964 in Pittsburgh, Pennsylvania, Morris earned a Bachelor of Fine Arts degree from Carnegie Mellon University's School of Design in 1986. He produced artwork for the United States Olympic Team, the 38th Montreux Jazz Festival, and the 2010 FIFA World Cup, and was commissioned to do work for Chanel, Absolute Vodka, Rolex, Kellogg's, Ford, and Coca-Cola (creating 100 different paintings for Coke's 100th anniversary of the 6.5 oz. glass bottle). His art and designs have graced the walls of renowned institutions like The Academy of Motion Picture Arts & Sciences, the White House, and the United Nations. In addition, Burton's artwork has helped to raise millions of dollars for charities worldwide.

George Rodrigue

The second-most-prolific artistic contributor to the set was George Rodrigue. He became famous with his *Blue Dog* book series and accompanying cover art paintings. Several of his works were prominently displayed in Central Perk: (1) *Blue Dog*, an inspirational tale about the Cajun character known as Blue Dog (Rodrigue) and its master with the paintings telling a story about love, art, and human nature; (2) *Blue Dog Man*, an American art and popular culture book that depicts 70 paintings featuring Blue Dog while also detailing the legends and inspirations behind his creation; and (3) *Blue Dog Love*, which highlights the paintings of Rodrigue who, particularly upon meeting his wife, often created artwork based on his life with her, though substituting a female blue dog in place of himself.

The Louisiana native began painting bayou landscapes in the 1960s and the Blue Dog series began in the early 1990s. Rodrigue used the shape and stance of his deceased dog, Tiffany, and his work was primarily influenced by the loup-garou (werewolf) legend. Blue Dog was made popular by Absolut Vodka in 1992 as part of its national ad campaign. The ghostly blue spaniel/terrier is often featured with a white nose and yellow eyes.

Jeff Schaller

The final artist to have work prominently featured in Central Perk is from Downingtown, Pennsylvania, and a Beaver College (Acadia University) graduate. Jeff Schaller's pop art paintings tie together his love of silk screen, encaustic and acrylic. He has the distinction of being the last artist to feature artwork in Central Perk. The displayed piece, entitled *Cup o Joe,* was specifically commissioned by the *Friends* producers for the finale. Schaller's work is collected both nationally and internationally and displayed in the Coca-Cola Museum and Lancaster Museum of Art. Another illustration of his artwork, entitled *Questions and Answers*, was prominently displayed in Ross' living room starting in the ninth season.

Schaller's artwork debuted in "The One with Ross's Inappropriate Song" (9.07) where he had a painting hanging in Richard's apartment. He owes a massive debt of gratitude to his good friend, pop artist and frequent *Friends* contributor, Burton Morris. When Morris was too busy to create new pieces for the hit TV series, he introduced Schaller to Greg Grande. "I remember getting the call and the set designer saying they needed a piece for Richard's apartment," the artist recalled. "I was so excited because I thought Monica and Richard were going to get back together! I was in the know!" Thereafter, Schaller became a regular art contributor for the final two seasons of the show.

Coffeemaker

The huge Central Perk coffeemaker actually comprises two entirely different machines. In order to create an instantly recognizable set piece, the art department found an antique inoperable cappuccino maker and placed it on top of a functional espresso machine. James Michael Tyler was hired as the barista who pretended to use the equipment.

The espresso machine prop was never really operated on the show (it would have been too loud), but the barista had to appear knowledgeable and experienced while pretending to use the equipment. Tyler never made one cup of coffee in Central Perk, and doubts that he could have, since it was such an obsolete coffee machine. The set designer purposely chose an outdated model because it was all he could afford on the show's shoestring budget.

Coffee Brand & Logo

Set decorator Greg Grande was integral in designing the Central Perk logo. "I'm really proud of the logo," he stated. "It's something that I had a hand in and that's everywhere now." Since the logo is almost symmetrical, the image is readable when overlaid on both sides of the coffee shop's window. Astute fans will notice the coffee steam is asymmetrical and therefore visible on the backside of the opposite logo.

Starting with the second season, Grande wanted to give Central Perk a genuine look so he worked with the art department to create logos for fake coffee brands that could be seen on packaging in the background. The coffee shop chalkboard then advertised the fictitious brands by listing them as menu items, highlighting special blends that were developed by the art department, such as the highly caffeinated Central Jolt or the robust Empire Roast. Central Perk had a flavor to satisfy any coffee lover's cravings.

Interior Chalkboard

The Central Perk chalkboard featured the cafe's signature line of specialty coffees. The chalkboard became quite famous in its own right. Its offerings changed on occasion but here is a sampling of what blends the coffeehouse sold in the first season (with purposeful typos added by the crew):

> *Long Island Cream*: A moovingly rich and creamy coffee straight from the mutter's utter.
>
> *Central Jolt*: Loaded with caffeine. We don't recommend doing needlepoint after a cup of this joe.
>
> *5th Avenue*: Going shopping? You'll need some fuel. Try this trendy blend while you spend.
>
> *Empire Roast*: Bursting w/flavor & energy. You won't be hanging around after drinking this stuff.
>
> *Ms. Liberty Blend*: A liberating blend. Light & sweet. You'll be crying "Freedom"! when you taste it.
>
> *N.Y. Classico*: The classic coffee taste you'd expect on a classic New York morning.
>
> *Tin Pan Java*: Filtered through the Fine St. skid row hankies, we get a brew so thin you'd think it's tea.
>
> *Manhattan Mocha*: A stimulating brew guaranteed to keep your eyes open until the wee hours.
>
> *Mocha Quartet*: A symphony of flavors blended together to make your day sing
>
> *Urban*: Robust and raw, this coffee will have you swinging from the lamp posts

Pop art prints by Jeff Schaller that were featured in seasons nine and ten

Of course, all the brands are fake and no coffee was ever brewed in Central Perk, but offstage the craft services department prepared a wide array of food and beverages for the cast and crew to eat and drink during working hours. Craft services (aka Crafty) provided hot meals for lunch and dinner as well as basic sustenance and snacks between meals. Typically, the backstage tables were located on the outskirts of the set and functioned as a place for crew members to take a moment and get fueled up for the workday.

Exterior Signage

On the sidewalk outside Central Perk, an A-frame sign promoted Phoebe as a regular performer every Friday and Saturday night. It also advertised the business' imported coffees and teas. During some establishing shots of Central Perk, the signage indicates "appearing today noon, Neighbor Tim," referencing an unidentified crew member named Tim whose on-set altruism went above and beyond the call of duty. Since then, "Neighbor Tim" remained a permanent fixture on the Central Perk message board.

Central Perk had one other advertising display: a wall sign to the left of the main logoed window. The board promoted daily events at the coffee shop: Wednesday—poetry reading, Thursday—open mic night, and Friday/Saturday—live performances (e.g., Phoebe Buffay).

Neighborhood

During the first season, there was no street set outside Central Perk. Not only did the construction department have a limited budget, but the Stage 5 soundstage was too small to accommodate a thoroughfare set. This created a problem because the set designer had to create a realistic view outside the coffee shop windows. "We got two backdrops from Warner Bros. that were all hand-painted and boy, were they old and tired. We tied them together and that was what was outside the main door of the coffeehouse," John Shaffner recalled. He quickly realized the tattered backdrop was inadequate, so he told the set decorator, "I have a horrible backdrop so we're going to put frosting on the lower part of the window. ... I think if we can hang a plant in here, anything you can think of to hang down in front of these windows because we don't want to look out there too much."

In the second season, the entire production crew moved to the much more expansive Stage 24. Kevin Bright immediately proposed discarding the painted backdrop. "Let's build a street outside the window so we can do things on the street and we're not looking at those crappy backdrops," he emphatically suggested. The new Central Perk set became one of the few soundstages with a real asphalt "street" which allowed for more realistic sound during "outdoor" filming. It also included underground plumbing to pipe-in real steam from the manholes. Having a city thoroughfare allowed the crew to film segments with the characters on the street, expand the show's scene locations, and reduce the number of on-location shoots on the Warner Bros. backlot.

The expansive street set allowed John Shaffner to build a small neighborhood outside Central Perk. The executive producers were responsible for naming some of the businesses. Free Being Records is homage to a Greenwich Village record store that Kevin Bright visited as a youth in New York during the 1970s. It was located at 129 Second Ave. just south of St. Mark's Place. At the time, it was one of the few businesses that partook in buying and selling used LPs. Locals dubbed it "Defwreckastow" because employees played the music mind-blowing loud. Joey Ramone even frequented the record shop and was photographed eyeballing Plácido Domingo's 1990 album *Be My Love*.

Central Perk paintings by George Rodrigue (left), Burton Morris (center), and Susan Winget (right)

David Crane also delved into the business-naming game. There was a florist shop on the street called Jeffrey's Flowers. It was across from Central Perk and named for his life partner, Jeffrey Klarik. "It's just a little chance to say hello," Crane playfully asserted. "I get a lot of points for getting his name into the script whenever I can."

Marta Kauffman was not to be outdone. She added a personal touch on two businesses. Dottie & Herman's Deli (finest imported kosher foods) was named after her mom and dad, Dorothy and Herman. As a tribute solely for her mother, Kauffman named an eatery Dot's Spot. Dorothy's nickname was "Dot" or "Dottie."

Central Perk Studio Tours

Generally, once a TV series ends, the production crew dismantles all the sets. In recent years, however, studios have started to realize the value in preserving the sets of popular shows. Although Warner Bros. was not foresighted enough to preserve any of the *Friends* sets, the studio eventually commissioned construction of a replica Central Perk set which it included as part of its studio tour. The knockoff was initially housed in a props warehouse where fans could sit on the trademark orange couch and have their picture taken. It later became a featured landmark in the studio's tour.

On July 16, 2015, WB opened Stage 48: Script to Screen, a behind-the-scenes tour of film and television production. The large, interactive museum is the final leg of the tour. Visitors can have a personal and professional photo taken on the burnt-orange Central Perk couch. The epochal atmosphere has frequently inspired visitors to propose marriage and has caused many tourists to cry. The immersive experience even offers a chance to recreate a *Friends* scene on the Central Perk set. Warner Bros. has retained nearly every *Friends* prop and set dressing, such as Pat the dog, the peephole picture frame, and other furnishings from Monica's apartment.

After the *Friends* reunion in May 2021, WB upgraded its fan experience. The menu for Central Perk Café was expanded to include foods typically devoured in a New York deli (e.g., corn beef melts, fries and pizza wedges) as well as the most important item: Central Perk coffee. The dessert offerings include Rachel's Thanksgiving trifle (without the meat or peas), cheesecake (but not off the floor), and other delectables. Guests can dine in recreated sets including Central Perk, Joey's apartment, Monica's apartment and Greenwich Village. As expected, the tour features *Friends*-themed merchandise, from kitchen and dining ware to apparel and other collectibles.

Central Perk Imitations

The popularity of *Friends* and its iconic Central Perk set has inspired various imitations worldwide, including the now-defunct Phoenix Perk in Dublin (named for Phoenix Park) and Riverdale Perk in Toronto. In 2006, Iranian businessman Mojtaba Asadian began a Central Perk franchise, registering the name in 32 countries, including Dubai. The *Friends*-inspired decor features replica couches, wooden bar counters, neon signage and brick walls. The coffeehouses also have paintings of various characters from the series, and the televisions air episodes from the series. In 2006, James Michael Tyler (Gunther) attended the grand opening of Friends Avenue Cafe (the flagship Dubai cafe in Umm Suqeim) and functioned as a spokesman for the company. Dubai has two additional *Friends*-themed shops: Cross Cultural Perks in Al Fahidi and Central Perk in Mirdif.

In India, there are six *Friends*-themed cafes, located in the cities of Chandigarh (Central Perk), Kolkata (F.R.I.E.N.D.S. Cafe) and West Bengal (F.R.I.E.N.D.S. Cafe). All six locations feature symbols from the original series, including Pat the dog, the orange sofa, Monica's purple door, and Phoebe's pink bicycle. There are two similarly themed cafes in Pakistan as well—one in Lahore, Punjab (Friends Cafe), and one in Peshawar, Khyber Pakhtunkhwa (Central Perk). Both offer the fabled couch, Phoebe's guitar, the guys' foosball table, and quotes from the show on the walls, with episodes airing on a projector.

Other venues have capitalized on the success of *Friends* and its quintessential coffee shop. Fully functional Central Perk replicas popped up in Beijing, China, in 2010 and then Liverpool, England, in 2012. Du Xin, a self-proclaimed *Friends* fanatic, opened the Beijing location in the Central Business District with an exclusive menu serving only food that was in the sitcom. It was so popular and successful that Xin purchased the building space next door to reproduce Joey's apartment.

In 2016, a Central Perk replica was opened in Outram, Singapore. It is the only Central Perk coffeehouse authorized by Warner Bros. that operates outside the United States. The cafe features replicas of the walls of the main characters' apartments with memorabilia and props used in the show. It even serves Monkeyshine lager, a fictional beer that debuted in "The One After the Superbowl, Part 1" (2.12). No other business establishment in the world is licensed to sell the beer.

Other Facts

During scenes in Central Perk, the cast is actually drinking coffee on set while filming the episodes. Craft services made cappuccinos and lattes for the cast to drink during live filming.

The oversize coffee mug evolved as a way to better warm the hands of the cast. During filming, the soundstage thermostat was set in the upper 60s to accommodate the audience. Having 300 attendees in close proximity had a tendency to generate a lot of body heat. The lower temperature made the six-hour production more tolerable. However, apart from the bleacher area, the lower thermostat setting made for a chilly soundstage. Thus, the oversize cup was meant to give the cast a larger surface area for warming their hands.

Although unrealistic, in the first season the gang always secured the best seat in the house (the orange sofa) whenever they visited Central Perk. When the media criticized this bizarre occurrence, the set decorator added a RESERVED sign and placed it on the coffee table (starting in season two). The writers then penned segments in three episodes where the orange couch was occupied by other customers. They even added a line of dialogue in one episode where one of the characters jokingly commented that the sofa was permanently reserved for them.

Salaries

The *Friends* creators wanted all six costars to be equally prominent in the series, and they held true to their dream, formulating what has been called "the first true ensemble show." Even the cast perpetuated the ensemble format to ensure that no one actor would be dominant—they entered themselves in the same acting categories for industry awards; during the first season, insisted on appearing together as a group on magazine covers; and after the second season, the cast opted for collective bargaining instead of individual salary negotiations.

The most important aspect of an ensemble cast is monetary equity. When an actor is signed to a series, it is generally a five-year contract at a set salary. In the first season, each of the six primary cast members signed for $22,500 per episode, except David Schwimmer who was paid $25,000 per episode. His agent negotiated an extra $2,500 per episode once it became apparent how much the creators wanted the actor to play Ross. "With *Friends*, the last actor to sign was David Schwimmer. Everybody loved Schwimmer, and his agent knew it," explained Harold Brook, executive vice president of business affairs for NBC. "We were $2,500 apart. We both dug in our heels. [NBC casting director] Lori Openden came to me and begged. I hated it, but we gave it to them."

Although she originally signed for $22,500, Courteney Cox actually made $25,000 per episode because her contract was guaranteed to match the highest-paid actor on the series. Since she was purportedly "the star" of the sitcom, her agent, Bernie Brillstein, shrewdly negotiated this clause for inclusion in the binding contract. "I was lucky I had the Richard Cunningham–Fonzie contract where no one could make more than me," Cox boldly stated.

Although the cast was under contract for five years, after the first season, Schwimmer's agent and Aniston's agent were mutually pressing for a contract renegotiation. Both actors were in strong bargaining positions because the Ross–Rachel unrequited-love story arc had captivated audiences and reinvigorated the show. Since Aniston had more Hollywood clout than Schwimmer, she was positioned to earn more than her colleague. Schwimmer, on the other hand, was in an excellent bargaining position vis-à-vis the other cast members. "For whatever reason, I was 'the breakout.' I was the guy who had the movie offers—everyone since then has had their time, their moment, but I was the first when the show started," Schwimmer proudly boasted. "And my agents were saying, 'This is the time when you go in for a raise.'"

Both actors' agents pushed NBC for more money, resulting in Schwimmer and Aniston receiving a salary bump to $40,000 per episode (though she was paid slightly more). Cox, of course, earned the same as Aniston, the highest-paid actor of the sextet. This resulted in a vast wage disparity since the lowest-paid actors (Kudrow, Perry and LeBlanc) remained at $22,500 per episode.

Following the second year, negotiations were being held to extend the contracts of the six principals. The Ross–Rachel romance was going strong and audiences continued to be enthralled by the couple. Aniston and Schwimmer knew they were the series' stars. Despite being an ensemble, they were prime to earn substantially more than their costars. "David was in the position to make the most money. He was the A-story—Ross and Rachel. He could have commanded alone more than anyone else," Matt LeBlanc acknowledged. Since the cast remained friends in real life, they openly shared their contract negotiations with one another. David Schwimmer later admitted, "I knew—because all of us were friends at this point—that, back when we started, each of us on the show had a different contract. We were all paid differently. Some had low quotes, some had higher."

Schwimmer's agent was telling him to demand a higher salary but he felt uncomfortable getting paid so much more than his costars. "I knew that I wasn't the highest-paid actor on the show, but I wasn't the lowest. And I thought, 'Okay, I'm being advised to go in for more money. But, for me, it goes against everything I truly believe in, in terms of ensemble,'" he confided. "The six of us are all leads on the show. We are all here for the same amount of hours. The storylines are always balanced." Schwimmer began to contemplate equal pay for the ensemble. "That was actually a by-product of how the impulse originated, which was from my ensemble theater," he pensively reflected. "[At Lookingglass] we all paid dues. We were all waiting tables and doing other jobs, but we all paid the same amount of dues, and we were all paid out equally. That idea was really important to me."

In his mind, the sextet were equals because they all functioned that way on set. Every episode had three storylines and all six costars were given an equal number of lines, jokes, scenes and plots. Of course, equal pay meant that higher paid costars (Aniston, Cox and Schwimmer) would have to take a pay cut to elevate the income of the lesser paid costars (LeBlanc, Kudrow and Perry). Schwimmer was near the top of the pay scale so he took the lead and consulted with his mother, Arlene Coleman, a respected divorce attorney. She was instrumental in unifying the cast.

John Agoglia, former head of business affairs at NBC, reflected upon the early contract negotiations with the cast. "We convinced ourselves that we'd be better off with the cast if we recognized their success early instead of waiting until their contracts ran out. Chemistry was crucial to that show, and it was important to keep the cast happy," he honestly stated. "We started giving them raises as they were going along. At one point David Schwimmer's mother convinced the cast to negotiate as a group. She's a prominent divorce attorney. Her license plate is EX BARRACUDA."

Armed with his mother's support, Schwimmer had to convince the cast it was a good idea. He gathered the comedy troupe for a confab and began the discussion. "Here's the deal. I'm being advised to ask for more money, but I think, instead of that, we should all go in together," he explained when addressing his colleagues. "There's this expectation that I'm going in to ask for a pay raise. I think we should use this opportunity to talk openly about the six of us being paid the same." This caught the attention of everyone. Schwimmer went on to say: "I don't want to come to work feeling that there's going to be any kind of resentment from anyone else in the cast down the line. I don't want to be in their position coming to work, doing the same amount of work, and feeling like someone else is getting paid twice as much. That's ridiculous." He concluded the monologue by stating, "Let's just make the decision now. We're all going to be paid the same, for the same amount of work."

Schwimmer was convinced it was the best decision for all. "I thought it was significant for us to become a mini-union because there began to be a lot of decisions that had to be made by the group in terms of publicity." Matt LeBlanc pondered the proposal in a political vein: "David Schwimmer quoted the idea of socialist theater to us." He then added: "Did he know ultimately there would be more value in that for all of us as a whole? I don't know. I think it was a genuine gesture from him, and I always say that. It was him." Lisa Kudrow suggested they threaten to walk off the set should their demands not be met. Although a seemingly outlandish proposal, the cast actually embraced the idea as a bargaining chip in the negotiation repertoire.

After the meeting, the six costars mutually agreed to enter salary negotiations united and demand equal pay for all. Despite the higher paid actors taking a pay cut, they agreed that a wage disparity was unconscionable. Aniston declared, "I wouldn't feel good going to work knowing someone was getting x amount and I was getting something greater." Cox felt the same way: "It was so important that we got paid the same amount of money. We were all working. The show used to be called "Six of One"—that's where it started—we were six of one. I mean, we were a team." Without cast unity, she feared the network would retaliate by firing two actors and only keeping four main costars. "It could have been an ugly situation, which [is why] we all stood by each other. It was everything. Any other way, it would have been too many hard feelings, too uncomfortable. It would just have been horrible." They vowed to honor a code: if one leaves, they all leave. Naturally, the lower paid actors were all in. "I was like, 'Yeah, that sounds good for me. I'm making the least amount,'" LeBlanc said, reflecting upon the situation.

It was the first time in television history that an entire cast jointly negotiated a contract. Although some sources claim *Seinfeld* holds that distinction for their contract negotiations earlier that same year in 1997, in truth, the show about nothing was not an ensemble, and only three costars, not the show's star, successfully negotiated as a group to secure equal pay for the final season of the series. There was one other major difference: *Seinfeld* was the most successful show on television, while *Friends*, although having ratings success, was a fledgling show two years out of the gate with a cast lacking sufficient power and influence to demand exorbitant salaries.

Naturally, production companies prefer to negotiate with actors individually because it gives them leverage and a tactical advantage. Since most actors don't know their costars' financial situation (e.g., salaries, contract offers, or the specifics from salary negotiations), some may be lowballed. A unified cast means that everyone knows the score so no one can be undersold. The *Friends* actors demanded $100,000 each per episode plus a percentage of the series' profits in syndication. Such a lofty request for a third-year show is usually laughable but the costars had an ace up their sleeve. Warner Bros. started a bidding war for syndication of the series and then publicly boasted about earning an astronomical (at the time) $4 million an episode. The deal, however, hinged on the sitcom continuing at least two more seasons to generate enough episodes for the catalog. With WB's big payoff on the line, the stars had a distinct tactical advantage.

Surprisingly, the cast aired their grievances publicly which ruffled a few feathers at the network. With no official demand on the table, NBC executives questioned why the cast went public. "It's a strange way to negotiate," said Don Ohlmeyer, the president of NBC's West Coast division. As negotiations dragged deep into the summer, the cast threatened "not to show up for the taping of the new season's shows." The parties ultimately agreed to $75,000 with a half percentage point of the show's syndication fees. This was the first of many salary impasses between the cast and network. It became an annual occurrence.

For the subsequent television seasons, each cast member earned the following salary per episode: $85,000 (fourth), $100,000 (fifth), $125,000 (sixth), $750,000 (seventh and eighth), and $1 million (ninth and tenth). The three female costars were the highest-paid TV actresses of all time in the final two seasons. In addition, the cast negotiated a share of the syndication royalties starting with the third season, a rarity in actor contracts. Production companies are quite reluctant to grant their employees an ownership stake in the show; the real money is made in syndication so parting with a portion of the profits is uncommon.

During the sitcom's decade run, there were contract negotiations almost every year, but two stalemates put the show's future in jeopardy. After the fourth season, the series was very close to being canceled. Enough episodes had been shot to complete the syndication deal, which meant the actors lost some of their bargaining power. "The problem was how *much* they wanted to be treated the same. The numbers were insane when it came time to renew their contracts," revealed Harold Brook, executive vice president of business affairs at NBC. On May 17, 1998, the night before NBC was scheduled to announce its fall lineup, contract negotiations continued into the early morning hours. Brook described the tense situation: "The night before we were going to announce the schedule, I was in the bathroom at a restaurant and got a call from Warner Bros. 'It's starting,' they said. The negotiation started around 10pm and closed around 3am. We had two promos made—one was the season finale, and one was the series finale." Although Warner Bros. held the upper hand, executives inexplicably acquiesced to the actors' demands.

Dick Wolf, the legendary writer-producer of *Law & Order*, was quite incensed about the *Friends* contract that year and made it known that he would have handled the negotiations much different: "When they made the *Friends* deal, the $100,000 apiece deal, I was pretty upset. What I would have done was come out the first day, say I was disappointed the cast had chosen to negotiate in the press, and I had the unpleasant news that Matt LeBlanc wouldn't be on the show next year. I guarantee that you'd never have gotten to a second name." David Schwimmer reminisced about the bitter contract negotiations, and had this takeaway: "That negotiation made us realize that the six of us *should* be making decisions as one and looking out for each other."

After the fifth season, the cast found themselves in another negotiation stalemate with NBC. Once again, the sextet made their demands public to garner additional support from the masses. The network agreed to a raise but it was a modest increase. Naturally, one year later, both sides were at the bargaining table, but this affair turned into a bitter battle.

Before agreeing to a seventh season, the cast demanded an 850% salary increase which exceeded the record-setting contract signed by *Seinfeld*'s costars three years earlier. After protracted negotiations, the cast would not back down from their $1,050,000 per episode salary demand, so NBC aired one earth-shattering program promotion with the voice-over "You've loved them for seven years, see how it all ends with the series finale of *Friends* this Thursday." The cast promptly agreed to lower their demand to $750,000 per episode (plus 2% syndicated royalties), which NBC accepted, but it insisted on a two-year contract.

After the eighth season, the cast and network were back to locking horns during their contract talks. *Friends* was still a top-flight show and the anchor for Thursday night. It was inevitable the cast would demand and receive a higher salary, the only question was how high they would go. The six cast members were determined to be the highest-paid actors on television. While negotiating their million-dollar contracts, there were some days the cast, as a whole, would protest the negotiation tactics being used. According to Matt LeBlanc, when studio or network executives tried to "beat up" on one person during the negotiations, the entire cast would walk off the set and refuse to rehearse. Fortunately, for the cast, the final arbitration hearing coincided with upfronts (when networks set advertising rates for their upcoming fall schedule). Thus, if NBC wanted to sell ads on a highly profitable show, like *Friends*, they didn't really have a lot of bargaining chips.

The sextet remained committed to their unified salary demand and ultimately settled for a one-year deal that equaled the record-setting salary negotiated by the *Seinfeld* costars five years earlier, $1 million per episode. Except for the cast of *The Big Bang Theory* (in 2018), the *Friends* cast was the only other ensemble to successfully use collective bargaining to negotiate their historic $1 million per half-hour episode for each costar.

Matt LeBlanc defended the cast's astronomical salary demand and contract. "Were we worth $1 million? To me, that's such a strange question. It's like, well, that's irrelevant. Are you worth it? How do you put a price on how funny something is? We were in a position to get it. If you're in a position in any job, no matter what the job is—if you're driving a milk truck or installing TVs or an upholsterer for a couch—if you're in a position to get a raise and you don't get it, you're stupid. You know what I mean? We were in a position and we were able to pull it off. 'Worth it' has nothing to do with it."

Like clockwork, four months into the television season, the media began speculating another salary standoff, knowing the costars would invariably demand more as the sitcom continued to be a ratings success. This time, however, NBC was determined to settle the dust quickly and efficiently. The producers wanted it resolved fast because every year it seemed the series faced inevitable cancellation, only to have it revived for one more year. It was like *Groundhog Day*. Miraculously, NBC was able to convince the cast to forego a pay raise in exchange for a truncated season, from 24 episodes to 18, which would allow the cast to work on outside projects.

NBC agreed to pay $10 million to Warner Bros. for the production of each episode in the tenth season, the highest price in television history for a 30-minute series. Although the network was unable to generate enough advertising revenue to offset the invoice, *Friends* had a spillover effect on other NBC programs which brought higher ratings and additional advertising revenue to the other less profitable shows on its Thursday night schedule, thus allowing the network suits to justify the expenditure.

Although *Friends* was immensely successful and extremely profitable, it was also very expensive to produce. When comparing 30-minute sitcoms to 60-minute dramas, *Friends* was No. 3 overall in expenses, with *ER* topping the list at $13 million per episode during its 1998-99 season. Comedies are often much cheaper to produce than dramas due to fewer sets, smaller casts, and shorter episode length. With each *Friends* star earning $1 million per episode, 60% of the production costs went to their salaries, so it was highly unlikely NBC could afford another round of contract negotiations for an eleventh season.

In total, each cast member earned upwards of $88 million during the show's decade run. The sextet was also among the first sitcom stars to receive residuals, i.e., a percentage of royalties from reruns and syndication. Unbeknownst to them, the series would remain popular a quarter century later and command lucrative syndication, streaming, DVD and merchandising deals exceeding a billion dollars in revenue per year. It's estimated that the cast earns $9 million annually in residuals. Many tabloids falsely report that the *Friends* castmates earn $20 million per year in residuals.

James Michael Tyler

Most *Friends* fans are dumbfounded to discover the vast income that James Michael Tyler (Gunther) earned playing a minor secondary character on the hit sitcom. During the first season, he earned $500 per episode appearance. His salary doubled in season two. For the third and fourth seasons, he earned $20,000 per episode. The next two seasons had a bump to $30,000. For the remainder of the series, he took home $40,000 per installment. Of course, Tyler was not paid for installments in which he did not appear, and his pay was much less when he did not have a speaking part. So these figures represent his average pay per installment. In sum, Tyler earned $4.65 million portraying Gunther. Moreover, since *Friends* is a SAG (Screen Actors Guild) show, he earned residuals from syndication which added another $1 million to his bank account. At the time of his death in 2021, Tyler's had an estimated net worth of approximately $4 million.

Series Cancellation

After the cast secured an exorbitant $1 million per episode for season nine, everyone (cast, crew, creators, producers, writers, etc.) was convinced it would be the final season of *Friends*. The costars began making plans for movies and other projects, not anticipating a tenth season. Even NBC was looking ahead to a new television season without *Friends*. The network was losing money on the current *Friends* contract, but using it as a loss-leader, hoping to recoup ad revenue on other less successful Thursday night sitcoms.

In December 2002, halfway into the television season, NBC noticed its new fledgling sitcoms were a bust and it had no hits to carry the network forward, primarily in a post-*Friends* world. NBC Entertainment President Jeff Zucker was in a panic, and foresaw only one solution to the problem—sign *Friends* to one more year. He made it his sole mission to expedite the process.

When negotiations began, the entire cast had projects in the works but they remained amenable to a tenth season. Jennifer Aniston was the only unknown variable. She was on the fence. "I had a couple issues that I was dealing with," she stated. At the time, she was married to Brad Pitt and he was eager to start a family. Aniston had previously stated that she wanted two or three kids, while Pitt proclaimed he'd like seven. Aniston, however, was not quite there emotionally. Plus, they were having other marital issues. Their conflict made for a tumultuous time, and Pitt did not support her career decision to return for the tenth season. "He just wasn't there for me," she confided.

Other factors weighed heavily on her mind. Aniston was pondering movie contracts and questioned whether another *Friends* season was feasible. "I wanted it to end when people still loved us and we were on a high," she confessed. "And then I also was feeling like, 'How much more of Rachel do I have in me? How many more stories are there to tell for all of us before we're just now pathetic?'" Aniston wanted the series to go out on top like *Seinfeld* and feared a lackluster season may tarnish the overall perception of her character and the series.

Despite Jeff Zucker's effort to expeditiously secure *Friends* for a tenth season, contract negotiations still lingered well into April. Bright was directing the last episode of the ninth season while also negotiating a tenth season with the costars. He would shoot a scene, call NBC, meet with the cast, they would discuss a number, and then Bright would call NBC back. It was a crazy way to negotiate. Everyone was feeling indignant. After five hours of filming, interspersed with contract talks between breaks, the parties officially finalized a deal for a tenth season, and it would be their last.

Aniston was the last domino to fall. She reached a compromise that she hoped would balance her home life and movie career—a truncated season. At the time, a typical sitcom season lasted 24 episodes, but she insisted on 18. A source close to her proclaimed, "Brad was really angry when she went back for another year. It's not like they or anyone else on *Friends* needs the money. ... The rest of the cast wanted one more year and she felt a lot of pressure. But she also wants to keep Brad happy. So Jennifer said she would do one more year, but insisted on only 18 shows and that filming would be done by January." Aniston's movie career was also a factor. It was kicking into high gear and she was already committed to shooting *Derailed* and *Rumor Has It* in 2004.

After the cast agreed to a tenth season, the executive producers had to be persuaded to return. "It took us a while to get on board with the idea of season ten," David Crane readily stated. "We had to really sort of examine what stories we have left to tell that would justify coming back. I'm glad we did, because I really liked this season a lot. But you don't want to overstay your welcome." The creators were in agreement that they would not have signed on for an eleventh season, even if all the cast members had wanted to continue.

Even before entering the final season, the creators, Marta Kauffman and David Crane, were more than ready to call it quits. They endured too many seasons of uncertainty. Each season the actors had intense contract negotiations, and especially in the latter years, it seemed as though, "Oh, season seven is the last season. Or season eight. Or season nine," Crane exasperatedly recalled, so the writers always had an eye on the series finale episode, and each year, at the last minute, the show was renewed for one more season. It was quite vexing. When season ten rolled around, the duo decided that was the final straw. "We can't keep stopping and starting and rethinking everything," he exclaimed. "And that also jived with what some of the cast was thinking."

In reality, there were numerous factors that weighed into the final decision to cancel the series: (1) coming up with fresh storylines; (2) exorbitant cost of production, especially cast salaries; (3) cast discontent, and desire to work on other projects; and (4) ending the series on a high note. Moreover, the *Friends* creators knew it was time to end the series because everybody was growing up. "This is part of why the show had to end. This was no longer that time in your life when your friends are your family. You're starting your own family," Kauffman elucidated. "You don't want them to feel like, 'Thank God it's over!' And leaving them wanting more is always a nice thing."

Although Aniston was the last holdout to commit to a tenth season, ironically, after shooting the finale in January she commented, "But now, of course, I don't want it to end at all." In retrospect, the cast agreed that if they had to do things again, they wouldn't have changed a thing. They would have ended the show after season ten rather than going on with more episodes, even though the show remained so successful.

As the series was nearing the end of its run, the creators were only sure of two things: Rachel and Ross had to get together, and they never wanted the show to have a television spinoff. "Never. We never, ever from the beginning ever wanted to do a spinoff or 'Grown-Up Friends' or 'Friends Kids' or 'Baby Friends,'" Marta Kauffman adamantly proclaimed. "We always knew and felt very strongly that not only would it never happen, we never wanted to be part of that, because it so rarely works. We just felt like this show is about a certain time in your life, and once you're past that time in your life, the show is over."

But not having a legacy to carry forward made ending the series even more difficult. The cast really felt like family, which made breaking up extremely hard to do. While Kudrow copped to feeling a pang of wistfulness when saying goodbye to other roles, "with *Friends*, I actually cried," she confided. "When I really thought we might not come back, I remember driving home and I burst into tears thinking, 'Oh, I'm going to miss Phoebe, and Monica and Rachel and Joey and Chandler,'" she openly shared. "I miss those people. I really do. They were fun."

Both she and Perry have gone on-record saying that just *maybe* they should have eked out a few more seasons. "If it were up to us, like, individually, oh, I would keep going," she said. "There would have come a time anyway when someone would have said, 'We've had enough.' But why not have fun until they do?" Perry said: "I find myself sort of reminiscing about how much fun the show was, and the hours that we worked. You know, you can see how much we laughed and everything." He then added, "I found myself saying, 'If I had a time machine, I would like to go back to 2004 and not have stopped.'" When asked what advice he'd give his younger self, he replied, "Do an eleventh season."

Courteney Cox offered a poignant perspective on the costars' time together. "It was an incredible time," she told her costars during the unscripted reunion special. "Everything came together. We became best friends through just the chemistry, the whole thing. It was life-changing and it forever will be—not just for us, but for people who watch it—and that's such a great feeling to carry forever. I'm really thankful, and I love you guys so much."

Series Finale

Prior to penning the first draft for the series finale, the *Friends* creators (David Crane, Marta Kauffman and Kevin Bright) watched the finales of other sitcoms, analyzing the good, the bad, and the ugly. They watched *Cheers* and *Seinfeld* and so many other timeless and classic shows. The creators decided the best finales were the ones that remained true to the series, such as *M*A*S*H*, *Newhart* and *The Mary Tyler Moore Show* (which they considered the "gold standard"). They aspired to have an emotional, powerful, gut-wrenching send-off. And although Crane claims *The Larry Sanders Show* finale "was brilliant," Kauffman opined that its celebrity-filled send-off was not the kind of finale the trio wanted for *Friends*. "We knew it had to be something where you *felt* something and where hopefully you laughed a lot," Crane stressed.

According to Crane, they did not want to do something "high concept, or take the show out of the show." In other words, the triumvirate wanted to avoid controversy or negativity, which is often attributed to the *Seinfeld* denouement. "Having seen the *Seinfeld* finale and knowing when you depart from who you are, it doesn't make the audience happy; let's deliver to the audience what they want and what they've earned," he opined.

Having a theoretical construct for the finale is one thing, making it a practical reality is another. The creators quickly realized that writing the first draft was an incredibly arduous task. They would go days without writing a single word, staring at their computers, unsure what to do. For a brief moment, they considered an alternate ending. "We did talk about, with Ross and Rachel, a gray area of where they aren't together, but we hint there's a sense that they might be down the road," Crane divulged. "But we thought, 'No, if we're going to do it, let's do it.' It's the nature of our show. It's not a show about grays. Let's deliver not just what the audience wants, but what we want, which was to see them finally together."

In reality, the showrunners always foresaw a happy ending for Ross and Rachel. "The only thing we absolutely knew from very early on was that we had to get Ross and Rachel together," Crane reiterated. "We had dicked the audience around for 10 years with their 'will they or won't they,' and we didn't see any advantage in frustrating them." The only problem was crafting a storyline to keep the audience invested. "The goal was to do it in a way that you didn't see where we were going, and it was kind of surprising," he elucidated. "It became all about execution. ... The end point isn't going to surprise anybody, but the journey is the question." The writing team completed the first draft in January 2004, weeks before filming, but four months before its original airing.

Stressful Finale

After filming the penultimate installment in mid-December 2003, the cast was given a three-week holiday break before returning to work on January 12th. It was an extremely emotional and stressful time for the entire cast. Matt LeBlanc openly acknowledged that the impending series finale was so stressful that he started smoking again. "I had quit smoking for four years, and in that final two weeks I started smoking again because we were so aware that our time together was coming to an end," he dolefully revealed. "Yes, I'll talk to you. Yes, I'll always know you. But I won't know you like this. I won't see you every day, all day. Eat lunch together every day. To have this awesome, awesome experience every week. It's coming to an end."

The cast treasured those fleeting memories. "So in those final two weeks, we would steal away these little moments. 'Hey, let's go hang out. Let's go sit in my room.' It was really ... a lot of Kleenex," LeBlanc said, fondly reminiscing about their final days together. The other castmates concurred that the final two weeks were filled with tears, laughter, smiles, hugs, and unforgettable memories.

Friends finale: The last supper (left) and giving an ovation to the audience (right)

Filming

At the time of its finale, *Friends* was the hottest sitcom on television. The world craved insider information about cast and crew activities, especially anything that occurred behind the scenes. Paparazzi tried to gather intel by frenetically following anyone associated with the series. A similar firestorm of media scrutiny accompanied the *Seinfeld* finale six years earlier. Tearing out a page from the *Seinfeld* playbook, the *Friends* producers proactively disseminated misinformation to send journalists on wild goose chases, such as claiming to have filmed multiple endings without an audience, when in fact, there was only one version and an audience was present. The showrunners blew enough smoke to glaze the eyes of hounding reporters.

Since the finale was an hour-long episode, the producers treated it like a typical double-length installment by scheduling the shoot over a two-week period, as if it were two totally separate episodes. The first half was filmed on January 16, 2004, and part two was shot the following week, on Friday, January 23rd. During production of part one, the cast was on set for a catered pre-filming dinner complete with steak and lobster, which was followed by an exchanging of gifts.

It was a bit like high school graduation. The production staff passed around custom-made *Friends* yearbooks with everyone signing each other's tome during filming breaks. The six stars banded together to present the creators with inscribed Cartier SA watches, while their bosses returned the sentiment with Neil Lane diamond earrings for Aniston, Cox and Kudrow, and cuff links for Schwimmer, Perry and LeBlanc.

Typically, at the commencement of filming, the cast would be introduced to the studio audience one at a time, but for this episode, the cast headed out for their precurtain bow together. "That made me cry," said Diane Newman, a *Friends* script supervisor. The hand-selected audience included the likes of Hank Azaria, David Arquette and Maggie Wheeler, among others. Brad Pitt skipped the affair, telling the producers he wanted to be surprised when the finale aired on television. In reality, he and Aniston were having marital troubles so he was not feeling supportive.

Kevin Bright fondly reflected upon the first night of filming: "We did the first take and everything went well. And then David [Schwimmer] mentioned to the rest of the actors the realization that this was the last coffeehouse scene that they were ever going to do together. Tears started to flow. It was kind of a benchmark that this would be the last time they would be in this set." Marta Kauffman added, "It was impossible to get through. We stopped several time because of tears."

James Michael Tyler (Gunther) specifically recalled his final coffeehouse scene. "It was really difficult to shoot. I had taken for granted over 10 years of walking onto that set. It felt like a second home," he said. "Jennifer and I, the first few takes, both of us were bursting into tears, so it was tough getting through and took a lot longer than it probably should have." He was particularly grateful the showrunners wrote a segment to give his *Friends* character closure.

Gushing eyeballs was a common theme among the producers. "It was three weeks of tears," Kauffman remarked. "Every time we did something, no matter how small, it would strike us. 'Oh, my God. This is the last time I'm going to have a bagel on Thursday morning while watching a scene.' Everything was filled with meaning. We shot the last coffeehouse scene on the next to last week and the actors could barely get through it."

At the end of filming, the cast gave an ovation to the audience to express their respect for having such a loyal fan base for an entire decade. After the studio audience exited, the Central Perk set was torn down so the crew could build an airport set for part two. Thus, in the final scene of the series, when Rachel asks if they want to go for coffee, and Chandler asks "Where?" it was actually sincere, since there was no longer a Central Perk set.

After the audience departed, the festivities started. "We tore down the coffeehouse at the end of the night and we ended up with an impromptu party, about 80 people—crew, cast, producers stayed, office staff—and we just watched it go down," Kauffman recalled. "It was like losing a little piece of yourself." The cast and crew drank tequila in celebration and lament for the show, and everyone signed the back of the coffeehouse set to memorialize the series and the moment. Matt LeBlanc's immortalized message for posterity: "I shit here —Matt LeBlanc."

Part two was filmed on January 23, 2004. The studio audience was 75% legitimate fans and 25% friends and family. "It was very important to us that it wasn't just friends and family because the laughs aren't the same," David Crane explained. "When you've got an audience of people who have all been invited, sometimes they go, 'Oh, yeah, sure,' instead of actually laughing. You want real people who will cheer and get emotionally involved."

Much like the filming of part one, the final episode was filled with waterworks. David Schwimmer, normally the rock of the group, was the first to crack during the preshow huddle. "That was the moment I was dreading for a long time because I knew that moment of just looking at everyone in their eyes, and saying 'Have a good show,' and knowing that was the last time we were going to be able to be in our little circle." Once he choked up, that was it, everyone lost it. Matthew Perry commented, "I didn't cry, but I felt like I was about to for like seven hours." Jennifer Aniston indicated it was "instant hysterics" when the cast walked out to a standing ovation from an audience filled with their family and friends.

Maggie Wheeler didn't guest star in the finale but she was on set to witness the affair. "The tears were flowing and the entire cast had to go back and have their makeup redone before starting," she revealed. Aniston added, "I don't think we've ever taken more time in hair and makeup in between scenes. ... We kept crying all our makeup off, over and over again." James Michael Tyler continued, "Those scenes really took their toll, especially for the makeup people. There were a lot of tears flowing and the director would call 'action,' then have to cut because someone would already be crying."

Filming the final episode of *Friends* was very emotional for everyone involved. After the final scene wrapped, the actors, creators, and most of the other people working on the show gathered on the set to hug, cry, and share in what was only the first of many goodbyes. "I mean, the last scene we just wept, cried our eyes out," Aniston proclaimed reminiscently. "And then a couple of us stayed really late and we crawled up to the roof of Stage 24 and we drank champagne and watched the sun rise. It was really wonderful."

Mementos

Security was tight the final two weeks of filming. Lisa Kudrow divulged that her car was searched every night before she left the studio lot to ensure she did not steal any props or set dressings. Although she didn't take anything, Matthew Perry pilfered a souvenir for her to keep as a memento—the Cookie Time cookie jar. Naturally, there was a story associated with the gift.

At one time in the past there was a scene where Phoebe had to check the time and then exclaim she was late and had to leave. However, Kudrow was not wearing a watch so she checked the time by looking at the Cookie Time clock, and then finished the scene. During the shoot, Matthew Perry asked, "Did you look at the cookie jar and say 'Look at the time?'" Hence, his wrap gift to Kudrow was meant to remind her of that hilarious moment.

After part one finally wrapped and the Central Perk set was dismantled, the cast and crew each received a chunk of the street outside the coffee shop mounted in a glass box as a keepsake. Marta Kauffman purloined the neon sign with "Service" inside an arrow, Kevin Bright swiped the big milk can sign, and Jennifer Aniston pilfered a neon coffee cup sign. When Matt LeBlanc was asked if he took anything from the show as a souvenir, he replied, "It's funny, I took a f*ck ton of cash!" He subsequently confided that he took a foosball from the gaming table in Joey's apartment. He kept it in his toolbox for some unknown reason. LeBlanc also walked off with the magna doodle that hung on the back of the door in Joey's apartment and gave it to Paul Swain, the crew electrician responsible for most of the doodle board messages and drawings that appeared on the show. LeBlanc joked that he "could have sold it for a lot more," but thoughtfully opted to give the piece of television history to a crew member.

Series finale: Jimmy Kimmel (left) and the *Friends* creators (right)

Others got into the action, too. David Schwimmer took a "Professor Geller" placard from Ross' office, Lisa Kudrow kept her studio security badge and then nabbed a few of Phoebe's rings, and set designer John Shaffner kept a mold of the iconic picture frame. Courteney Cox didn't take anything from the set but wishes she had.

Wrap Parties

There were three separate wrap parties to commemorate the finale: (1) dinner at the Aniston–Pitt residence on January 19, 2004, (2) sit down event at Il Sole in West Hollywood on January 22, and (3) blowout party for everyone associated with the show at Los Angeles' Park Plaza Hotel on January 24th.

The first was an intimate gathering at the home of Jennifer Aniston and then husband Brad Pitt. Executive producer Kevin Bright treated the guests to vintage bottles of Haut-Brion that he had been saving for a decade (he bought the wine at the start of season one). The second wrap party was held three days later but it was an intimate gathering for the cast members. They celebrated at Il Sole, which was one of their favorite hangouts.

The big send-off took place on Saturday, January 24th, the night after filming part two of the series finale. Warner Bros. hosted the lavish event and used the venue to announce that Stage 24, where the *Friends* sitcom was filmed, was being renamed The *Friends* Stage. Nearly 1,000 guests attended the soiree at Los Angeles' Park Plaza Hotel featuring musical guests Sheryl Crow and The Rembrandts (who naturally performed the show's theme song). Some of the cocktails served at the bash had names such as Smelly Cat and Ugly Naked Guy, in honor of glorious moments from the show. The highlight of the evening was the cast reenacting the runaway bride scene from the pilot episode.

Promotion & Advertising

NBC heavily promoted the series finale, which was preceded by weeks of media hype. *Dateline NBC*, a weekly television news magazine, devoted two episodes to the finale, one of which ran for two hours. When the epochal day finally arrived, local NBC affiliates planned viewing parties, including an event at Hollywood's Universal CityWalk featuring a special broadcast on an outdoor Astrovision screen. As many as 3,000 fans flocked to New York's Times Square to watch the finale on the big screen, and another 3,000 gathered at Hudson River Park's Pier 25. A 60-minute retrospective clip show aired prior to the finale, and then following the double-length episode, a prerecorded installment of *The Tonight Show with Jay Leno* was broadcast from the set of Central Perk, which featured the *Friends* cast as guests.

The advertising rates for the *Friends* series finale neared Super Bowl levels, averaging $2 million for 30 seconds of commercial ad time (double the rate during its tenth season), breaking the $1.7 million record held by *Seinfeld* for its finale six years earlier. NBC made $70 million from the final night of *Friends* in a record-setting haul for an entertainment program. In the UK, ads sold for nearly £1.2M ($1.8 million), making it the most expensive commercial slot of any British TV entertainment (nonsport) program.

Ratings

The May 6, 2004 series finale had 52.46 million viewers (17.9% of the US population), making it the most watched entertainment (nonsport) telecast in six years (since *Seinfeld*'s finale). It was the fourth-most-watched series finale in television history, behind *M*A*S*H*, *Cheers* and *Seinfeld*, which were watched by 105 million, 80.4 million and 76.2 million viewers, respectively. The finale was the second-most-watched television show of the year; only the Super Bowl had more viewers.

The sitcom's depressed numbers were somewhat expected. With the fragmentation of society and the prolific availability of cable networks and satellite transmissions, viewers had virtually unlimited viewing options. It was no longer the Big Three networks; instead, there were literally hundreds of television signals and cable networks from which to choose. When the *M*A*S*H* finale garnered an unprecedented viewership in 1983, only 37% of the homes had cable television with very few channel options, as opposed to 81% in 2004 with hundreds of channels. In addition, personal computers, internet surfing, and home video-games further eroded the television viewing audience. Thus, it was not too surprising that the *Friends* viewership numbers were somewhat underwhelming.

The *Friends* finale had a 29.8 rating (percentage of television households watching the program) and 43 share (percentage of television sets in use). However, these numbers are dwarfed compared to *M*A*S*H* (60.2/77) and *Cheers* (45.5/64). Even the *Seinfeld* numbers illustrated a severely fragmented audience. Just six years earlier there were 8% fewer cable subscriptions, and the sitcom had a 41.3 rating and 58 share.

In the UK, 8.6 million fans watched the series finale, which was more than a third of the island country's television viewing audience. It set three records for Channel 4, the UK's distributing channel for *Friends*: (1) highest-rated program of 2004, (2) highest-rated non-British program, and (3) second-highest-rated program (excluding films, sports and special events), trailing the third series finale of UK's *Big Brother* (2000), which had over 10 million viewers.

Although the *Friends* series finale attracted the eyes of 52.46 million viewers, it was not the most watched episode in the series' catalog. That distinction goes to "The One After the Superbowl" (2.12, 2.13), which aired in 1996 and set the series record with 52.9 million viewers. The one-hour extravaganza featured guest appearances by Julia Roberts, Brooke Shields and Jean-Claude Van Damme.

Reviews

The *Friends* series finale had mixed to positive reviews from critics. Robert Bianco of *USA Today* described the send-off as entertaining and satisfying, and praised it for deftly mixing emotion and humor while showcasing each of the six stars. Sarah Rodman of the *Boston Herald* praised Aniston and Schwimmer for their acting, but felt their characters' reunion was "a bit too neat, even if it was what most of the show's legions of fans wanted." Roger Catlin of the *Hartford Courant* indicated that first-time viewers to the series would be "surprised at how laughless the affair could be, and how nearly every strained gag depends on the sheer stupidity of its characters." Ken Parish Perkins, writing for the *Fort Worth Star-Telegram*, pointed out that the episode was "more touching than comical, more satisfying in terms of closure than knee-slappingly funny."

The cast members gathered in Los Angeles to watch the finale. They enjoyed the episode and were confident that fans would react similarly. "It's exactly what I had hoped," David Schwimmer surmised. "We all end up with a sense of a new beginning and the audience has a sense that it's a new chapter in the lives of all these characters." According to IMDB, the second half of the series finale is the highest-rated episode by viewers.

Final Reflections

Matt LeBlanc had heartwarming words when reflecting upon his decade on the series: "More important than anything else is the look on people's faces when you cross paths with them in the street, or in the store, or in the grocery line. You can always tell that you were —maybe still are, maybe always will be—a part of their family. Movies have this thing where it's an event. You get dressed up, you go to dinner, and you go to the movies. You're outside of your element. But with television, people are watching you in bed, at their kitchen table eating. You're in their house. I did not want it to end."

In a singular moment of emotional vulnerability, Matthew Perry reminisced about those cherished moments on the sitcom. "There's only five people in the world who know exactly what being on *Friends* was like, other than me. There's five of them. David, Matthew, Lisa, Courteney, and Jen. That's it," he confided. "Marta and David were close, but when they left the stage, no one knew what they did. We could never leave the stage, metaphorically speaking. Still can't. Still on that stage. That will follow us around forever."

Success, Ratings & Awards

After the *Friends* pilot was picked up and the network ordered 12 additional episodes, the producers didn't have overinflated expectations. "When we started producing the show, we only had a commitment for six episodes on the air," Kevin Bright recalled. "We were only hoping it would get picked up for the rest of the season." In October 1994 NBC ordered the back 11 for a full 24-episode season. From there, the series' potential was limitless and it quickly reached unprecedented heights.

Series Success

Even before the series debuted, *Friends* was given every opportunity to succeed. It was anointed with the second-most-coveted timeslot on NBC's schedule, preceding *Seinfeld*. Only *Madman of the People* had a better pole position, following *Seinfeld*. Squeezed between *Mad About You* (No. 14, 23.2 million) and *Seinfeld* (No. 2, 32.8 million), the *Friends* debut garnered 21.5 million viewers, making it the 15th-most-watched program of the week. A solid outing for a freshman show, faring especially well at holding the lead-in audience, dropping only 1.7 million viewers.

Despite a strong start, over the next five weeks *Friends*' audience slowly trickled away. When "The One with the Butt" (1.06) aired, viewership was down to 18.2 million, which meant the series had lost over 15% of its original pilot audience. "I remember sweating the ratings of *Friends* the first few weeks. It was falling off more than anybody wanted it to," frankly stated Jamie Tarses, NBC's senior vice president of primetime series. "Outside of development, there was a lot of doubt about *Friends*." Tarses was an instrumental advocate for the series during its early stages of development. Despite serious network concern over the future viability of the series, the following week NBC ordered a full season of episodes.

During production of "The One with the Blackout" (1.07), the creators summoned the cast and crew to the stage to announce that they had bad news and good news. "The bad news is that we did not get picked up for the back nine," Marta Kauffman revealed. The crowd was astonished. There were rumblings. The natives were getting restless. She toyed with them a moment longer before finishing her thought: "The good news is we got picked up for 11." (Typically, after the pilot is picked up, 12 additional episodes will be ordered, followed by the remaining 9, if the ratings were high enough. This arrangement is referred to as the "Front 13" and "Back 9." Currently, a full television season for a program is 22 episodes.)

Cast members were crying with joy at the powerful vote of confidence from NBC. Cosimo Fusco (Paolo) plaintively noted, "Jennifer Aniston basically cried in my lap because nothing like that had ever happened to her before." (Aniston had previously costarred in four failed sitcoms that never lasted an entire year.) The next morning, after everyone arrived at work, NBC President Warren Littlefield was dressed in an apron and serving omelets to the cast and crew.

NBC's decision to sign the series for an entire year proved wise because "The One with the Blackout" (1.07) became the show's highest-rated installment to date with 23.5 million viewers. The guest star appearance by model Jill Goodacre was the impetus for increased viewership but the show's future success hinged on the Ross–Rachel unrequited-love story arc that captivated the masses and propelled the show's ratings to new heights. "The first couple of scripts after the pilot, we were struggling with scripts and struggling with story," Tarses said. "Then it was a soap opera, and it was hilarious. The Ross-and-Rachel thing set the tone for that, and you got thrust into a sort of soapy storytelling."

The original timeslot for *Friends* was nestled behind *Mad About You*. Halfway through the first season, *Friends* started beating *Mad About You* in the weekly ratings so the shows swapped positions in the schedule. This was NBC's subtle acknowledgment of the series' success; it effectively ordained *Friends* as the network's anchor program on Thursday night.

Signs of Success

The writing staff believes "The One with the Blackout" (1.07) was the first episode that had the public buzzing about *Friends*. Matthew Perry credited this episode as the moment he first realized the series was going to be a huge success. Since he didn't share any scenes with his castmates, Perry was able to see what the show looked like from a distance, and this fresh perspective helped him realize it would be a hit.

NBC President Warren Littlefield realized *Friends* was a pop phenomenon about six to eight episodes into its run. "These scripts were brilliant, funny, soap operas," he declared. "*Seinfeld* outrageously went for funny. *Friends* went for 'We're going to grab your heart and we're going to make you laugh.'"

Matt LeBlanc's epiphany came during the summer hiatus following the first season. He can't remember a precise moment but he was sitting in a traffic jam when he noticed a girl in a convertible rocking out to a song. This piqued his curiosity so he promptly rolled down the window, only to discover it was "I'll Be There for You" by The Rembrandts, the *Friends* theme song. After the girl recognized the sitcom star, she was so astonished that she let her foot off the brake and crashed into the car in front. "I felt terrible," LeBlanc said. "But as a personal marker of the show's success, it's one I remember."

Jennifer Aniston had an entirely different experience that made her assess and rethink the definition of success. "When somebody follows you 20 blocks to the pharmacy, where they watch you buy toilet paper, you know your life has changed," she said disconcertingly. The incident in question occurred while she was visiting a friend in San Francisco. A few die-hard fans of the show recognized the actress as she sauntered down the street so they followed her to a local pharmacy.

Lisa Kudrow's initial revelation occurred on *The Oprah Winfrey Show*. "I think that first summer, [Oprah] showed us all of these people in internet cafes. People were online talking about the show, which was the first time that people were using the internet to connect with each other, like the new watercooler. I thought, 'Okay, this is something then. This is a big deal.' That's when I got it."

The showrunners' moment of enlightenment occurred around Thanksgiving 1994. While dining with his parents and partner, Jeffrey Klarik, David Crane first realized that *Friends* was a success when he overheard people at the next table discussing "The One with the East German Laundry Detergent" (1.05). Marta Kauffman then commented that her first realization of the show's success was the next day when Crane recapitulated the dinner conversation anecdote. But the monumental success of the show did not register to them until the summer of 1995 when they saw the cast's visages on dozens of magazine covers. "*Dream On* was great but it was under the radar. *Friends* was over the top with publicity," David Crane recalled.

Overall, the creators indicated that the show's sudden fame did not affect their work per se, but it did affect the schedule of the actors because they started getting other gigs as a result of their stardom. Director Thomas Schlamme noticed the change, too. "The cast of *Friends* became so famous it was like *Friends* was their second job," he observed. "They had so many other commitments that it was difficult to get them all to rehearsals at the same time."

Struggling with Success

The first season of *Friends* propelled the cast into the stratosphere of popularity, media attention and professional success. The costars handled fame differently and had varying perspectives on their stardom. Most of the cast members coped with their celebrity status rather effectively, except for Matthew Perry and David Schwimmer, where the former turned to substance abuse and the latter reverted to isolationism.

Lisa Kudrow resented her warp-speed rise in popularity. "Fame doesn't feel like a warm hug. It really feels like an assault," she revealed. "I think before you are famous you think, 'Oh, if you're famous, you're loved and adored.' Then when you really experience that attention and everyone cares what you're doing and wants pictures of you. ... Then, not long after, you start to realize, this has almost nothing to do with me, and I better do the work." She recalled one harrowing experience in particular to illustrate her point. "We did a photo shoot for *Entertainment Weekly*. When we walked out of it, our cars were all the way across the street, and there were tons of paparazzi, and it was nighttime, and we were blinded by all the flashing. It was scary, because we hadn't had that before. It was unnerving, because they yell at you. It's more of an assault than any kind of congratulations, or 'We love you.' That's not ever how it feels. So, that was jarring, and then I think all of us understood, 'Oh, I get why people get so antagonistic with paparazzi.'"

Despite the pitfalls of success, Kudrow offered a fresh perspective for aspiring actors: "Fame doesn't cure whatever is going on inside of you, however you feel about yourself." She felt blessed having five close friends to share the experience. "The lucky thing was that the six of us had each other to go through it." She felt bad for actors who had to do it on their own.

Matt LeBlanc also experienced the negative side effects of being a Hollywood celebrity. "I remember I was living in an apartment in Beachwood Canyon. ... I had to move so quickly. It was unbelievable. All of a sudden, the people in the building were banging on my door. People knew I lived there. I was like, 'I've got to get a house. I need a house with a gate, because I need to be able to hide.'" Regarding his status as a role model for kids, LeBlanc eloquently stated, "I never set out to be a role model. I set out to pay the rent."

Matthew Perry

Even prior to *Friends*, Matthew Perry abused alcohol. Stardom did not precipitate the issue, it merely exacerbated the problem. It didn't become a serious matter until he started mixing alcohol with Vicodin, which was first prescribed for a wisdom tooth extraction in 1995. He moderately increased his use and abuse of substances over the next two years, which was painfully obvious to the *Friends* cast and crew, though he claims he was first reintroduced to the drug in 1997 following a jet ski accident. However, observant fans will notice Perry's significant weight loss in episodes that aired in late 1996. The jet ski accident was merely the tipping point where his addiction pushed him over the edge.

A few months later, he checked himself into the Hazelden Foundation rehabilitation center in Minnesota to partake in a 28-day inpatient program. The treatment didn't take. Perry continued to abuse alcohol and drugs which commenced a three-year blackout (1998, 1999 and 2000). He lost all recollection of those years including his tenure on *Friends*. "I don't remember three years of it. ... Somewhere between season three and six ... I was a little out of it."

During those three illusory seasons, Perry's weight began fluctuating dramatically. The six-foot-tall actor normally weighed about 165 pounds, but dropped to 145 pounds in 1997 and again in early 2000. He checked into Cedars-Sinai medical center in May 2000, and stayed for two weeks, purportedly for pancreatitis, a potentially chronic condition that he later admitted was probably caused by his abuse of alcohol and prescription drugs. But this medical scare didn't temper his behavior.

In February 2001, Perry finally hit rock bottom. He was filming the feature film comedy *Serving Sara* in Dallas when he showed up to work painfully hungover and incapacitated due to severe abdominal pain. He contacted a local doctor who advised him to enter rehab immediately. Perry called his parents from a hotel room and asked for help. "It was scary. I didn't want to die," he professed. "But I'm grateful for how bad it got. It only made me more adamant about trying to get better." Perry promptly checked into Daniel Freeman Hospital, in Marina del Rey, California, where he received inpatient treatment for his addiction to various drugs including alcohol, amphetamines and opioids.

After his stint in rehab, Perry publicly proclaimed his unwavering abstinence, but the entire production team knew he was continuing to abuse alcohol and drugs. Over a year later, at the start of the ninth season, the showrunners observed Perry's erratic behavior on set so they decided to reformulate the story arc for his onscreen character, Chandler. The same disconcerting behavior occurred in 1998 at the end of season four, and at that time the producers contemplated relocating Chandler to Minnesota (comedic irony since Perry spent 28 days in rehab in the gopher state). It was déjà vu four years later, but this time the creators pulled the trigger by having Chandler transferred to Tulsa during season nine. This was a precautionary move in case Perry relapsed because his character could easily be written out of entire episodes if he happened to enter a rehab facility again. At this point, the showrunners seriously contemplated firing Perry from the series. Fortunately, his drug usage stabilized during the final two years of the show so no drastic measures had to be taken.

David Schwimmer

Fame was a double-edged sword for David Schwimmer. Sitcom success brought great financial rewards but at the cost of increased media attention and public scrutiny. He never craved the celebrity limelight, at least not to the level that accompanied *Friends*; instead he preferred to be a wallflower or a background extra in the stage called life. When *Friends* was an instant success, he was vastly ill-prepared. "I didn't feel like my character had changed, but suddenly people were treating me in a very, very different way, that sometimes was flattering, but mostly very evasive," he said. "Because you are in their home. There's something very approachable about actors on television, and I think especially in a half-hour comedy, where there's something very comforting about it."

His cyclonic success resulted in bizarre street encounters: "I had never been a part of the entertainment industry. I didn't know anyone famous. I'd never seen it. I had a girlfriend at the time, and I remember walking down the street with her, holding her hand, when some girls came up, pushed her out of the way, and asked for my number. They were like, 'Oh my God, can you come out with us right now?' As if my girlfriend just didn't exist. I found it very difficult to handle." For Schwimmer, the hardest part was coping with his immense popularity. "For me, the fame is something I've wrestled with and struggled with since it happened. I don't think I responded very well to the sudden celebrity, the sudden fame, and the loss of privacy. There were several moments that were quite traumatic for me. I remember in the early days of just going to the airport and walking to my gate when I heard bloodcurdling screams, and I thought someone was being killed. Before I knew it, a group of girls was running at me and literally grabbing me and wouldn't let me go," he said of the harrowing incident.

All the training as an actor never prepared him for the consequences of fame. "As an actor, the way I was trained, my job was to observe life and to observe other people, and so I used to walk around with my head up, and really engaged and watching people," he said. "The effect of celebrity was the absolute opposite: it made me want to hide under a baseball cap, not be seen. And I realized after a while that I was no longer watching people; I was trying to hide. So I was trying to figure out: how do I be an actor in this new world, in this new situation? How do I do my job? So that was tricky." It even impacted his personal life. "It was pretty jarring and it messed with my relationship to other people in a way that took years, I think, for me to kind of adjust to and become comfortable with," he thoughtfully confided.

As a celebrity, his stature made him a target for greedy charlatans. For example, in 1997, celebrity fundraiser Aaron Tonken alleged that Schwimmer "demanded two [Rolex] watches, worth $26,000, for himself and his father in exchange for attending a 'Friends Helping Friends' event," according to the *Los Angeles Times*. Schwimmer maintained that he did no such thing and Tonken eventually admitted that he had supplied the *Times* and *National Enquirer* the false story. Schwimmer profited $400,000 from a defamation lawsuit; his accuser, on the other hand, received five years in prison.

Of the six *Friends* costars, Schwimmer was the one who shied away from the limelight. Although he continued to perform after the show ended, he spent many years behind the scenes doing voice work, directing, and producing. Of course, part of the reason was being typecast. Schwimmer stated: "There was a period that I was very, very frustrated by being pigeonholed in this one genre, this one idea. I got *Friends* when I was 27 but I had done all this work on stage. But all that was just eradicated. As far as the public was concerned, I came out of the womb doing sitcom. So that was frustrating, as if it obliterated all the other training, all the other roles I had done." It took over 15 years before he finally declared, "I think I'm kind of over that."

Second-Season Backlash

Friends was an instantaneous success, but at times during the first season it struggled in the ratings, hovering in the mid-teens. NBC did everything to blow wind into its sails, including switching timeslots with *Mad About You*, and then later sandwiching the series between two megahits, *Seinfeld* and *ER*. The latter move boosted ratings but executives wondered whether *Friends* was a bona fide contender or a timeslot pretender. After season one wrapped in early April 1995, the *Friends* producers felt they needed to get the word out about their show to increase its popularity. They did a full-fledged media, advertising and promotional assault starting with a high-profile feature story in *Rolling Stone* magazine with the cast spotlighted on the May 1995 cover issue. During the summer months, the cast hit the talk show circuit which attracted intense media attention. At the same time, the show's theme song bombarded the airwaves, the associated music video dominated MTV and VH1, and reruns attracted droves of new viewers. Even the newly evolving internet capitalized on the *Friends* frenzy. An entire cottage industry of discourse was devoted exclusively to the show, the actors, and the fans with countless articles in the popular media and press, fan books, and a vast number of internet newsgroups, homepages and websites. At one point, *Friends* had more websites devoted to it (98) than any other TV show.

Not to be outdone, Warner Bros. Television and NBC threw their hats into the ring by collaborating on tie-ins, promotions, and contests, and the studio commissioned a massive merchandising program so an endless stream of companies could plaster the *Friends* logo and characters' visages on every store shelf in America (and across the globe). The *Friends*-stamp was blazoned on every conceivable consumer product or collectible, such as coffee mugs, cookbooks, CDs, hats, t-shirts, calendars, and there was even a coffee line. It was impossible to walk into a bookstore or gift shop without bumping into something *Friends*-related. There was a media onslaught from gossip columns and news features to magazine covers and endless television interviews.

The *Friends* cast became the talk of the town—the haircut and fashion, the actors and their movies, the theme song and video. It was overwhelming. Even the costars' side gigs were splattered across every media outlet around the world. Kevin Bright was involved with an annual telethon sponsored by the Hasidic Jewish sect Chabad to raise money for their drug and alcohol rehabilitation centers, so he persuaded the *Friends* cast to appear. Matt LeBlanc signed a contract with Saks Fifth Avenue to model for their spring 1996 catalog. Matthew Perry and Jennifer Aniston appeared in a 60-second TV commercial introducing Windows 95 and its 60-minute instructional video guide to the new operating system. The female costars filmed a promotional video for the NBA from Monica's living room where they expressed enthusiasm for old-school NBA short-shorts and ogled Utah Jazz point guard John Stockton. Lisa Kudrow and Aniston were featured in the highly popular Got Milk? advertisements. David Schwimmer starred in an AT&T commercial and signed a seven-figure, four-picture deal with Miramax, one of which he planned to direct as well as cowrite. Even the *Friends* writers were featured in a print ad for Waterman pens, presumably their writing utensil of choice when creating scripts.

The promotional blitzkrieg worked to invigorate fans. According to Vincent Ventresca (Fun Bobby), "The first season, they had a show that was doing pretty well on the air, and it looked like they were going to do more, but they weren't The Beatles. And then they came back the second year, and they *were* The Beatles." To further take advantage of the *Friends* resurgence, the producers arranged a deal with Coca-Cola for the cast to appear as their sitcom characters in several Diet Coke commercials. The advertisement plot involved the gang being interrogated by police about a missing Diet Coke. The beverage giant paid an estimated $10 million for use of the show's name and cast. The producers succumbed to the lure of a large paycheck and admitted to manipulating the cast into accepting the deal (the sextet was paid somewhere between $250,000 and $500,000 each).

The creators commissioned their staff writers to draft ideas for the proposed television commercials and print ads, in which the six friends touted the splendor of the low-calorie soda. They were given one week. The campaign "Who's Gonna Drink the Diet Coke?" was a mystery suspense game premised on who "stole" a Diet Coke from Monica and Rachel's apartment. One commercial staged mock police lineups and mug shots of the principal characters. During interrogation, Phoebe recommended candles to lighten the mood and Monica ranted about how she had no alibi because she did not have a boyfriend. All six friends swore their innocence.

The promotional bombardment started on January 1, 1996. Coca-Cola put together an advertising crusade to lure younger consumers who previously switched from Diet Coke to other beverages such as iced teas, sports drinks and coffee. It sponsored a "watch and win" campaign, which included online promotions (e.g., trivia contest and a behind-the-scenes room visited by *Friends* production workers), and a select on-campus publicity drive with displays at 260 bookstores and 2,500 college viewing parties. Participants could mail in bottle caps for a chance to win an all-expense paid trip to Los Angeles to watch the filming of a *Friends* episode.

Each bottle cap contained the name of a *Friends* character. Purchasers were instructed to watch *Friends*, but more specifically, the accompanying Diet Coke commercial which revealed one of the characters drinking the low-calorie beverage. If the name under the cap matched the character in the ad, the cap holder won a prize. The contest installments aired on January 11th, 18th, 25th, and following the Super Bowl XXX on January 28th. The final TV commercial was broadcast during "The One After the Superbowl, Part 2" (2.13) where it revealed the diabolical villain—Rachel.

The contest lasted only four weeks, but to television viewers, it felt like a lifetime. The media barrage was intolerable: the Super Bowl episode, the A-list guest stars, the Diet Coke contest, David Schwimmer's Skittles commercial—everything came to a boil. The show and cast were officially overexposed and the backlash began. A *Chicago Tribune* writer called the episode, "The One Where the Show Crosses the Line from Promiscuity into Prostitution."

For Diet Coke, the campaign was a great success: sales increased and continued to rise, and the soda brand reasserted its claim on the youth market. For *Friends*, the campaign was a bust. The series did not lose viewers but everyone associated with the program had to work hard to win back its cool factor and reestablish audience trust. The showrunners quickly realized that their avarice and shameless promotion of the show came with a steep price tag. They were too naive to comprehend the most important cardinal rule: avoid overexposure and overcommercialization. The Super Bowl extravaganza was the last straw. The world needed a break from *Friends*.

There was a torrential backlash among media critics and fans, claiming the cast had sold out. Incessant criticism prompted the producers to limit publicity, hoping to derail the recoil that was gaining momentum. "None of this has ever happened to us before," Marta Kauffman said. "We're like kids in a candy store." She convened a meeting with the cast the following week to pronounce a moratorium on media interviews. "We said, 'Let's try to be a little cool right now.'"

NBC was on board, too, by refusing press opportunities for fear of further overexposure. Network President Warren Littlefield recollected the tumultuous time: "For the first time in my memory at NBC, we had to worry about overexposure. We became gatekeepers for the *Friends* cast. Everybody wanted a piece of them—an electronic interview, a photo shoot, something. We realized the cast was so white-hot that we had to pull back, to help protect both them and their show."

Although the series' ratings stayed strong, the costars did not fare well at the box office. Matt LeBlanc's *Ed* debuted on March 15, 1996, followed by Jennifer Aniston's *Dream for an Insomniac* on April 18th. Both crashed and burned at the box office. The May 3rd release of David Schwimmer's *The Pallbearer* also floundered, though it fared a little better due to the waning reverberations associated with the sitcom and its stars.

Of all the decisions that David Crane made as cocreator of *Friends*, he most regrets the Diet Coke advertising campaign. Fortunately for him, and everyone involved in the series, as the production team continued to crank out great episodes throughout the remainder of season two, the scathing criticism slowly subsided. By the time *Friends* returned to the air for its third season, very few people remembered the Diet Coke fiasco.

Series Reviews

The pilot was often called a rip-off of *Seinfeld* and *Ellen*—though much less funny—but as the series unfolded, reviewers began to slowly change their perceptions. Noel Holston of *Newsday*, who initially dismissed the episode as a "so-so *Seinfeld* wannabe," retracted his earlier review after rewatching the episode and felt like writing an apology to the creators. Heather Havrilesky of Salon.com thought the series "hit its stride" in the second season, though most reviewers rank the fifth season near or at the top with season three very close behind. Even the latter seasons were mostly lauded by critics. Bill Carter of The *New York Times* called the eighth season a "truly stunning comeback." Liane Bonin of *Entertainment Weekly*, however, felt that the direction of the ninth season was a "disappointing buzzkill," claiming its nonstop celebrity guest spots had the series treading jump the shark territory. The last season of the show often ranks in the middle of the pack.

In the grand scheme of network television, time has been kind to the overall perception of the series. *Friends* made *Time*'s 2010 list of The 100 Best TV Shows of All-Time, *Rolling Stone*'s 2016 list of the 100 Greatest TV Shows of All Time (No. 26), *TV Guide*'s 2013 list of the 60 Best Series of All Time (No. 2), and *Empire*'s 2008 list of the 50 Greatest TV Shows of All Time (No. 7).

Notwithstanding the critics' views, the power of public opinion cannot be understated. A vast majority of viewers list *Friends* as one of the best TV shows of all time. As of November 2021, IMDB users voted the series the top non-animated sitcom of all time. *Friends* was No. 2 (behind *The Office*) on Ranker.com's May 2021 list of the Greatest Sitcoms in Television History. A 2013 poll by *60 Minutes* and *Vanity Fair* named *Friends* the third-greatest sitcom of all time. A 2011 *TV Guide* readers' poll named *Friends* the Best Comedy Cast of All Time (29% of the votes), beating *Seinfeld* (18%). Even the entertainment industry views *Friends* in high regard. A 2015 *Hollywood Reporter* survey of 2,800 actors, producers, directors, and other industry people named *Friends* as their No. 1 favorite show. Staff writer Adam Chase reflected upon the show's seemingly endless popularity: "When I was home sick from school I watched *The Odd Couple*. When my kids and my grandkids are home sick from school, they're going to watch *Friends*. That is the coolest thing in the world to me."

Cast publicity that precipitated the second-season backlash

Ratings—Ten Seasons

When *Friends* debuted on September 22, 1994, its future success was not guaranteed. It ranked No. 15 for the week and then viewership slowly waned for the next five weeks. It had a resurgence once the Ross–Rachel unrequited-love storyline arc captivated audiences, beginning with "The One with the Blackout" (1.07). Three episodes later, on December 15, 1994, "The One with the Monkey" (1.10) surpassed its lead-in show, *Mad About You*, in the weekly ratings. *Friends* was slowly finding an audience and gaining momentum.

As the newbie comedy continued to beat the veteran sitcom, NBC had visions of shoring up its Thursday night lineup with a fresh anchor series. But first it had to build a stronger audience base for the Manhattan-based sextet. On February 23, 1995, NBC implemented its ratings-boosting agenda by placing *Friends* in the timeslot previously occupied by its original sitcom darling, *Madman of the People*. NBC introduced *Friends* to a new timeslot (following *Seinfeld*) using a unique approach: it aired a two-part episode on the same night but with one installment before *Seinfeld* and the other after. The gimmick worked. *Friends* held its own, losing only a small fraction of *Seinfeld*'s lead-in audience, thereby becoming a top-five show.

Although NBC was hopeful about the future success of *Friends*, executives were unsure whether the elevated ratings were only temporarily propped by its cushy timeslot following *Seinfeld*. Nevertheless, they decided to take a chance on the freshman sitcom as its new anchor on Thursday night. When the 1995-96 television season kicked off in September, *Friends* replaced *Mad About You* at the 8pm (EST) timeslot, a position it never relinquished until retiring in 2004. The network's strategy was a success. During the second season, *Friends* viewership roller-coastered between 20 and 30 million and remained a permanent top-five show for the rest of its run. There were several factors that contributed to its early achievements: (1) a summertime promotional blitz by NBC, (2) timeslot placement behind *Seinfeld*, (3) continuous media coverage of the cast, and (4) nonstop radio airplay of the *Friends* theme song. It was the perfect storm for attracting legions of new viewers to the twentysomething sitcom.

At the end of the fifth season, *Friends* had its highest rating as the No. 2 program in the country. It seemed perched to overtake *ER* for the No. 1 position, but the following season viewership dropped 12% and the series had its lowest rating since its inaugural season. Rumors began swirling that *Friends* was fading. Monica and Chandler's courtship appeared to revitalize the series in season seven so CBS brazenly attempted a programming kidney punch to cripple the aging sitcom. In January 2001, CBS announced it was moving its top series (No. 2 overall), the reality show *Survivor*, in direct competition with *Friends*, starting on February 1st.

Jeff Zucker, NBC's newly appointed entertainment president, was faced with his first major programming test. He devised a promotional stunt of using supersized episodes. A typical sitcom is 30 minutes (with commercials) and has two act breaks; a supersized show is up to 40 minutes with three act breaks. The unconventional programming format was meant to eliminate weaker sitcoms by extending the runtime of more popular shows. NBC executives thought he was crazy but soon all the networks were doing it to their broadcast schedules.

Despite Zucker's unique approach, on the first week of competition *Survivor* crushed *Friends* in the weekly ratings—29 million viewers to 22.2 million—and continued to easily dominate the rest of the season. Although *Friends* ended the season ranked No. 5, it had its smallest average audience (20.2 million) during its decade run. *Survivor* was No. 1 for the season. The following year the table turned. *Friends* took control and subjugated *Survivor*—the sitcom was No. 1 while the reality show, which had two seasons, finished No. 8 and No. 6. NBC even abandoned its supersized episode strategy. The following two years both shows remained top-10 programs. During the *Friends* farewell season, CBS knew it would lose the ratings battle so it switched *Survivor* to Sunday night.

Friends became the only sitcom in modern television history to last a minimum of 10 years while spending its entire series run in the network ratings top 10. The following is the series ratings by year, season rank, and average number of viewers per episode:

Season One (1994-95)—No. 8, 24.3M

Season Two (1995-96)—No. 3, 30.0M

Season Three (1996-97)—No. 4, 24.9M

Season Four (1997-98)—No. 4, 24.0M

Season Five (1998-99)—No. 2, 23.5M

Season Six (1999-2000)—No. 5, 20.7M

Season Seven (2000-01)—No. 5, 20.2M

Season Eight (2001-02)—No. 1, 24.5M

Season Nine (2002-03)—No. 2, 21.8M

Season Ten (2003-04)—No. 4, 22.8M

In addition to being a top-five series for nine straight seasons, *Friends* was the No. 1 comedy for six straight years. Though not as industry-recognized as *Frasier* or critically acclaimed as *Seinfeld*, *Friends* remains a beloved sitcom having an equally notable impact on popular culture.

Super Bowl Episode

The double-length Super Bowl installment is officially known as "The One After the Superbowl" (2.12, 2.13), which aired January 28, 1996. It was aptly named because both episodes aired after Super Bowl XXX, where the Dallas Cowboys defeated the Pittsburgh Steelers, 27–17. The installment title "Superbowl" was purposely misspelled to prevent a trademark infringement claim or the need for special permission from the NFL. The league's trademark is two words. The sporting event was named by Lamar Hunt, then owner of the Kansas City Chiefs, after observing his son playing with a Super Ball (toy bouncy ball based on a type of synthetic rubber invented in 1964).

NBC aired this episode directly after Super Bowl XXX hoping to make it the "highest-grossing ad revenue day in television history." Big-name guest stars were cast to bolster viewership, which executives touted to justify their unprecedented advertising rates. In past years, networks had exploited the post-Super Bowl timeslot to launch a new series. NBC made an exception with *Friends*, knowing it could attract more advertising revenue than a series premiere. The advertising rates for "The One After the Superbowl" averaged $600,000 for a 30-second spot. At the time, this was the highest rate ever for a non-series-ending sitcom episode. "For the night, NBC averaged a 42.0 rating and a 62 share. It ended up being the most watched night in television history with 140 million Americans tuning in," NBC President Warren Littlefield gleefully exclaimed. "No network had ever accomplished that."

Awards

To maintain the series' ensemble format, the *Friends* cast members jointly decided to enter themselves in the same acting categories for awards. Beginning with the series' eighth season, however, the actors submitted themselves in the lead actor balloting, rather than the supporting actor fields. In 10 seasons, *Friends* was nominated for 62 Primetime Emmy Awards (winning six) including six nominations (1995, 1996, 1999, 2000, 2002 and 2003) for Outstanding Comedy Series, winning in 2002. The series also won an American Comedy Award (14 nominations), one Golden Globe Award (10 nominations), one GLAAD Media Award (3 nominations), two Logie Awards (3 nominations), eleven People's Choice Awards (11 nominations), one Satellite Award (9 nominations), and two Screen Actors Guild Awards (14 nominations).

In the Emmy race, only Lisa Kudrow and Jennifer Aniston won an award. Courtney Cox was the only costar who did not receive a nomination. She was particularly woeful in 2000 when both Aniston and Kudrow received a nomination but she was excluded. "I had a hard time not taking it personally when it was both Lisa and Jennifer at the same time. One guy, one girl, whatever. But both girls and not me? It hurt. I'm very sensitive," Cox confessed. Matt LeBlanc had three nominations, and the other two male leads had one each.

When Jennifer Aniston gave her 2001 Emmy Award acceptance speech for Outstanding Lead Actress in a Comedy Series, she thanked the usual suspects—her husband, the cast and creators—and then thanked Inger. The obscure adulation was for Inger Johnson, the show's craft services staffer, who kept the *Friends* happy with her homemade soups. "She's just the most amazing chef," James Michael Tyler (Gunther) said. "She kept everyone very happy. She made these outstanding organic soups, all from scratch. She kept everyone in high spirits. She was like a mother to everyone."

Only Aniston, Kudrow and LeBlanc received nominations for a Golden Globe Award; Aniston was the sole victor, winning in 2003.

Syndication & Streaming

In fall 2001, Warner Bros. Domestic Cable (WBDC) made a deal with sister network TBS (both are owned by Time Warner) to televise *Friends* in syndication. A decade later, WBDC announced that it had sold additional cable rights to Nick at Nite which began airing the series on September 5, 2011. Unlike the TBS syndication airings, Nick at Nite broadcasts replaced the end credit tag scenes with marginalized credits featuring promotions for the sitcom and other Nick at Nite programs. Warner Bros. was expected to make $200 million in license fees and advertising from the deal. Nick at Nite paid $500,000 per episode to air the show after 6pm (EST) for six years through fall 2017. The sitcom jumped to Paramount Network in 2018 and 2019, and on October 12, 2019, Comedy Central began airing reruns of *Friends*.

In total, *Friends* has been broadcast in more than 200 countries and translated into more than 15 languages. As of 2016, through syndicated reruns, the US weekly audience, not including streaming, was remarkably impressive with 16 million viewers. In fact, rerun viewership actually exceeded the original broadcast audience for "The One with the Vows" (7.21) in 2001. Moreover, the *Friends* rerun audience was nearly four times larger than the total number of viewers who tuned in to see the original first-run broadcast of the 2020 series finale of *Modern Family*, a series that lasted 11 years.

Friends may be one of the most profitable shows in television history, but the money didn't come pouring in right away. Warner Bros. Television licensed the 30-minute comedy to NBC, however, for the first four years of broadcast, the production company actually lost money on the show, gambling that it would pay off after the series went into syndication. By the time the series entered its fifth season, NBC was so intent on keeping the sitcom in its Thursday night lineup that it agreed to cover the cost of production. During the show's 10-year broadcast run, the overhead costs included an estimated $70 million in producer fees for Bright/Kauffman/Crane Productions and roughly $88 million for the stars, whose salaries rose from a modest $22,500 per episode in the first season to an astronomical $1 million a show in the final two years.

The real payoff began once the show entered syndication. With 97 episodes banked over those first four years, Warner Bros. had enough shows to begin selling its *Friends* catalog to local stations, cable networks and channels outside the US, and eventually to streaming services, in a string of deals that *Forbes* estimates amounted to some $4.8 billion for the production company, as of 2021. That does not include any revenue from DVD sales. This translates to $1.4 billion for the cast and creators ($136 million for each costar and over $550 million for Bright/Kauffman/Crane Productions).

Besides traditional syndication, modern technological advancements have broadened the field to make television programs more accessible to the public. Streaming services offer programming on demand so viewers can watch shows when they want, without waiting for a live broadcast or DVR recording of the series. Plus, subscribers can binge-watch as many episodes as they desire. Traditional formats limit broadcasts to usually one or two episodes per day. This revolutionary service changed the syndication game for the betterment of all, including production companies, broadcasters and viewers.

Knowing the money to be made, Warner Bros. was sure to capitalize on the new format. In late 2014, WB signed a $30 million per year deal with Ted Sarandos and Co. allowing Netflix to begin airing all 236 *Friends* episodes starting on January 1, 2015. This broadcast arrangement introduced a new generation of teenagers to the show. Moreover, its reach extended to all corners of the world, exponentially expanding viewership. In 2015, the UK experienced a 10% annual increase in its *Friends* syndicated audience, and three years later it was the country's most streamed series on Netflix. From 2017 to 2018, *Friends* was the second-most-streamed series in the US having been watched 31.8 billion minutes (*The*

Office amassed 45.8 billion minutes). This level of sustained viewership is unprecedented in television history. But it is not just longtime fans who are streaming the show. Nearly half the *Friends* viewers on Netflix are under the age of 35, and around 11% of them have just started watching it for the first time, according to the firm Branded Entertainment Network, which conducts tracking studies of Netflix users every month.

Friends fanatics went crazy in late 2018 after news broke that their beloved sitcom was leaving Netflix in 2019. They began circulating a Change.org petition to keep the show on Netflix and #Justice4Friends started trending. The digital petition garnered nearly 90,000 signatures, compelling the streaming service to pay $100 million to retain the show for one more year. In contrast, four years earlier the company shelled out $30 million per year for the streaming rights, which is three times less than the 2019 fee. The executive producers of *Friends* credit streaming for the show's resurgence among a new generation of viewers. "We'll stay indebted to Netflix for making this all happen," Kevin Bright declared. "It's really been an incredible revival of the show, and they have to get a lot of credit for that."

The series remained so popular that Warner Bros. launched a new streaming platform, HBO Max, in part to control the dissemination of *Friends* and to reap the profits from the timeless sitcom. WarnerMedia dropped a reported $425 million to take the rights back from the other platforms, but only for five years. The sitcom's debut on HBO Max coincided with the launch of the platform on May 27, 2020. The original plan was for it to coincide with the much-anticipated *Friends* reunion special, but due to COVID-19 concerns, production was delayed a year. *Friends: The Reunion* was taped in April 2021 and aired the following month on May 27th, one year after its originally scheduled airdate. A survey conducted by CableTV.com in May 2020 determined that *Friends* was the top show in the US during the bleakest days of the pandemic. The sitcom was named the most popular series in 11 states, including 7 of the 10 most populated ones. As of 2021, the show has been watched more than 100 billion times across all platforms, and is credited for influencing everything from fashion to hairstyles.

There are many theories addressing the timeless popularity of *Friends* among teenagers who were not even born when the series expired. Marta Kauffman describes the series as "comfort food" because "It's warm. It's inviting. You want those people in your house." Amid societal chaos in recent years, the 1990s seem like simpler times. Youths seek and find solace in the 22-minute program. It is relaxing and a good way to unwind. Although the characters' problems appear trivial, the themes are universal and transcend generations. Teens can use the series as a snapshot of what the future holds—first jobs, first romance, first time living on your own, etc., and doing it all with supportive friends every step of the way.

One cannot discount the vast popularity of *Friends* being somewhat associated to the generational and technological gap. Teens especially love the technology gaps—cell phones rarely exist, apartments are equipped with landline telephones and answering machines, everything is recorded on VHS tapes, which corresponds with using a VCR, the videogame graphics are substandard, laptops and computers are archaic, etc. Matt LeBlanc called the show "timeless" but then qualified the remark: "The only thing that dates the show is when someone makes a phone call, you see them pull the antenna on the phone." Even the older viewers enjoy spotting the antiquated clothes, accessories, hairstyles, slang, concepts and technologies.

International Broadcasts

Friends debuted in the US on September 22, 1994. After reaping huge initial success, Warner Bros. decided to broadcast the show in Europe. It premiered in the UK on April 28, 1995, and aired first-run installments until September on Channel 4 at 9:30pm on Friday nights. It was an instant success, and propelled the theme song to No. 3 on the UK Singles chart in September 1995. The popularity of the show led to a double-length episode being produced in London at the end of the fourth season.

The following year, Sky One purchased the rights to the hit series and licensed delayed rebroadcasts (by several weeks) to Channel 4. Miraculously, *Friends* still remained one of Channel 4's most popular shows, averaging 2.6 million viewers per episode. Unlike many of its imported series, such as *ER*, *Frasier* and *NYPD Blue*, Channel 4 never moved *Friends* from its peak-time position. Networks aired *Friends* in its original, unedited international version, not the edited version used for US broadcast and syndication airings. These uncut episodes have aired on such stations as Channel 4, Sky One, E4, and Comedy Central UK.

Ron Leibman (Dr. Green) (left) and cast members goofing around (right)

In 1999, Channel 4 signed a £100M ($138 million) deal to regain the rights to *Friends* and *ER* from Sky One. The three-year contract allowed Channel 4 to air first-run episodes of the hit series in the UK, and to negotiate pay-TV airings with other UK broadcasters. On September 4, 2011, *Friends* reruns officially ended on E4 after being aired for seven years. Comedy Central UK took over the syndication rights and began broadcasting episodes the following month. Since 2018, Channel 5 also started broadcasting the program.

In the Republic of Ireland, each season of the show made its European debut on RTÉ2. After 2004, RTÉ2 began to repeat the series from the start before moving over to TV3 and its digital channel 3e in 2010. As of February 2015, reruns of the show returned to RTÉ2 and also air on Comedy Central Ireland.

The first season of *Friends* premiered on Australian television in 1996 on the Seven Network. The following year the Nine Network began broadcasting the second season, and it continued to air first-run episodes through the series finale in 2006. Network Ten aired the series in syndication from 2007 to 2009 on GEM (a sub-channel of the Nine Network), and on pay-TV channel TV Hits (formerly aired on Arena, 111 Hits). TV2 began broadcasting the sitcom in New Zealand in 1995 and aired all 10 seasons, and continues to televise repeats. *Friends* is only one of three imported television shows to be broadcast year-round in New Zealand (the others being *The Simpsons* and *King of the Hill*).

In Canada, the hit series was broadcast on Global. In later years, it was syndicated on several of its sibling cable networks, including Slice, DTour, and TVTropolis, its previous incarnation. In India, the show is broadcast by Comedy Central at various times. It is the most watched English language show in the country. In the Philippines, the show originally aired on ABC-5 from 1996 to 2005 and ETC from 2005 to 2014. In Greece, the show was broadcast on Star Channel. In Cyprus, *Friends* aired on CyBC 2 while reruns were shown on TVOne. Today, the series is available in most countries around the world.

Friends has a massive following in China, with many Chinese millennials crediting the show with introducing them to American culture and teaching them the English language. One day after the *Friends* reunion show aired, the topic "*Friends* reunion" attracted over 180 million hits on Weibo, China's version of Twitter.

Translated Telecasts

Friends is broadcast in non-English-speaking countries such as Japan, Sweden and Germany. In most countries, voice-over artists are hired to dub the dialogue into the native language of the country. In Sweden, however, they watch the episodes with subtitles. To prepare for each voice-over performance, the actors take the script home to memorize and scrutinize the English version of the episode, along with a translated copy. At the studio, they rehearse only once with the help of a director before recording the first take.

Voice-over artists occasionally edit the script to comport with their culture. When there is a huge outburst of laughter in the episode, the actors play around with the joke in their native tongue to make it funnier to match the track.

Production of the German version of *Friends* is an expedited process. Since Germans have a similar sense of humor to New Yorkers—straight, fast and spontaneous—the voice-over artists must perform the script without rehearsal. "We don't get the books before. We get everything in the studio and then we have to be ready, prepared for what we have to do," remarked one of the actors. "It is our great concern to be as close to the original. We are like an ensemble of actors and we are really friends."

Remastering

Beginning on March 5, 2012, high definition (HD) versions of all 236 *Friends* episodes were made available to local broadcast stations, starting with the pilot installment. For the remastered episodes, Warner Bros. restored previously cropped images on the left and right sides of the screen, using the original 35 mm film source, to comport with the entire 16:9 widescreen frame. However, because the show was not originally filmed for widescreen, but rather in 4-perf format (4:3), some cropping problems were evident because the expanded shots revealed unintentional continuity errors, including set edges, boom mics, and stand-ins replacing some of the main cast.

Prior to 2012, in early versions of the HD remasters, there were a few shots, including chroma effects shots, that were sourced from standard-definition 480i videotape sources because not all of the footage had been tracked down in time for the remaster (the original film sources for these shots were later rescanned for future broadcast and release). These remasters have been airing in New Zealand on TV2 since January 2011 and the earlier HD prints continue to air on Comedy Central UK as of 2020. Netflix added all 10 seasons of *Friends* in high definition to their US streaming service on January 1, 2015.

Timelessness

Great writing, great acting, great cast chemistry, and relatable themes. That is what makes a sitcom timeless. "[*Friends* is] about people in a phase of your life—that sort of after college and before your life starts," Matt LeBlanc said. "There's always going to be a new generation going through that, and they can identify with it because we kind of dealt with a lot of the issues that you deal with where your friends are your family. I think it's good. I'm proud of it." Matthew Perry had a similar take on the subject: "It was a character-driven funny, not timely funny," he noted. "They didn't make timely jokes. They didn't make jokes about OJ Simpson. They made character-driven jokes about people—and people are going to come back time and time again and watch that." Contrary to his statement, the writers actually penned one notable current events bit.

In "The One Where Rachel Finds Out" (1.24), as Chandler is eating cereal and reading the newspaper, he asks Joey if something is going on with OJ. This bit is often deleted from syndicated versions because of the negative connotation associated with the infamous OJ Simpson murder trial and acquittal. The spectacle—often characterized as the trial of the century because of its international publicity—spanned nearly 11 months, from the jury's swearing-in on November 9, 1994, until the acquittal verdict on October 3, 1995.

The perpetual success of *Friends* can also be attributed to the young viewers' addiction to online streaming services and their desire for serialized storytelling while binge-watching episodes. When the sitcom debuted, story arcs were discouraged by networks. "At the time, the network was nervous about arcs, but we felt strongly about them," Marta Kauffman said. "And they help with the streaming services now. You can get involved in a story, and not suddenly be in a whole new episode where they dropped that thing that was happening with Monica." David Crane continued with the thought: "We were just telling stories that we liked. But when we did pursue arcs, it really helped the show because Marta and I really cared. We cared because it had to be funny, but also because we were both very invested in how much you cared about these characters, and you needed ongoing stories to really be able to do that."

A 2019 survey of British children aged 9 to 16 discovered that *Friends* was their favorite series, even though most of them were born long after the final episode aired. Since most youths are first experiencing the series on streaming services, they actually believe *Friends* is a newly released program, not one from a quarter century ago. In 2021, Marta Kauffman recounted an anecdote from 2015 that encapsulates the timelessness of *Friends*. "A few years ago, my youngest daughter, who was in high school at the time, said a friend of hers came up to her and said, 'Have you seen that new show called *Friends*?'" Kauffman stated. "Girl thought it was a period piece."

Tributes, Reunions & Merchandising

One indication of a show's timelessness is the presence and quantity of tribute shows as well as events and reunion telecasts that captivate the masses. In addition, the sheer volume of series-related merchandising is another criteria to consider when assessing a show's continued popularity, especially when sales remain steady for many years after the show retired. Although *Home Improvement* was a No. 1 megahit sitcom and top-10 show throughout the 1990s, there is never a tribute special or celebrated reunion show and its product merchandising is practically nonexistent. Although the sitcom may be present in some syndicated markets, it is dwarfed by comparable period pieces such as *Friends* and *Seinfeld*.

UK Tributes

A *Friends* musical launched in the UK at Everyman Theatre in Cheltenham on July 15, 2019, to commemorate the 25th anniversary of the show. *Friendsical*, created by Miranda Larson, is a musical parody inspired by the 1990s hit sitcom. It commences from the very beginning, right around the time Carol leaves Ross for Susan, and Rachel ditches Barry at the altar. The musical numbers include "(He's her) Lobster," "Richard's Moustache" and "You're Over Me? When Were You Under Me?" The production also has the gang taking on naked Thursdays, a power cut (blackout), and a dinosaur convention. The musical received positive reviews, and with its ensuing success, the show went on tour with dates extending into 2024.

FriendsFest started in 2015 as a five-day pop-up event in London to celebrate one of Comedy Central UK's most popular shows and help bring the series closer to its audience. According to Amanda Browne, head of public relations for the broadcaster, "Experiential events are incredibly popular with our audience and we felt *Friends* was the perfect show to create this type of interactive event for, as it has so many iconic moments and sets." The extravaganza sold out in minutes with more than 250,000 people applying to get tickets. Due to the phenomenal interest and demand from fans, Comedy Central UK brought the event back the next year, turning it into a six-week outdoor countrywide touring festival. By 2018 it morphed into an annual 12-week extravaganza with additional sets and *Friends*-themed activities being added each year.

US Tribute

Friends! The Musical Parody officially debuted off Broadway at St. Luke's Theatre on November 2, 2017. Composer Assaf Gleizner wrote the music, and the book and lyrics were penned by Bob and Tobly McSmith, the creative pair behind other unauthorized sitcom satires like *Bayside! The Saved by the Bell Musical, Full House! The Musical!* and *The Office! A Musical Parody.* The production comically celebrates and lovingly pokes fun at the series while musically sharing the adventures of the sextet as they navigate the pitfalls of work, life and love in 1990s Manhattan. The performance recreates many favorite moments from all 10 years of the show through an uncensored, fast-paced, music-filled romp with added commentary where the cast members mock each other about their real-life choices, such as Jennifer Aniston losing Brad Pitt to Angelina Jolie. Reviews were mixed but mostly tepid, yet popular enough that the stage show continues to have revivals every year with multi-city tours across North America.

25th Anniversary Celebration

In 2019, Warner Bros. joined forces with Fathom Events to celebrate the milestone 25th anniversary of *Friends* featuring a three-night special event. "*Friends* 25th: The One with the Anniversary" gave recognition to the cultural phenomenon by bringing 12 fan-favorite episodes to movie theaters across the US over three nights: September 23, September 28 and October 2. The event was screened in more than 1,000 movie theaters nationwide at 7pm local time through the Fathom Network. Each episode was remastered in 4K from the original 35 mm camera negative. The screenings also included exclusive interviews and never-before-seen content. A few of the popular episodes were "The One Where No One's Ready" (3.02), "The One with Chandler in a Box" (4.08) and "The One Where Ross Got High" (6.09).

Pop artist Burton Morris, whose work was often featured in Central Perk, collaborated with Warner Bros. to stage an exhibition with all his famous pieces that appeared on the show and several new creations inspired by the occasion. The exhibition took place from September 19 to October 16, 2019 in New York. To benefit from the *Friends* reunion special on May 27, 2021, he auctioned a line of *Friends* pop art from June 3 through June 7, 2021.

Las Vegas had its own way of celebrating the 25th anniversary of *Friends*. At New York–New York casino, artist Nathan Sawaya designed a full-size replica of Central Perk using roughly 975,000 Lego bricks. In addition, *Friends* fans could take part in several interactive elements, pose for selfies on the famed orange couch, and meet Katie, the capuchin monkey who starred as Marcel. The Sin City events included a new *Friends*-inspired show at the Fountains of Bellagio and a special performance by Blue Man Group.

Kirkbi authorized a special edition Lego Central Perk set for $59.99. The 1,070-piece set comprised many special elements of the coffee shop like the orange couch and the stage where Phoebe debuted her most beloved song, "Smelly Cat," complete with her guitar and microphone. It also added special details like Rachel with a tray and coffee cup (from her earlier years as a server), Ross with the keyboard (which fueled his infamous "sound"), and Joey with his beloved pizza, not to mention Gunther with a broom and espresso machine.

Replicas of the iconic Central Perk orange couch began a two-month journey around the globe, hitting US locations like New York City, New Orleans and Los Angeles, as well as international destinations such as London and Madrid.

On July 30, 2019, Pottery Barn launched a 25th anniversary *Friends*-themed collection that included Rachel and Phoebe's famed apothecary table; however, it did not sell for $150 like it supposedly did at the Colonial flea market, it cost $1,099. The anniversary collection included tea towels, throw pillows, mugs, glasses, and prints featuring memorable dialogue, catchphrases and objects from the series. The collection also contained items with classic *Friends* quotes like "You're my lobster" and products depicting indelible imagery, like the purple door.

Retail giant Target jumped into the foray by releasing a *Friends*-inspired clothing line that was full of references from the sitcom. From a "Pivot!" couch hoodie to a "You're My Lobster" gray cropped t-shirt to black sweatpants emblazoned with the characters' names. The Minneapolis-based retailer offered a wide sampling of *Friends*-related garments.

In August 2019, Alex and Ani released seven jewelry items featuring quotes from the beloved NBC sitcom. The collection offered fans necklaces and bangle charms with classic *Friends* phrases (such as "You're My Lobster" and "How You Doin'") as well as pieces that boast the logos for the series and Central Perk.

Broadcaster TBS held a fan-vote *Friends* marathon dubbed "The One Where Fans Take Over TBS." The special television event was held from September 16th to the 21st, where viewers could watch all of the most treasured *Friends* episodes, which were selected based on fan votes.

Giphy unveiled an entire *Friends* GIF channel where fans of the series could text friends their favorite character's reactions. It's an entire GIF channel dedicated to the series. There are over 2,300 new GIFs pulled from every episode and then added to the channel.

For the first time ever, Warner Bros. auctioned official *Friends* props, costumes, and production materials from the series. The proceeds benefited The Trevor Project, the world's largest suicide prevention and crisis intervention organization for LGBTQ young people. The Prop Store offered more than 100 items that spanned across all 10 seasons of the sitcom at auction houses based in London, England, and Valencia, California, from December 3-17, 2019. The auction raised $241,675. A studio-edition authorized reproduction of the Central Perk couch raked in $11,000, far more than the anticipated $6,000 to $8,000. Joey and Chandler's wood canoe and two paddles commanded $10,500, which was expected to bring home $4,000 to $6,000. Joey's stuffed penguin pal (Hugsy) was expected to raise $1,000 to $1,500 but sold for a whopping $8,500. However, not all the items exceeded expectations. A studio-edition reproduction of Ross' Holiday Armadillo costume pulled in $4,100, much less than the expected $10,000 to $15,000.

Two stage parodies: *Friendsical* **(left) and** *Friends! The Musical Parody* **(right)**

Pop-ups

The 15th anniversary of *Friends* commenced a pop-up tradition. From September 24 to October 7, 2009, a Central Perk replica was based at Broadwick Street in Soho, London. The cafe itself was an exact copy of the one from the series with a burnt-orange velvet sofa, green armchair, oriental rugs, brick walls and neon lighting. The coffeehouse sold coffee to customers but no food was available. The pop-up featured a display of *Friends* memorabilia and props, such as Rachel's wedding gown, her pink bridesmaid dress, Ross' *Science Boy* comic book cover, a copy of the porn movie *Buffay the Vampire Layer*, Joey's "best buds" bracelet, and the Geller Cup trophy.

As the pop-up tradition continued, the extravaganza became bigger and better. By the time the show reached its silver anniversary, Warner Bros. capitalized on the resurgent popularity of *Friends* by collaborating with entertainment and creative company Superfly to create a giant 8,500-square-foot pop-up filled with real props from the show and special areas dedicated to each of the show's main characters. Ardent fans enjoyed an immersive experience, such as sitting on the famed orange couch in Central Perk, lounging on Joey and Chandler's leather recliners, and even sticking their noggins inside a Thanksgiving turkey. The pop-ups appeared in most major US cities, such as New York, Los Angeles and Chicago. Eight O'Clock Coffee provided original and unique blends at the pop-up shops. The NYC Central Perk pop-up opened for one month (September 7 to October 6, 2019) and the entire event sold out in three hours.

Naturally, the tourist trap also contained a massive retail store to sell *Friends*-themed merchandise, such as mugs, ornaments, shirts, bags and keychains, as well as bracelets from Alex and Ani. The pop-ups offered a variety of food and beverages. There were several themed pastries on the menu:

> Joey's NY Apple Pie: $6
> *Friends* Branded Donuts: $6.50
> Ross's Mini Blueberry Bribe Muffin Basket: $4.50
> Joey's Blackberry Jam Turnovers: $6.50
> Monica's "Good time" Chocolate Cake: $6
> Rachel's Oops I Dropped the Cheesecake: $6
> Chandler's Licked Banana Nut Muffin: $4.50
> Phoebe's Great Great Grandma's Famous Cookies: $4.50

Other *Friends* pop-ups followed suit. The Coffee Bean & Tea Leaf company celebrated the 25th anniversary by opening two Central Perk pop-ups in Southern California: on the Third Street Promenade in Santa Monica and on Beverly Boulevard in West Hollywood, the latter operated August 16-23, 2019. The chain joined forces with Warner Bros. to introduce a limited-edition line of coffees and teas available on its website and on Amazon.com. A 12-ounce bag cost around $10. Three flavors were available: (1) Central Perk Medium Roast with a walnut aroma and a sweet, smooth finish; (2) Central Perk Dark Roast made from Brazilian and Colombian coffee with a cocoa flavor; and (3) Central Perk Tea using freshly steeped black tea with bright citrus. Specialty mugs were also available with unique puns on cafe-themed catchphrases from the show like "We were on a coffee break" and "How you brewin'?"

James Burrows Reunion

On February 21, 2016, the *Friends* cast (minus Matthew Perry) reunited on NBC for a tribute to director James Burrows, where they discussed a few of their favorite moments on the show. The special, *Must See TV: An All-Star Tribute to James Burrows*, commemorated the 1,000th episode of TV that Burrows directed, and reunited stars from his most famous shows—*Taxi*, *Will & Grace*, *The Big Bang Theory*, *Frasier*, *Cheers* and, of course, *Friends*. Matthew Perry missed the event because he was in London starring in a play he wrote, but the actor did appear via a pre-taped message to offer a personal tribute to the renowned director.

The reunion was panned as uninformative, unfunny, and a boring waste of two hours. Basically, five *Friends* stars sat on a sofa on national television and nothing happened. All the hype and publicity called the special a comedy, but not one chuckle was evoked from the insipid dialogue. It was a major disappointment to *Friends* fans.

HBO Reunion

Since *Friends* ended in 2004, the show's creators, Marta Kauffman and David Crane, have consistently and adamantly resisted any reboot or revival of the series. They even avoided being part of the *Joey* spinoff because they did not want to tarnish the sitcom's legacy. "There are two reasons for that," Kauffman explained. "One of them is, this is a show about that time in your life when your friends are your family and once you start having family that changes, so it wouldn't be what's at the heart of the show anymore. But the other reason is, it's not going to be what we did." Crane added, "If you visited those characters now, it would just have a different DNA. It would just not be the same show. Chances are it wouldn't be as good a show. Why go back to the well?"

The tandem also realized that nothing good could come from a reunion or reboot. "All we'd be doing is putting those six actors back together, but the heart of the show would be gone," Kauffman earnestly stated. "I don't know what good it does us. The show is going just fine, people love it. [A reunion] could only disappoint." (The creators resisted a scripted show where the actors would play their original characters; they did not oppose other ideas, such as an unscripted talk show format.) The creators were not alone. The male leads have always resisted a reunion. Matt LeBlanc was "firmly against" a major *Friends* storyline, and even a talk show reunion took a lot of convincing. Matthew Perry concurred: "I have this recurring nightmare. ... When I'm asleep, I have this nightmare that we do *Friends* again and nobody cares."

A *Friends* reunion was discussed for some time but it didn't officially take shape until the cast was first approached in July 2019. According to director Ben Winston, if there was ever going to be a reunion show, David Schwimmer was the linchpin because he had been involved in the sitcom more creatively than the others, so he would have the most to say about bringing everything back. "He was the one I had to win over first," Winston said. "He heard my ideas and then vouched for me." Once Schwimmer was on board, the director met with Lisa Kudrow, Courteney Cox, and Matt LeBlanc as a group. He then conversed with Matthew Perry over FaceTime. The last to be contacted was Jennifer Aniston, and she was excited from the get-go, Winston claimed.

On November 12, 2019, *The Hollywood Reporter* announced that Warner Bros. TV was developing a *Friends* reunion for HBO Max that would feature the cast and creators. On February 21, 2020, HBO confirmed that the unscripted reunion special, tentatively named "The One Where They Got Back Together," was scheduled to be released on May 27, 2020. On March 18th, it was announced that the special, which was set to film on Stage 24 (The *Friends* Stage) from March 22-24, had been postponed indefinitely due to the coronavirus pandemic.

Friends: The Reunion, officially known as *The One Where They Get Back Together*, was filmed over a three-day period during the first week of April 2021; the 104-minute event premiered May 27, 2021 on HBO Max. It brought together the six original cast members for an unscripted special hosted by talk show host James Corden. Celebrity guests included recognizable faces from the series, such as Elliott Gould, Christina Pickles, Tom Selleck, James Michael Tyler and Maggie Wheeler, as well as avid fans of the show like BTS, Justin Bieber, Lady Gaga and Kit Harington. Special appearances by director James Burrows and comedian Bob Newhart were cut from the original broadcast but later used as bonus clips in the HBO Max release.

Scheduling the shoot on Stage 24 was a logistical nightmare. "Studio 24 is one of the main studios at Warner Bros. that they use for sitcoms. It was a three-week load-in and light [setup], a 10-day strike-out [set deconstruction] and a three-day shoot," Winston said. "So you're looking at, 'How do you get Studio 24 for five weeks?'" Once it was time to film, they rebuilt the show's biggest sets: the two main apartments (Joey's and Monica's) and Central Perk. "They pulled those [sets] out of storage," David Crane noted. "It all had to be reconstructed. They pulled props from the Warner Bros. tour, *Friends* pop-up experiences. They wanted all the original pieces." The series' art director John Shaffner and set designer

Greg Grande both returned to ensure everything was exactly where Monica left it. And if it was not, they scoured the internet. "Anything that was missing, Grande found on eBay," Kevin Bright stated, "including the cookie jar in Rachel and Monica's kitchen, which Lisa took home at the end of the show." Fortunately, most everything had been archived or used in the official studio tour at Warner Bros. Bright estimated that the crew "got about 75% of the furnishings from the boys' and the girls' apartments. And almost everything from the coffeehouse because it was in the museum." Past photos, shopping and a little creativity filled in the rest.

Creating the magic of the reunion's first moments—with the cast entering the stage one at a time and seeing the iconic sets (and then one another)—wasn't easy. "I always wanted them to be apart that morning," director Ben Winston declared. So imagine his panic when he showed up and all their trailers were lined up right next to one another. "I was so upset. I really wanted that moment to be real. So I immediately got the team and we built tents outside of their doors so that they wouldn't see each other." Winston then texted the cast, begging them to avoid contacting their fellow friends. "Luckily they played along, so that moment when they see each other on set is the first time they've all six been together [since the show ended], apart from one dinner," he added. It was extremely emotional for all of them. "I don't think any of us had any idea how emotional we would be when we walked onto the set," said Courteney Cox. "To see it exactly the way it was, … it was exactly the same. And it was so emotional that we just started crying."

Getting a seat in the studio audience was a matter of luck. It was not filled with family and friends like the series denouement 17 years prior. "We were very low-key about what they were doing," Winston stated. "An audience company found us an audience, but they didn't know until the day before what they were going to be watching, because we didn't want any leaks. So we found huge *Friends* fans but they didn't know what they were seeing until everybody could go through the COVID protocol." TMZ reported that a live audience consisted of union actors who were hired as extras for the shoot.

Prior to filming, director Ben Winston asked Kudrow if she would sing "Smelly Cat" and she said, "Yeah, that would be fun." They went through a few names, and both agreed that Lady Gaga, if they could get her, "would be the ultimate one because she associates with and feels close to Phoebe in so many ways." The pop star jumped at the chance to do it, but the singer barely had time to rehearse. "We sat there with the two guitars with Lisa and her and worked it out there and then," Winston said. After agreeing to a duet, Kudrow realized she did not remember the chords to the melody so she searched the internet to refresh her memory.

There were a couple noteworthy cameos. Soccer player David Beckham proclaimed, "I'm most like Monica because I'm a clean freak!" and then divulged his favorite *Friends* episode, "The One Where No One's Ready" (3.02): "It's one of those episodes that when I'm away and I'm feeling a little bit low, I put it on and it makes me smile, almost to the point of crying." Nobel Prize winner Malala Yousafzai said a friend got her hooked on the comedy, and BTS honored the series with a brief video message. Leader of the pop boy band, RM, stated, "My mom bought me the DVDs of the whole series when I was in elementary school. *Friends* really had a big hand in teaching me English and the show really taught me the things about life and true friendship." The other band members shouted "We love *Friends!*" Other celebs, such as Mindy Kaling and Kit Harington, opened up about their love for the sitcom in prerecorded interviews.

In a mini fashion show, model Cara Delevingne wore Rachel's appalling pink bridesmaid dress (underwear mishap included) from "The One with Barry & Mindy's Wedding" (2.24), and then sported Ross' winter-holiday armadillo costume from "The One with the Holiday Armadillo" (7.10). Singer Justin Bieber stepped out in the full Spudnik costume from "The One with the Halloween Party" (8.06), and model Cindy Crawford walked the runway in Ross' fantabulous formfitting leather pants from "The One with All the Resolutions" (5.11). Matt LeBlanc even recreated the scene where he wore all of Chandler's clothes from "The One Where No One's Ready" (3.02).

The main cast did a few intimate table reads from pivotal episodes like "The One Where Everybody Finds Out" (5.14), "The One Where Ross Finds Out" (2.07) and "The One with the Jellyfish" (4.01). Even in these short scenes, the actors managed to snap right back into their old rhythm with an almost eerie recall. (Aniston, it seems, can still recite most of her old lines from memory.) They also partook in a trivia game that paralleled the scene in "The One with the Embryos" (4.12), and Matt LeBlanc had a sketch where he tried to identify Joey's identical hand twin (he did). Larry Hankin (Mr. Heckles), Thomas Lennon (Joey's identical hand twin) and Tom Selleck (Richard Burke) joined the trivia game segment.

Friends reunion: director Ben Winston (left) and backstage activities (right)

The first edit of the reunion show was three hours, which was finally pared down to 104 minutes. In reference to the edited footage, director Ben Winston stated, "It was rubbish." He then added, "I believe if it didn't make it in, it wasn't good enough. There are no extras." Thus, do not expect a director's cut to be released in the future.

Although it was a wonderful trip down memory lane, Courteney Cox indicated the cast probably wouldn't do another reunion like this. "This will be the last time that we're ever asked about the show as a group, that we will do this," she stated. "We're not going to do this again in 15 more years." Lisa Kudrow agreed. "I once heard Marta and David say, and I completely agree, that they ended the show very nicely, everyone's lives are very nice, and they would have to unravel all those good things in order for there to be stories," Kudrow stated. "And I don't want anyone's happy ending unraveled. Also, at my age, to be 'floopy?' Stop. You have to grow up."

While the *Friends* reunion was seemingly uncontroversial, the international community censored parts of the special. China cut a number of celebrity cameos for political reasons. Lady Gaga, Justin Bieber and the band BTS had their spots cut, apparently because they had insulted Beijing in the past. Lady Gaga has been banned from touring in China since 2016 after she met with the Dalai Lama and showed her support for the Tibetan spiritual leader, who advocates separatism. Canadian pop star Justin Bieber has been banned from performing in China after posting a 2014 photograph of himself visiting the controversial Yasukuni Shrine in Tokyo, which honors fallen Japanese warriors. China and South Korea view the shrine as a symbol of Japan not being sorry for its empire's past warmongering. Bieber has since apologized and removed the picture but the ban has not been lifted. K-pop boy band BTS has been banned from Chinese social media since 2020 because a member of the band made controversial remarks regarding the Korean War. BTS band leader RM referenced South Korea's shared "history of pain" with the US over the 1950-53 campaign. His remarks angered Chinese social media users, as Beijing had backed North Korea in the conflict. A number of LGBTQ references, deemed highly controversial in China, were also censored.

Friends: The Reunion was watched by an estimated 29% of US streaming households on May 27, 2021, the first day of its release, as measured by TVision, a connected-TV analytics provider. The viewing audience was 55.4% female, and more than 50% were in the 35 to 54 age demographic. By comparison, DC's *Wonder Woman 1984* reached 32% of US streaming households when it premiered on Christmas Day 2020 on HBO Max.

The reunion was equally popular in the UK. It was available exclusively on Sky One and its Now streaming service where it broke viewership records, becoming the network's most watched show with more than 5.3 million rabid viewers. The special was second to *Game of Thrones* for the most watched piece of content in its first 24 hours from launch on Now, but stands alone as the best organic performing content across Sky and Now's social channels, and the #FriendsReunion tag trended locally as well as globally on the day of launch.

Reactions to the special have been broadly positive, although many critics noted some elements of the show worked better than others. *Rolling Stone* fittingly described it as "an overproduced affair with too many guest stars and detours," but added, "When it lets the iconic gang of six just talk amongst themselves, it hits the nostalgic sweet spot." The HBO special currently has a C grade on Rotten Tomatoes with a 66% critic's score, and a 94% audience score.

Reunion guests: Lady Gaga, David Beckham, Malala Yousafzai and K-pop band BTS

Friends: The Reunion received four Emmy nominations (but no awards): Outstanding Variety Special (Pre-Recorded), Outstanding Directing for a Variety Special, Outstanding Production Design for a Variety Special, and Outstanding Lighting Design/Lighting Direction for a Variety Special. According to *Variety*, the six costars each received between $2.5 million and $4 million for appearing in the special broadcast.

Merchandising

The most obvious *Friends* merchandising is the release of its entire catalog on DVD and Blu-ray. All 10 seasons of *Friends* have been issued on DVD individually and as part of a box set. Blu-ray is only available as a box set. Each individual season release on DVD has special features and footage originally cut from the series. The most recent releases have episodes updated with color correction and sound enhancement.

Friends released two soundtrack albums. In October 1995, WEA Records distributed *Friends Original TV Soundtrack*, containing music featured in previous and future episodes. Between some tracks there is spoken dialogue from scenes during the show's first season. The soundtrack debuted on the Billboard 200 at No. 46, selling 500,000 copies in a single month (November 1995), but only peaked at No. 41, selling 1 million copies worldwide. In 1999, a second soundtrack titled *Friends Again* was released, which never charted because it only sold 500,000 copies worldwide.

Three soundtracks were released after the show ended: (1) *Friends: The One with All the Party Music* (2004), a six-track EP; (2) *Friends: The Ultimate Soundtrack* (2005), a double CD containing the best hits and some new unreleased tracks from the show; and (3) *Friends: 25th Anniversary Soundtrack* (2019), an exclusive album released on the silver anniversary of the series, containing 171 tracks with cast performances and dialogue. None of the LPs charted.

Fans can find practically any *Friends*-themed merchandise imaginable being marketed and sold somewhere. The list is endless so here is a sampling: Central Perk trivia games, Central Perk spoon and travel mug, smelly cat cell phone case, Joey doesn't share his food mug, classic golden peephole picture frame (also as a keychain), stuffed lobster, posters, orange couch necklace, lobster watercolor art (lobsters mate for life), throw pillows, turkey head t-shirts, tote bags, cross stitch, cookbooks and bobbleheads. There is also a *Friends* version of the DVD game Scene It?, and the quiz computer game *Friends: The One with All the Trivia*, hosted by Christina Pickles, Elliott Gould, Maggie Wheeler, and James Michael Tyler, as their respective characters from the series.

The *Friends* reunion special prompted other businesses to jump on the bandwagon. For example, Porsche announced the Porsche Tribbiani Edition with an Instagram post: "Could we BE any more excited about the *Friends* reunion? So much so, in fact, that we present: the Porsche Tribbiani edition. Careful, she's sleeping. #FriendsReunion."

Celebrity Equinox created a weeklong *Friends*-themed cruise that set sail on May 15, 2022, with stops at Key West, Grand Cayman, and Cozumel. Fares ranged from $1,648.66 per person for an inside stateroom up to $3,048.66 for a Sky Suite with a balcony view to the ocean below. The cruise ship events included costume contests, trivia games, and other surprise goodies.

Reunion: Trivia game reenactment (left) and Matt LeBlanc picking his hand twin (right)

On September 14, 2020, UK-based Revolution Beauty introduced an official *Friends* makeup line featuring three 9-shade eye-shadow palettes and three creamy bullet lipsticks inspired by the female leads. For example, the packaging for the Phoebe Palette is plastered with a picture of the taxicab she inherited from her grandmother. Inside, it has primarily pastel hues in varying finishes with names like Smelly Cat, Lobster and Triplet. A little over six months later, on April 1, 2021, the beauty company launched a new collection for the male leads, which features colors influenced by their apartments. For example, the Ross Eyeshadow Palette contains sensible neutrals with shade names like Leather Pants, Break, and My Sandwich. The cosmetic line includes sheet masks, named for each character and decorated with a symbol that represents them. There's even a blue lip balm that nods to Joey's unforgettable appearance in a Japanese "lipstick for men" commercial.

Societal Impact

Although the producers have claimed that *Friends* is "only a TV show," sociologists and psychologists have investigated the cultural impact of the series ever since it premiered in 1994. There is no denying the widespread influence *Friends* had on pop culture, fashion, hairstyles, and vernacular, but it also extended to other aspects of life, such as infertility, adoption, condom efficacy, safe sex practices, and a slew of other topics. To understand the scope of *Friends'* influence one must first discover the breadth of its reach.

Lexicon

Friends is credited for inventing words and catchphrases that are now part of modern dictionaries, and for popularizing obscure references that are now part of urban vernacular. Examples include friend zone, BFF and going commando. The list is vast, so a few notable illustrations will suffice.

The term "friend zone" refers to one member of a friendship who desires to enter into a romantic or sexual relationship, while the other does not. It is the moment when the pair are forever "just friends" with no prospect of a romantic coupling. This term first appeared in "The One with the Blackout" (1.07) when Ross was told that Rachel was unattainable because he waited too long to ask her for a date which forever relegated him to the friend zone.

The acronym BFF was another *Friends* invention. Phoebe was the first character to use the acronym BFF (Best Friends Forever) on national television in "The One at the Beach" (3.25). The abbreviation became so popular it was added to some international dictionary databases, such as Cambridge and Oxford, and is still widely used today, especially in the age of texting.

"Going commando" was first uttered in "The One Where No One's Ready" (3.02). It is a phrase used to connote not wearing any underwear. Going commando refers to the Vietnam War and was first documented as a slang term on American college campuses in 1974 at the University of North Carolina. During wartime activities, soldiers sweat a lot and can't take showers for days. Their uniforms are loose to allow for ease of movement, and they don't wear underpants in order to minimize skin eruptions and fungal infections.

Here are a few other examples:

- "We were on a break!"—Ross
- "Smelly cat, smelly cat, what are they feeding you?"—Phoebe
- "It's a moo point."—Joey ("It's like a cow's opinion. It just doesn't matter. It's moo.")
- "It's *not* that common, it *doesn't* happen to every guy, and it *is* a big deal!"—Rachel
- "I'm not so good with the advice. Can I interest you in a sarcastic comment?"—Chandler
- "Pivot! PIVOT!"—Ross
- "Here come the meat sweats."—Joey
- "Unagi"—Ross (state of total awareness in karate; it is really a type of sushi)
- "My diamond shoes are too tight."—Chandler
- "Could I *be* any more ..."—Chandler
- "How you doin'?"—Joey (ranked No. 4 in *TV Guide*'s 2005 list of TV's 20 Top Catchphrases)
- "Smell-the-fart acting"—Joey (actor technique to recall script lines)
- "He's her lobster."—Phoebe (basically, a soul mate)
- "This is brand new information!"—Phoebe

- "Oh. My. God."—Janice (her famous catchphrase to express incredulity)
- "They don't know that we know they know we know."—Phoebe (explaining the convoluted game of trickery used to expose Monica and Chandler's romantic relationship)
- "I wish I could, but I don't want to."—Phoebe (on helping Ross assemble furniture)
- "I'm fiiine."—Ross (pretending he is totally cool with Rachel and Joey dating)
- "Whoooopaah"—Chandler (trying to make the "whipped" sound)
- "Big dull dud"—Chandler (in reference to Rachel's boss Joanna)
- "Joey doesn't share food!"—Joey
- "I'm breezy."—Monica (leaving a casual message for Richard on his answering machine)
- "Mmm, noodle soup."—Joey (repeatedly misspeaking during a soup commercial audition)
- "laminated list"—Ross (preserving his celebrity freebie list)
- "My eyes! My eyes!"—Chandler and Phoebe (expressing astonishment after seeing something traumatic)
- "kidney stooones"—Joey's doctor

Vernacular

Friends not only invented and popularized numerous catchphrases that quickly became permanently affixed to modern vernacular, but also changed the way society spoke those words by mimicking the actors' delivery techniques (e.g., inflections, word emphases and vocal tics). Many *Friends* fans say "How you doin'?" by pronouncing the words exactly like Joey. The same applies to Janice's trademark "Oh. My. God" or Chandler's vocal tic, "Can I *be* more ...?" *Friends* taught an entire television subculture what to say and how to say it. It is known as Friendspeak.

Naturally, the global expanse of *Friends* prompted numerous research studies related to the sitcom and its influence on the English language. According to an article by Dr. Sali Tagliamonte, a linguistics professor at the University of Toronto, the characters used the emphasized word "so" to modify adjectives far more often than other intensifiers, such as "very" and "really." As in "that's *so* yesterday" to signal staleness or "that is *so* not true." That preference had already worked its way into American vernacular, but usage on the show, she thought, would play a role in accelerating the change—a testament to the series' unparalleled influence. Tagliamonte also found that the three main female characters used "so" as an intensifier considerably more than their male counterparts. "The sociolinguistic (academic) literature has shown over and over again that women lead in linguistic change," she said. "Women are also thought to use more intensifiers than men."

Chandler's habit of halting his dialogue midsentence for sarcastic effect also influenced viewers' speech habits. Robert Thompson, a media and popular culture expert at Syracuse University, claimed it's usually the hit shows that affect language. The legacy of *Friends*, he says, will be its attitude, conveyed by half-completed sentences dripping with irony, as in, "And I needed to know that be-cause ...?" He referred to it as "the Chandler Bing-ing of America."

The creators claim that societal perpetuation of Chandler's unique manner of speaking was an unexpected consequence. "Oddly, that didn't really register with us at the time," Kauffman said. "You write the show and you want the characters to be funny and specific, and then the actors bring their own spin to it, but as far as how the rest of the world responds to that, all you can do is go, 'Hmmm, that's kind of interesting.'" They claim it's all happenstance. "We don't set out to create a kind of lexicon," Crane definitively stated. "I think, actually, that it kind of evolved organically out of us as well as the other writers in the room and the actors themselves. I wasn't really aware of it all until one day someone I knew said to me, 'Oh, so you're the reason my kids talk this way!' I had no conscious awareness until then."

Although the showrunners may not have intentionally set out to create Friendspeak, as a general rule, sitcom writers fervently strive for accolades associated with penning the next big catchphrase. However, it is not as easy as it may seem. Success depends on a variety of factors, such as the quality and context of the phrase, actor delivery and popularity of the show, and there is no guarantee it will be picked up or perpetuated by fans. For example, in *Seinfeld*, the writers purposely created the word "anti-dentite" hoping it would be the latest catchphrase but instead fans latched onto another phrase in the episode, "yada yada yada."

Besides creating Friendspeak, *Friends* has been credited in helping many non-English-speaking students to grasp the English language. In 2012, Kaplan International English Colleges found that 26% of its students claimed the sitcom "helped them the most of any series in understanding the language." The list of disciples include Liverpool FC manager Jürgen Klopp, BTS band member RM, and Belgian professional golfer Thomas Pieters.

Scientific Studies

Besides linguistic experts, the intense popularity of *Friends* has caught the attention of researchers in other disciplines. Numerous studies have been performed over the decades to find links between the TV series and various aspects of life, whether social, cultural or sexual.

Unconventional Family

One unique aspect of *Friends* was its portrayal of a new way of living life and developing relationships that was not normally exhibited in conventional society. According to Jillian Sandell, assistant professor at San Francisco State University in the Women and Gender Studies department, the sitcom presents the idea that friends are an alternate family. "The promise of the show," she suggested, "is that in the face of heterosexual failure and familial dysfunction, all you need are good friends." The sitcom is about the construction of families as voluntary institutions, or, in other words, "families we choose." And choice makes them alternate families that "can substitute for badly paid jobs and dysfunctional relationships."

The idea of friends as family was not a novel concept when *Friends* debuted in 1994. Nearly a quarter century earlier, *The Mary Tyler Moore Show* (1970-77) was premised on the belief that the title character's coworkers were her surrogate family. Over two decades later, *Seinfeld* became the first series to articulate the notion of friendship propinquity—a group of young adults sharing an urban neighborhood—with no real authority figures (parents or bosses) offering guidance. "*Seinfeld* was the innovator, *Friends* the imitator when it comes to television and the urban tribe," said Robert J. Thompson, founder of the Center for the Study of Popular Television at Syracuse University. "But as more and more people in their 20s delayed marriage and traditional families during the 1990s, *Friends* was the one that best reflected and celebrated that lifestyle—offering a utopian version of it. *Friends* spoke to Generation X the way *Mary Tyler Moore* did to their baby boomer parents."

Therapeutic

According to Dr. Marc Hekster, Clinical Psychologist at The Summit Clinic in Highgate, London, watching *Friends* can be therapeutic and help relieve stress and anxiety. "Having worked for over a period of 20 years with those experiencing anxiety, I can conclude that among other factors, it is the repetitive and relational nature of programs such as *Friends* and *The Big Bang Theory* that will be doing the trick," he concluded.

According to Hekster, watching *Friends* "is about an experience of repair—of watching the characters in the show repeatedly having worries, which then get repaired and soothed, usually in the context of other relationships in their lives." He added, "Complex problems are made the focus of each episode, and then they are resolved within the relationships which are the essence of the shows. It is pure escapism."

Basically, it is more about the healing nature of repetition. Studies show that seeing a similar outcome every time and knowing you can depend on it acts as a quick boost to the brain and tricks the mind into believing that complex situations can be solved by calming the mind, believing in yourself, and working as a team. In effect, the show's predictability makes it soothing: "Yes, it is soothing to see the same outcome every time and know you can depend on it. This is at the heart of human development. So, when grownups are anxious, they can have child-like feelings of fear and worry, and these can be soothed by repetition," Hekster surmised.

Culture Changing

In the opinion of Elayne Rapping, a professor of American studies at the University at Buffalo, *Friends* is "one of those rare shows that marked a change in American culture." It is a well-defined youthful culture where the characters portray a lifestyle that centers on creating and sustaining relationships between friends, while running their own lives and seeking help from each other. "*Friends* stands out as a sign that we are now living in a culture where youth rules, where the image of youth has become the dominant image of our culture," says Rapping. "*Friends* will be remembered as the show that made America aware that being in your 20s is really being in the prime of life."

Ross holding his son Ben (left) and Rachel crushing on her assistant, Tag (right)

According to Rapping, *Friends* and *Beverly Hills, 90210* were among the first shows to depict independent youths who were on their own without significant parental interaction. Prior sitcoms were almost always centered on the lives of nuclear families, where father and mother knew best. "The characters in *Friends* and *90210* pretty much were running their own lives and looked to each other for moral guidance," she stated. "They constructed their own family among each other. This became a dominant theme on many programs, and it is a mainstream trend in our society."

This theme, she surmised, grew partly from an acute awareness that, for the first time in American history, an entire generation of young people would not be better off than their parents. "And so you had sitcoms like *Friends* and *Seinfeld*, where the characters lived in apartments, not in houses, where the characters were not upwardly mobile, and where they had the same friends forever and never grew up," Rapping noted.

The premise of these shows, she says, often centered on trivial matters in the fictional characters' lives—sending the message that it is alright to not be serious about anything because nothing really bad is likely to happen in a young person's life. Since 9/11—and with the country's current economic problems—that attitude has changed, which may be one reason why sitcoms are losing favor and experiencing major ratings declines. "What we are seeing now, instead, is the immense popularity of TV reality shows, with their depictions of corporate, cut-throat values, whose characters are concerned solely with competing and getting ahead of other people. That's the opposite of what *Friends* was about," Rapping stated.

Although sitcoms seem to be waning in popularity in the 2020s, *Friends* is credited with spawning a generation of copycat comedies. *Vox* magazine stated that *Friends* impacted the development of other good-natured "hangout sitcoms" with groups of adult friends who are funny and have similar character traits. One perfect illustration is *How I Met Your Mother*, which shares the same Manhattan setting with *Friends*. Other examples include *The Big Bang Theory*, *New Girl* and *Happy Endings*.

Birth Control

A study in *Pediatrics* medical journal measured whether the condom message in "The One Where Rachel Tells Ross" (8.03) positively influenced teen behavior. Forty percent of the viewers watched with an adult and ten percent discussed with an adult condom efficacy as a result of the show. Compared with other viewers, youths who conversed with an adult were more likely to report learning about condoms from the installment and appeared less likely to reduce their perceptions of condom efficacy after the episode.

Due to Ross' astonishment that condoms are not 100% effective, RAND Health oversaw research in 2003 regarding teenage condom use. It concluded that this episode positively affected teenage condom use because adolescents understood that condoms alone are not necessarily 100% effective. In fact, two-thirds (65%) remembered that the episode storyline depicted an unplanned pregnancy caused by condom failure.

Kaiser Family Foundation did a formal study about the effect of sexuality on television and concluded that *Friends* had one of the most positive effects on sexuality and the use of birth control, primarily due to Ross and Rachel's condom discussion. In the segment, Ross asserts, "We used a condom," and she responds, "But, you know, condoms only work like

97% of the time." Utterly astonished, he interjects, "Well, they should put that on the box," to which she retorts, "They do!" A follow-up survey six months later found that teens who watched the installment about condom efficacy were more likely to rate condoms as 95% to 100% effective than teens who did not view the episode (30% versus 18%).

Marta Kauffman felt "vindicated" by these studies. The sitcom was often vilified as being "overtly sexual" but she always believed the producers were "very, very responsible."

Female Erogenous Zones

"The One with Phoebe's Uterus" (4.11) has a classic scene where Monica lists the seven female erogenous zones and then passionately utters the proper order necessary to achieve orgasm. Women's health sites have designated the erogenous zones as the ears, lips, neck, breasts, buttocks, inner thighs and vagina. Chandler was shocked by the number, and his surprised reaction is most likely to the ears. On the other hand, Webmd.com has a different perspective, claiming the e-zones are inner wrist, nape of neck, buttocks, scalp, behind the knees, earlobe, and feet (one of Rachel's zones). In truth, there is no right or wrong answer; it is really a matter of personal preference.

Sex

The *American Journal of Pediatrics* conducted a study on the popular hit sitcom *Friends* and concluded the sitcom was responsible for "glamorizing sex while hardly mentioning its downsides, such as pregnancy and sexually transmitted diseases." Marta Kauffman often took umbrage to these types of studies, noting her constant battle with network censors to include condoms or condom wrappers in episodes. Contrary to the study's findings, the series did address serious social issues, such as the harrowing life of a single mother and the stigma and ostracism associated with VD (venereal disease). The creators inexorably strived to advocate safe and responsible sex because they were well aware of their role as television producers. They knew the content of the show would influence teen behavior so they made every effort to be responsible in their programming.

Rather than glamorizing sex, *Friends* became a trailblazer in changing attitudes toward sex. The creators' commitment to adult entertainment transformed network programming for the 8pm to 9pm timeslot, which had been characterized as television's primetime family hour, a period deemed appropriate for children. At the forefront was the topic of sex. What really ruffled the feathers of conservatives was the sitcom's advocacy of youthful sexuality— sex out of wedlock, condom usage, and the laissez faire attitude that sex was common and acceptable behavior. Columnist George Will wrote the following in a 1996 piece about an episode where Rachel and Ross slept together for the first time: "More depressing than what *Friends* considers wit, which rises only from the cretinous to the sophomoric, is the fact that the program transmits to teenagers the message that such shallow sexuality is not only acceptable, it is expected of them."

The vast popularity of *Friends* helped soften societal perceptions of sex on television. In 1992, there was a conflagration of national controversy surrounding *Murphy Brown* when the title character, played by Candice Bergen, had a baby out of wedlock. A decade later, Rachel did the same on *Friends* and the ordeal was barely a blip on the radar. "We were concerned initially that people were going to say, 'Hey, what kind of a role model is that?'" Crane said. "But that didn't happen. And I think it's because there is so much love between the characters on the show and this baby is so loved—with Ross still in the picture. But we never got one letter."

Musical Influence

Prior to being eternally linked to *Friends*, The Rembrandts were relatively unknown, having only one modest hit "Just the Way It Is, Baby" (#14, 1991). The duo did not mind performing the theme song, but resented their record label demanding the tune be included on their newly issued album, *L.P.*, because the track did not fit their concept. Nonetheless, the single helped sell a lot of albums, to which they are thankful, but the duo refused to release the track as a single because they didn't write the song. Miraculously, based on airplay alone, the song peaked at No. 17 on the US Billboard Hot 100 singles chart and topped the Hot 100 Airplay chart for eight weeks.

In the 1995 episode "The One with Five Steaks and an Eggplant" (2.05), Monica, Ross and Chandler go to a rock concert to watch Hootie & the Blowfish perform. During the audience bleacher scene, the song "I Go Blind" is heard in the background. The tune was originally released a year prior as a B-side on the band's "Hold My Hand" single. Two years later it was added to the *Friends* soundtrack and skyrocketed to No. 13 on the US Billboard Hot 100 chart.

The following week, in "The One with the Baby on the Bus" (2.06), Chrissie Hynde had a guest starring role as a musician who replaces Phoebe as Central Perk's primary source of entertainment. As a condition for appearing on the sitcom, Hynde wanted to premiere the release of her latest single, a cover of "Angel of the Morning," by performing it live in Central Perk. The track was included on the *Friends* soundtrack album, and her cameo coincided with the LP's release. The sitcom showrunners were hoping to exploit her popularity as the lead singer of The Pretenders to bolster sales but the ploy backfired. Despite 30.2 million episodic viewers, the song never cracked the US Billboard Hot 100 chart, and her rendition failed to generate sustained interest in the soundtrack.

Lawsuit

In December 1999, less than two months after being fired, *Friends* writers' assistant Amaani Lyle (an African-American) filed a formal complaint with the Department of Fair Employment and Housing, alleging race discrimination, sexual harassment, retaliation and wrongful termination. She subsequently filed a civil suit. Ironically, the producers claimed she had been fired after four months of employment for failing to grasp the writers' lewd exchanges fast enough. The California Supreme Court unanimously dismissed the claim. According to the justices, miming sexual gratification, drawing graphic pictures and words, detailing sexual preferences, and bragging about exploits was not harassment. In fact, the lewd and crude behavior of the writers (Adam Chase, Greg Malins and Andrew Reich) was a necessary part of their job. The justices claimed the suit was without merit for two reasons: none of the writers' offensive conduct was aimed at the plaintiff, and due to the nature of the writers' work, the pervasive sexual atmosphere was necessary for the creative process of writing an adult-themed show.

Even the *Friends* cast was not immune from sexual harassment. Lisa Kudrow was the recipient of an incredibly misogynistic comment while working with an unnamed celebrity who appeared in a guest role. During the week of production, the costars would arrive on set without makeup or hairstyling. On the night of filming, Kudrow was hair-and-makeup ready, and she was told, "Oh wow, *now* you're f*ckable." She refused to name the celebrity but hinted that "big brother" Matt LeBlanc put the actor in his place.

Although not a *Friends*-related incident, Jennifer Aniston joined the #MeToo movement to publicize harassment she encountered in the workplace. "I've definitely had some sloppy moves made on me by other actors, and I handled it by walking away," she said. "I've never had anyone in a position of power make me feel uncomfortable and leverage that over me. In my personal experience, I've been treated worse verbally and energetically by some women in this industry."

Criticism

History has a way of rewriting the legacy of legends. It applies to humankind, art, and even fiction. As society becomes more inclusive, period pieces are perceived with altered perceptions. *Friends* is not immune from such intense scrutiny. Recent revisionists have re-evaluated the show's legacy by identifying problematic storylines and criticizing the sitcom for its lack of cultural diversity, as well as being sexist, homophobic, transphobic, and so much more.

In the whitewashed world of comedy, *Friends* is a period piece, a product of its time—eschewing political correctness and sprinkling offensive or inappropriate one-liners here and there throughout every installment. Purists accept it for what it is. Revisionists tear it down and label it as vile and heinous. Although *Friends* was often hailed as hilarious and progressive at the time, and some of the jokes remain timeless, a considerable swatch of its content would never be aired on network television today.

Diversity

After the first season, the media began castigating *Friends* for featuring six all-white protagonists and depicting "a fictional Manhattan where black people are strangely absent from restaurants, museums, health clubs and the streets." Although most network dramas included integrated casts and racially incisive stories, comedies like *Friends* rarely featured nonwhite characters, even in recurring, supporting or guest starring roles. Of course, this racially divisive format was systemic to most television programming at the time.

In 1996, of the 64 comedies that appeared on the six major networks, only 12 featured racially mixed casts, with 40 all-white and 12 all-black programs. *Friends* was 3rd in the Nielsen ratings, but ranked 99th in African-American households. The same applies for *Seinfeld*, 2nd in the Nielsen stats but 79th in black homes. The reverse was true as well. African-American comedies like *Living Single* and *Martin* were extremely popular in black households but were rarely watched by whites. *Martin* ranked 6th in black households, but 104th for white audiences. *Living Single* was 2nd in black homes, but 107th among white viewers.

In the 1990s, racial divisiveness in viewership was not necessarily attributable to a lack of cast diversity. Other predominately black sitcoms—*Family Matters, Moesha, Sister, Sister* and *The Fresh Prince of Bel Air*—had strong white audience bases. The issue wasn't race, it was economics. Advertisers target a narrowly defined, demographically desirable group of viewers: young, white, educated and affluent. Since white viewers account for over 60% of the population, they are the primary consumers of goods and services.

Although there are legitimate justifications for racial divisiveness, it still does not fully excuse the prodigious lack of diversity on *Friends*. According to Jillian Sandell, assistant professor at San Francisco State University in the Women and Gender Studies department, in some respects *Friends* is groundbreaking but in other ways it "still offers a racially and ethnically homogeneous network" despite being set in New York City, one of the most multi-cultural areas in the US. In other words, in some spheres like sexual and gender roles it offers a view of changing patterns, while in others, such as race and class, it perpetuates stereotypes.

David Schwimmer always believed that *Friends* should have had more diversity. "It felt wrong that there was not enough representation on the show," he said. In fact, he actually pushed for his character to date more women of color on the show. "I was well aware of the lack of diversity and I campaigned for years to have Ross date women of color. One of the first girlfriends I had on the show was an Asian-American woman, and later I dated African-American women. That was a very conscious push on my part."

Some critics claim Asian-American actress Lauren Tom was introduced as a recurring character because the *Friends* executive producers were feeling pressure from media outlets clamoring about the show's lack of diversity. In truth, her appearance was precipitated by director Gail Mancuso, who recommended Tom for the part. The creators remembered her starring role in *The Joy Luck Club* (1993) which influenced their final decision to cast her as Julie, with no audition required. Tom had a seven-episode story arc but she was never a strong supporting character. Unlike Aisha Tyler's role as Charlie, Tom was mostly relegated to simple sentences or setting up jokes to be delivered by the main cast.

It took over seven years before another ethnic recurring character was cast on *Friends*. Aisha Tyler (Charlie Wheeler) had the first recurring role played by an African-American, and she didn't appear until the ninth season. Although the character wasn't written for a specific ethnicity—Tyler auditioned against a multitude of other women of different ethnic backgrounds—she was primarily cast to address criticism that *Friends* showcased too few ethnic minority actors. Tyler made it clear, though, that she did not believe she was hired because of her race. Prior to Tyler, there was only one episode featuring a black guest star, Gabrielle Union, in "The One with the Cheap Wedding Dress" (7.17).

When asked if they would have done anything differently in terms of their casting, the creators have adamantly proclaimed and resoundingly stated, "No!" They cast the best six actors, which happened to be all white. "We didn't intend to have an all-white cast. That was not the goal, either," Kevin Bright explained. "Obviously, the chemistry between these six actors speaks for itself." Marta Kauffman added, "Back then, there was no conscious decision. We saw people of every race, religion, color. These were the six people we cast. So, it was certainly not conscious."

Kevin Bright was very pleased with the final result. "I don't have any regrets other than hindsight. I would have been insane not to hire those six actors," he concluded. "What can I say? I wish Lisa [Kudrow] was black? I've loved this cast." Marta Kauffman, on the other hand, has regrets. "There are probably a hundred things I would have done differently. I've talked about it in the past and I do have very strong feelings about my participation in a system, but it comes down to I didn't know what I didn't know," she candidly confessed. "I have more regrets about things that remained than things that we took out."

One thing is for sure, if the show were made today, it would look entirely different. "We would be so aware. It would be integral to the chemistry and the conversation that these guys would be having. Do they get together as much as they do on the show, or is this more of a social media back and forth?" Bright pondered. "So much would change, but to get them to behave realistically within this time, there would be a lot that would change about them. And the racial makeup of them would change because of that. If we did *Friends* today, no, I don't imagine they would probably end up being an all-white cast."

David Crane has often stated that racial diversity was not prioritized on network shows in the 1990s. "I think you have to look at it through the lens of when we started. If you look at *Seinfeld*, *Mad About You* and *Frasier*, no one was prioritizing that. Should they have? Probably," he freely confessed. "It's something that, in a contemporary way, you're aware of. I think if you were approaching the show today, you would certainly approach it differently. But on the other hand, these were absolutely the six people who felt perfect for these parts, so it's hard to get into a time machine and imagine it differently." Marta Kauffman agreed. "It was, to a certain extent, a product of the time period and of my own ignorance," she stated. "There were black shows and there were white shows. There weren't a lot of shows that were interracial."

Sexism

There is no debate that *Friends* was extremely sexist. By definition, sexism is prejudice, stereotyping or discrimination based on one's sex or gender. As the proverbial womanizer, Joey was sexist in that he initially viewed women as objects, or more aptly, sex toys to play with and discard. His perception of women somewhat evolved after he developed feelings for Rachel, but for the most part he never truly changed his spots.

There were many instances of sexism in *Friends*, though less overt than Joey's lothario contrivances. For example, (1) Joey was derided for sporting a man purse; (2) Chandler was perceived as feminine for a variety reasons, e.g., liking show tunes, watching parades and not knowing about sports; (3) women were deemed inferior to compete in backlot football, so Phoebe exposed her breasts to level the playing field; and (4) a male nanny was labeled inherently gay (or at least bi) based solely on him being highly sensitive and emotional.

Although men were the most frequent sexist offenders, the female protagonists were not without their faults. Rachel, for instance, was most likely to utter sexist remarks. On many occasions she objectified men by making bawdy remarks about their butts as they bent over in front of her. The male character most objectified was Joshua (a client of Rachel's when she was a personal shopper for Bloomingdale's).

Gender Stereotyping

The official definition of gender stereotyping is an overgeneralization of characteristics, differences, and attributes, of a certain group based on their gender. *Friends* was definitely in violation of this standard. A prime example occurred in "The One with the Metaphorical Tunnel" (3.04), where Ross tirelessly attempts to dissuade Ben from playing with a Barbie doll by encouraging him to play with stereotypical male-oriented toys such as a monster truck or G.I. Joe army soldier. There are a few other illustrations as well. In "The One with the Male Nanny" (9.06), Ross refuses to have his child raised by a male nanny because the guy is highly sensitive and emotional. Likewise, in "The One Where Chandler Takes a Bath" (8.13), Chandler initially perceives a bath as unmanly and then reacts equally sexist about receiving a facial. Finally, in "The One with Joey's Bag" (5.13), Joey is derided for carrying a purse because it is perceived as a feminine accessory.

Sexual Harassment

Sexual harassment involves behavior characterized by the making of unwelcome and inappropriate sexual remarks or physical advances in a workplace or other professional or social situation. Once again, the number of instances is too voluminous to detail so a few examples will highlight the point. Joey, for instance, was known to hit on female coworkers using his famous pickup line, and in one episode a restaurant owner uttered lewd sexual innuendos during Monica's audition for a chef position. Other than Joey, Rachel was the worst offender of them all. On multiple occasions she objectified a fellow coworker (Tag) by making suggestive remarks about his derriere as he bent over in front of her, and then she sexually harassed him by telling everyone in the office that he was gay to prevent women from pursuing him. Although Ross' romance with a college student was neither unwelcome nor inappropriate, and Elizabeth was not a student in his class when they started dating, it still constitutes sexual harassment since he was a professor in a position of authority and power, while she was a student, and therefore a subordinate.

Sexual Assault

By definition, sexual assault is any type of nonconsensual sexual activity or contact which may involve physical force or threats of force or the use of drugs or alcohol as part of the assault, and includes rape and sexual coercion. Naturally, *Friends* seldomly ventured down this road for a chuckle, but one prime instance was Paolo sexually assaulting Phoebe by grabbing her ass during a massage and then intentionally exposing his genitalia to her after the incident. Technically, by its definition, Ross was guilty of this infraction when he passionately kissed a woman without her consent while she was sleeping. His behavior was even more offensive and morally objectionable since he did it to his sister, even though he thought it was Rachel.

Sexual Objectification

The act of treating a person solely as an object of sexual desire is construed as sexual objectification, though more broadly it means treating a person as a commodity or an object without regard to their personality or dignity. On *Friends*, both sexes did this repeatedly. Rachel was guilty of leering at and making comments about Tag and Joshua's butts, while Mr. Waltham exhibited the same behavior toward Joshua. Additionally, all three guys made objectifying comments every time they saw an attractive woman, Monica once checked out a woman's ass for Joey, and even Phoebe entered the foray—she went out with a fireman and a school teacher primarily due to their brute physicality and chiseled physiques.

Homophobia

This concept encompasses the entire gamut of negative attitudes and feelings toward homosexuals or people who are identified or perceived as being lesbian, gay, bisexual or transgender. Chandler is often characterized or mistaken as gay which is a classic example of this notion. Ross expresses innumerable negative remarks and connotations about the sexual orientation of his ex-wife and her lover. Also, his resistance to hiring a male nanny actually fits into multiple offensive categories, including homophobia, because he negatively characterizes a sensitive male as being gay.

Transphobia

Transphobia is a collection of ideas and phenomena that encompass a range of negative attitudes, feelings or actions towards transgender people or transness in general. Naturally, the most obvious offender was Chandler due to his remarks about his father, Charles Bing (aka Helena Handbasket), a transgender Las Vegas drag queen. Chandler was constantly embarrassed by his father so he pervasively joked about Charles' sexuality. Rachel was also an offender. During the rehearsal dinner for Monica and Chandler's wedding, she mistakes a woman named Amanda as being transgender, and then remarks, Oh, I get it. A … Man … *Duh.*"

Body Shaming

This is the action or practice of humiliating someone by making mocking or deprecatory comments about their body shape or size. The obvious illustration is Fat Monica. One of the most common themes throughout the series was fat shaming Monica for her childhood obesity. For example, when Chandler observes her high school bathing suit, he quips, "Oh, I thought that's what they used to cover Connecticut when it rained." In another example, while watching Monica's high school prom video, Joey does not recognize her so when he observes a fat girl in the shot, he screams, "Some girl ate Monica!" Body shaming was a comedy crutch for the staff writers.

Intelligence Shaming

This is the act of mocking someone who is less intelligent than others. Joey was often a little slow intellectually, especially when it came to connecting the dots to get from point A to B in matters of deduction, as well as most inferences and nonsexual innuendos. Joey's inability to learn French is a primary example because Phoebe cannot tolerate tutoring him due to his slow comprehension. In fact, she refers to him as being "a bit retarded" (though this remark is excised from syndicated telecasts). Phoebe is also the butt of jokes due to her flakiness, though much less frequent.

Emotional Abuse

Emotional or psychological abuse is a way to control someone by subjecting or exposing them to criticism, embarrassment, shame, blame, or forms of manipulation. Although this form of abuse was rarely exhibited in *Friends*, at least one instance is glaringly apparent. In the aptly titled episode, "The One with All the Jealousy" (3.12), Ross exhibits unrelenting jealousy toward Rachel's coworker Mark, and his resulting treatment of Rachel borders on emotional abuse. He constantly calls her, unexpectedly visits her workplace, shows a lack of trust, and manifests obsessive and controlling boyfriend behavior; basically, he treats her like chattel. In another episode, "The One Where No One's Ready" (3.02), Ross orders Rachel to get dressed for a museum benefit dinner, as if she were a child, and then throws her shoes in anger when she objects to his command.

Groundbreaking Storylines

Any television series that is dissected and micro-scrutinized is likely to be found guilty of cultural insensitivity and possess other offensive attributes, especially as society evolves and changes its definition of what is acceptable and proper behavior and content. However, each TV show must also be judged by the totality of the work for which it represents, aside from its inherent flaws. In this light, *Friends* has an equally impressive number of laudable progressive characteristics that define the show as groundbreaking, for its time. *Friends* pushed boundaries, challenged perspectives, and championed equality. Sure it has flaws in retrospect, but its aim was to be relatable to everyone as a slice-of-life sitcom.

Matt LeBlanc defended *Friends* for what it represented in its totality. "We steered clear of any sort of political content, nothing too topical. *Friends* was about themes that stand the test of time—trust, love, relationships, betrayal, family and things like that." That's why the show resonates on such an emotional level. That's why it still makes us laugh. That's why it is finding a resurgence with droves of new youthful viewers, and keeps older faithful fans coming back for more. The characters are real, flawed, and relatable, just like real-life friends.

Kevin Bright concurred. "I think, probably, if anything would change about the show, it would just be to reflect more what's going on in the world that's happening today, but not in a topical way—more in a cultural way. So I think it would reflect that. But other than that, I don't think much would change," he definitively declared. "It's a universal story. It was never about gimmicks, or aliens. ... It was about simple stories about relationships and people trying to make it in the world—loves won and lost." According to Claire Sisco King, associate professor in the department of communication studies at Vanderbilt University, the characters "are not all married, or where they want to be in their careers, and so you see a little bit of that uncertainty with which probably a lot of people, regardless of cultural or national context, could identify." She came to the conclusion that it was this simplistic, universal theme that resonated with viewers.

Multifaith Acceptance

Friends never overtly addressed religion but offered subtle, symbolic references. Most of the characters were Jewish but their faith was never an issue. At least half the *Friends* staff writers were Jewish, yet the storylines rarely reflected it. There was mention of bat mitzvah and circumcision, the winter holiday had menorahs, dreidels and Star of David symbols, and characters occasionally wore Magen David necklaces, but the Jewish faith was never thrust on the public.

David Schwimmer was proud of how the writers tackled other religions. "It's interesting also how the show handled the Judaism of the characters," he propounded. "I don't think that was earth-shattering or groundbreaking at all, but I for one was glad that we had at least one episode where it wasn't just about Christmas. It was also Hanukkah and, even though I played the Hanukkah armadillo, ... I was glad that we at least acknowledged the differences in religious observation." In that episode, "The One with the Holiday Armadillo" (7.10), Ross dressed in a holiday armadillo costume to teach Ben about Judaic custom and tradition. The Judaism plot, however, was tempered with Christian and secular symbols, like a Christmas tree and Santa Claus.

The multifaith household and joint holiday celebration was inspired by Kevin Bright's home life. He is Jewish and his wife is not. Their family celebrates both holidays, Christmas and Hanukkah, so he could really relate to the Holiday Armadillo installment. Due to this multifaith familial arrangement, he purposely added Jewish and Christian symbols to all of the winter holiday–themed episodes.

Homosexuality Acceptance

Another groundbreaking attribute of *Friends* was its inclusion of a lesbian couple. In the 2020s, having a lesbian character is practically mandatory when casting a television show, but back in the 1990s, it was revolutionary. Susan and Carol were inspired by the creators' best friends in New York. "We didn't create them for any particular political reason or because of lesbian chic," Marta Kauffman declared. "It was just an opportunity to tell a really interesting story." GLAAD called the characters a "positive example of a gay couple on television."

Susan and Carol were also written as strong, independent characters, not just comedic props. The showrunners made sure to include plots related to the couple. In fact, they were featured in the aptly titled episode "The One with the Lesbian Wedding" (2.11), which has the distinction for being the first LGBTQ wedding ceremony on television. At the time, the state of New York did not recognize or authorize same-sex marriage (this ruling was not overturned until Martinez v. County of Monroe in 2008), so showcasing a lesbian wedding in a sitcom was remarkable, especially when viewed in context.

In anticipation of the lesbian wedding broadcast, NBC expected hate mail and tens of thousands of telephone calls so they hired 104 people to answer all the complaint calls. The network received 11 calls and only two complaints by phone. *Friends* actually received more criticism for Kathleen Turner's portrayal of Chandler's transgender father, which many fans perceived as being transphobic.

Due to the controversial nature of a lesbian wedding, the episode was banned in some foreign countries, and two US network affiliates refused to air it (KJAC-TV in Port Arthur, Texas, and WLIO in Lima, Ohio), citing objectionable content, although the decision drew little press attention, partly due to the small size of the markets in question. Lesbian and gay groups, most notably GLAAD, decried the stations' censorship of the episode. David Schwimmer characterized the series "groundbreaking, in its time, for the way in which it handled ... gay marriage and relationships," and proclaimed, "The way they portrayed gay marriage on the show and how we as a family made it work, I thought was great."

Transgender Acceptance

It is undeniable that Chandler's transgender father received the brunt of the offensive jokes. But, on the upside, the character was portrayed as a strong individual—successful, resolute, confident and likable—with a positive self-image and unwavering resolve to never feel ashamed, guilty or regretful for being transgender.

Unconventional Childbirths

Each female protagonist was purposely given a unique pregnancy storyline to spread a positive social message—that surrogacy, adoption and single motherhood are all common and acceptable, and represent beautiful and normal paths to motherhood. Case in point, Phoebe served as a surrogate for her half brother and sister-in-law, Monica and Chandler experience infertility so they adopt, and Rachel and Ross have a daughter out of wedlock. The creators made it their mission to present alternative methods and acceptable means for having a child and establishing a family.

Phoebe's surrogacy story arc touched on issues of in vitro fertilization (IVF), which is a complex series of procedures used to help with fertility or prevent genetic problems and assist with the conception of a child. In television, infertility has always been a taboo topic, especially for a sitcom. *Friends* changed the playing field and allayed those misconceptions.

The issue of infertility was closely examined when Monica and Chandler decided to start a family in season nine. She was diagnosed as having a "hostile" uterus and he had low sperm motility. The inability to conceive was shared because the writers didn't want the blame to be shouldered by one person, which may cause resentment. Thus, adoption was chosen as an alternative means of parenthood.

Finally, Rachel became unexpectedly impregnated after a one-night stand with Ross. Although not controversial like teen pregnancy, the show spotlighted the fears and logistical issues surrounding a single mother. Of course, the creators still kept it happy and upbeat by having a supportive and actively involved father. This may not be an accurate depiction of many single fathers, but, according to the producers, a deadbeat-father character is a theme better suited for a television drama than a comedy.

Female Sexuality

On television, as well as in real life, human sexuality often has been treated as a double standard—womanizing is acceptable and encouraged among men but manizing is improper and discouraged among women. Men are championed as gods or heroes for their number of sexual conquests, whereas women are castigated as sluts and whores for having more than one sexual partner.

Right out of the gate, in the pilot installment, the *Friends* creators addressed this sexual hypocrisy and never let off the gas pedal. Although female casual sex is commonplace and acceptable today, in the 1990s it was purposely swept under the rug. *Friends* was groundbreaking in its treatment of casual sex by pushing the envelope even further than *Seinfeld*. The female protagonists enjoyed one-night stands (Rachel asks Chandler to find a suitable coworker for her to bed), practiced safe sex (Monica and Rachel fight over the last condom), and dated a lot of guys during their journey toward finding Mr. Right.

The most groundbreaking sexual activity was the issue of female masturbation. There are many illustrations: Phoebe announcing her hippity hop is a "godsend, if you know what I mean," Monica repurposing the massaging showerhead, Rachel owning an erotic novel, and Monica explaining female erogenous zones which prompts the horny listeners to seek private quarters to finish what she started. Even female orgasms were championed, not only with Monica's euphoric erogenous zone depiction, but also through Kathy, Chandler's girlfriend at the time, who tearfully thanking Monica for teaching him the art of pleasuring a woman.

Safe Sex

The showrunners were proud of their efforts to advocate safe and responsible sex. Two installments featured the topic as a major plotline. In "The One Where Dr. Ramoray Dies" (2.18), Monica and Rachel discuss who gets the last condom. Both want to have sex but only one will do the deed—no condom, no sex. NBC refused to allow the characters to say the word "condom" or show the prophylactic wrapper, and only a plain, nondescript box could be shown.

In "The One Where Rachel Tells Ross" (8.03), Rachel's unexpected pregnancy bewilders Ross because he used a condom. The staff writers penned an entire scene related to the revelation that condoms are not 100% effective. The theme is then extended throughout the episode as he informs Joey of the startling news. Joey hilariously removes a string of 12 linked condom wrappers to check if the packaging actually discloses that condoms are only 97% effective.

Career-Driven Women

Friends cannot be labeled as groundbreaking in its portrayal of women having careers or lofty occupational aspirations. In fact, strong, independent female leads were present for decades in *That Girl* and *The Mary Tyler Moore Show*. However, *Friends* can be lauded for its authentic depiction of female dreams, goals and accomplishments. Monica knew she wanted to become a chef from the moment she got her first Easy-Bake Oven and opened Easy Monica's Bakery. She followed her dream, commencing with an entry-level job as a waitress, then slowly advanced as a caterer, until reaching her goal as head chef at a top restaurant. She even functioned as the household breadwinner while Chandler pondered his future as an advertising intern.

Similarly, Rachel was a spoiled, rich daddy's girl who chose waitressing to survive and pay the bills. She found her niche in fashion and slowly ascended the corporate ladder as a personal assistant, purchaser, and personal shopper, en route to becoming a valuable asset as an executive at Ralph Lauren. Moreover, she balanced single parenthood and a career, and thrived at both.

Toxic Masculinity

This is defined as a set of attitudes and stereotypical behaviors often associated with or expected of men that have a negative impact on men and society as a whole. An excellent illustration of this concept appears in the episode "The One with the Male Nanny" (9.06) where Ross uncharacteristically displays hostile tendencies toward a male nanny (Sandy) by insolently asking about Sandy's sexual preference and then insisting that the emotional, hypersensitive caretaker has to be bisexual to explain choosing such a "girly" profession.

On the other side of the spectrum, the episode also characterizes Ross as the ignorant buffoon and portrays Sandy as the lovable, caring and understanding victim. Moreover, Ross ultimately seeks solace and comfort through Sandy by explaining the reason why he feels uneasy around a sensitive male. Ross recounts the emotional abuse he experienced from his father for not living up to the masculine ideal. It's a creative means of illustrating the fact that so many men feel forced to quell their emotions, which may have a damaging effect on them and society as a whole.

Strong Female Friendships

Long before *Sex and the City*, *Girls* and *Parks and Recreation*, *Friends* brought strong female friendships to the fore on television. Throughout the years, the girls were there for one another to offer comfort, support, advice and love. "The One on the Last Night" (6.06) features a storyline to highlight their tight-knit bond. Chandler is set to move in so Rachel has to move out. Despite Monica and Rachel spending most of the evening bickering, they share a poignant moment as they relive wonderful memories before tearfully parting ways. It's a theme that resonates with every twentysomething woman for its honesty and realism.

Female Empowerment

Besides the female friends controlling their careers and sex lives, the staff writers also penned a couple episodes where they take back control of their romantic relationships. In one episode, "The One Where Eddie Won't Go" (2.19), the girls try to harness their wind to become goddesses by not allowing the lightning bearers (men) to steal it. In another show, "The One with the Candy Hearts" (1.14), the girls reclaim control of their future romantic relationships by performing a boyfriend-cleansing ritual. They gather in Monica's abode and form a circle around the coffee table where they place personal mementos from past lovers in a garbage can and then burn the entire lot. The goal is to break the bad-boyfriend cycle and focus on finding good men to date.

Keeping It Real

Regardless of all the criticism of *Friends* being racist, homophobic, sexist, etc., the fact remains that those misguided ideas, thoughts and concepts still exist today in the hearts of many Americans, and society as a whole. Whitewashing TV comedies and excluding any reference to offensive content denies its existence in the modern world. Ignoring it doesn't make it go away. Similarly, joking about it may not be right but that doesn't make it wrong. If anything, it illustrates the ignorance of those uttering those words, which can make it a topic for discussion, rather than pretending it doesn't exist until it boils over like a festering wound.

Although *Friends* failed to have a diversified cast, there are innumerable enclaves of society with exclusively single-race friendships. Not every group of friends is mixed race. That is a reality. Just because the US population is 60.1% white, 18.5% Hispanic, 12.2% black, and 5.6% Asian does not mean every group of friends has the same proportionate composition. Likewise, just because 50.8% of the US population is female does not equate to every group of friends being half female and half male.

There is a sizable portion of the population that is homophobic, transphobic and sexist, and even more people who partake in gender objectification, body shaming, and intelligence shaming. It exists. *Friends* merely expressed inner thoughts that most people are too afraid to utter. This is one possible reason why *Friends* remains so popular today. Viewers enjoy the opportunity to have those inappropriate words vocalized because, outside the fictional realm of television, those concepts cannot be verbalized or expressed in any public forum. It is their personal escapism and evil indulgence.

9/11 Tributes

The terrorist attack on the World Trade Center in New York occurred on September 11, 2001. Since *Friends* was set in New York, many wondered if the show would address the incident. The executive producers debated the issue and chose to not mention it directly; instead, they incorporated subtle references in episodes. "We're a comedy show, and there is nothing funny about September 11. Dramas are much better equipped to handle that subject matter," Kevin Bright declared. "We thought about doing something momentarily, and decided it was best to stay away from. When people come to a show to laugh and enjoy themselves, the last thing they need is September 11. It was in enough places."

Thus, in the *Friends* universe, the 9/11 attack never happened. However, that didn't stop the show from honoring the victims and heroes through props and set dressings. The magna doodle in Joey's apartment contained frequent sketches and messages of support—Statue of Liberty with the letters FDNY (Fire Department of New York), basketball with USA flag overlaid, lunar surface with US flag, I ♥ NY, etc. Several cast members wore FDNY t-shirts, while others wore New York–themed attire, including a t-shirt embroidered with the name Captain Billy Burke, as a tribute to a real-life firefighter who died battling the blaze on September 11th. In addition, American flags were placed in Joey's apartment, Rachel's office, and Central Perk to express sympathy and sorrow.

Cultural References

The popularity and universal appeal of a television program can often be measured by the number of times it is referenced in other shows. Jokes are only funny if the subtext is relatable to the audience. The sheer volume of *Friends* references in other television shows heralds its timelessness and mass recognition. As they say, imitation is the sincerest form of flattery, and if that is the case, then the *Friends* series would be blushing. There are over 1,000 *Friends* references in other television shows. Here is a sampling:

- On November 11, 2021, the new sitcom *Ghosts* (ep Flower's Article) was the latest series to reference *Friends* in its script. In the episode, Pete repeatedly touts the perks of being in the "friend zone."

- In the Hulu series *The Handmaid's Tale* (ep Unwomen), June finds a *Friends* DVD box set and secretly watches "The One with Phoebe's Uterus" (4.11), specifically, the scene where Monica explains female erogenous zones to Chandler.

- In the horror series *Supernatural* (ep Hammer of the Gods), Dean hits on a girl in a diner using Joey's pickup line, "How you doin'?" Singer Camila Cabello even referenced the line in the opening verse to her 2017 chart-topper "Havana" ("He didn't walk up with that 'How you doin'?'"). In Scrubs (ep My Missed Perception), during his Dr. Acula fantasy, JD repeats Joey's line "How you doin'?"

- The popular medical comedy *Scrubs* had at least five *Friends* allusions. For example, in the episode "My Fault," the janitor describes JD's relationship with Elliot as "not exactly Ross and Rachel" and in "My Cold Shower" Dr. Cox compares Elliot and J.D. to Ross and Rachel.

- During the 100th episode of *One Tree Hill* (ep Lucas' and Lindsay's wedding), a character references Ross saying the wrong name at the altar during his wedding vows to Emily. This is a direct tribute to "The One with Ross's Wedding, Part 2" (4.24).

- *Murder, She Wrote* (ep Murder Among Friends) was purposely penned to parody *Friends* in retaliation after the drama series was moved from Sunday to Thursday, opposite the sitcom. In the installment, amateur sleuth Jessica Fletcher (Angela Lansbury) investigates the murder of a writer for *Buds*, a fictional television series about the daily lives of a group of city friends. Lansbury had "a bit of an attitude" about the move to Thursday so she was instrumental in the storyline. Series staff writer Jerry Ludwig researched the "flavor" of *Buds* by watching installments of *Friends*.

- In *The Family Guy* (ep Petergeist), Stewie references the *Friends* series finale along with its spinoff, *Joey*, when he's talking to the television possessed by Native American poltergeists, saying, "Oh, you didn't see it? Ross and Rachel got back together. It wasn't that great, and Joey got his own spinoff but eeehhh ... it's not going so well."

- Phoebe's proclamation that Ross and Rachel are lobsters is referenced in *How I Met Your Mother* (ep Lobster Crawl) when Lily tells Robin that Barney is like her lobster. Of course, in *Friends* it means soul mate, whereas in *HIMYM* it means wanting someone only because you can't have them. In another installment (ep Something Borrowed), Ted says "I'm not Ross" after Marshall asks about the page length of the wedding list. This is an allusion to "The One with the Jellyfish" (4.01) where Rachel writes an 18-page letter, front and back, concerning thoughts about her and Ross' prior romantic relationship.

- "The One with the Jellyfish" (4.01) is also referenced in *Archer* (ep Skytanic) where Cyril walks in on Archer and Lana in a compromising position, and, in the ensuing fight, Lana exclaims, "We're on a break!" to which Cyril responds, "Fine by me!" A similar exchange occurred between Ross and Rachel; she states, "We are so over!" to which he replies, "Fine by me!" And of course, *Friends* invented the popular expression "We were on a break!"

- The term "going commando" is referenced in *The Middle* (ep Halloween III: The Driving) where Sue is picking out a keychain and states, "This one says 'I'm going commando.' I don't really get it, but I do support the military."

- The *Friends* episode "The One with the Jam" (3.03) is referenced in *Carter* (ep Harley Gets Replaced) where David Arquette claims he played Phoebe's stalker on the show which made him a huge star.

- In *Parks and Recreation* (ep Telethon), Leslie Knope, attempts to fill an entertainment void in a telethon by discussing her favorite *Friends* episodes. She describes the plot of "The One with Chandler in a Box" (4.08) and claims it is her second-favorite *Friends* episode.

- "The One with Mac and C.H.E.E.S.E." (6.20) is referenced in the webseries *The Cinema Snob* (ep Exorcist II: The Heretic) through the dialogue: "This machine makes me think of *Mac and C.H.E.E.S.E.* No, not THAT mac and cheese." *Mac and C.H.E.E.S.E.* was the short-lived TV series where Joey costarred with a robot.

- In *Mr. Robot* (ep eps2.7_init_5.fve), Angela hacks Joseph Green's e-corp account, and his password is "holidayarmadillo." This is a direct credit to "The One with the Holiday Armadillo" (7.10).

- "The One with Monica and Chandler's Wedding" (7.23, 7.24) is referenced in *The Vampire Diaries* (ep Woke Up with a Monster) where Caroline Forbes tells her mother Liz: "So if you start the *Friends* box set now, I'll be back in time for Monica and Chandler's wedding."

- The movie *Up in the Air* (2009) has a scene where Natalie proclaims that due to her new computerized system, they will not have to spend any more Christmases in a hotel room in Tulsa. This is an allusion to the *Friends* episode "The One with Christmas in Tulsa" (9.10).

- In the British dramedy *Skins* (ep Katie), Katie notices the phrase "You are my lobster" on the blackboard which is written by either Naomi or Emily. In another installment (ep Maxxie and Anwar), a Russian girl learns English from watching *Friends*, and uses many of the catchphrases (e.g., "How you doin'?" and "We were on a break,") as a recurring joke.

- Nickelodeon's *Game Shakers* (ep The One with the Coffee Shop) has many *Friends* themes and references, and even offers a version of "Smelly Cat."

- NBC's comedy *The Good Place* (2016-20) had several *Friends* references during its four-year run. In the episode "What We Owe to Each Other," Michael mentions the show by name, and in "The Funeral to End All Funerals" he says six is the original number of friends.

- The British comedy *Chums* features numerous short sketches parodying *Friends*. Its three characters, Ant, Dec and Cat, play fictionalized versions of themselves while living together in a Newcastle flat. The installment titles mimic the *Friends* format by beginning with "The One ..."

Baby Names

Another indicator of a show's popularity is the societal use of character names for their children. Using this category of influence, *Friends* has proven its cultural imprint on the masses, primarily in the naming of US children. Such an inference can be made based on records from the Social Security Administration (SSA).

Ross

In 1994, when *Friends* premiered, Ross was No. 311 on the popularity list for boys, a continuation of a general downward pattern that began in the 1980s. But the following two years, it seems the name took a break from its overall drop in popularity. In 1995, it rose to No. 268, and in 1996, it was No. 271. But in 1997, Ross dipped back to No. 331 and moved down every year until it fell off the Top 1,000 list after 2012. So it seems the *Friends* bump was short-lived.

Rachel

The *Friends* character inspired a hairstyle craze and may have influenced the name's popularity among American parents. Either that, or the name Rachel coincidentally hit its all-time peak as the ninth-most-popular name for girls in 1996—two years into the show's run—its only year in the top 10. The following year, it ranked No. 13 and mostly declined from year to year after that. In 2020, Rachel was ranked No. 227.

Emma

Perhaps the most popular baby name from *Friends* is Emma. In "The One Where Rachel Has a Baby, Part 2" (8.24), Monica reveals that she wants to give her future daughter the name, but ultimately lets Rachel use it. The episode aired in May 2002, and while it cannot be definitively declared how much it affected parents' choices, it more than likely boosted Emma's appeal. In 2001, the name ranked No. 13 on the SSA's popularity list, but in 2002 it jumped up to the fourth-most-popular name for girls. In 2003, Emma was No. 2, and it's been in the top three every year since.

Chandler

The funster of the group saw his name have a huge boost in popularity after *Friends* debuted. In 1994, it was No. 348 for boys, up 10 spots from the previous year and 61 spots higher than it was the year before that. But in 1995, it jumped a staggering 171 places to No. 177, suggesting Chandler Bing may have accelerated the appellation's rise. The name ultimately peaked at No. 151 in 1999 before descending to No. 569 in 2020. Chandler rose and fell slightly as a name for girls over the course of the show until it fell off the Top 1,000 list after 2002. In 2020, however, it was the 977th-most-popular name for newborn girls in the US.

Monica

The appellation Monica peaked in popularity in the 1970s and then followed a general pattern of decline. However, it saw a couple tiny bumps during the *Friends* era—from No. 88 in 1994 to No. 87 in 1995, No. 82 in 1996 and No. 79 in 1997. But in 1998 the name dropped back down to 105 and then 151 in 1999. It's impossible to attribute the decline to *Friends*, especially since the Bill Clinton–Monica Lewinsky scandal came to light in 1998, which put the name in a flurry of negative news headlines.

Phoebe

The *Friends* effect seems probable with the name Phoebe. It rose sharply from 1994 to 1995; in fact, it jumped 239 spots from No. 819 to No. 580. Then, from 1998 to 1999, it bumped up again from No. 605 to No. 494, perhaps due to the premiere of *Charmed*, which also featured a Phoebe character. These days, it's still climbing the charts, most recently hitting No. 256 in 2020.

Joey

Joseph, aka Joey, is a classic name, so it's difficult to attribute its popularity to a TV show. Joseph was the 11th-most-popular name for baby boys in 1994, and after a steady climb, it reached No. 6 in 2003 for the first time since the early 20th century. The name has since fallen a bit, hitting No. 26 in 2020. Meanwhile, the moniker Joey as a forename instead of a nickname has also declined since the 1990s. In 1994, it ranked No. 411, but in 2020, Joey was down to No. 895.

Other Names

Similar to the Joseph/Joey moniker, the name Ben/Benjamin (Ross' son) is a classic that doesn't reflect any discernible *Friends* influence. In 2020, Benjamin was the 7th-most-popular moniker for boys and Ben was No. 770. The same seems likely with Chandler and Monica's son Jack, although the name rose from No. 42 in 2004 to No. 34 in 2005 after the show ended. Their daughter, Erica, on the other hand, experienced a decline in popularity.

World Record

In 2009, *Friends* fanatic Steve Misiura watched every episode of the sitcom in a single sitting and managed to smash the *Guinness* world record for watching nonstop television. He suffered from nausea, stomach cramps and hallucinations during the marathon, which lasted a whopping 83 hours and 40 minutes. It was worth it, though. Misiura raised £1,500 ($2,050) towards his acting course at London's Central School of Speech and Drama. "I love *Friends*, but this hurt," he admitted at the time. "At around 72 hours, I wanted to die."

Jewish Connection

While *Friends* has Jewish roots, the creators and writers did not venture into the world of religious beliefs too often. Subtle references, minor dialogue, and a few symbolic images were the extent of the show's Judaism. Nevertheless, the series had an abundant undertow of Judaic influence lurking below the surface.

Friends creators David Crane and Marta Kauffman were raised in Jewish households, and she also went to Jewish summer camp, visited Israel, and remained kosher growing up. Her Jewish husband Michael Skloff composed the music for the *Friends* theme song and Jewish lyricist Alta "Allie" Willis wrote the lyrics.

While Ross, Monica and Rachel are Jewish, the creators didn't write the characters as strongly affiliated with their religious identities. "When we were creating the show, we were not thinking about Jewish characters," David Crane proclaimed. "In the initial character breakdowns, we never mentioned religion. We wanted funny, caring, and real characters with stories you invest in. But a lot of it has to do with the actors you cast."

Despite not "thinking about Jewish characters," Crane said the writers room was about half Jewish and they often told stories from their lives. "Ross emerged out of a room where a lot of people had a Jewish background," Crane said. "So his Jewish plotline was probably influenced by that." The actor who portrayed Ross, David Schwimmer, is Jewish. His acting debut at age 10 was playing the fairy godmother in a Jewish version of *Cinderella*. Cutely, his older sister's name is Ellie.

Chandler's most vexing romantic relationship involved Janice Litman Goralnick (née Hosenstein), who was raised in a secular Jewish household in Manhattan. The surname Goralnick was inspired by a Jewish friend of the creators, Deborah A. Franzblau (it was her mother's maiden name). Maggie Wheeler, the actor who portrayed Janice, was raised in a secular Jewish home and now directs the Golden Bridge Community Choir in Los Angeles.

Phoebe was portrayed by Jewish mother and actress Lisa Kudrow. Raised in a Jewish family in Los Angeles, Kudrow had a bat mitzvah, and her grandparents were Holocaust survivors.

The hit sitcom also welcomed a host of Jewish celebrity guest stars over its 10 seasons, including Paul Rudd as Mike Hannigan, Phoebe's boyfriend and future husband; Hank Azaria as David the scientist, a Ladino-speaking Sephardic Jew; Selma Blair as Wendy, Chandler's seductive coworker; and Winona Ryder as Melissa, Rachel's sorority sister. Recurring regular Elliott Gould, who played Jack Geller, claimed to have a very deep Jewish identity.

Seinfeld Influence

Whether fans admit it or not, the success of *Friends* is intricately linked to *Seinfeld*. In many ways, the series about nothing laid the foundation and then directly influenced the twentysomething sitcom. The *Seinfeld* inspiration began immediately after NBC ordered a pilot script for "Insomnia Cafe." Prior to writing the installment, David Crane and Marta Kauffman spent countless hours going over unproduced *Seinfeld* episodes to help get their voice. But the *Seinfeld* influence didn't end there.

The creators came up with the idea of descriptive episode titles from *Seinfeld*, which used succinct monikers like "The Pony Remark" or "The Junior Mint." The *Friends* creators opted for comparably simplistic titles but added a little more descriptiveness, naming most episodes with the lead-in phrase "The One with..." or "The One Where...."

Friends was groundbreaking in its treatment of casual sex but *Seinfeld* set the standard by having its main characters, including Elaine, frequently engaging in casual sex. This laid the groundwork for *Friends* to push the envelope further and expand the concept. Joey may have been an unabashed womanizer, but the female protagonists had their fair share of casual sex.

Youthful sexuality was another uncharted area of network television. *Seinfeld* opened the door for NBC and other networks to explore casual sex on primetime television. Despite tackling taboo subjects such as female sexuality, the sitcom about nothing remained a top-rated program. This invariably influenced NBC executives into becoming more lax in their acceptance of similar practices. Although *Friends* staff writers still experienced network resistance, especially in the early years, after the show became a universal phenomenon, the series became more aggressive in its assault on sexual conservationism. However, had it not been for *Seinfeld* paving the way, *Friends* would have encountered heavy resistance and censorship from NBC executives.

The use of three equally weighted storylines was another product of *Seinfeld*. Although *Seinfeld* was not an ensemble, its episode structure treated the costars as equals because they had the same number of scenes, lines, and jokes, as the headliner. *Friends*, banking on being an ensemble comedy, did the same thing for all six cast members. In nearly every episode, each character was intricately involved in the major plots.

Another major *Seinfeld* influence was the structure of episodes. It was the first sitcom to run multiple storylines within an installment, often dovetailing each one so all the plots came together at the end of the episode. The *Friends* executive producers wanted to mimic this approach. Though most *Friends* episodes did not unite all three storylines in a clever, succinct ending, each was crafted to intersect the stories throughout the episode.

Finally, if not for Courteney Cox's guest appearance on *Seinfeld*, the ensemble comedy *Friends* may have been an entirely different show. The *Seinfeld* experience changed Cox's perception on how actors can work together to improve their performances. She suggested using the collaborative *Seinfeld* acting technique to her colleagues and they embraced the idea. Thereafter, the entire cast worked together as a cohesive unit.

Mad About You Influence

When Lisa Kudrow was cast as Phoebe on *Friends*, she already had a recurring role on *Mad About You* playing the ditzy waitress, Ursula. Normally, an actor playing different roles in two different shows is an annoyance, not an issue. However, when *Friends* was picked up and scheduled to televise immediately after *Mad About You*, this posed a problem. David Crane and Marta Kauffman feared viewers may be confused seeing Lisa Kudrow portraying two different characters in back-to-back sitcoms on the same night. Although the creators encouraged her to keep the other gig and agreed to work around her schedule, they did feel the need to address the issue on the show. After a brainstorming session, the duo came up with the idea of creating a crossover between *Mad About You* and *Friends* by having Phoebe and Ursula being characterized as twins.

Since the pilot was already shot, they used the very next episode to lay the foundation for a series crossover. In "The One with the Sonogram at the End" (1.02), Phoebe mentions her estrangement from an unnamed twin sister who is a waitress. Fans of both hit sitcoms could then infer that Phoebe and Ursula were sisters without it being explicitly spelled out (which would require permission from the creators of *Mad About You*). At the time, NBC had only ordered 13 episodes of *Friends* so Kauffman and Crane had no other plans for Ursula. However, once *Friends* was picked up for the rest of the season, the showrunners wanted to settle the issue once and for all by definitively dispelling any viewer confusion.

The showrunners approached *Mad About You* cocreator Danny Jacobson to discuss whether he would be amenable to a twins crossover. Fortunately, David Crane was dating *Mad About You* writer Jeffrey Klarik, which may have helped unite the two sitcom creators. Jacobson consented to the crossover, though Crane later admitted that had the table been turned, he would not have agreed to a crossover.

NBC loved the idea. The twins concept opened the door to a variety of story possibilities and crossover segments involving both casts. Ursula made her official *Friends* premiere in "The One with Two Parts, Part 1" (1.16). In one segment, Joey and Chandler dine at Riff's restaurant (the *Mad About You* eatery) where their server is Ursula. Later in the episode, Helen Hunt and Leila Kenzle, appearing as their *Mad About You* characters, enter Central Perk and mistake Phoebe for Ursula. With the twins crossover settled once and for all, in future episodes Phoebe was able to freely discuss her sister in more detail.

Lisa Kudrow portrayed Ursula in eight *Friends* installments. When asked to choose her favorite twin character, Kudrow was unsure. "They were both fun for completely different reasons," she stated diplomatically. In 1999, the *Mad About You* series finale featured a tag scene set 22 years in the future. In the segment, Ursula became the Governor of New York after a successful career as a porn star. Naturally, *Friends* capitalized on this revelation by crafting an episode where Ursula appears in a porn movie using Phoebe's name.

Series Spinoff

Although Marta Kauffman and David Crane adamantly refused to partake in a series spinoff, that did not dissuade their partner from pursuing the idea. Kevin Bright agreed to executive produce the series with *Friends* staff writers Scott Silveri and Shana Goldberg-Meehan. The spinoff series featured Joey after he moved to Los Angeles to pursue an acting career. Many *Friends* fans are surprised to learn that Matt LeBlanc was not the first choice for a spinoff series—he was the third. NBC desired Jennifer Aniston to lead a spinoff but she wanted to pursue a film career so they approached Courteney Cox and Matthew Perry, but they didn't want to play their *Friends* characters anymore.

NBC heavily promoted *Joey* and gave it *Friends*' Thursday 8pm (EST) timeslot. The pilot premiered on September 9, 2004, with respectable numbers, 18.6 million viewers, but its audience faded over the next two seasons, averaging 10.2 million viewers in the first season and 7.1 million in the second. The final installment aired on March 7, 2006, attracting an audience of only 7.09 million. NBC canceled the series on May 15, 2006, and eight episodes were left unaired. While the Complete First Season of *Joey* was released on DVD in the US, poor sales led to the second season only being released abroad.

Kevin Bright claimed too many suits ruined the spinoff show. It became a collaboration of network executives, studio executives, and other producers. They totally changed the dynamic of the show. "On *Friends*, Joey was a womanizer but we enjoyed his exploits. He was a solid friend, a guy you knew you could count on," Bright opined. But the spinoff was completely different. "Joey was deconstructed to be a guy who couldn't get a job, couldn't ask a girl out. He became a pathetic, mopey character. I felt he was moving in the wrong direction, but I was not heard."

Reboot

After *Friends* retired, the creators remained firmly committed to their original position: no spinoff, no reunion, and no reboot. "The characters are done," David Crane exclaimed. "We feel like we put them to bed." When asked whether they would be amenable to another creative team carrying on the legacy, both responded with an emphatic "No!" Surprisingly, Warner Bros. supported the decision. "They've been incredibly respectful of us throughout this entire process," Marta Kauffman acknowledged. "We'd said early on that we didn't want to do a reunion or a reboot, and they've never asked. We won't be able to beat what we've done, and what was magical about the show was those six actors. So I can't see how we could improve on what we did."

Random Facts & Trivia

Series

- In the year 2024, *Friends* turned 30, which made Ben 29, Phoebe's triplets 27, Emma 22, and Monica and Chandler's twins 20.

- The full names of the characters are Chandler Muriel Bing, Rachel Karen Green, Ross Eustace Geller, Monica E. Geller (the full middle name is never revealed), Joseph Francis Tribbiani Jr., and Phoebe Buffay (she did not know her middle name; her birth certificate was taken by Ursula and sold to a Swedish runaway).

- In Old English, Chandler, and its variant spellings, is a family name that began as an occupational surname in medieval England. It applied to a person involved in making or selling candles and similar articles. Since the character Chandler was named after a friend of the creators, they hoped he didn't take offense when Joey listed multiple reasons "Chandler" is a terrible name.

- In the series, Monica says the first line and Chandler utters the last. The first line of dialogue in the pilot episode was "There's nothing to tell." The last line in the finale was "Where?"

- In every episode of *Friends*, the word "friend" is uttered at least once.

- With respect to episode titles, Rachel's name appears the most (21 times), followed by Ross (19), Joey (13), Phoebe (10), Chandler (9), and Monica (7).

- There have been 11 Oscar-winning actors who have appeared on *Friends*: Fisher Stevens, Charlton Heston, Reese Witherspoon, Sean Penn, Susan Sarandon, Jim Rash, Helen Hunt, Julia Roberts, Robin Williams, George Clooney and Brad Pitt.

- The establishing shot for Phoebe's apartment is 5 Morton St., New York. However, the invitation she received for Ross' wedding was addressed to 143B Howton Ave., New York, NY 10001. In real life, this address is located in Staten Island, New York. Phoebe's apartment number is 16, but she once told the mystery cell phone guy that she lived in apartment 14, and when her grandmother lived there the designation was 12B.

- Rachel is the only character that never lived alone during the series. Monica lived solo between having Phoebe as a roommate (prior to the pilot episode) and then rooming with Rachel (starting with the pilot episode). Phoebe and Ross lived alone for a majority of the show but each had Rachel as a roommate for a brief period. Joey and Chandler briefly lived alone after Joey joined *Days of Our Lives* and moved into his own apartment. Joey also had the place to himself after Chandler cohabited with Monica in season six.

- On filming day, the cast and crew drank 32 pots of regular coffee. During a typical week, they went through 100 cases of water.

- Phoebe drank more coffee than anyone on the show—227 cups throughout the 10 seasons.

- All six of the friends changed jobs at least once. Chandler was the only one never to be fired.

- Out of the six friends, Chandler is the only one without siblings. Rachel has two sisters, Monica and Ross are siblings, Phoebe has a twin sister and a half brother, and Joey has seven sisters.

- After totaling all the money Joey owed Chandler over the years, it comes to about $120,000.

- Marcel earned a starring role in a movie before any of the six costars capitalized on their *Friends* stardom. The simian was featured in *Outbreak* (1995), which grossed more revenue than all six lead actors' first films combined.

- Most of the friends have been in love triangles with each other: season two: Ross–Julie–Rachel, Monica–Jean-Claude Van Damme–Rachel; season four: Joey–Kathy–Chandler; season seven: Joey–Kristin–Ross; season eight: Joey–Rachel–Ross; season nine: Joey–Charlie–Ross; and season ten: Joey–Rachel–Ross.

- In one assessment of the sexual activity of the *Friends* characters (assigning 1 point to each definite or strongly suggested sexual partner and 0.5 points to each probable but uncertain sexual partner), the six friends collectively bedded about 138 lovers over 10 seasons. The results from least to most: Chandler (10.5 sex partners), Ross (14), Monica (14.5), Rachel (15.5), Phoebe (32.5), and Joey (51.5).

- Even before Monica and Chandler became a couple on the show, Courteney Cox admitted in an interview that if she had to "do" (sleep with) one of the other male friends, she would choose Chandler.

- All six of the main characters have kissed each other on the show. Many sources indicate that Monica and Phoebe never kissed but they did in fact smooch when Monica said goodbye before leaving for London. Even Ross and Monica kissed at a college party.

- Matthew Perry is the only *Friends* costar to never marry or have children. But, on November 26, 2020, he announced his engagement to Molly Hurwitz, a literary manager for Zero Gravity Management, who was 22 years his junior. They started dating in 2018 and called off the engagement on June 1, 2021.

- David Schwimmer was the only costar to direct an episode. In fact, he directed 10 from season six through the last season: The One on the Last Night (6.06), The One with Rachel's Assistant (7.04), The One with Ross's Library Book (7.07), The One with All the Candy (7.09), The One with the Truth About London (7.16), The One with the Red Sweater (8.02), The One with the Stripper (8.08), The One Where Joey Dates Rachel (8.12), The One with Phoebe's Birthday Dinner (9.05) and The One with the Birth Mother (10.09).

- Director Betty Thomas inspired Kevin Bright as a director. For physical comedy, he learned from Abbott and Costello, Laurel and Hardy and The Three Stooges.

- The number 27 is frequently used in the series: (1) Rachel tells a date that Monica labels her cups, and provides the example, cup 27; (2) the girls wear three firemen hats that have 27 on them; (3) Chandler gives Ross $27 when he feels guilty about dating Monica; (4) Joey tells everyone he weighed 27 pounds when he was born; (5) when Chandler needs to replace Monica's broiling pan, she tells him to order it from page 27 of the catalog; (6) Monica says 27 is a dangerous eye age; (7) Monica claims to be 27 years old when dating a high schooler; (8) the gang traveled along highway 27 on a ski trip; (9) Chandler paid $27 for three pizzas; and (10) Joey's age was 27 on a sperm donor form.

- According to the costars, Lisa Kudrow was the smartest of all of them. Although she deftly portrayed a ditzy character, Kudrow once planned to obtain a doctorate degree in neurobiology.

- Courteney Cox struggled to remember her lines and was known to write them on the dining table and keep episode scripts in the sink. Matt LeBlanc recounted an on-set incident for Cox. "You had this big speech," he said. "You were struggling with it all weeklong, and you wrote it on the table. And when you weren't looking I erased it and you got so mad at me!" Cox laughs about it now, but candidly said, "I have memory issues!"

- Kevin Bright did editing, sound mixing, schedule budgets, casting of guest stars and directing. He is credited for selecting most of the music for the series. David Crane loved doing standards and practices meetings (where network executives try to censor script content). Marta Kauffman was intricately involved with the stage activities.

Actors

In the second season, Matt LeBlanc started going gray around the temples so he began regularly dyeing his hair black, which he continued doing until the series ended. Once, he tried coloring his locks at home because it took two hours at the studio. The next day, he arrived at work with the back of his ears entirely black so thereafter he routinely visited the set hairdresser.

Believe it or not, when Matt LeBlanc watches *Friends* in syndication, often he cannot remember filming some of the shows. The hit series amassed 236 episodes, so to him, the whole experience felt like "one long episode." He openly confessed: "I remember obviously loving everybody there and having fun, and I remember certain times in my life that I was there, but I don't remember episodes."

In the early days of the series, Matt LeBlanc had a crush on Jennifer Aniston. In an interview, he honestly admitted this fact. "I had a little crush on Jen in the very beginning, but I think the whole world did too, so what are you going to do?" Child actor Cole Sprouse (Ben Geller) also confessed to having a crush on her.

LeBlanc is repeatedly approached by youthful fans of the show who look at him and say, "What's with the gray hair? Are you Joey's dad?" Instead of having a cool Hollywood comeback, LeBlanc would say "Scram," which, he pointed out rather ironically, "That's like what an old guy says!"

David Schwimmer never believed the Ross–Rachel romantic reunion was realistic in the series finale: "The whole arc of the relationship was weird then, because for him to be able to move on enough to marry someone else and then go back to being in love with Rachel later, [that] just went a bit too far."

Lisa Kudrow did not like bringing her son (Julian) to the set. "Here's what was difficult about having a child: when he visited the set, it was hard to be in character," Kudrow said. "Because I didn't want him to ever experience me as anything *other* than his mother." FYI: During his on-set visits, Julian, like most boys (and men) in the world, was infatuated with Jennifer Aniston, so he would run over to her and sit in her lap. When he was at home and saw her on TV, he would yell, "Mommy!"

Kudrow hated playing guitar. To prepare for the role, a tutor taught her the instrument but it did not go well. "I didn't like the guitar. I wasn't getting it," she confessed. "I think I even asked, 'What if she plays the bongos?'" The executive producers rejected the idea, and instead hired a renowned teacher to provide lessons. That also failed. Kudrow was only able to learn a few chords before firing the instructor. Thereafter, she refused to take any further lessons and settled on playing only the few chords she knew. "You know, I don't want the guitar lessons anymore. I've learned a few chords, that's enough, that's all Phoebe would know anyhow. So I'll make everything do with just these chords," she told the producers. Kevin Bright thought it was a great idea because her musical ineptitude made the comedy better. She performed 47 original songs over the 10-year span of the series. Since the show ended, Kudrow has only touched the guitar a couple times, usually for *Friends* events.

Matthew Perry and Courteney Cox are actually distant cousins. MyHeritage ancestry discovered the pair are 11th cousins; they share distant relatives: William Osbern Haskell III and Ellen Haskell, who were married and lived in England around 500 years ago. Ellen and her two sons emigrated from England to America in 1635. One son, Roger, is a direct ancestor of Cox, and the second son, William, is a direct ancestor of Perry. The connection is through Cox's mother, Courteney Copeland, and Perry's father, John Bennett Perry. It also found that both actors are distantly related to Lady Gaga. Cox is a 17th cousin once removed and Perry a 14th cousin thrice removed.

When Jennifer Aniston joined Instagram in October 2019, she nearly broke the social media platform with her first post—a selfie with her former *Friends* castmates. Aniston did set the record for the fastest time to reach 1 million followers on Instagram, as recognized by *Guinness World Records*.

Set & Props

In several episodes, *Friends* characters were seen smoking Morley cigarettes, a fictitious brand. The packaging has been featured in hundreds of movies and TV shows, including

Seinfeld, Frasier and *The X-Files*, though it first appeared in the movie *Psycho* in 1960 and TV series *Naked City* in 1961. As of 1998, tobacco advertising was banned in both movies and television so Morley became the go-to prop brand. Its packaging resembles the original packaging of Marlboro. The name "Morley" is a play on words for "Marleys," the nickname for Marlboro cigarettes. There is also a Morley Lights version with gold-and-white packaging (similar to Marlboro Lights), marked "Lights." The fictional prop brand is sold to production companies by The Earl Hays Press, a century-old Hollywood prop packaging service. FYI: Magnolia Props reproduces Morley brand cigarettes for $26 a pack but the item cannot be shipped to the US.

When Rachel returns to her childhood home, in "The One Where Joey Speaks French" (10.13), the exterior establishing shot uses stock footage from the movie *Planes, Trains and Automobiles* (1987). The real-life address is 230 Oxford Rd. in Kenilworth, Illinois. Built in 1916, it has six bedrooms, four baths, over 3,500 square feet, and sold in 2009 for $1.4 million.

Although *Friends* never used an establishing shot to represent Monica and Chandler's suburban home, in "The One with Princess Consuela" (10.14), the neighborhood includes the McCallisters' residence from *Home Alone* (1990). A view outside the living room window shows the same blue-and-white garage for the house across the street. *Friends'* production company simply purchased the stock footage. It is common for studios to reuse footage that already exists rather than paying to create their own, especially for negligible background images. It can be very costly to film backplates so using stock footage is cost effective. The real-life *Home Alone* house address is 671 Lincoln Ave., Winnetka, Illinois. Built in 1921, it has six bedrooms, four and a half baths, 4,243 square feet, and sits on a half-acre lot with an estimated home value of $1.9 million. The home sold for $1,585,000 on March 19, 2012, but the original asking price was $2.4 million.

Bizarre Encounters

The cast and creators experienced bizarre encounters with the public so the writers used this as an opportunity to craft one memorable scene. In "The One with Joey's New Brain" (7.15), Cecilia Monroe exits Joey's bedroom wearing nothing but his t-shirt yet that doesn't stop doting fans (Monica and Rachel) from approaching and behaving like it's an ordinary encounter. Although not based on an actual event, the scene is gleaned from real-life encounters by the six costars. They have been approached by fans in every location, including bathrooms. David Schwimmer admitted to being badgered by women demanding that he kiss them—even when their boyfriend was there.

Marta Kauffman had an encounter with a youthful fan as the sitcom neared its finale. "A teenager came up to me and said, 'You've got to tell me how this ends with Ross and Rachel.' And I said, 'I don't even tell my children,'" she proclaimed. "People really wanted them together. People over that summer would come up to me, if I had my *Friends* jacket on, total strangers, and say, 'Listen to me, please. You got to tell me. Are Rachel and Ross going to get together? I won't tell anybody, I promise.' Total strangers."

Kauffman was floored at the level of interest among fans of the show. "That was one of the things that was so shocking about the success of the show was how people invested in the characters as if they were real," she declared. "They existed and they had to be together. How could you not put them together?" Her encounters were not limited to strangers on the street. "My rabbi would stop me every Sunday when I drove the kids to Hebrew school, and say 'What's with Ross and Rachel? You gonna get them together?'"

Cocreator Kevin Bright recalled being recognized by Japanese tourists in Santa Monica, California, who said they knew him because of interviews in the *Friends* DVD extras. David Crane revealed that a flight attendant saw his name on an airline ticket and spent a six-hour flight talking to him.

Lawsuit

In August 2019, Graham Chase Robinson was fired and ultimately sued for spending "astronomical amounts of time" binge-watching *Friends* episodes while at work. Robinson, the former vice president of production and finance at Canal Productions, was also accused of embezzling money. The civil lawsuit by Canal Productions, Robert De Niro's production company, demanded $6 million. The petition declared: "Over the four-day period between Tuesday, January 8 and Friday, January 11, 2019, 55 episodes of *Friends* were accessed." Robinson filed a separate $12 million lawsuit accusing De Niro of leading an abusive workplace toward women and making gratuitous unwanted physical contact. The cases are still pending.

Porn

Due to the success of *Friends*, a porn movie was made to parody the sitcom. *Friends: A XXX Parody* (2009) has a fountain scene title sequence with a theme song ("these friends go all the way / these friends love to screw") and Rachelle (Rachel) even flashes her breasts. The movie parodies several episodic themes: (1) Russ (Ross) enters Canoga Perk (Central Perk) to announce his wife is lesbian, then Carol and Sandra (Susan) want a three-way; (2) Moanica (Monica) and Sandler (Chandler) are getting married and having sex all over the place; (3) Freebie (Phoebe) and Joe (Joey) have sex; and (4) the girls organize a bachelorette party where the stripper is Naked Guy (Ugly Naked Guy).

In 2018, adult video website YouPorn reportedly offered David Schwimmer $1 million to star in a *Friends* porn parody. The offer letter reads: "We at YouPorn, like so many others, miss that time you awkwardly proved to Rachel and Joey that you were 'fine!' Or that time you tried to teach Rachel and Phoebe about the state of total awareness ... Unagi! To make everyone's dreams come true, we want to bring those talents back to the screen and are offering you a $1 million contract to star in your very own *Friends* porn parody. We know it's not the 'silver screen' but we already have a Rachel on board and think it's the perfect PIVOT in your career." They added: "We'll even let you wear those leather pants again!"

Mistakes, Errors & Goofs

The *Friends* cast was known for their jocularity on set, which included jokes, pranks and playful banter. Although they are trained professionals, that does not mean they are impeccable actors. "The audience loves when they mess up. They enjoy that thoroughly," Marta Kauffman said. "The cast curses and it's the funniest thing ever. Funnier than any joke we could ever write. All they have to do is say a curse word when they miss a line and to the audience it is absolutely hysterical." Of course, mistakes are expected but after final editing, the finished product should be near flawless. But that was not always the case with *Friends*.

A study revealed that *Friends* had more mistakes per season (149) than any television show in network programming history, surpassing *Buffy the Vampire Slayer* (90) and *Red Dwarf* (81). In other words, there are at least six mistakes per episode for a total of nearly 1,500 errors over the course of the series. Obviously this is enough to fill a book so only a couple highlights will be mentioned.

Numerous times an actor stand-in was captured on camera. For example, "The One with the Mugging" (9.15) had two such errors, including two stand-ins in the same frame, and "The One in Massapequa" (8.18) had the stand-in for Elliott Gould caught on camera. Of course, many of the errors first became visible after some DVD and Blu-ray releases showed the episodes in the original 16:9 format, as opposed to the standard 4:3 format that is used when broadcasting television programs.

The cast frequently broke character during filming. The show's editor tried to splice the film to excise the errors but often it was unavoidable. There were a few notable examples. In "The One with the Worst Best Man Ever" (4.22), Matt LeBlanc is keeling over laughing as the guys confront the stripper about stealing a wedding ring. In "The One with Joey's New Brain" (7.15), both Jennifer Aniston and Lisa Kudrow cannot contain their laughter while Ross is playing the bagpipe.

The exterior view from Monica's kitchen and balcony window changed throughout the series. In the kitchen, the backdrop varied between a cityscape, plain brick wall, laundry line, neighbor's balcony and window, and a cardboard wall in the series finale. The balcony window used different painted backdrops such as a distant apartment building, which changed in design and color, and other times there was a wing attached to the building.

Chandler and Rachel meet for the first time on three separate occasions. In the pilot episode, Monica introduced Rachel to the gang, including Chandler (who supposedly never met the runaway bride). However, they previously met in "The One with the Flashback" (3.06) (in a tavern one year prior) and in "The One with All the Thanksgivings" (5.08) (at the Gellers' residence when he was in college).

Ross' birthday was a fluid concept. In various installments he was born in March, then December, and finally October 18th. Moreover, three years in a row he celebrated his 29th birthday (seasons three, four and five). In the third season, he declines Chandler's offer for chocolate milk by saying, "No thanks, I'm 29." In the fourth season, when the guys realize they don't like partying as much as they used to, Joey says to Ross and Chandler "We're 29." In the fifth season, Ross wonders what to do about Emily, and fears getting divorced for the second time before age 30.

In "The One Where Chandler Doesn't Like Dogs" (7.08), Ross claims he doesn't like ice cream because it's too cold. Yet, several scenes contradict this fact: (1) he is seen holding a spoon as the gang eats ice cream in "The One with the Thumb" (1.03); (2) he is sharing a cone with Marcel in "The One After the Superbowl, Part 2" (2.13); and (3) he is holding a cone while on a date with Elizabeth in "The One Where Ross Dates a Student" (6.18).

Rachel's surname was spelled two different ways. On the invitation to Ross and Emily's wedding, her last name was spelled "Greene" ("The One with the Invitation," ep 4.21), which is consistent with the sign on her office door ("The One Where Rachel Goes Back to Work," ep 9.11). However, in the closing credits, her parents have the surname "Green" ("The One with Two Parties," ep 2.22), which is also the spelling on the bakery box for Emma's cake ("The One with the Cake," ep 10.04).

In "The One with the Baby on the Bus" (2.06), when Phoebe is seated outside Central Perk, some random guy asks if he can retrieve a condom from her guitar case. The actor is Giovanni Ribisi, who later appears as Frank Jr., Phoebe's half brother. The role of Condom Boy was supposed to be a one-time part but the producers liked him so much they cast him in a recurring role.

Rachel's ex-fiancé's surname changed. In the pilot episode he was Barry Finkle. In all future episodes, his surname was Farber.

Phoebe mentions that her father abandoned her before she was born. However, when her father showed up in "The One with Joey's Bag" (5.13), he mentioned reading bedtime stories to lull her to sleep.

Phoebe's family appears in several episodes but none are present for her wedding. Prior episodes featured her mother Phoebe Sr., half brother Frank Jr., sister-in-law Alice, the triplets, father Frank Sr. and sister Ursula. They were purposely omitted to cut costs and because there simply weren't enough storylines for all the characters.

Ross' son vanishes entirely from the show. Ben, played by Cole Sprouse, was last seen in season eight, "The One Where Joey Dates Rachel" (8.12), but his scene with dialogue was cut. There were 55 more episodes after that, and not one of them had Ben as a character. A lot of things happen in those installments that would normally precipitate Ross' son being present, like, for example, the birth of his half sister.

Monica's secret closet changed over time. In season one it was a walk-in closet but by season six it was a standard-size hall closet. In addition, the door knob changed from left to right. In season one, the knob was on both sides of the door (mostly on the left), and since season two, it was consistently on the right. Moreover, in the first season the closet was a tidy regimented space but in season eight it was a disorganized storage area for all sorts of junk.

Where Are They Now?

The showrunners and cast have pondered the evolution of the *Friends* characters and made a few predictions on how their lives turned out since the show ended in 2004. Marta Kauffman stated, "I think Monica and Chandler are together. They have their twins, they're doing great." Matthew Perry then chimed in, Chandler "would be a wonderful father. And a wonderful comedy writer." According to Cox, in some ways her character didn't change. "I always just feel like Monica would be doing something competitively with other mothers and trying to outdo them. Whether it's the bake sale at school or something. I mean, she'd be so annoying. She'd be at the head of the PTA or something." After realizing she forgot to mention Chandler, Cox promptly told Perry, "And you are still making me laugh every day." He quickly retorted, "Just wanted to make sure I factored in somewhere."

Marta Kauffman believed Ross and Rachel were still together, though Jennifer Aniston opined that the couple had one more child after finally getting married. The creators agreed with her but added that "Ross and Rachel's daughter, Emma, is in therapy because she didn't get quite as much parental attention in those formative years." Aniston had further thoughts about her character: "I would like to have maybe started a clothing line of my own, and it's sort of a small franchise. Like a Nili Lotan. And I live in New York City on the Upper East Side."

Matt LeBlanc indicated that Joey is married with six kids and gave up acting. "I think he probably opened a sandwich shop on Venice Beach," he proclaimed. "And eaten all the sandwiches," quipped Matthew Perry. Naturally, David Schwimmer had to include his two cents so he remarked that Ross "would've invested in Joey's sandwich shop and lost a lot of his savings for his kids." LeBlanc then slightly modified his original idea, "Dinosaur-themed sandwich shop. Bronto-burger."

Lisa Kudrow opined that Phoebe "is living in Connecticut with Mike and their kids, and she's in charge of the arts program for the school." In addition, Phoebe is "the advocate for her kids because they're different like she was." Kauffman added, "Phoebe and Mike are definitely still together and she's got, like, four foster kids. She still plays music whenever possible, but she's very busy with the kids." Kevin Bright did not foresee the same idyllic future. "Phoebe's got a cult," he said, before modifying his statement, "It's a very positive cult." Kudrow then chimed in, "I honestly think Phoebe would be a super-competitive tiger mom. She doesn't do anything by half measure."

Episode Index

Note: Entries without page numbers are not cited in the text

General Index

www.ingramcontent.com/pod-product-compliance
Lightning Source LLC
Chambersburg PA
CBHW021946120726
47992CB00001B/160